Petfluencers and Pet-Powered Branding

Luzia Arantes
University of Aveiro, Portugal & Polytechnic University of Cávado and Ave, Portugal

Bruno Sousa
Polytechnic University of Cávado and Ave, Portugal

IGI Global
Scientific Publishing
Publishing Tomorrow's Research Today

Vice President of Editorial	Melissa Wagner
Director of Acquisitions	Mikaela Felty
Director of Book Development	Jocelynn Hessler
Production Manager	Mike Brehm
Cover Design	Jose Rosado

Published in the United States of America by
IGI Global Scientific Publishing
701 East Chocolate Avenue
Hershey, PA, 17033, USA
Tel: 717-533-8845 | Fax: 717-533-7115
Website: https://www.igi-global.com E-mail: cust@igi-global.com

Library of Congress Cataloging-in-Publication Data

Names: Arantes, Luzia, 1994- editor | Sousa, Bruno Barbosa editor
Title: Petfluencers and pet-powered branding / edited by Luzia Arantes, Bruno Sousa.
Description: Hershey, PA : IGI Global Scientific Publishing, 2026. | Includes bibliographical references and index. | Summary: "This book examines the rise of petfluencers and pet-powered branding, exploring how brands leverage pet-driven marketing to enhance consumer engagement and loyalty"-- Provided by publisher.
Identifiers: LCCN 2025029138 (print) | LCCN 2025029139 (ebook) | ISBN 9798337343426 hardcover | ISBN 9798337343433 paperback | ISBN 9798337343440 ebook
Subjects: LCSH: Pet industry | Pet supplies--Marketing | Animals in advertising | Pets--Psychological aspects
Classification: LCC SF414.7 .P55 2025 (print) | LCC SF414.7 (ebook)
LC record available at https://lccn.loc.gov/2025029138
LC ebook record available at https://lccn.loc.gov/2025029139

British Cataloguing in Publication Data
A Cataloguing in Publication record for this book is available from the British Library.

Table of Contents

Detailed Table of Contents

This chapter proposes a sustainable tourism route in Barcelos, integrating its cultural and historical landmarks with a special focus on the iconic Barcelos Rooster. Through heritage interpretation, the route aims to enrich visitor experiences, raise community awareness, and promote sustainable tourism aligned with the UNESCO Creative Cities Network. The methodology includes a literature review and qualitative surveys of residents and visitors to gather diverse insights. The outcomes involve identifying the best practices for sustainable tourism, analyzing Barcelos' current tourism landscape, and designing an itinerary centered on the Barcelos Rooster. The research also evaluates potential impacts on local communities and heritage, ensuring this route reflects local values. Innovative digital marketing strategies are trying to promote the route, emphasizing Barcelos' cultural identity. The chapter contributes to a sustainable tourism model that may serve as a benchmark for other UNESCO Creative Cities.

In modern times, companies are coming to realize more and more how important it is to employ relationship marketing techniques to stand out in highly competitive markets. Brands employ emotional and value-driven strategies to connect with their audiences more closely rather than depending only on product attributes or cost. The use of animal imagery is a tactic that, if well-planned, can create emotions in consumers. This chapter explores how marketing campaigns can use themes such as the emotional value of animal companionship to build relationships with consumers. This study highlights the growing importance of relationship marketing using animals by examining a few campaigns.

In sport (and football), animals represent an important symbol of a club's identity, representing values of society and local culture (such as strength, passion, loyalty or courage). The use of animal imagery in sports marketing can be highly effective due to its ability to evoke strong emotional responses and create memorable brand associations. This chapter aims to illustrate two representative examples of the importance that some animals (real or imaginary) may represent in a sports club in Portugal, as a differentiating symbol in the brand, identity and products associated with the club. Thus, this chapter aims to present some insights for sports marketing, but also for the importance of animals in the domain of sports companies (and sports clubs in particular - FCPorto and Gil Vicente FC). Finally, limitations and lines of future research will be presented.

This chapter places petfluencers in the context of the emotional economy of consumption and explores their function in modern branding. Through anthropomorphism, nostalgia, and parasocial interaction, it makes the case that animals are dynamic emotional agents rather than passive mascots that promote attachment, trust, and brand love. The chapter uses examples like Grumpy Cat, Nala Cat, and Doug the Pug to show how petfluencers are different from conventional animal symbols in that they co-create meaning with audiences and create commercial value through digital engagement, merchandising, and sponsorship. A conceptual model of pet-driven branding is proposed, integrating symbolic representation, identity mediation, emotional activation, and consumer outcomes. The chapter also discusses market saturation, ethical issues, and the growing popularity of AI-generated pets, pointing out both advantages and disadvantages. All things considered, it reinterprets animals as relational actors at the core of post-human branding.

In the ever-evolving world of social media, new trends and influential personas emerge regularly, reshaping the way content is consumed and brands connect with audiences. Among these trends, one of the most intriguing and heartwarming phenomena is the rise of "petfluencers" — animals who have become online celebrities with massive followings across platforms like Instagram, TikTok, YouTube, and Facebook. These charismatic pets, often cats, dogs, rabbits, or even exotic animals, are more than just adorable faces; they are now powerful marketing tools, brand ambassadors, and cultural icons in their own right.The concept of influencer marketing is not new. For over a decade, brands have collaborated with popular social media figures to promote products and services in a more authentic, relatable way. However, the evolution from human influencers to animal influencers signals a fascinating shift in consumer psychology and digital engagement. Unlike human influencers, petfluencers evoke a unique emotional appeal.

This chapter explores how pet-powered branding intersects with sustainability in digital marketing, focusing on pets as symbolic mediators of trust, empathy, and ecological responsibility. As consumers demand authenticity, pets and petfluencers provide affective capital that supports imaginaries of care, adoption, and eco-friendly lifestyles. At the same time, their symbolic use can trivialise sustainability, enabling performative practices and masking weak commitments. Drawing on theories of performativity, affective capitalism, and ethical branding, the chapter proposes a framework showing how pets may both enhance authenticity and facilitate

Preface

INTRODUCTION

The ways in which humans engage with animals have undergone a profound transformation in recent decades. Once primarily valued for companionship, labor, or symbolism, animals now occupy prominent spaces within the domains of branding, marketing, and digital culture. This evolution is particularly evident in the phenomenon of "petfluencers," animals whose personalities, images, and online presences resonate with global audiences in ways that rival—and often surpass—human influencers. By tapping into emotional economies and cultural identities, these animals extend beyond their physical presence to become active agents in branding strategies, consumer behavior, and sustainable narratives.

This volume, *Petfluencers and Pet-Powered Branding*, emerges at the intersection of communication, marketing, cultural studies, and sustainability research. It provides a comprehensive and interdisciplinary exploration of how animals—whether real, symbolic, or digitally mediated—are leveraged within branding practices. Through a collection of chapters contributed by international scholars, the book presents diverse perspectives ranging from tourism development and sports marketing to social media strategy, emotional economics, and even honey tourism.

Our intention as editors has been to assemble a resource that not only highlights the novelty and charm of pet-driven branding but also interrogates its ethical, cultural, and economic dimensions. We invite readers—whether academics, practitioners, or students—to critically engage with the opportunities and challenges posed by this growing field. By considering both the benefits and potential pitfalls of petfluencer culture, we hope this book will serve as a springboard for future research and responsible practices in marketing and communication.

CHAPTER OVERVIEW

Chapter 1 examines cultural heritage and sustainable tourism in Barcelos, Portugal, showcasing how the iconic Barcelos Rooster functions as a powerful cultural and branding symbol within the UNESCO Creative Cities Network.

Chapter 2 explores the emotional role of animal imagery in brand marketing, revealing how strategically deployed representations of animals foster deeper consumer connections.

Chapter 3 investigates the symbolic use of animals in sports clubs in northern Portugal, focusing on how animal imagery reinforces cultural identity and loyalty within fan communities.

Chapter 4 situates petfluencers within the emotional economy, offering a conceptual model of pet-driven branding and considering issues such as anthropomorphism, parasocial interaction, and the emergence of AI-generated pets.

Chapter 5 analyzes the rise of petfluencers in social media marketing, tracing how they transform digital engagement, shape consumer psychology, and offer unique opportunities for brands.

Chapter 6 explores the relationship between pet-powered branding and sustainability, addressing both its potential for authentic ecological communication and its risks of greenwashing.

Chapter 7 highlights the rise of petfluencers as modern branding agents, unpacking their emotional appeal, ethical implications, and influence on consumer engagement.

Chapter 8 shifts focus to airline innovations in international pet-onboard services, demonstrating how pet-inclusive travel policies impact brand positioning and consumer loyalty.

Chapter 9 deepens the analysis of petfluencers' marketing power, illustrating their cross-industry appeal and strategies for effective campaign design.

Chapter 10 turns attention to bees, positioning them as critical agents in food security, biodiversity, and honey tourism, while also reflecting on branding opportunities grounded in sustainability.

Chapter 11 delves into the psychology of pet-driven consumer behavior, examining how humanization of pets and attachment theory shape purchasing decisions and industry growth.

Chapter 12 concludes with a broad view of digital marketing trends in the pet industry, highlighting platforms, strategies, and opportunities for authentic consumer engagement.

CONCLUSION

Taken together, these chapters reveal the extraordinary breadth of ways in which animals contribute to contemporary branding and consumer culture. From symbolic roosters and sports mascots to social media celebrities and airline policies, the case studies and analyses presented in this volume underscore that animals are no longer marginal elements of marketing—they are central actors in shaping emotional, cultural, and commercial value.

Yet, with this growing prominence comes responsibility. Petfluencers and pet-driven branding raise ethical questions around commodification, sustainability, authenticity, and animal welfare. Readers will notice that many contributions address not only the opportunities but also the risks inherent in this phenomenon. As editors, we emphasize the importance of approaching pet-powered branding with critical awareness and ethical sensitivity.

Finally, this book reflects the collaborative effort of an international group of scholars united by curiosity and commitment to advancing knowledge in an emerging field. We extend our gratitude to the contributors for their thoughtful research, and to the readers who will continue this conversation through their own practices, scholarship, and reflections. We hope that *Petfluencers and Pet-Powered Branding* will inspire innovative thinking, responsible branding, and renewed appreciation for the many ways animals shape our shared cultural and economic landscapes.

Luzia Arantes

University of Aveiro (UA), Portugal & Polytechnic University of Cávado and Ave (IPCA), Portugal

Bruno Sousa

Polytechnic University of Cávado and Ave (IPCA), Portugal

Chapter 1
From Heritage Interpretation to Sustainable Tourism Routes:
The Barcelos Rooster Case Study Within the UNESCO Creative Cities Network

Francisco Joaquim Gonçalves
https://orcid.org/0000-0003-1965-7427
Polytechnic University of Cávado and Ave, Portugal

Carlos Manuel Costa
University of Aveiro, Portugal

ABSTRACT

This chapter proposes a sustainable tourism route in Barcelos, integrating its cultural and historical landmarks with a special focus on the iconic Barcelos Rooster. Through heritage interpretation, the route aims to enrich visitor experiences, raise community awareness, and promote sustainable tourism aligned with the UNESCO Creative Cities Network. The methodology includes a literature review and qualitative surveys of residents and visitors to gather diverse insights. The outcomes involve identifying the best practices for sustainable tourism, analyzing Barcelos' current tourism landscape, and designing an itinerary centered on the Barcelos Rooster. The research also evaluates potential impacts on local communities and heritage, ensuring this route reflects local values. Innovative digital marketing strategies are

DOI: 10.4018/979-8-3373-4342-6.ch001

trying to promote the route, emphasizing Barcelos' cultural identity. The chapter contributes to a sustainable tourism model that may serve as a benchmark for other UNESCO Creative Cities.

INTRODUCTION

Barcelos, a member of the UNESCO Creative Cities Network, holds significant cultural and tourism potential as Portugal's capital of crafts and the birthplace of the iconic Barcelos Rooster (*Galo de Barcelos*), one of the most recognized symbols of Portuguese tourism. This research investigates how heritage interpretation, through educational activities and community involvement, can contribute to the development of a sustainable tourism route in Barcelos, leveraging the Barcelos Rooster as a central branding element within the framework of the UNESCO Creative Cities Network.

Despite its cultural richness, previous studies indicate that only a small fraction of visitors are aware of Barcelos's UNESCO designation (Gonçalves & Costa, 2020). This study forms part of a post-doctoral research project that uses Barcelos's membership in the UNESCO Creative Cities Network and its association with the Barcelos Rooster as a case study. The project aims to design a sustainable tourism route that integrates the city's key cultural and historical attractions, with a particular focus on the Barcelos Rooster as a unifying symbol and brand.

LITERATURE REVIEW

The Barcelos Rooster (Galo de Barcelos) is an emblematic figure deeply embedded in the cultural identity of Barcelos, Portugal. Known for its vibrant artisanal traditions, the city stands as a hub of creative expression, with the Barcelos Rooster emerging as a powerful symbol that resonates with both locals and visitors. Rooted in folklore, this figure not only embodies the region's rich storytelling heritage but also exemplifies its capacity to communicate cultural narratives through art.

Barcelos is widely celebrated for its strong craftsmanship, particularly in pottery, ceramic figurines, embroidery, and woodworking. These artistic practices reflect the community's deep-rooted skills and contribute to a dynamic, sustainable creative economy. Local artisans play a vital role in preserving and evolving the city's cultural identity, skillfully blending tradition with innovation to keep these crafts alive and relevant. Creative tourism has become a key strategy in safeguarding these traditions. By fostering this form of engagement, Barcelos not only supports emerging artisans but also ensures that its artistic legacy remains a vibrant part of the local economy. This approach aligns closely with the goals of UNESCO's Creative Cities

Network, which recognizes cities that place culture and creativity at the heart of their development strategies (Gonçalves & Costa, 2022).

Within the rich tapestry of local crafts, the creation of pottery and ceramic figurative objects, such as oxen, pigs, horses, roosters, and religious figures like saints and devils, has long been a defining tradition in Barcelos. Among these, the rooster holds a particularly esteemed place. In an 1899 study, ethnographer Rocha Peixoto highlighted the rooster's prominence in local art, describing it as the most noble and intricately crafted of all animal representations. He also emphasized its symbolic significance in folklore and mythology, referencing Greek traditions, the miracles of Jesus Christ and Saint James, and the belief that the rooster's crow dispels demons and heralds the dawn (Rocha Peixoto, 1966).

The Barcelos Rooster has become a profound element of intangible cultural heritage and a symbol of both local and national identity, deeply rooted in two ancestral traditions: the artisanal crafting of rooster figurines and the Jacobean legend of the miraculous rooster associated with the Camino de Santiago. These traditions converged in the 1960s, largely due to the efforts of Barcelos' mayor, Luís Figueiredo, who unified them under a shared mythological and cultural symbol to prevent the private registration of the "Galo de Barcelos" brand. Furthermore, prominent political figures such as António Ferro and António Salazar played key roles in promoting the Barcelos Rooster as a cornerstone of Portuguese folk art. Their initiatives capitalized on the rooster's commercial appeal, enabling the mayor of Barcelos to more explicitly link it to the Jacobean legend. This strategic association helped regionalize and legitimize the rooster as a culturally significant emblem. Tourism played a pivotal role in embedding the rooster within Portuguese cultural consciousness. As tourism expanded, so too did the socioeconomic importance of the Barcelos Rooster. Through the cultural policies of António Ferro and António Salazar, these ancestral customs were transformed into a unified tradition, elevating the rooster from a local craft to a national icon. Today, the crafts associated with the Barcelos Rooster and the Jacobean legend are inseparably inked through this shared mythological figure, the rooster. This connection is continually reinforced by the local community and the cultural landscape of Barcelos, solidifying the rooster's status as an enduring symbol of both regional identity and broader Portuguese heritage (Gonçalves, 2018). Indeed, António Salazar employed ethnography to legitimize the nationalist ideology underpinning his regime (Melo, 2001).

Regarding the historical origin of the Barcelos Rooster, this study also explores its significance as an important element of intangible cultural heritage and a symbol of local identity. It investigates whether the community identifies with this icon and why this connection has endured over time. The findings reveal that the Barcelos Rooster originated from two longstanding traditions: the craft of creating rooster figurines and the Jacobean legend of the miraculous rooster on the Camino de Santiago. These traditions were primarily unified in the 20th century through the influence of tourism and cultural promotion. Both legend and the craft share several core elements: the mythological animal, the rooster, the geographical region of Barcelos, and the local community. While the legend dates to medieval times, the tradition of producing ceramic rooster figurines has an even longer history, spanning several centuries. Historically, local pottery depicted a variety of domestic animals such as oxen, pigs, horses, and hens, but roosters became prominent due to their cultural associations with virtues and miracles (Gonçalves & Costa, 2016).

Regarding the morphological evolution of the Barcelos Rooster, the early "proto rooster" of the 19th century was a small figurine, approximately 15 centimeters tall, characterized by a compact body, a small comb, and wattles, features that resemble those of the modern Barcelos Rooster. This early version also bore similarities to weathervanes, a common regional motif. Advancements in pottery techniques during the 1930s led to changes in both size and detail, as exemplified by pieces housed in the Museu de Olaria in Barcelos. The version of the rooster presented at the 1940 Portuguese World Exhibition was a larger, wheel-thrown ceramic figure, approximately 25 centimeters tall. By the late 1940s, the traditional morphology of the Barcelos Rooster had become well established. Throughout the 1950s, a new form emerged—known as the "elegant rooster", characterized by a slenderer body, a taller and more graceful neck, and a more detailed comb and tail featuring serrated edges, though not as pronounced as in earlier versions (Mimoso, 2010). Furthermore, around 1955, the local painter Gonçalves Torres was commissioned to redesign the rooster for a promotional poster for the *Festas das Cruzes* pilgrimage. In doing so, he introduced a distinctive decorative style featuring prominent red heart-traditional motifs from the Minho region as central elements. These features were soon adopted by local craftspeople in Barcelos, enhancing the rooster's visual appeal and commercial success. This new design quickly gained widespread popularity, particularly through international interior design magazines, most notably in France. As a result, the Barcelos Rooster became increasingly recognized and appreciated both nationally and internationally (Gonçalves, 2018).

The promotion of the Barcelos Rooster as a symbol of Portuguese folk art was significantly bolstered by the efforts of influential political figures such as António Salazar and António Ferro. Their cultural policies, combined with the growing commercial success of the ceramic rooster, motivated local authorities to formally associate the figure with the Jacobean legend of the miraculous rooster. This deliberate linkage not only reinforced the rooster's symbolic value but also helped to regionalize and legitimize it as a vital emblem of local cultural heritage. As a result, the convergence of these two ancient traditions, artisanal craftsmanship and legendary narrative, gained increasing prominence, particularly in the context of the expanding tourism industry in Barcelos. The rooster evolved into a powerful cultural icon, embodying both the creative identity of the region and the broader narrative of Portuguese heritage, while also contributing to the socioeconomic development of the local community (Gonçalves & Costa, 2019a; Gonçalves & Costa, 2019b).

The Jacobean legend of the miraculous rooster, associated with the Camino de Santiago and Saint James' miracles, represents a pivotal aspect of Barcelos' cultural identity, symbolizing divine justice and the community's enduring faith. According to ethnographer Rocha Peixoto (1966), the cultural, religious, and mythological significance of the rooster is deeply embedded in ancient traditions. The longstanding practice of crafting ceramic representations of roosters and other domestic animals has endured for centuries, highlighting their sustained cultural and artisanal importance within the region.

In Barcelos, this artisanal tradition became closely intertwined with the Jacobean legend, primarily through the influence of tourism and deliberate cultural promotion. The earliest documented references to the legend date back to the 19th century, including an 1867 article by Amaral Ribeiro in *Notícia Descriptiva de Barcellos*, and the *Memoria Histórica da Villa de Barcellos, Barcellinhos e Villa Nova de Famelicão*, authored by Domingos Joaquim Pereira, also known as the "Abbot of Louro." Chapter XI of Pereira's work discusses the gallows of Barcelos and a stone cross (*cruzeiro*) associated with the legend. Ribeiro's article remains one of the most important early sources documenting these traditions (Gonçalves, 2018).

Also, on display at the *Museu Arqueológico de Barcelos* is a granite *cruzeiro* carved in relief, which visually evokes the Jacobean legend of the miraculous rooster. The sculpture depicts a pilgrim awaiting judgment, with Saint James supporting his feet below and Jesus Christ crucified above. A prominently featured rooster affirms the pilgrim's innocence, serving as a powerful symbol of divine intervention. According to the legend, the story unfolds as follows: "In the town of Barcelos, a crime was committed, and the perpetrator remained unidentified. A pilgrim, traveling along the Camino de Santiago to fulfill a vow, arrived in the town. As a stranger, he was falsely accused, arrested, and sentenced to death. The man proclaimed his innocence and prayed fervently for justice. As a final request before his execution, he asked to be brought before the Magistrate. When presented to the Judge, the pilgrim once again declared his innocence. At that moment, a roasted rooster lay on the judge's table for his lunch. As the pilgrim spoke, the rooster miraculously stood up and crowed loudly its cry affirming the man's innocence. His life was spared, and later, in gratitude to the Virgin Mary and Saint James, he returned to Barcelos to erect a monument commemorating this miracle." This legend has become a foundational element of Barcelos' cultural identity, symbolizing divine justice and the enduring power of faith. Over time, both the story and its central symbol, the rooster, have been deeply integrated into local traditions and cultural narratives, reinforcing the town's image as a place where myth, history, and spirituality converge. Through tourism and cultural promotion, the legend continues to play a vital role in preserving Barcelos' intangible heritage and fostering a strong sense of collective identity (Pires de Lima, 1965).

In sum, this study highlights the deep connection between cultural heritage and community identity by examining the significance of the Barcelos Rooster as a symbol of intangible cultural heritage. It explores whether the local community continues to identify with this emblem and investigates the reasons behind its enduring cultural relevance.

The research concludes that the Barcelos Rooster emerged from the convergence of two ancient traditions: the artisanal craft of producing rooster figurines and the Jacobean legend of the miraculous rooster. These traditions became closely intertwined during the 20th century, largely due to the growing influence of tourism and strategic cultural promotion. Both the legend and the craft share key elements that reinforce their cultural resonance: the mythological figure of the rooster, the geographical identity of Barcelos, and the collective memory and participation of the local community. While the legend dates to medieval times, the ceramic tradition spans several centuries. Historically, local pottery featured a variety of domestic animals, such as oxen, pigs, horses, and hens, but the rooster gradually gained prominence due to its symbolic associations with virtues, miracles, and divine justice.

Through this fusion of myth and material culture, the Barcelos Rooster has become a powerful emblem of regional identity and a lasting representation of Portugal's intangible heritage.

Heritage interpretation: it plays a pivotal role in connecting people with the cultural and natural values of a place. According to the International Charter for Cultural Tourism (ICOMOS, 1999), cultural and natural heritage, diversity, and living cultures are among the most significant future tourist attractions. These elements serve not only as sources of identity and memory but also as key drivers of creative and cultural tourism. Despite the clear connection between heritage and tourism, supported by scientific evidence and the increasing demand for cultural experiences, practical integration remains challenging. In Portugal, for instance, empirical data show that cultural and heritage elements are often underrepresented in the tourism sector (Costa, 2005).

Heritage interpretation effectively acts as the "voice" of territorial resources (Gonçalves & Costa, 2019). Heritage interpretation also links natural and cultural heritage, diversity, and living cultures as major tourism attractions (ICOMOS, 1999) The emotional bond between the host community and its heritage is fundamental to creating meaningful tourism experiences. Therefore, heritage interpretation should be an integral component of tourism activities, as it is crucial for transforming local resources into sustainable and enriching attractions (Coelho, Figueira & Costa, 2014).

Tilden (2007, p. 163) stated that interpretation is "an educational activity which aims to reveal meanings and relationships through the use of original objects, by firsthand experience, and by illustrative media, rather than simply to communicate factual information". It plays a significant role in tourism by transforming endogenous resources into sustainable attractions, adding value to visitor experiences, and fosters socioeconomic benefits while contributing to the well-being of local communities (Knudson, et al., 2003). Interpretation transcends mere communication; it acts as the voice of heritage, revealing the meanings and values embedded in both tangible and intangible assets. This process enables visitors to engage with places in meaningful and transformative ways (Gonçalves & Costa, 2019b).

The Ename Charter (ICOMOS, 2008) emphasizes the importance of training and employing local interpreters to ensure that interpretation reflects community voices and promotes sustainable development. Similarly, Yu, et al. (2025) highlight that integrating local knowledge and perspectives is vital for building resilient, inclusive tourism models. Taken together, these perspectives highlight that heritage interpretation plays a crucial role not only in enriching visitor experiences but also in advancing sustainable development by forging meaningful connections between tourists and cultural or natural heritage. To fully realize these benefits, stakeholders should prioritize the inclusion of community voices and the capacity-building of local interpreters. Such an approach ensures that tourism models are not only inclusive and resilient but also capable of showcasing the unique assets of each destination while enhancing local well-being.

While traditional cultural tourism often involves passive observation of heritage sites, creative tourism encourages visitors to actively engage with local traditions, crafts, and stories, transforming sightseeing into immersive experiences (Gonçalves & Costa, 2022; Richards, 2011). Therefore, heritage symbols like the Barcelos Rooster exemplify this approach, serving as powerful icons that reflect local identity and cultural richness. Developing tourism routes that highlight these symbols and associated practices allows tourists to meaningfully connect with the territory's intangible and tangible heritage, fostering deeper understanding and appreciation. Sustainable tourism development must rely on the endogenous resources of the territory (Fazenda, 2014).

The concept of territory goes beyond its physical attributes; it embodies a shared space shaped by the community, a synthesis of natural landscapes, built environments, cultural dynamics, and the intangible heritage that imbues it with identity (Umbelino, 2014). Tourists are drawn to destinations by these distinctive features: immovable resources such as landscapes, heritage symbols, and local craftsmanship, all of which contribute to the territory's unique character. Considering this, tourism organizations should embrace a philosophy rooted in community engagement and knowledge exchange, leveraging local assets to foster innovation and gain a competitive advantage. Furthermore, building resilient tourism networks requires forging connections not only within the region but also with external stakeholders, national and international, across diverse sectors. This collaborative approach facilitates the infusion of new knowledge and ideas, paving the way for the development of innovative tourism services and products (Brandão & Costa, 2014).

Route and itinerary planning: it focusses on creating experiences that deepen the essence of territories. This strategic approach encourages tourists to appreciate both traditional and contemporary heritage by identifying resources, transforming them into attractions, and presenting them effectively through thoughtfully designed cultural experiences. Digital databases with tools for data management, analysis, and multimedia development support comprehensive inventories, accommodate new attractions, and enhance tourism experiences. These efforts produce unique tourism products that reflect a destination's character, foster stakeholder cooperation, and stimulate economic growth. Routes serve as both promotional tools and networks, promoting local resources, differentiation, and territorial promotion. Their creation is fundamental for sustainable tourism development, supporting territorial differentiation, resource mobilization, and the building of cooperation and competition networks, which ultimately promote and strengthen the tourism industry (Figueira, 2010;2013).

Creating well-defined tourism routes and itineraries is essential for sustainable development, as they directly contribute to territorial differentiation, the promotion of local resources, and socio-economic vitality. These routes serve as tangible expressions of local identity, exemplified by historic paths such as the Camino de Santiago, which has evolved from a religious pilgrimage in the 11th and 12th centuries into a leading cultural itinerary recognized by UNESCO, first in Spain (1993) and later in France (1998) (Cravidão, 2014). Ultimately, integrating heritage symbols, active cultural participation, and community-driven resource development into route planning is key to fostering authentic and sustainable tourism experiences. This approach not only preserves and enhances local identities but also promotes broader economic and social well-being.

The success of sustainable cultural and creative routes depends heavily on effective promotion through digital marketing. To maximize its impact, tourism promotion must utilize tools such as social media platforms, targeted advertising, multimedia storytelling, and interactive websites, as highlighted by Arantes and Sousa (2021). Their case study on Barcelos demonstrates how digital marketing enhances visibility and engagement with heritage assets like the Barcelos Rooster and pilgrimage routes, enabling destinations to reach broader audiences and provide real-time updates that foster visitor interaction. Furthermore, Gonçalves *et al.*(2022) argue that digital tourism strategies contribute to the preservation and valorization of intangible cultural heritage while promoting sustainability. When properly implemented, these strategies not only amplify the visibility of local heritage but also support its preservation and sustainable development, fostering more inclusive and enriching tourism experiences. In short, digital marketing tools boost visibility, engagement, and sustainability for heritage tourism. When used effectively, they help preserve cultural assets while creating more inclusive and resilient tourism experiences.

METHODOLOGY

This study adopts a qualitative research design, as it is best suited to explore the meanings, perceptions, and cultural significance embedded in heritage and community narratives. As Collis and Hussey (2005) note, the choice between qualitative and quantitative methods depends on the nature of the research problem. Given this study's focus on cultural identity, symbolic representation, and community engagement, a qualitative approach is both appropriate and necessary. Following Creswell (2013), the research design integrates multiple qualitative methods, including a case study, literature review, qualitative digital survey, and thematic content analysis. This multi-method strategy allows for triangulation, enhancing the credibility and depth of the findings.

The research is framed within an interpretivist paradigm (Resende, 2016), which emphasizes understanding the subjective experiences and cultural contexts of individuals. This paradigm supports the study's aim to investigate how heritage interpretation and community involvement can contribute to sustainable tourism development in Barcelos, particularly through the symbolic use of the Barcelos Rooster. The research question for this study is the following: "how can heritage interpretation, through educational activities and community involvement, contribute to developing a sustainable tourism route in Barcelos, leveraging its main tourism asset, the Barcelos Rooster, as its brand, within the framework of the UNESCO Creative Cities Network"? Its main goal is: "to develop a sustainable tourism route in Barcelos that integrates its key cultural and historical attractions, with a special focus on the Barcelos Rooster as its brand, within the framework of the UNESCO Creative Cities Network". And its objectives are the following: i) explaining the historical and cultural significance of the Barcelos Rooster and its connection to Barcelos' status within the UNESCO Creative Cities Network; ii) analyzing the tourism and cultural assets in Barcelos; iii) evaluating the best practices for developing sustainable tourism routes; iv) creating an itinerary that integrates all key cultural and historical tourism attractions in Barcelos under the "Barcelos Rooster brand"; v) developing innovative digital marketing strategies aimed at promoting the "Barcelos Rooster Tourism Route", with a particular emphasis on preserving and showcasing the cultural heritage of Barcelos.

Primary data were collected through semi-structured qualitative digital surveys containing open-ended questions designed to capture participants' perceptions, experiences, and ideas related to the research question (Creswell, 2013). Participants were purposively sampled to ensure the collection of rich and relevant data (Altinay & Paraskevas, 2008). The sample included community members, local tourism stakeholders, cultural experts, and visitors. A total of ten participants took part in the study, comprising six residents and four foreign participants, six males and four females. All respondents were purposively selected based on their professional or academic engagement with themes directly related to the research question, including cultural heritage, heritage interpretation, and sustainable tourism development. Their diverse backgrounds, ranging from tourism business management and tour guiding to academic roles in tourism and cultural studies, ensured a rich and contextually relevant dataset aligned with the study's objectives. The participants represented a broad age range, from 21 to 67 years, contributing intergenerational perspectives to the understanding of heritage and tourism in Barcelos.

Data Analysis: The qualitative data gathered throughout the research process were subjected to a detailed and systematic thematic content analysis. This analytical approach was primarily guided by the methodological framework proposed by Bardin (1977) which emphasizes a rigorous and structured process for interpreting qualitative information. The method involves several key stages, including an initial phase of familiarization with the data, followed by the systematic coding of textual elements, the categorization of these codes into broader conceptual groupings, and finally, the development of overarching themes. This process allows for a nuanced and in-depth exploration of the meanings embedded in participants' responses, capturing both explicit and implicit dimensions of their perspectives. In addition to Bardin's foundational approach, the analysis was further informed by the widely recognized framework developed by Braun and Clarke (2006). Their contribution to the field of qualitative research highlights thematic analysis as a versatile and accessible method that is particularly well-suited for identifying, analyzing, and reporting patterns within qualitative datasets. Despite being frequently employed in psychological and social research, thematic analysis has often been under-theorized and inconsistently applied. Braun and Clarke's work addresses this gap by offering a clear and coherent set of guidelines that support researchers in conducting thematic analysis in a more deliberate, transparent, and theoretically grounded manner. Their framework also draws attention to common challenges and methodological pitfalls, thereby enhancing the overall rigor and credibility of the analysis.

The data collection and subsequent analysis were facilitated using Microsoft Forms, a digital platform that enabled the efficient organization, storage, and preliminary categorization of participant responses. This technological support contributed to the systematic handling of qualitative data and ensured consistency throughout the analytical process. Furthermore, the entire procedure was conducted in alignment with the methodological principles articulated by Altinay and Paraskevas (2008), which emphasize the importance of maintaining a strong connection between the research objectives and the analytical strategies employed. Their guidance helped ensure that the analysis remained both methodologically sound and responsive to the specificities and subtleties of the data collected.

The thematic analysis focused on identifying and interpreting themes that emerged in relation to three central areas of interest: heritage interpretation, community involvement, and digital marketing strategies. These thematic areas were examined within the broader context of designing and implementing a sustainable tourism route in the municipality of Barcelos. To structure the analysis, five core research objectives were established, each of which was represented by a distinct analytical theme. These themes served as interpretive lenses through which the data were examined, allowing for a coherent and comprehensive understanding of participants' insights and experiences.

The findings derived from this analytical process reveal a rich tapestry of cultural values, highlight the untapped potential for tourism development in the region, and point toward strategic directions for promoting sustainable and digitally integrated tourism practices. Finally, it is worth noting that content analysis, as emphasized by Vala (1986), continues to be one of the most widely utilized and adaptable techniques in empirical research across the Human and Social Sciences. Its enduring relevance lies in its capacity to combine methodological rigor with analytical flexibility, making it particularly suitable for studies such as this one.

Table 1. Thematic Analysis of Participant Responses Aligned with Research Objectives

Theme / Research Objective	Key Insights	Citations
Theme 1. Cultural and Historical Significance of the Barcelos Rooster	National symbol of Portuguese tourism	10
	Traditional piece of Barcelos handicraft	8
	Symbol of the Camino de Santiago legend	7
	Local cultural heritage icon	6
	Representation within UNESCO Creative Cities Network	5
Theme 2. Mapping Barcelos' Cultural and Tourism Assets	Medieval Downtown	10
	Barcelos Rooster	9
	Barcelos Pottery Museum	7
	Local artisan workshops	5

continued on following page

Table 1. Continued

Theme / Research Objective	Key Insights	Citations
	Legend of the Rooster on the Camino de Santiago	5
	Shrine of Senhor da Cruz	3
Theme 3. Best Practices in Sustainable Tourism Development	Preservation of cultural heritage	9
	Environmental sustainability	9
	Community involvement	8
	Accessibility and inclusivity	7
	Visitor experience and satisfaction	4
	Economic development	2
Theme 4. Designing the Barcelos Rooster Tourism Itinerary	Guided cultural and historical tours	10
	Wine and gastronomy tours	8
	Live storytelling performances of the Barcelos Rooster legend on the Camino de Santiago	8
	Artisan demonstrations	6
	Pottery and handicraft workshops	6
	Culinary experiences featuring the Barcelos Rooster	3
Theme 5. Digital Promotion and Cultural Preservation	Social media (Instagram, Facebook)	11
	Official tourism websites	9
	Online travel blogs and forums	9
	Mobile apps with interactive maps	8
	Augmented reality (AR) experiences	3
	Email newsletters	1

Source: Author's own elaboration based on qualitative data collected in 2025.

The thematic analysis conducted in this study reveals a profoundly embedded cultural identity centered around the iconic figure of the Barcelos Rooster. This symbol emerged consistently across participant responses as a powerful and unifying emblem, representing not only national pride but also the unique local heritage of Barcelos. It is widely perceived as a tangible artifact of artisanal tradition and a vessel for spiritual and historical narratives. Its legendary association with the Camino de Santiago was frequently mentioned, suggesting that the Rooster functions as a symbolic bridge between regional folklore and the broader cultural context of international pilgrimage. Moreover, its formal recognition through inclusion in the UNESCO Creative Cities Network further affirms its global cultural significance and underscores the community's deep commitment to its preservation and promotion.

Participants repeatedly emphasized the richness of Barcelos' cultural and tourism assets, identifying them as foundational elements of the city's appeal to both domestic and international visitors. The Medieval Downtown was particularly celebrated for its architectural elegance and historical atmosphere, often described as the "soul" of the city. The Pottery Museum and various artisan workshops were not only appreciated as tourist attractions but also recognized as dynamic spaces that preserve and perpetuate local craftsmanship. These venues were viewed as essential for sustaining cultural continuity and for providing immersive, hands-on experiences that connect visitors with the living traditions of the region. The legend of the miracle of the Rooster, interwoven throughout local landmarks and narratives, was consistently cited as a central storyline that reinforces and unifies the city's cultural identity.

In relation to sustainable tourism development, participants advocated for a comprehensive and integrated approach. The preservation of cultural heritage was regarded as a fundamental priority, with several respondents expressing concern about the risks of cultural dilution and loss of authenticity due to excessive commercialization. Environmental sustainability also emerged as a key theme, with calls for the implementation of eco-conscious infrastructure and the promotion of responsible tourist behavior. Community involvement was identified as a critical success factor, with strong support for participatory planning processes and the empowerment of local stakeholders. Additionally, issues of accessibility and inclusivity were highlighted as areas requiring further attention, particularly in terms of accommodating the diverse needs of visitors and ensuring that cultural experiences are equitably accessible to all.

The legend of the Rooster, embedded in various landmarks and stories, was frequently cited as a narrative thread that ties the city's identity together.

In the realm of sustainable tourism development, respondents emphasized a holistic approach. Preserving cultural heritage was seen as non-negotiable, with many expressing concerns over the potential loss of authenticity due to commercialization. Environmental sustainability was also a recurring theme, with calls for eco-friendly infrastructure and responsible visitor behavior. Community involvement was highlighted as a cornerstone of success, with participants advocating participatory planning and local empowerment. Accessibility and inclusivity were noted as areas needing improvement, particularly to accommodate diverse visitors' needs and ensure equitable access to cultural experiences.

When conceptualizing a potential "Barcelos Rooster tourism route," participants expressed a clear preference for tourism experiences that are immersive, narrative-driven, and rooted in cultural authenticity. Rather than passive sightseeing, respondents favored guided tours that offer educational value and contextual depth, allowing visitors to engage meaningfully with the historical and cultural significance of the region. Gastronomic experiences, particularly those featuring locally produced wines and traditional dishes inspired by the symbolism of the Barcelos Rooster, were highlighted as memorable and sensorially rich components of the itinerary. These culinary encounters were seen not only as enjoyable but also as powerful vehicles for cultural storytelling and identity reinforcement.

Live storytelling performances, especially those dramatizing the legend of the miracle of the Barcelos Rooster along the Camino de Santiago, were praised for their ability to animate historical narratives and foster emotional connections with visitors. Similarly, artisan demonstrations and hands-on workshops, such as pottery-making and handicraft sessions, were valued for their role in preserving traditional skills and providing direct economic support to local creators. These activities were consistently described as essential tools for cultural transmission, offering both entertainment and education while reinforcing the community's intangible heritage.

In the domain of digital promotion and cultural preservation, participants demonstrated a strong inclination toward dynamic, interactive, and technologically enhanced platforms. Social media channels, particularly Instagram and Facebook were identified as the most effective tools for engaging diverse audiences, with a special emphasis on reaching younger travelers who are more responsive to visual and real-time content. Official tourism websites and well-established travel blogs were appreciated for their credibility, depth of information, and ability to convey a coherent narrative about the destination.

Mobile applications featuring interactive maps and geolocated content were considered indispensable for enhancing the on-site visitor experience, offering practical guidance and enriching exploration. Notably, there was growing enthusiasm for the integration of augmented reality (AR) technologies, which were seen as innovative tools for animating historical sites and delivering immersive educational content. This interest reflects a broader shift toward digitally enhanced storytelling as a strategic means of both attracting tourists and safeguarding intangible cultural heritage, ensuring that local traditions remain vibrant and accessible in an increasingly digital world.

RESULTS AND DISCUSSION

This section presents and interprets the empirical findings of the study considering the literature reviewed. The discussion is structured thematically, aligning with the five core research objectives, and integrates critical reflection supported by academic sources. The results of this study are organized around five thematic areas aligned with the research objectives: (1) the cultural and historical significance of the Barcelos Rooster, (2) the mapping of cultural and tourism assets, (3) best practices in sustainable tourism development, (4) the design of a themed tourism itinerary, and (5) digital promotion and cultural preservation. These findings are discussed in light of relevant literature on heritage interpretation, creative tourism, territorial identity, tourism route planning, and digital marketing.

1. The Cultural and Historical Significance of the Barcelos Rooster: Participants consistently identified the Barcelos Rooster as a powerful symbol of local and national identity. It was described as a handcrafted artifact, a national emblem, and a representation of the Camino de Santiago legend of the miracle of the Rooster. These findings align with Gonçalves and Costa (2016, 2022), who argue that the Rooster embodies a convergence of two traditions: the artisanal production of ceramic figurines and the Jacobean legend of the miraculous rooster. This dual heritage reinforces the Rooster's symbolic power and its role as a vehicle for cultural storytelling.

The Rooster's transformation into a globally recognized icon, particularly after its stylized redesign by Gonçalves Torres in the 1955, demonstrates how cultural symbols evolve through tourism and strategic promotion (Gonçalves, 2018). As Rocha Peixoto (1966) noted, the Rooster has long held a privileged place in local art and mythology, symbolizing virtues such as justice and divine protection. Its inclusion in the UNESCO Creative Cities Network further affirms its cultural relevance and the pride the community places in its preservation.

2. Mapping Barcelos' Cultural and Tourism Assets: Participants highlighted key cultural assets such as the Medieval Downtown, the Pottery Museum, artisan workshops, and the Shrine of Senhor da Cruz. These sites were valued not only for their historical and aesthetic appeal but also for their role in preserving and transmitting local identity. This reflects Umbelino's (2014) concept of territory as a space shaped by community, memory, and intangible heritage.

The mapping of these assets supports the idea that tourism development should be grounded in territorial differentiation, the unique combination of cultural, natural, and symbolic resources that define a place (Figueira, 2010, 2013). These findings also align with the literature on endogenous development, which emphasizes the importance of leveraging local resources and knowledge to foster sustainable tourism (Brandão & Costa, 2014).

3. Best Practices in Sustainable Tourism Development: Participants advocated for a holistic approach to sustainability, emphasizing the preservation of cultural heritage, environmental responsibility, community involvement, and accessibility.

These priorities reflect the principles outlined by Coelho, Figueira, and Costa (2014), who argue that sustainable tourism must be rooted in local values and inclusive planning.

Heritage interpretation emerged as a key strategy for achieving these goals. As Tilden (2007) and Knudson et al. (2003) suggest, interpretation is not merely about conveying information but about revealing the deeper meanings and relationships embedded in heritage. It fosters emotional connections between visitors and places, transforming tourism into a meaningful and transformative experience. The Ename Charter (ICOMOS, 2008) and Yu et al. (2025) further emphasize the importance of involving local interpreters and community voices to ensure that tourism development is inclusive and resilient.

4. Designing the Barcelos Rooster Tourism Itinerary: Participants envisioned a themed itinerary that includes guided tours, gastronomy, live storytelling, artisan demonstrations, and handicraft workshops. These activities were praised for their immersive and educational qualities, aligning with the principles of creative tourism, which encourages active participation and co-creation (Richards & Raymond, 2000; Gonçalves & Costa, 2022). This approach also reflects best practices in tourism route planning, which aim to deepen the visitors' understanding of a territory by transforming local resources into coherent and engaging experiences. The success of the Camino de Santiago as a cultural route, evolving from a medieval pilgrimage into a UNESCO-recognized itinerary, demonstrates the potential of such models to promote both heritage preservation and socio-economic development (Cravidão, 2014).
5. Digital Promotion and Cultural Preservation: Participants expressed strong support for digital tools such as social media, mobile apps, and augmented reality (AR) to promote and preserve cultural heritage. These tools were seen as essential for reaching broader audiences, enhancing visitor engagement, and animating historical narratives. This aligns with Arantes and Sousa (2021), who highlight the role of digital marketing in increasing the visibility of heritage assets and fostering real-time interaction. Moreover, digital strategies contribute to the preservation and valorization of intangible cultural heritage, as noted by Gonçalves et al. (2022). When effectively implemented, these tools not only amplify the reach of local traditions but also support their sustainability by creating more inclusive and resilient tourism experiences.

Taken together, the findings of this study affirm Barcelos Rooster's role as a multidimensional cultural symbol that bridges tradition and innovation, local identity and global recognition. The integration of this symbol into a creative, sustainable, and digitally enhanced tourism strategy offers a compelling model for other destinations seeking to balance cultural authenticity with contemporary visitor expectations. The study underscores the importance of heritage interpretation, territorial identity, strategic route planning, and digital innovation as key pillars of inclusive and resilient tourism development. By leveraging local assets, engaging communities, and embracing technological tools, destinations like Barcelos can foster tourism models that are not only economically viable but also culturally meaningful and socially sustainable.

CONCLUSION

This study has examined the development of a sustainable tourism route in Barcelos, with a particular focus on the iconic Barcelos Rooster as a central cultural symbol and unifying brand for the region's heritage. The findings underscore the deep-rooted cultural identity of the area, shaped by artisanal craftsmanship, mythological narratives, and a strong sense of community. These elements are further reinforced by the strategic use of digital technologies designed to enhance heritage interpretation and visitor engagement.

The research confirms that the Barcelos Rooster functions not only as a powerful emblem of local heritage and national pride but also as a cohesive branding element that encapsulates the diverse cultural assets of the region. It highlights the critical importance of integrating cultural resources, sustainable tourism practices, and interpretive strategies to foster tourism experiences that are meaningful, resilient, and inclusive.

By embracing creative and immersive forms of tourism, Barcelos is well-positioned to expand its appeal to a wide range of visitors while preserving its distinctive cultural landscape. This study contributes to broader academic and policy discussions on the role of intangible heritage, community participation, and digital innovation in shaping sustainable tourism development. Ultimately, it demonstrates how heritage-based tourism can serve as a catalyst for cultural continuity, economic vitality, and social cohesion.

Recommendations

To support the sustainable development of tourism in Barcelos, the following strategic recommendations are proposed:

Develop Interpretive Programs: Establish comprehensive training initiatives for local interpreters and storytellers to deliver compelling, authentic narratives that connect visitors with the cultural and historical richness of Barcelos. These programs should emphasize emotional engagement and cultural sensitivity.

Enhance Digital Engagement: Invest in the development and maintenance of digital tools such as mobile applications, augmented reality (AR) experiences, and targeted social media campaigns. These technologies can significantly increase the visibility of the Barcelos Rooster and related heritage assets, while also enriching the visitor experience.

Support Artisan Communities: Provide sustained financial support, capacity-building programs, and marketing assistance to local artisans. This will help preserve traditional crafts, foster innovation, and attract tourists interested in creative and participatory cultural experiences.

Implement Inclusive Tourism Strategies: Ensure that all tourism infrastructure and services are designed with accessibility and inclusivity in mind. This includes physical access, multilingual resources, and culturally appropriate content to guarantee equitable participation for all visitors.

Foster Community Participation: Actively involve local residents in tourism planning, decision-making, and implementation processes. Community engagement is essential for building local ownership, preserving cultural authenticity, and ensuring long-term sustainability.

Create Thematic Routes: Design and promote integrated tourism itineraries that combine key elements such as traditional crafts, regional gastronomy, live storytelling, and historical landmarks. These routes should be centered around the Barcelos Rooster and curated to offer immersive, educational, and memorable experiences.

REFERENCES

Altinay, L., & Paraskevas, A. (2008). *Planning Research in Hospitality and Tourism* (1st ed.). Elsevier, Ltd.

Arantes, L., & Sousa, B. (2021). Digital Marketing and Tourism. *Case Study Applied to Barcelos.*, (June), 23–26.

Bardin, L. (1977). *Análise de Conteúdo*. Presses Universitaires de France.

Brandão, F., & Costa, C. (2014). Inovação em Turismo: Uma Abordagem Sistémica e Territorial. In Z. Costa, Carlos; Brandão, Filipa; Costa, Rui; e Breda (Ed.), *Produtos e Competitividade do Turismo na Lusofonia* (pp. 69–91). Escolar Editora.

Braun, V., & Clarke, V. (2006). Using thematic analysis in psychology. *Qualitative Research in Psychology*, *3*(2), 77–101. DOI: 10.1191/1478088706qp063oa

Coelho, J., Figueira, L., & Costa, C. (2014). O Turismo Militar e a Ativação Turística do Património: Conceitos, Perspetivas e Tendências. *Revista Turismo & Desenvolvimento (Aveiro)*, *I*, 113–120.

Collis, J., & Hussey, J. (2005). *Pesquisa em Administração* (2ª). São Paulo: Artmed Editora.

Costa, C. (2005). Turismo e cultura: Avaliação das teorias e práticas culturais do sector do turismo (1990-2000). *Analise Social*, *XL*(175), 279–295.

Cravidão, F. (2014). Velho(s) Território(s): Novo(s) Turismo(s). In R. B. Costa, Carlos; Brandão, Filipa; Costa (Ed.), *Turismo nos Países Lusófonos: Conhecimento, Estratégia e Territórios* (pp. 59–69). Escolar Editora.

Creswell, J. W. (2013). Qualitative inquiry and research design: choosing among five approaches (3rd Edition). *SAGE Publications.* ENAME Charter, 1 (2008).

Fazenda, N. (2014). Turismo em Portugal: Reflexões para uma Política Nacional de Turismo. In Costa, C. (Ed.), *Turismo nos Países Lusófonos: Conhecimento, Estratégia e Territórios* (pp. 293–312). Escolar Editora.

Figueira, L. (2010). *Manual para Elaboração de roteiros de Turismo Cultural.* Instituto Politécnico de Tomar.

Figueira, L. M. (2013). Roteirização do Turismo: Uma Abordagem Preliminar à "apresentação-interpretação" do território. *Revista Turismo & Desenvolvimento (Aveiro)*, *1*(20), 121–133.

Gonçalves, A. R., Dorsch, L. L. P., & Figueiredo, M. (2022). Digital Tourism: An Alternative View on Cultural Intangible Heritage and Sustainability in Tavira, Portugal. *Sustainability (Switzerland), 14*(5). Advance online publication. DOI: 10.3390/su14052912

Gonçalves, F. (2018). *A Interpretação do Património como fator de desenvolvimento do Turismo Cultural e Criativo. O caso do Galo de Barcelos*. Tese de Doutoramento, Universidade de Aveiro.

Gonçalves, F., & Costa, C. (2016). Galo de Barcelos: Património e destino turístico. *Revista Turismo & Desenvolvimento (Aveiro).*

Gonçalves, F., & Costa, C. (2019a). Modelo de Desenvolvimento e Implementação do Turismo Criativo. O caso do Galo de Barcelos. *Revista Turismo & Desenvolvimento (Aveiro), 32*(52), 25–36.

Gonçalves, F., & Costa, C. (2019b). O Contributo da Interpretação do Património Para o Desenvolvimento do Turismo Criativo. O Caso do Galo de Barcelos. *Revista Portuguesa de Estudos Regionais, 52*, 25–36.

Gonçalves, F., & Costa, C. (2020). Contribution of Caminos de Santiago to the sustainable development of Tourism, in Barcelos. *Journal of Tourism & Development, 34*, 65–79.

Gonçalves, F., & Costa, C. (2022). Barcelos, Cidade Criativa da UNESCO: Contributo para o desenvolvimento sustentável do Artesanato através do Turismo Criativo Creative City sustainable development Creative Tourism. *Revista Turismo & Desenvolvimento (Aveiro)*, •••, 107–128.

ICOMOS International Cultural Tourism Charter. (1999). https://www.icomos.org/charters/tourism_e.pdf

Knudson, D., Cable, T., & Beck, L. (2003). Interpretation of Cultural and Natural Resources. In *2ª Ed., Pennsylvania, Venture Publishing, Inc.*

Melo, D. (2001). *Salazarismo e Cultura Popular (1933 - 1958)*. Instituto de Ciências Sociais da Universidade de Lisboa.

Mimoso, J. M. (2010). Origem e Evolução do Galo de Barcelos. *Olaria: Estudos Arqueológicos, Históricos e Etnológicos*, 143–159.

Pires de Lima, F. (1965). *A Lenda do Senhor do Galo de Barcelos e o Milagre do Enforcado*. Gabinete de Etnografia da FNAT.

Resende, R. (2016). Técnica de Investigação Qualitativa: ETCI. *Journal of Sport Pedagogy & Research, 1*, 50–57.

Richards, G. (2011). Creativity and tourism. The state of the art. *Annals of Tourism Research, 38*(4), 1225–1253. DOI: 10.1016/j.annals.2011.07.008

Rocha Peixoto. (1966). *As olarias de Prado*. Museu Regional de Cerâmica.

Tilden, F. (2007). Interpreting our Heritage (4th Ed.). The University of North Carolina Press. (Original publicado em 1957).

Umbelino, J. (2014). Os Valores do Território no Lazer e no Turismo. In Z. Costa, C. Brandão, F., Costa, R., & Breda (Ed.), *Produtos e Competividade do Turismo na Lusofonia* (pp. 203–216). Lisboa: Escolar Editora.

Vala, J. (1986). A Análise de Conteúdo. In Santos Silva, A., & Madureira Pinto, J. (Eds.), *Metodologia das Ciências Sociais* (pp. 101–128). Edições Afrontamento.

Yu, J., & Meng, T. (2025). Image Generative AI in Tourism: Trends, Impacts, and Future Research Directions. *Journal of Hospitality & Tourism Research (Washington, D.C.)*. Advance online publication. DOI: 10.1177/10963480251324676

KEY TERMS AND DEFINITIONS

Barcelos Rooster Brand: A cultural symbol and identity marker of Barcelos, rooted in local craftsmanship and the Jacobean legend. It represents values such as faith, justice, and tradition, and serves as a central element in the city's tourism branding and heritage promotion.

Camino de Santiago: A historic pilgrimage route leading to Santiago de Compostela, recognized by UNESCO as a cultural itinerary. In Barcelos, it intersects with local heritage through the legend of the miraculous rooster, reinforcing the city's spiritual and cultural significance.

Digital Marketing: The strategic use of digital tools, such as social media, multimedia storytelling, and interactive websites, to promote tourism destinations. It increases visibility, fosters engagement, and supports the sustainable development of cultural heritage.

Heritage Interpretation: An educational approach that reveals the deeper meanings and connections of cultural and historical assets. It enhances visitor experiences by using storytelling, original artifacts, and interactive media to go beyond information.

Sustainable Tourism Route: A thoughtfully designed travel itinerary that promotes environmental responsibility, cultural preservation, and community engagement. It aims to generate long-term benefits for both visitors and local populations while minimizing negative impacts.

Chapter 2
Building Emotional Bonds:
The Power of Animal Imagery in Brand Marketing

Marina Joice Chalupa
https://orcid.org/0009-0005-7242-195X
Polytechnic Institute of Cávado and Ave, Portugal

ABSTRACT

In modern times, companies are coming to realize more and more how important it is to employ relationship marketing techniques to stand out in highly competitive markets. Brands employ emotional and value-driven strategies to connect with their audiences more closely rather than depending only on product attributes or cost. The use of animal imagery is a tactic that, if well-planned, can create emotions in consumers. This chapter explores how marketing campaigns can use themes such as the emotional value of animal companionship to build relationships with consumers. This study highlights the growing importance of relationship marketing using animals by examining a few campaigns.

1. INTRODUCTION

Building strong, long-term customer relationships is becoming essential to brand success and survival in today's competitive marketplace (Grönroos, 2004). Emotive, high-level relationships with brands are driving customers more than ever before, beyond price or functional value, to become the byproduct of the capability of products and services. As such, companies are shifting away from transactional promotion frameworks to relationship marketing frameworks that focus on creating

DOI: 10.4018/979-8-3373-4342-6.ch002

long-term interaction and client loyalty (Berry, 1983). Because loyal customers are champions of the company who can influence others, relationship marketing places considerable attention on customer satisfaction, retention, and lifetime value (Payne & Frow, 2013). Keeping intimate, long-term customer relationships has become the brand's success and survival secret in the competitive business today (Grönroos, 2004). Consumers are increasingly driven by emotional experiences rather than purely functional attributes, a shift that favors long-term relationship marketing, making secondary to the existence of products and services. Therefore, companies are shifting from paradigms of transaction promotion to paradigms of relationship marketing that seek to establish long-term interaction and loyalty among consumers (Berry, 1983). Loyal consumers often act as persuasive ambassadors, whose influence extends beyond their own purchasing behavior and helps shape broader public perception. Relationship marketing places tremendous importance on customer satisfaction, retention, and lifetime value (Payne & Frow, 2013). Differentiation is challenging in such a scenario. It is the responsibility of the marketers to find new means of grabbing attention, building trust, and forming emotional bonds to differentiate themselves from the rest of the businesses (Kotler & Keller, 2016).

One beneficial and rapidly changing strategy within this area is the use of animal imagery in brand promotion. Animals occupy a unique and powerful place within human psychology and culture, and should be capable of engendering high emotional reactions such as affection, empathy, warmth, and trust (Serpell, 2000). Humans form bonds with animals from a very early age, and these carry over into adult life and influence attitude and behavior in many contexts. Brands are therefore leveraging the very natural connections by employing animal imagery for their communications and adverts. There are different facets for such a tactic: animals can make adverts more aesthetically pleasing, convey certain brand traits such as loyalty and concern, and even support major social causes of animal welfare and conservation (Holbrook & Hirschman, 1982). Strategic use of animals thus allows companies to tell stories that are emotionally and morally resonant with people. Moreover, it is the universal appeal of animals across cultures and languages that makes them an appropriate choice for representing international marketing campaigns. Such cross-cultural convergence translates into their capacity to resonate with wide-ranging audiences, evoking a sense of universal humanity and shared values. Animals' natural innocence and vulnerability will also elicit a consumer's protective urge, further rooting emotional ties. If a brand aligns itself with such good qualities, it can implicitly communicate its integrity and reliability, creating a reputation beyond and outside of product details. This intense but unspoken communication is particularly valuable in an oversaturated marketplace when consumers are increasingly wary of overt promotional approaches.

The implied reason that animal imagery is used in marketing strategy is to create and build emotional bonds with customers. By associating a brand with the good feelings animals can generate, companies strive to build the image of warmth, trust, and values shared, which are more than the functional attributes of goods or services (Batra & Ahtola, 1991). Such emotional connections can enhance preference for the brand, enhance loyalty, and ultimately shape purchasing behavior in a positive direction (Oliver, 1999). Such causes generally pertaining to animals include promoting adoption, stopping cruelty against animals, and honoring the companionship of animals. Such narratives touch consumers' hearts and evoke their empathy and sympathy, ultimately putting them in a positive frame of mind concerning the brands that promote and sponsor such causes (Thompson & Malaviya, 2013). Also, the narrativity of animal imagery is immense. Companies can create powerful narratives through an animal mascot or animal theme that engagingly highlight their purpose and principles. A good example is an eco-brand that may utilize endangered species as a means of representing its sustainability and conservation measures subtly. This not only makes one aware of significant issues but also makes a brand socially responsible, appealing to those who seek ethical consumption. The imagery of animals is also very shareable across social media, imparting a brand's message and reach organically.

The current research aims to examine the strategic application of animal symbolism in relationship marketing. It aims to extend the understanding of how the application of stories and animal symbolism may be applied in evoking emotional involvement and loyalty. The research also aims to provide practical guidelines for marketing practitioners who would want to conduct moral and effective campaigns with the use of animal imagery. By comparing several campaigns and their matching theoretical perspectives, the chapter seeks to contribute to the debate on relationship marketing strategies that are responsive in today's emotionally charged marketplace. The study will offer insights into the nuances of using animal imagery, considering not only its possible benefits but also ethical concerns such as avoiding exploitation or misrepresentation. Finally, understanding how to tap into the natural energy of animals in marketing can provide brands with a solid competitive advantage in establishing authentic and lasting relationships with customers.

2. CORPORATE SOCIAL RESPONSIBILITY

These days, people care a lot more about social issues, which is pushing companies to act more responsibly. Businesses aren't just out there to make money anymore; they need to be part of the community. Corporate Social Responsibility (CSR) is a reaction to this change; it is an ethical framework that, if used correctly and strategically, can be the key for companies to stay ahead of their competitors (Rexhepi et al., 2013). As Alves (2019) points out, companies are part of the community, so they can't just ignore what's happening around them. CSR means moving beyond just chasing profits and considering how their actions affect society.

This shift has encouraged businesses to include social and environmental issues in what they do, making it possible for them to succeed while also being good for the community. More and more, consumers are looking at what a brand stands for, not just the quality of what they're selling. More and more studies show that CSR (Corporate Social Responsibility) strategies that involve consumers directly tend to work better than the more traditional top-down approaches. For example, Lee, Kim, and Kim (2021) found that when companies let consumers take part in decision-making, it creates a sense of interaction. This leads to stronger engagement and helps build a better relationship between the consumer and the company. When consumers see a brand's social efforts as genuine, they are more likely to support it, affecting their purchasing choices.

Companies can't just focus on selling their products anymore; they need to provide value in other ways too. CSR plays a big role in building communities around shared values, which helps keep customers loyal and turns them into advocates for the brand. Loureiro and Lopes (2019) stress how key it is to engage stakeholders through digital platforms. They point out that social media not only spreads the word but also gives people a chance to communicate and collaborate. Nowadays, with people having shorter attention spans and lots of content out there, engaging stakeholders has become essential. Those who used to just watch are now getting involved, and successful CSR campaigns need to adapt to this change.

Adding interactive features like user-generated content, polls, and virtual events can help brands connect better and be more transparent. This active participation builds community ties and allows companies to get real-time feedback to improve their CSR efforts. The emotional side of CSR is another important point that's been getting a lot of attention. Xu et al. (2025) found that emotional content, especially when paired with good product quality, creates a warm glow effect. This connection makes consumers more willing to support the brand and strengthens their bond.

Emotional storytelling is a technique that can create empathy and personal connections. This helps consumers feel that the brand's social mission is part of their own identity, which is intended to create loyalty that goes beyond simply purchasing a product. Mansoor et al. (2025) go further, suggesting that if companies incorporate CSR into their business model, consumers can become brand advocates. Their research shows that when a company's values meet consumers' expectations, it creates deeper loyalty and encourages them to share positive experiences, both online and through word of mouth.

This relationship not only increases the brand's social impact but also helps it succeed in the market over time.

As people's expectations change, brands are expected to match social and political realities in their identities. Luna-Amador et al. (2025) highlight the importance of presenting themselves as genuine. Today's consumers are quite skeptical and pay close attention to whether a brand's activism is genuine or just lip service. If a brand's actions don't match its social messaging, you can quickly lose trust. According to the value theory approach, CSR activities focus on a company's core values, and therefore, it is important to determine the value priorities behind the company's actions.

There is also a strong link between CSR and corporate reputation from a public relations perspective, given that CSR is often defined as a component of corporate reputation, which can lead to a good or bad reputation depending on how it is planned (Aksak et al., 2016). That's why being transparent and consistent in communication is key to earning trust in social campaigns. Francioni et al. (2025) back this up, warning that inconsistency in social campaigns can hurt a brand's reputation. Unlike operational mistakes that might be forgiven, ethical failings in CSR get judged much harshly.

Many well-known brands have learned how quickly trust can slip away when their social messages don't align with their actual behavior. For instance, brands that promote eco-friendly initiatives while having unsustainable supply chains face intense scrutiny. This makes it clear that companies need to align their CSR messaging with their business practices to avoid confusing consumers. Cultural context also matters a lot when it comes to how CSR messages resonate. Saluja and Chan (2025) point out that activist branding can be seen differently in various regions.

Ethically unsuccessful attempts in CSR are looked at much more seriously than operational errors, which can be neglected (Francioni et al., 2025). When the advertisement and the practice are erratic, there may be an instant backlash. This backlash is exacerbated by social media, where customers swiftly express their dissatisfaction. Companies are frequently exposed if they start campaigns over female empowerment while facing allegations of internal disparities in wages, or when they stand for sustainability while going on to use high-carbon supply chains. In addition to eliminating the campaign's investment, this publicity can negatively impact the company's reputation in the long run (Aksak et al., 2016). Therefore, authenticity is a strategic requirement that necessitates consistency between a brand's actions and words at every stage of its operations, as opposed to just being a communication tactic.

Consumer scrutiny has increased in combination with the growing demand for ethical positioning. Individuals of today are particularly wary of advertisements that appear fake or performative (Luna-Amador et al., 2025). Frequently referred to as “woke-washing” or “greenwashing,” this phenomenon occurs when a business primarily uses social or environmental causes in its communications to improve its public image, without the discourse reflecting in its business practices. A brand runs a serious risk of losing consumers' trust if it promotes social messages but has inconsistent internal processes (Francioni et al., 2025).

In individualistic societies like the U.S., bold campaigns may be welcomed. But in collectivist cultures, like those in Southeast Asia, messages that focus on community and harmony might get a better response. These insights suggest that global brands need to adjust their CSR strategies to fit local cultures and avoid miscommunication. Tailoring campaigns not only makes them culturally relevant but also shows respect for different values, which can improve brand acceptance in diverse markets.

Sansome, Conduit, and Wilkie (2025) argue that transparency is crucial for effective CSR. Today's consumers expect brands to be consistent across all their platforms—websites, social media, and customer service, and they want the messaging to line up. Emotional triggers like fear or surprise can boost engagement with transparency efforts, but they have to be used carefully. Misusing these tactics can lead to manipulation, which can destroy trust. Once trust is lost, it's very hard to rebuild. So, ethical transparency should strike a balance between great storytelling and facts, encouraging genuine consumer participation instead of manipulation.

Ben Lahouel and Taleb (2025) take a strategic view, seeing CSR as a way to align business goals with what stakeholders want. When done with sincere intentions, CSR can offer a competitive edge and operational benefits. But this raises a key ethical concern: can CSR really be genuine if it's driven by profit? Today's organizations face the challenge of balancing strategic goals with ethics. As CSR is increasingly seen as essential for modern business, its success will hinge on being genuine, emotionally appealing, and culturally attuned. This ongoing change calls for businesses to keep reflecting on and adjusting their CSR approach, ensuring it makes a real impact on society rather than just serving as a marketing gimmick.

Hasudungan and Saragih (2023) found that consumers' perceptions of economic, environmental, and social CSR initiatives have a direct impact on increasing brand awareness, as well as strengthening their intention to build relationships with the brand. There is a direct positive correlation between CSR and brand awareness in developing markets (Ismael, 2022). Gálvez-Sánchez et al. (2024) report that different dimensions of CSR (economic, social, and environmental) contribute uniquely to brand equity, reputation, and how consumers feel about paying. Muniz et al. (2019) demonstrated that CSR communications have the power to increase brand awareness and loyalty, with the effect being greater if consumers perceive the campaign as voluntary and authentic.

It is important to note that internal CSR activities are important and can improve employee satisfaction and contribute to a stronger internal brand reputation and equity. Growing public concern about animal welfare and environmental issues has led companies to adopt ethical marketing strategies for animal products (Borkfelt et al., 2015). Consumers are increasingly willing to pay more for products that are more animal-friendly and environmentally friendly (Liang et al., 2022). Companies are recognized as moral actors with a responsibility to consider animal welfare in their practices, particularly in sectors such as food production (Janssens, 2021).

Public concern for animal welfare is high, but understanding is often limited, suggesting the need for greater transparency and education to align marketing with genuine welfare improvements (Cornish et al., 2016). Animal ethics can be integrated into consumer value systems, significantly influencing attitudes and behaviors towards the consumption of animal products, especially among those with strong ethical positions (Hölker et al., 2019).

3. BRAND AWARENESS AND SOCIAL RESPONSIBILITY

Brand awareness, or the extent to which consumers recognize and recall a brand, is a fundamental objective of marketing strategy. It is the foundation upon which all other brand initiatives are built, including consumer trust, loyalty, and advocacy.

As initially conceptualized by Aaker (1996), brand awareness is one of the key dimensions of brand equity, influencing consumer choice and preference. In today's saturated markets, with abundant and often equal-quality product offerings, strong brand awareness becomes an ultimate competitive advantage. It is a cognitive shortcut for consumers, leading to quicker and more confident purchase decisions.

Brand awareness means that people know about and remember a brand. This helps buyers determine what to buy more quickly and more reliably (Hoyer & Brown, 1990). For example, when we buy a commonly used product, the choice is made more readily. Knowing the brand alone, however, is not enough to prompt individuals to buy. The brand should also take into account other valences, such as having a positive image, being trustworthy, and being liked by the customers (Azzari & Pelissari, 2020). In addition to that, brand salience, i.e., the presence of a brand in the consumer's mind while making the purchasing decision, is closely linked to awareness.

High salience brands are those that are readily remembered in particular consumption situations. Research by Romaniuk and Sharp (2004) demonstrates that brands with greater salience enjoy greater market shares as they remain top-of-mind when consumers think of product categories. This finding underscores the benefit of ongoing brand visibility and distinctiveness to enable customers to associate the brand with particular needs or occasions. Emotional connections also play a vital role in reinforcing brand awareness. As the work of Thomson, MacInnis, and Park

(2005) demonstrates, emotionally engaging brands form stronger and more enduring memories. These affective connections can be established on the basis of storytelling, brand personality, and values that resonate with the target clientele. When customers are emotionally connected to a brand, they remember it and recommend it to others, facilitating organic growth through word-of-mouth.

The rise of digital technologies and social media sites has transformed the dynamics by which brand awareness is created and reinforced. Traditional advertising media, such as television and print, while still relevant, have been supplemented or even supplanted by digital approaches offering greater engagement and targeting precision.

As Keller (2013) maintains, effective brand awareness strategies employ a multichannel approach involving paid, earned, and owned media to create a common brand narrative. It is the integration that subjects consumers to brand messages repeatedly across touchpoints to establish recognition and recall.

Nowadays, through the internet and social media, brands can reach more people and spread messages quickly, which helps to create even more awareness and interest (Barreda et al., 2015). Second, each country and market is different, and thus brands cannot use generalist strategies (Romaniuk et al., 2004; Romaniuk et al., 2017).

Studies have established that social media sites allow brands to reach a larger number of users, provide interactive areas, and increase the engagement of users (Dabbous & Barakat, 2020; Suparto, 2024; Saputra et al., 2025).

Valuable, interesting content and frequent communication with users are very good at increasing brand awareness as they increase consumer engagement with the brand (Dabbous & Barakat, 2020; Oleárová & Bačík, 2023; Faisal & Ekawanto, 2022). One thing that has been shown to work particularly well is influencer partnerships and employee engagement that get the consumer closer (Suparto, 2024; Saputra et al., 2025). Frequent and well-managed brand activities on social media have been shown to improve consumer brand awareness, although overexposure should be avoided, and there needs to be a plan (Tchelidze, 2023). The rise of user-generated content and influencer marketing also challenges traditional notions of brand awareness. Consumers are increasingly relying on peer advice and social proof, rather than brand messaging alone. A study by De Veirman, Cauberghe, and Hudders (2017) found that influencer endorsement plays a significant role in brand awareness, particularly with youth audiences. This reality forces marketers to develop strategies incorporating authentic voices and collective engagement, rather than the exclusive application of broadcast-style advertising. Campaigns based on animal appeals have been shown to enhance brand recall through the combination of moral messaging and memorable animal imagery (Mardani et al., 2019).

Kronenberg & Bocian (2022) put forward the argument that as companies leverage this to make money or improve their brand image, they should return or repay this value, possibly through assisting in animal conservation or the environment.

Companies that use animals in their advertisements ought to have an ethical obligation to ensure the welfare of the animals (Jannsens, 2021).

The majority of companies continue to treat animals as mere resources (Merskin, 2021). In tourism and entertainment, animals are typically employed for human pleasure without their rightful moral consideration (Winter, 2020). Companies do have a moral responsibility to treat animals as stakeholders and address animal welfare as part of their corporate social responsibility, but this is not what happens (Merskin, 2021).

4. PET MARKETING

Animal imagery has also been extensively utilized in advertising to gain attention, elicit emotions, and modify consumers' behavior. There is a body of literature on the effects of animal imagery and metaphors on the persuasive effectiveness of advertising and brand beliefs, as well as the underlying psychological processes driving the effects.

Animal imagery and metaphors applied in advertising produce emotional and cognitive reactions that change consumer behavior, making advertisements more convincing (Abeer & Malkawi, 2025). Metaphors in visual forms, including animals, tend to be associated with greater positive responses and purchase intentions compared to non-metaphorical adverts (García-Madariaga et al., 2020). Comparative marketing strategies based on animals or animal metaphors have the potential to create memorable and emotionally evocative adverts that have the end result of brand loyalty and purchasing behavior (Kaushik et al., 2024).

Animal metaphors can support brand symbolism with consumers through the use of cultural and psychological meanings, creating a more realistic and distinctive brand within the consumer's mind. Well-taken and well-thought-out metaphors must be used to ensure compatibility with values for brands (Noble et al., 2013).

Animals are used to push sales and target new markets as well as express specific emotions. They can be depicted in a natural form, anthropomorphized, or as mascots to establish brand recognition and emotional connection (Lloyd & Woodside, 2013; Wong, 2017). Marketers will select specific animals, and whether to utilize anthropomorphic or non-anthropomorphic imagery is organized in advance in terms of setting, aware of which will be most impactful (Spears et al., 1996). We see brands using animal mascots and logos, using anthropomorphism to render brands more familiar (Wong, 2017).

Choosing a pet typically relies on desired brand characteristics, whether it is loyalty, affection, trust, or humor. According to Kirk (2019), consumers attribute greater economic value to dogs than to cats. The impact is underpinned by consumers' affective bonds with the pet. Jia, Yang & Jiang (2022) explain that dogs tend to elicit promotion-oriented frames, whereas cats elicit prevention-oriented frames that influence consumer judgments and purchase intentions towards non-pet products.

A study by Liu, Chang, Yang, Li and Wu (2024) indicates that there are significant benefits of having animals for businesses; retailers need to account for targeting pet owners as a market segment for their services and goods. Pets are indeed described as much-loved family members, using their imagery helps brands become family-friendly and trusted even though their products do not relate to pets (Mayo et al., 2009; Laurent-Simpson, 2021).

Anthropomorphic mascots are often used in a digital era on social media platforms as virtual influencers that shape perception and even encourage interaction (Wandel, 2017; Dabiran et al., 2024). In comparing pet influencers and human influencers, the result was that the animal influencer was more effective than the human influencer in terms of consumer response (Keller et al., 2020; Lavertu et al., 2025). Pet influencers are also a consideration for companies and the future of influencer marketing as they are a cheap alternative to human influencers (Myers et al., 2022). What gives animal influencers good results is that they emotionally show up in advertisements, especially when used with humor, and this makes the campaign credible. Besides, the value added is not only felt by pet owners (Di Cioccio, Pozharliev, & De Angelis, 2024).

Pet influencers can establish strong bonds with their followers on the basis of emotional content, which, as mentioned earlier, operates in the interest of brands through building trust and emotional connection (Jacobson, Hodson & Mittelman, 2022). It is, however, worth observing that obvious advertising cues undermine engagement, which means that subtlety is optimal (Myers et al., 2022).

A study by Zhang et al. (2023) discovers that animals appear to be more tangible and lovable compared to humans, resulting in campaigns being emotional. However, when the message is informative, human-based narrators become more engaging. The "cuteness economy" has increased over recent years in digital marketing, especially with pet influencers on social media. Wei Wei et al. (2025) note how the "cute" nature of animals triggers a strong emotional connection with followers as a valuable tool for fashioning consumer behaviors.

The study by Xie-Carson et al. (2023) is the first to explore the new trend of non-human social media influencers. It also classifies these influencers into eight categories, which are: living things of animals and plants, and non-living things of objects, toys, mascots, robots, licensed characters, and virtual influencers. The authors note that, though not human, users approach these influencers in the same way as human beings, applying concepts such as source credibility, product-endorser fit, and parasocial relationships.

Worthy of note is the observation that the use of animal metaphors can turn out differently than expected, especially in health-focused advertising, as it creates the feeling of self-dehumanization, which is less successful in contrast to other markets (Huang, 2024). Caution should be used with the tactics utilized when using mascots for advertising. These should have great attributes and stories so that they can fulfill the ultimate purpose: building trust and long-term commitment, because, as other authors had stated previously, incompetently managed mascots may not evoke positive feelings (Palladino et al., 2022; Brown, 2010). In general, the strategic use of anthropomorphic animal mascots not only promotes brand recognition and differentiation but also creates lasting emotional bonds that create long-term brand loyalty (Reddy et al., 2024; Ko et al., 2022; Deligoz & Ünal, 2021).

Holding up the use of animals to carry messages can inspire people towards more positive behaviors, such as tidying up the garbage in a proper way. In essence, if people spot an endearing animal taking the lead or pleading, they will most likely respond appropriately (Sun et al., 2024).

Depictions of animals in marketing are reflections of broader societal discussions of nature, gender, and human-animal relations that frequently contradict or support cultural norms (Burton & Collins, 2014).

Marketers have to deal with the troublesome ethics brought about by the rapid growth of the pet influencer marketing industry. Companies have an ethical obligation to safeguard these animals despite the huge amount of engagement they create (Jannsens, 2021). Animals can be put in stressful situations and made to act in unnatural ways due to the need to produce content all the time. There has to be a balance between having real moments and taking advantage of a living creature for profit. Even though anthropomorphism is employed well in advertising (Epley, Waytz, & Cacioppo, 2007), it also results in animals being used as actors or objects, without consideration of their biological and behavioral needs, which could have long-term negative effects on their welfare (Mota-Rojas et al., 2021).

The target audience (the people a campaign is reaching out to) is very important in quantifying how they will react. Consumer research in India found that metaphors aid in understanding the conscious or subconscious perceptions individuals have towards foreign brands and products, and these perceptions rely heavily on culture (Martin, Palakshappa and Woodside, 2019).

Secondly, the effectiveness of animal metaphors is also dependent on their consistency with local culture, values, and symbolic meanings attributed to animals in the society. The metaphors can gain emotional value and cultural identity and propel purchase intentions higher when they are grounded on established cultural symbols (Liu and Zhao, 2024).

A study by Trivedi and Teichert (2020) found that animal usage in advertisements generated more positive attitudes, especially when the animals appeared alone, as opposed to human models.

Young people are among the primary audiences of authentic, pet-based social media content like influencer partnerships and user-generated content, which leads to higher interaction. Such online interaction plays a critical role in developing and maintaining long-term loyalty (Cai, 2025).

5. CASE STUDIES

In this section, we take a close look at some effective marketing campaigns that have successfully utilized animal imagery to create intense emotional responses among audiences. These campaigns are good illustrations of how brands can create strong emotional connections through relationship marketing through animals, positioning themselves not just as goods manufacturers but as assets in society.

Among the most powerful emotional marketing weapons is storytelling, creating narratives appealing to the cognitive and emotive sides of the audience. As the main characters for these stories, animals serve as the medium for marketers to take advantage of anthropomorphism: inferring human traits, emotions, or intentions onto animals (Epley, Waytz, & Cacioppo, 2007).

Budweiser – "Puppy Love" (Super Bowl 2014)

Budweiser's "Puppy Love" Super Bowl 2014 advertisement is a prime example of emotional storytelling through animal imagery. The advertisement documents the bond of a young golden Labrador Retriever puppy and a Clydesdale horse as they form an unlikely but profound friendship. The tale is a progression of themes of loyalty, friendship, and pain of separation, for the puppy keeps escaping to visit the horse, culminating in a dramatic rescue set against communal solidarity. The use of animals is deliberate: the dog traditionally symbolizes love, loyalty, and friendship, while the horse recalls strength, tradition, and reliability. Through this pairing, Budweiser sends its brand messages of timelessness and fidelity, effectively humanizing the product and bringing it into the web of daily emotional living. The use of narrative allowed the brand to transcend mere brewery status, positioning itself as an icon of universal human values. The campaign's scope was great, the top-rated Super Bowl ad in 2014 according to USA Today's Ad Meter (Luckerson, 2014), and it went viral with over 60 million YouTube views shortly after release. The occurrence of a follow-up commercial, "Lost Dog," indicates that Budweiser was able to successfully incorporate an emotional branding model supporting long-term customer interaction (The Marketing Explainer, 2024).

John Lewis – "Monty the Penguin" (2014)

In 2014, British department store John Lewis developed a master Christmas campaign called "Monty the Penguin." The ad is about the developing relationship between a young boy and his imaginary best friend, a penguin named Monty. The boy notices that Monty is sad and lonely, apparently because he wants a friend. The boy, concerned about the emotional welfare of Monty, purchases a friend on Christmas morning. The final twist discloses that Monty is actually a stuffed toy, one that the boy vividly imagines as real and as his pet.

The campaign used the symbolism of penguins to reflect ideas of love, sympathy, and emotional richness. The use of animals, especially in anthropomorphized form, allowed the brand to discuss human issues in a disarming and emotive way without the usual frills of animal advertising. The advert attracted over 36 million viewers in its first month alone and had a real impact on business performance: John Lewis posted a 5.5% increase in Christmas sales that year, ahead of the wider market, which rose by just 1.5%. Further, the ad generated 350 million impressions in the holiday season, an increase of 320% compared to last year, highlighting the tight link between emotional storytelling and brand awareness, which is beneficial for the brand in the long term (Bowler, 2022).

Subaru – "Dream Weekend" (2014)

As Subaru navigates the auto business amidst the cutthroat competition, it has always tread the path of divergence with a focus on emotional connection and family. The "Dream Weekend" campaign, launched in 2014, is another excellent example of the same strategy. The advertisement revolves around an older dog and his escapades with his owner, doing all his favorite things. The journey is emotional, conveying the silent bond between humans and animals, and also touching upon the death of an animal, which later makes the whole strategy more emotive. What's most notable about this campaign is the subtlety of tone and the deep emotional realism. Noam Murro directed the commercial, and Carmichael Lynch produced it, as part of Subaru's #MakeADogsDay campaign that encouraged pet owners to honor and care for their pets. Though the campaign's exact sales figures are not publicly released, the commercial racked up millions of views and was popularly shared and praised on social media (Stewart, 2015).

Erste Bank – "What Would Christmas Be Without Love?" (2018)

In the year 2018, banking group Erste Bank released an energetic Christmas advert that captured the hearts of everyone across Europe and the globe.

The advert, "What would Christmas be without love? ", is about a young hedgehog who is struggling with social isolation. Because of his quills, he is unable to connect with other creatures in the usual way, play with a ball, or snuggle with his friends. The ad tracks his loneliness until another student comes up with the idea of creating protective pads for his quills, so he can finally be like everyone else and join things. There is no single spoken word in this ad, as it depends entirely on visual narration.

What's so unique about this campaign is the fact that it has a multi-layered emotional narrative. The hedgehog is employed as a symbol for somebody who has ever been ostracized or been different. Employing animals rather than human characters adds an air of innocence and universality to the narrative that makes it all the more engaging.

Even though it is a financial brand, a business category not normally considered to be emotive storytelling, Erste was successful in humanizing its brand and communicating with consumers on a very deep emotional level. The campaign became viral, reaching millions of views and over 50 global awards. Since 2018, the Christmas campaigns of Erste Group have garnered over 200 million views worldwide, proving that banks can get into winning, emotionally charged relationship marketing, too, when creativity meets intention (LBBOnline, 2021).

Amazon Prime – "An Unlikely Friendship" (2021)

The Mill, CyW and Blur Films/Outsider director Chris Balmond have teamed up to create a Christmas ad for Amazon Prime. The commercial follows the companionship of a zookeeper and complaining hyena Hattie, who finds herself laughing with her human friend while watching Amazon Prime content (positioning the product in an unconscious and emotional light). The message was meant to convey the idea that "every smile tells a story" through the relationship between a human and an animal. Within two minutes, the viewer identifies with the narrative, as though it were a movie. Prime didn't stop there and has also pledged to donate £100,000 to Pets As Therapy, a UK charity that works with volunteers and therapy animals to give people access to an animal's affection, utilizing social responsibility as opposed to relationship marketing by using pet marketing (Amazon Prime Video, 2021; The Mill, 2021).

These five campaigns demonstrate the power of animal imagery to create emotional resonance with audiences. All brands use animals not just as living beings, but as emotional comforts that convey values, tell stories, and build relationships. From the loyalty of a hyena to the healing friendship of a hyena and a zookeeper, these campaigns demonstrate how animals can cross species to embody our most human feelings.

Ultimately, these emotionally charged narratives serve as powerful tools in relationship marketing, all with the same goal: fostering brand loyalty and strong customer relationships. By exploring the universality of animal symbolism and anthropomorphism, brands utilize marketing to humanize themselves, moving beyond being seen as mere service/product providers. This fosters empathy and creates lasting emotional bonds. In such a saturated digital age, it's an excellent way to differentiate themselves from their competitors. We can see that it is more recurrent for brands to make campaigns like this during Christmas time for brands to launch this type of advertisement, because people are more sensitive and receptive.

6. CONCLUSION

In today's market, where customers are more educated, mindful, and emotionally driven, using animal portrayals has become an effective strategy for brands seeking deeper connections. We have discussed the strategic role of animals in relationship marketing, focusing on CSR, brand awareness, and pet marketing. The data shows that not only does animal-related content attract attention, but it also helps build strong emotional bonds with brands.

One of the contributions of this research is the emotional power that animals possess over consumers. As ingrained concepts in human culture and psychology, animals trigger emotions such as trust, empathy, care, and warmth. These feelings are essential in relationship marketing, where the objective extends beyond attracting consumers to forging intimate, long-lasting relationships.

From Budweiser's "Puppy Love" to Amazon Prime's "An Unlikely Friendship," a recurring theme becomes evident in the case studies analyzed: animal-based advertising campaigns effectively appeal to consumers' moral values, cultural symbolism, and emotional memory. These companies go beyond conventional advertising by crafting stories that reflect ethical issues and feelings found in everyday life. By doing this, they gain the support and trust of customers, which are becoming more and more elusive in a crowded market. The importance of relationship marketing in modern branding strategies is further supported by these examples, which show how emotional content improves brand recall and positive customer sentiments.

This chapter additionally explores the constantly shifting nature of corporate social responsibility. CSR is now an essential component of how customers analyze a brand's worth and credibility, not just a flimsy branding campaign or a supplementary marketing tool. Consumers of today look for brands to stand up for ethical principles like community involvement, environmental preservation, and animal welfare. Higher consumer engagement, greater commitment, and enhanced brand equity are the outcomes of using animal imagery in campaigns that are consistent with genuine CSR values. On the other hand, they manage the risk of criticism and harm to their reputation when messages about animals seem false or unconnected to their real business practices.

Plenty of advantages and disadvantages are linked to the convergence of emotional marketing and corporate social responsibility. The ethical ramifications of using animals in advertising campaigns must be considered by brands. Using animals as metaphors or imagery is insufficient; businesses also need to show the fact that they are actively working to promote animal welfare and incorporate these ideals into every aspect of their operations. Businesses that complement their marketing with sincere CSR commitments are more likely to keep customers' trust and thrive in the long run, whether through advocacy for animal rights, sustainable sourcing, or charitable donations.

Most importantly, the pet industry is not alone in being affected by this phenomenon. Businesses from a variety of industries, including finance, fashion, automotive, and hospitality, are increasingly using content about animals to humanize their brands while creating an emotional bond with their intended consumers. Real, animated, or anthropomorphized animals all work well for this because they are nonverbal representations of tenderness, purity, and sincerity.

However, there are moral dilemmas associated with this emotional effectiveness. Despite its impact, anthropomorphism sometimes serves to uphold stereotypes or impossible expectations. Achieving a balance between responsible representation and emotional appeal is critical for marketers. The way that animal imagery is viewed is also greatly influenced by the cultural setting. Global brands must thus localize their strategies while keeping ethical standards, customs, and cultural quirks in mind.

The development, distribution, and consumption of content with an animal theme have all changed as a result of the integration of digital platforms. Pet marketers can create organic reach through user-generated content, virtual mascots, and interactive features on platforms like YouTube, Instagram, and TikTok. These tactics promote communities based on common values and emotional experiences in addition to raising brand awareness.

Limitations

There are however some limitations to this research. First of all, the chapter fails to employ primary data collection methods like surveys or interviews, even though it draws from a range of case studies and academic publications. Therefore, it fails to offer concrete evidence for the behavior of consumers in real-time situations.

Second, most of the examples provided come from Western countries, particularly the US and the UK. The results might not be completely applicable to non-Western cultures, where opinions on CSR and the symbolic meaning of animals differ significantly.

Additionally, as digital marketing shifts quickly, trends like petfluencer culture are always shifting. What is effective now may not be effective in a few years, and this study lacks the ability to accurately predict how consumer behavior or platform dynamics will evolve in the future.

A second important limitation concerns the potential desensitization effect of repeated exposure to animal-themed advertising. Since animal imagery is more and more utilized, consumers become desensitized to its emotional power. What was initially distinctive and affecting can be viewed as cliche or manipulative. Brands risk falling into a trap of overusing emotional triggers so that they become less authentic and, ultimately, less effective. Furthermore, few empirical data have been gathered on how different demographic subgroups are being reached by animal-focused campaigns. Age, culture, socioeconomic level, and prior exposure to pets may all affect the way people are receiving and responding to such messages.

Without context-specific information, there is a possibility that marketers might deploy generic strategies not always effective on segments. Yet another limitation is there is very little research on the ethics of using animals in marketing for those against the exploitation of animals. Such groups would find even symbolic use of animals problematic except with avowed advocacy or welfare. Ignoring such a segment can cause reputational risk among ethically active consumers.

Suggestions for future research

This research presents a significant contribution to the study of relationship marketing and pet marketing. These areas have been studied more as their importance for the success of companies has been recognized today.

Several recommendations can be made to enhance the findings' robustness in future research. First, access to company-provided internal data may be useful for future research. A deeper investigation of the strategic implications of animal-based emotional marketing and corporate social responsibility programs would be possible by combining consumer-driven qualitative and quantitative data with internal brand insights.

Furthermore, although this study shows several examples of effective campaigns from well-known brands around the world, doing comparable analyses for other kinds of businesses might provide fresh perspectives on how emotional branding with animals operates for various business models and marketing budgets.

One area of research that should be further investigated is the psychological mechanisms involved in the consumer's mindset when they see images of animals in advertising. Psychological principles can be used as an explanation for why the repeated association of animals with specific attributes of a brand elicits a favorable response from humans. Animals, and especially "cute" or socially familiar animals, trigger innate protection and caretaking behaviors. These primal reactions, developed through evolution, can be extended by marketers to products and brands.

Finally, though this study focused on the ethical and emotional aspects of using animals in brand marketing, longitudinal methods could be used in future research that aim at the long-term effects of this imagery on consumer advocacy, loyalty, and purchasing behavior. This could assist to determine whether the emotional bonds created by content about animals result in long-lasting relationships between consumers and brands.

In conclusion, expanding further research in these areas will benefit the academic field of relationship marketing and provide useful information to companies seeking to engage with ethically and psychologically committed customers in a competitive and values-driven market.

REFERENCES

Aaker, D. A. (1996). Measuring Brand Equity across Products and Markets. *California Management Review*, *38*, 102–120. DOI: 10.2307/41165845

Abeer, H., & Malkawi. (2025). The use of conceptual metaphors in advertising: A cognitive approach to persuasive language. *Journal of Humanities and Political Science*, *5*(2). Advance online publication. DOI: 10.63332/joph.v5i2.469

Aksak, E. O., Ferguson, M. A., & Duman, S. A. (2016). Corporate social responsibility and CSR fit as predictors of corporate reputation: A global perspective. *Public Relations Review*, *42*(1), 79–81. DOI: 10.1016/j.pubrev.2015.11.004

Alves, M. C. A. (2019). *Relação de Trabalho Responsável: Responsabilidade social empresarial e a afirmação dos direitos fundamentais no trabalho*. Editora JH Mizuno.

Amazon Prime Video. (2021, 25 de novembro). Prime Video celebrates an unlikely friendship in its first ever Christmas advert for Europe [Press release]. https://press.aboutamazon.com/uk/2021/11/prime-video-celebrates-an-unlikely-friendship-in-its-first-ever-christmas-advert-for-europe

Azzari, V., & Pelissari, A. S. (2020). Does brand awareness influence purchase intention? The mediation role of brand equity dimensions. *Brazilian Business Review*, *17*(6), 669–685. DOI: 10.15728/bbr.2020.17.6.4

Barreda, A. A., Bilgihan, A., Nusair, K., & Okumus, F. (2015). Generating brand awareness in online social networks. *Computers in Human Behavior*, *50*, 600–609. DOI: 10.1016/j.chb.2015.03.023

Batra, R., & Ahtola, O. T. (1991). Measuring the hedonic and utilitarian sources of consumer attitudes. *Marketing Letters*, *2*, 159–170. DOI: 10.1007/BF00436035

Ben Lahouel, B., & Taleb, L. (2025). Beyond the linear link: Threshold effects of CSR on financial performance. *International Review of Economics & Finance*, *100*, 104086. Advance online publication. DOI: 10.1016/j.iref.2025.104086

Berry, L. L. (1983). Relationship Marketing. In Berry, L. L., Shostack, G. L., & Upala, G. D. (Eds.), *Emerging Perspectives on Services Marketing* (pp. 25–80). American Marketing Association.

Borkfelt, S., Kondrup, S., Röcklinsberg, H., Bjørkdahl, K., & Gjerris, M. (2015). Closer to Nature? A Critical Discussion of the Marketing of "Ethical" Animal Products. *Journal of Agricultural & Environmental Ethics*, *28*, 1053–1073. DOI: 10.1007/S10806-015-9577-4

Bowler, H. (2022, June 14). World's best ads ever: 'Monty the Penguin' becomes John Lewis's most iconic. The Drum. https://www.thedrum.com/news/2022/06/14/world-s-best-ads-ever-43-monty-the-penguin-becomes-john-lewis-s-most-iconic

Burton, L., & Collins, F. L. (2014). Mediated animal geographies: Symbolism, manipulation and the imaginary in advertising. *Social & Cultural Geography, 16*(3), 276–298. DOI: 10.1080/14649365.2014.979863

Cai, T. (2025). Analysis of digital marketing strategies in the pet food industry: A comparative study of different brands. Advances in Economics [AEMPS]. *Management and Political Sciences, 151*. Advance online publication. DOI: 10.54254/2754-1169/2024.19411

Cornish, A., Raubenheimer, D., & McGreevy, P. (2016). What We Know about the Public's Level of Concern for Farm Animal Welfare in Food Production in Developed Countries. *Animals (Basel), 6*. Advance online publication. DOI: 10.3390/ani6110074

Dabbous, A., & Barakat, K. (2020). Bridging the online offline gap: Assessing the impact of brands' social network content quality on brand awareness and purchase intention. *Journal of Retailing and Consumer Services, 53*, 101966. DOI: 10.1016/j.jretconser.2019.101966

Di Cioccio, M., Pozharliev, R., & De Angelis, M. (2024). Pawsitively powerful: Why and when pet influencers boost social media effectiveness. *Psychology and Marketing*. Advance online publication. DOI: 10.1002/mar.22000

Epley, N., Waytz, A., & Cacioppo, J. T. (2007). On seeing human: A three-factor theory of anthropomorphism. *Psychological Review, 114*(4), 864–886. DOI: 10.1037/0033-295X.114.4.864

Faisal, A., & Ekawanto, I. (2022). *The role of Social Media Marketing in increasing Brand Awareness, Brand Image and Purchase Intention*. Indonesian Management and Accounting Research., DOI: 10.25105/imar.v20i2.12554

Francioni, B., De Cicco, R., Curina, I., & Cioppi, M. (2025). *The strength of stance: The impact of brand activism on resistance to negative information, purchasing, and premium paying intents across different types of failures*. University of Urbino Carlo Bo., DOI: 10.1016/j.jretconser.2024.104102

Gálvez-Sánchez, F. J., Molina-Prados, A., Molina-Moreno, V., & Moral-Cuadra, S. (2024). Exploring the three-dimensional effect of corporate social responsibility on brand equity, corporate reputation, and willingness to pay: A study of the fashion industry. *Journal of Retailing and Consumer Services*. Advance online publication. DOI: 10.1016/j.jretconser.2024.103836

García-Madariaga, J., Moya, I., Recuero, N., & Blasco, M.-F. (2020). Revealing Unconscious Consumer Reactions to Advertisements That Include Visual Metaphors. A Neurophysiological Experiment. *Frontiers in Psychology*, *11*, 760. DOI: 10.3389/fpsyg.2020.00760

Grönroos, C. (2004). The relationship marketing process: Communication, interaction, dialogue, value. *Journal of Business and Industrial Marketing*, *19*(2), 99–113. DOI: 10.1108/08858620410523981

Hasudungan, A., & Saragih, H. S. (2023). Brand awareness and relationship intention: The moderating role of perceived corporate social responsibility dimensions. *Asia Pacific Journal of Marketing and Logistics*. Advance online publication. DOI: 10.1108/APJML-03-2022-0184

Holbrook, M. B., & Hirschman, E. C. (1982). The experiential aspects of consumption: Consumer fantasies, feelings, and fun. *The Journal of Consumer Research*, *9*(2), 132–140. DOI: 10.1086/208906

Hölker, S., Meyer-Höfer, M., & Spiller, A. (2019). Inclusion of Animal Ethics into the Consumer Value-Attitude System Using the Example of Game Meat Consumption. *Food Ethics*, •••, 1–23. DOI: 10.1007/S41055-019-00036-6

Hoyer, W. D., & Brown, S. P. (1990). Effects of brand awareness on choice for a common, repeat-purchase product. *The Journal of Consumer Research*, *17*(2), 141–148. DOI: 10.1086/208544

Huang, W.-H. (2024). I am not an animal: How animal metaphors backfire in product advertising. *Psychology and Marketing*, *41*(12), 3009–3023. DOI: 10.1002/mar.22100

Ismael, Z. N. (2022). Marketing strategy: The influence of corporate social responsibility on brand awareness. *International Journal of Engineering Business Management*, *6*(5), 43–48. DOI: 10.22161/ijebm.6.5.6

Jacobson, J., Hodson, J., & Mittelman, R. (2022). Pup-ularity contest: The advertising practices of popular animal influencers on Instagram. *Technological Forecasting and Social Change*, *174*, 121226. DOI: 10.1016/j.techfore.2021.121226

Janssens, M. (2021). Animal Business: An Ethical Exploration of Corporate Responsibility Towards Animals. *Food Ethics*, *7*. Advance online publication. DOI: 10.1007/s41055-021-00094-9

Jiang, Y., Yang, X., & Jia, L. (2022). The Pet Exposure Effect: Exploring the Differential Impact of Dogs Versus Cats on Consumer Mindsets. *Journal of Marketing*.

Kaushik, M., Choudhary, S., & Choudhary, M. (2024). Impact of emotional marketing on consumer decision making: A review (Article No. IJFMR240213659). [IJFMR]. *International Journal for Multidisciplinary Research, 6*(2). https://www.ijfmr.com

Keller, B., & Gierl, H. (2020). *Effectiveness of Animal Images in Advertising*. Marketing ZFP.

Kirk, C. P. (2019). Dogs have masters, cats have staff: Consumers' psychological ownership and their economic valuation of pets. *Journal of Business Research, 99*, 414–429. DOI: 10.1016/j.jbusres.2019.02.057

Kronenberg, J., & Bocian, M. (2022). Animal and plant images in corporate marketing communications are ecosystem services that should be paid for. *Ecosystem Services, 55*, 101464. DOI: 10.1016/j.ecoser.2022.101464

Laurent-Simpson, A. (2021). "This Is My Son Rosenberg". In Just Like Family.

Lavertu, L., Kulow, K., Cowan, K., & Marder, B. (2025). Petfluencers, the fur-mula for sincere endorsements: Examining how and when pets exhibit greater persuasion as influencers. *Journal of Consumer Behaviour*. Advance online publication. DOI: 10.1080/00218499.2025.2463707

LBBOnline. (2021). How Erste Group's Christmas ads became a festive favourite. https://lbbonline.com/news/how-erste-groups-christmas-ads-became-a-festive-favourite

Lee, S. Y., Kim, Y., & Kim, Y. (2021). Engaging consumers with corporate social responsibility campaigns: The roles of interactivity, psychological empowerment, and identification. *Journal of Business Research, 134*, 507–517. DOI: 10.1016/j.jbusres.2021.05.062

Liang, Y., Xu, Y., Lai, D., Hua, G., Huang, D., Wang, H., Li, H., & Han, L. (2022). Emerging market for pork with animal welfare attribute in China: An ethical perspective. *Meat Science, 195*, 108994. DOI: 10.1016/j.meatsci.2022.108994

Liu, L., & Zhao, H. (2024). Research on consumers' purchase intention of cultural and creative products—Metaphor design based on traditional cultural symbols. *PLoS One*. Advance online publication. DOI: 10.1371/journal.pone.0301678

Liu, Y., Chang, X., Yang, S., Li, Z., & Wu, Y. (2024). "Pets make you spend more!" Impact of pet ownership on consumer purchase decisions. *Journal of Business Research, 174*, 114838. DOI: 10.1016/j.jbusres.2024.114838

Loureiro, S. M. C., & Lopes, J. (2019). How corporate social responsibility initiatives in social media affect awareness and customer engagement. *Journal of Promotion Management, 25*(3), 378–403. DOI: 10.1080/10496491.2019.1557815

Luckerson, V. (2014, february 3). This was the most successful commercial of the Super Bowl. TIME. https://time.com/3870/budweiser-puppy-love-super-bowl-commercial

Luna-Amador, J., Caraballo-Payares, A., & Escobar-Espinoza, A. (2025). *Brand activism: Research trends and cluster analysis*. Departamento de Economía y Administración, Universidad de Cartagena., DOI: 10.1016/j.iedeen.2025.100279

Mansoor, M., Paul, J., Khan, T. I., Abukhait, R., & Hussain, D. (2025). Customer evangelists: Elevating hospitality through digital competence, brand image, and corporate social responsibility. *Journal of Business Research, 165*, 113181. DOI: 10.1016/j.ijhm.2025.104085

Mardani, P. B., Ayuningtyas, F., & Putri, J. N. (2019). Creative Strategies to Drive Brand Awareness (Case of "Forever Against Animal Testing Campaign" The Body Shop Indonesia). International Journal of Multicultural and Multireligious Understanding.

Martin, D., Palakshappa, N., & Woodside, A. (2019). Consumer metaphoria: Uncovering the automaticity of animal, product/brand, and country meanings. *Australasian Marketing Journal, 27*(2). Advance online publication. DOI: 10.1016/j.ausmj.2018.08.001

Mayo, D. T., Helms, M., & Mayo, C. (2009). Pets in Print Advertising-Are We Seeing More of Rover and Fluffy? A Content Analysis of Four Popular Magazines. *Academy of Marketing Studies Journal.*

Merskin, D. (2021). Circle of responsibility: Animals as stakeholders. In Bowen, D., Hayward, A. M., & James, K. (Eds.), *Public relations for social responsibility*. Emerald Publishing., DOI: 10.1108/9781800431676

Mota-Rojas, D., Mariti, C., Zdeinert, A., Riggio, G., Mora-Medina, P., Reyes, A. del M., Gazzano, A., Domínguez-Oliva, A., Lezama-García, K., José-Pérez, N., & Hernández-Ávalos, I. (2021). Anthropomorphism and its adverse effects on the distress and welfare of companion animals. *Animals (Basel), 11*(11), 3263. DOI: 10.3390/ani11113263

Muniz, F., Guzmán, F., Paswan, A. K., & Crawford, H. J. (2019). The immediate effect of corporate social responsibility on consumer-based brand equity. *Journal of Product and Brand Management*. Advance online publication. DOI: 10.1108/JPBM-09-2018-2036

Myers, S., Sen, S., Syrdal, H., & Woodroof, P. (2022). The impact of persuasion knowledge cues on social media engagement: A look at pet influencer marketing. *Journal of Interactive Advertising*, *22*(1), 43–60. DOI: 10.1080/10696679.2022.2093224

Noble, C. H., Bing, M. N., & Bogoviyeva, E. (2013). The effects of brand metaphors as design innovation: A test of congruency hypotheses. *Journal of Product Innovation Management*, *31*(1), 32–45. DOI: 10.1111/jpim.12067

Oleárová, M., & Bačík, R. (2023). A Relationship Between Social Media Marketing and Brand Awareness Increase. 15TH GLOBAL CONFERENCE ON BUSINESS AND SOCIAL SCIENCES ON 14 - 15 SEPTEMBER 2023. *NOVOTEL BANGKOK PLATINUM PRATUNAM, THAILAND.*, *184*. Advance online publication. DOI: 10.35609/gcbssproceeding.2023.1

Oliver, R. L. (1999). Whence consumer loyalty? *Journal of Marketing*, *63*(Special Issue), 33–44. DOI: 10.2307/1252099

Palladino, A., Lee, M., & Zhou, X. (2022). An analysis of Olympic mascot design toward attitude and purchase intention. *International Journal of Sport Communication*, *15*(3), 190–196. DOI: 10.1123/ijsc.2022-0052

Payne, A., & Frow, P. (2013). *Strategic customer management: Integrating relationship marketing and CRM*. Cambridge University Press., DOI: 10.1017/CBO9781139057417

Rexhepi, G., Kurtishi, S., & Bexheti, G. (2013). Corporate social responsibility (CSR) and innovation: The drivers of business growth? *Procedia: Social and Behavioral Sciences*, *75*, 532–541. DOI: 10.1016/j.sbspro.2013.04.058

Romaniuk, J., Wight, S., & Faulkner, M. (2017). Brand awareness: Revisiting an old metric for a new world. *Journal of Product and Brand Management*, *26*(5), 469–476. DOI: 10.1108/JPBM-06-2016-1242

Saluja, G., & Chan, E. Y. (2025). Going against the tide: How self-construal moderates receptivity towards popular brand activism. *Journal of Business Research*, *171*, 114129. DOI: 10.1016/j.jbusres.2025.115228

Sansome, K., Conduit, J., & Wilkie, D. (2025). Consumers demand transparency… but do they actually engage? Exploring motives and interactions with brand transparency information. *Journal of Business Research, 194*, 115386. DOI: 10.1016/j.jbusres.2025.115386

Saputra, O., Azhar, A., & Saputa, O. (2025). ANALYSIS OF THE ROLE OF SOCIAL MEDIA IN BRAND MANAGEMENT AND MARKETING. Pedagogic Research-Applied Literacy Journal. https://doi.org/.DOI: 10.70574/tdbrer63

Spears, N. E., Mowen, J. C., & Chakraborty, G. (1996). Symbolic role of animals in print advertising: Content analysis and conceptual development. *Journal of Business Research, 37*(1), 87–95. DOI: 10.1016/0148-2963(96)00060-4

Spears, N. E., Mowen, J. C., & Chakraborty, G. (1996). Symbolic role of animals in print advertising: Content analysis and conceptual development. *Journal of Business Research, 37*(2), 87–95. DOI: 10.1016/0148-2963(95)00051-1

Sun, D., Yang, D., Wang, J., & Tan, F. (2024). How animal metaphors increase tourists' waste classification intention. *Environmental Research Communications, 6*(10), 105012. DOI: 10.1088/2515-7620/ad82b0

Suparto, Y. (2024). *The Role of Social Media in Increasing Brand Awareness: A Literature Review*. Maneggio., DOI: 10.62872/bry58b32

Tchelidze, L. (2023). Influence of Brand Activities through Social Media on Consumer Awareness. Journal of International Business Research and Marketing. https://doi.org/.DOI: 10.18775/jibrm.1849-8558.2015.81.3001

The Marketing Explainer. (2024, july 2). Budweiser's marketing strategy explained. https://www.marketingexplainers.com/budweisers-marketing-strategy-explained/

The Mill. (2021). Amazon Prime – Unlikely Friendship [Portfólio de produção]. https://www.themill.com/the-mill/work/amazon-prime-unlikely-friendship/

Wei, W., Zhang, L., Ying, T., & Zheng, Y. (2025). Pet influencer marketing appeal in hotel booking: Exploring the power of message appeal and boundary conditions. *International Journal of Hospitality Management, 126*, 104094. DOI: 10.1016/j.ijhm.2025.104094

Winter, C. (2020). A review of research into animal ethics in tourism: Launching the Annals of Tourism Research curated collection on animal ethics in tourism. *Annals of Tourism Research, 84*, 102989. DOI: 10.1016/j.annals.2020.102989

Wong, W. (2017). Brand Mascots and Other Marketing Animals, Stephen Brown & Sharon Ponsonby-McCabe (Eds.). Journal of Design History, 30(2), 241–242. https://doi.org/DOI: 10.1093/jdh/epx015

Woodside, A., & Lloyd, S. (2013). Animals, archetypes, and advertising (A3): The theory and the practice of customer brand symbolism. Journal of Marketing Management.

Xie-Carson, L., Benckendorff, P., & Hughes, K. (2023). Not so different after all? A netnographic exploration of user engagement with non-human influencers on social media. *Journal of Business Research*, *167*, 114149. DOI: 10.1016/j.jbusres.2023.114149

Xu, J., Tong, Z., Rehman, M., & Hussain, T. (2025). Informational or emotional? The influencing mechanism of digital corporate social responsibility related interactive content on product purchase intention. *Journal of Business Research*. Advance online publication. DOI: 10.1016/j.actpsy.2025.104988

Zhang, L., Wei, W., Rathjens, B., & Zheng, Y. (2023). Pet influencers on social media: The joint effect of message appeal and narrator. *International Journal of Hospitality Management*, *110*, 103453. DOI: 10.1016/j.ijhm.2023.103453

Chapter 3
The Use of the Animal as an Identity Symbol of the Culture and History of Sport Clubs From Northern Portugal

Bruno Barbosa Sousa
https://orcid.org/0000-0002-8588-2422
Polytechnic University of Cávado and Ave (IPCA), Portugal & UNIAG, Portugal

Luzia Arantes
https://orcid.org/0000-0003-1179-9113
University of Aveiro, Portugal & Polytechnic Institute of Cávado and Ave, Portugal

ABSTRACT

In sport (and football), animals represent an important symbol of a club's identity, representing values of society and local culture (such as strength, passion, loyalty or courage). The use of animal imagery in sports marketing can be highly effective due to its ability to evoke strong emotional responses and create memorable brand associations. This chapter aims to illustrate two representative examples of the importance that some animals (real or imaginary) may represent in a sports club in Portugal, as a differentiating symbol in the brand, identity and products associated with the club. Thus, this chapter aims to present some insights for sports marketing, but also for the importance of animals in the domain of sports companies (and sports clubs in particular - FCPorto and Gil Vicente FC). Finally, limitations and lines of future research will be presented.

DOI: 10.4018/979-8-3373-4342-6.ch003

1. INTRODUCTION

Animals and pets represent a lot to contemporary societies, due to their importance in the context of nature but also in family contexts and personal domain. Likewise, in sport (and football), animals represent an important symbol of a club's identity, representing values of society and local culture (such as strength, passion, loyalty or courage). The use of animal imagery in sports marketing can be highly effective due to its ability to evoke strong emotional responses and create memorable brand associations (Kwak et al., 2011). Animals often symbolize specific traits such as strength, agility, and resilience, which align well with the values and aspirations of sports teams and athletes (Lloyd & Woodside, 2013). This symbolic representation can enhance team identity, foster fan loyalty, and increase merchandise sales. Additionally, the anthropomorphism of animals can make sports brands more relatable and engaging, appealing to a broader audience and enhancing overall marketability. Thus, and from an exploratory perspective, this chapter aims to illustrate two representative examples of the importance that some animals (real or imaginary) may represent in a sports club in Portugal, as a differentiating symbol in the brand, identity and products associated with the club. Thus, this chapter aims to present some insights for sports marketing, but also for the importance of animals in the domain of sports companies (and sports clubs in particular). Finally, limitations and lines of future research will be presented.

2. THEORETICAL BACKGROUND

2.1. Sports Marketing

Sports marketing refers to the strategic application of marketing principles and techniques to promote sports events, teams, athletes, and related products or services (da Silva & Las Casas, 2020). It encompasses both the marketing of sports as a product and the use of sports as a platform to market other goods and services (Shank & Lyberger, 2014). This dual nature makes sports marketing a unique and dynamic field, requiring a deep understanding of consumer behavior, brand management, and fan engagement. It plays a critical role in shaping the public image of sports entities and in generating revenue through sponsorships, merchandise, media rights, and ticket sales (Chen & Zhang, 2011). The evolution of sports marketing has been closely tied to technological advancements and the globalization of sports. Initially focused on local promotions and event attendance, the field expanded significantly with the advent of television broadcasting in the mid-20th century (Vieira & Sousa, 2020). The digital era further transformed sports marketing, introducing social media, data analytics, and immersive technologies such as virtual and augmented reality. These innovations have enabled more personalized and interactive fan experiences, while also offering brands new avenues for engagement and monetization (da Silva Pereira & Sousa, 2020).

The importance of sports marketing lies in its ability to build strong emotional connections between fans and sports entities. Marketing strategies can enhance fan loyalty, increase brand equity, and drive long-term financial sustainability (Bühler & Nufer, 2015). For sports organizations, marketing is not merely a support function but a core component of strategic planning. It influences decisions related to branding, partnerships, community outreach, and international expansion (Ferrand & McCarthy, 2008). Moreover, it plays a vital role in attracting and retaining sponsors, who seek visibility and alignment with the values and reach of sports properties. In contemporary sports management, sports marketing is indispensable for navigating a highly competitive and commercialized environment (Gashi, 2025). Organizations that invest in innovative marketing approaches are better positioned to capitalize on emerging trends, such as esports, influencer marketing, and sustainability initiatives. Sports marketing contributes to the broader societal impact of sports by promoting inclusivity, health, and social causes. As the industry continues to evolve, the integration of marketing with data science, fan engagement platforms, and global branding strategies will be essential for sustained success (Leite, 2025).

2.2. Animals as an emotional element in sport

The presence of animals in sports contexts - whether as mascots, competitors, or companions - has been shown to elicit strong emotional responses from both participants and spectators. This emotional engagement often transcends the competitive nature of sport, fostering a sense of empathy, attachment, and identity (Marvin et al., 2022). For instance, equestrian sports, dog agility competitions, and falconry not only rely on the physical capabilities of animals but also on the emotional bond between human and animal, which can significantly influence performance outcomes and audience perception (Dashper, 2016). Animals also serve as powerful symbols within the sporting domain, often embodying traits such as strength, loyalty, and resilience (Tymowsk, 2013). Mascots, both live and symbolic, are strategically used by teams to cultivate emotional connections with fans, enhance team identity, and create a sense of tradition and continuity (Schultz & Sheffer, 2018). These emotional associations can increase fan loyalty and engagement, contributing to the commercial and cultural success of sports organizations. The anthropomorphization of animals in these roles often leads to heightened emotional investment and narrative development within sports media (Keen, 2011).

From a psychological perspective, the inclusion of animals in sport can act as a buffer against stress and anxiety for athletes, particularly in high-pressure environments (Guo et al., 2025). The presence of therapy animals or companion animals in training and competition settings has been associated with improved mood, reduced cortisol levels, and enhanced focus (Beetz et al., 2012). This emotional support function underscores the broader role of animals not merely as participants or symbols, but as integral contributors to the emotional ecology of sport. The incorporation of animal figures into the visual identity of sports clubs plays a significant role in shaping the emotional landscape of fan engagement (Omasta & Chappell, 2015). Animals are often selected for their symbolic attributes, such as courage, agility, or dominance (which are then projected onto the team's image).

This symbolic association fosters admiration and emotional resonance among supporters, who internalize these traits as reflective of their own identity and values. As a result, the animal emblem becomes more than a decorative element; it serves as a conduit for emotional expression and collective pride, reinforcing the psychological bond between the club and its fan base (Cottingham, 2012). Animal-based symbols contribute to the construction of a cohesive and enduring brand identity, which in turn cultivates loyalty and long-term affiliation among fans (Liang & Cheong, 2025). The consistent use of animal imagery across merchandise, stadium design, and media narratives enhances brand recognition and facilitates emotional continuity across generations of supporters (Smith et al., 2017). This symbolic continuity strengthens the affective ties between fans and the club, promoting a sense of belonging and shared heritage. In this context, the animal figure functions as a powerful semiotic tool that not only differentiates the club in a competitive market but also anchors the emotional and cultural identity of its community (Michailidis et al., 2016).

2.3. The Role of Sports in Regional Economic Development

Sports play a pivotal role in stimulating regional economies by generating employment, attracting investment, and promoting tourism. The construction and maintenance of sports infrastructure (e.g. stadiums, training centers, and recreational facilities) create direct and indirect job opportunities (Raso & Cherubini, 2024). Additionally, sports events, both amateur and professional, draw visitors who contribute to the local economy through spending on accommodation, food, and transportation. These economic activities can lead to long-term benefits by enhancing the region's visibility and attractiveness to investors and tourists alike. Beyond economic impacts, sports contribute significantly to social development at the local level. They foster community identity, pride, and cohesion by bringing people together across diverse backgrounds (Skinner, Zakus & Cowell, 2008). Participation in sports activities promotes inclusion, reduces social inequalities, and encourages civic engagement. Local sports clubs and events often serve as platforms for volunteerism and intergenerational interaction, strengthening the social fabric and enhancing the quality of life in communities (Skinner et al., 2008).

Sports are also instrumental in improving public health and developing human capital. Regular physical activity reduces the prevalence of chronic diseases, lowers healthcare costs, and enhances mental well-being (Bailey et al., 2013). Therefore, sports programs in schools and communities support the development of essential life skills such as teamwork, discipline, and leadership (Dickson & Zhang, 2021). These benefits contribute to a healthier, more productive population, which is a key driver of sustainable regional and local development.

3. METHODOLOGY AND CONTEXT

This chapter adopts a qualitative, exploratory case study approach to investigate the symbolic and emotional significance of animal figures in the visual identity and cultural narratives of Portuguese sports clubs. Specifically, the research focuses on two clubs - Futebol Clube do Porto (F. C. Porto) and Gil Vicente Futebol Clube - as illustrative examples within the national sports context. These clubs were selected due to their distinct use of animal symbolism in their emblems and branding, which provides a relevant basis for examining the emotional and cultural impact of such imagery on fan identity and club heritage. Data collection will involve a combination of document analysis, semi-structured interviews, and visual content interpretation. Official club materials (e.g., logos, merchandise, historical archives) will be analyzed to trace the evolution and symbolic framing of animal figures within each club's identity. Interviews with club representatives, sports historians, and fans will provide insights into the perceived emotional and cultural relevance of these symbols. This triangulated approach aims to capture both institutional and individual perspectives, thereby enriching the understanding of how animal imagery contributes to affective loyalty and brand identification in the sports domain.

By focusing on F. C. Porto and Gil Vicente as case studies, the research seeks to generate context-specific insights that reflect broader patterns in Portuguese sports culture. While not intended to be generalizable, the findings will offer illustrative examples of how animal symbolism operates within club identity construction and fan engagement. The exploratory nature of the study allows for the emergence of nuanced interpretations and contributes to the growing body of literature on emotional branding and symbolic communication in sport.

4. ANALYSIS

The dragon, as a central figure in the emblem of Futebol Clube do Porto, serves as a potent symbol of strength, courage, and resilience. Unlike real animals commonly used in sports branding, the dragon is a mythical creature, which amplifies its symbolic power and mystique. Its presence in the club's identity is not merely decorative; it conveys a narrative of dominance and fearlessness, qualities that are deeply embedded in the club's competitive ethos.

The dragon's fierce and majestic representation aligns with the club's aspiration to assert superiority both nationally and internationally. Historically and culturally, the dragon also resonates with the identity of the city of Porto and the broader northern region of Portugal. The North is often characterized by its industrious spirit, historical resistance, and cultural pride, traits that are metaphorically encapsulated in the image of the dragon. By adopting this symbol, FCPorto reinforces a collective identity that transcends sport, linking the club's values with regional narratives of perseverance and autonomy. The dragon thus becomes a cultural ambassador, bridging the club's sporting mission with the socio-historical identity of its community.

The emotional impact of the dragon on supporters is significant. It fosters a sense of admiration and loyalty, as fans often perceive the symbol as a reflection of their own values and aspirations. The dragon's presence in stadium iconography, merchandise, and media communications reinforces a shared mythology that strengthens fan engagement and emotional investment. This symbolic continuity contributes to the club's brand equity, making the dragon not only a visual marker but also a central element in the affective and cultural experience of being a F. C. Porto supporter. From a semiotic perspective, the dragon functions as a multidimensional signifier within the club's identity system. It encapsulates abstract values such as bravery and determination while also serving as a visual anchor for storytelling and brand differentiation. Its integration into the club's emblematic and communicative practices exemplifies how imaginary animals can be leveraged to construct powerful emotional and cultural narratives in sport. In the case of F. C. Porto, the dragon is not just a symbol - it is a strategic and affective tool that embodies the spirit of the club and the identity of its region. "Dragon Stadium" (Estádio do Dragão), the home stadium of the Portuguese football club FC Porto in Porto, Portugal. The name "Dragão" (dragon) refers to the mythical creature that is a symbol of both FC Porto and the city. The dragon is featured in the club's logo and the city's coat of arms, representing strength and pride. The stadium, with a capacity of over 50,000, was inaugurated in 2003 and has hosted numerous high-profile matches, including the 2021 UEFA Champions League Final. It's also known for its distinctive architectural features, such as the extensive use of azulejos (tiles) and a transparent polycarbonate roof that, when viewed from above, is said to resemble a dragon's back.

The rooster, prominently featured in the emblem of Gil Vicente Futebol Clube, serves as a culturally resonant symbol deeply rooted in Portuguese folklore and national identity. Its inclusion in the club's visual identity reflects not only a connection to the legendary figure of Gil Vicente, a symbol of justice and civic courage, but also to the broader cultural motif of the rooster as a guardian and herald of truth. In this context, the rooster transcends its zoological identity to become a metaphor for vigilance, pride, and moral integrity—qualities that the club seeks to embody on and off the field.

The symbolic use of the rooster also aligns with the regional identity of Barcelos, the city where the club is based. The "Galo de Barcelos" (Rooster of Barcelos) is one of the most iconic symbols of Portuguese popular culture, associated with a legend of miraculous justice and national pride. By incorporating this figure into its emblem, Gil Vicente FC reinforces its local heritage and strengthens its cultural ties to the community. This symbolic anchoring enhances the club's authenticity and fosters a sense of belonging among supporters, who see the rooster as a reflection of their own values and historical narratives.

From a branding perspective, the rooster functions as a distinctive and emotionally charged element that differentiates Gil Vicente FC within the competitive landscape of Portuguese football. Its visual and symbolic consistency across club communications, merchandise, and fan rituals contributes to a coherent brand identity that resonates with both local and national audiences. The rooster's assertive posture and vibrant symbolism evoke admiration and emotional attachment, reinforcing fan loyalty and enhancing the club's cultural capital.

The rooster's role in the club's identity illustrates how animal symbolism can serve as a strategic tool for emotional engagement and cultural storytelling in sport. It encapsulates a set of values—honor, resilience, and justice—that are not only relevant to the club's ethos but also deeply embedded in Portuguese collective memory. In this way, Gil Vicente FC's use of the rooster exemplifies how sports organizations can leverage culturally significant animal figures to construct meaningful narratives that unite fans, reinforce regional pride, and sustain long-term brand loyalty.

The legend of the Galo de Barcelos holds a central place in the cultural identity of the Barcelos community, symbolizing justice, faith, and divine intervention. According to the tale, a pilgrim wrongfully accused of theft was sentenced to death but proclaimed his innocence by declaring that a roasted rooster would crow as proof. Miraculously, the rooster sang at the moment of his execution, leading to his salvation.

This narrative has been preserved across generations and is deeply embedded in local folklore, serving as a moral exemplar and a symbol of hope and righteousness. The rooster thus transcends its literal meaning to become a cultural icon that reflects the values and historical consciousness of the region. For the people of Barcelos, the Galo is more than a folkloric figure—it is a symbol of civic pride and regional identity. It is prominently featured in public art, tourism branding, and local celebrations, reinforcing a shared sense of belonging and cultural continuity.

The monument erected by the pardoned pilgrim in honor of Saint James and the Virgin Mary remains a tangible link to this legend, anchoring the community's historical narrative in a physical and spiritual space. Through its enduring presence, the Galo de Barcelos continues to inspire admiration and emotional connection, functioning as a unifying emblem for the city and its inhabitants.

In conclusion, the analysis of Futebol Clube do Porto and Gil Vicente Futebol Clube reveals that animal symbolism plays a critical role in shaping the emotional and cultural identity of sports organizations in Portugal. The dragon and the rooster, respectively, serve not only as emblematic figures but also as carriers of regional values, historical narratives, and collective aspirations. These symbols transcend their visual function, becoming integral to the clubs' storytelling, branding, and emotional engagement strategies. Both case studies demonstrate how animal figures can foster a deep sense of belonging and loyalty among supporters. The dragon, with its mythical connotations of strength and fearlessness, reflects the resilient spirit of the city of Porto and the northern Portuguese identity. Similarly, the rooster, rooted in the legend of Barcelos, embodies justice, pride, and cultural heritage, reinforcing Gil Vicente's connection to its local community. These symbolic associations enhance the affective bond between fans and clubs, contributing to sustained engagement and intergenerational support.

In conclusion, the use of animal imagery in sports club emblems is not merely aesthetic—it is a strategic and culturally embedded practice that reinforces brand identity, emotional resonance, and regional pride. The exploratory case study approach has provided illustrative insights into how symbolic animals function within the Portuguese sports context, offering a foundation for future research on emotional branding and cultural semiotics in sport. Further comparative studies could expand this framework to other clubs and regions, deepening our understanding of the interplay between symbolism, identity, and fan culture.

5. DISCUSSION

The symbolic use of animals in sports club emblems serves as a powerful emotional anchor that fosters affective bonds between clubs and their supporters. In the case of Futebol Clube do Porto, the dragon represents strength, courage, and resilience—qualities that resonate deeply with the cultural identity of the city of Porto and the northern Portuguese region. Similarly, Gil Vicente Futebol Clube's use of the rooster, rooted in the legend of the Galo de Barcelos, evokes values of justice, pride, and local heritage. These animal figures are not merely decorative;

they function as emotionally charged symbols that encapsulate the ethos of each club and its surrounding community. These symbols also play a crucial role in cultivating intergenerational loyalty and emotional continuity among fans. The dragon and the rooster become part of family traditions, passed down through stories, rituals, and visual representations that reinforce a shared identity. Children grow up identifying with these symbols, associating them with moments of pride, celebration, and belonging. This emotional inheritance strengthens the clubs' cultural presence and ensures that the symbolic animals remain relevant across generations, contributing to the long-term sustainability of fan engagement. Local sports clubs serve as vital institutions for fostering territorial cohesion by creating shared spaces for interaction, collaboration, and identity formation. These organizations often transcend socio-economic and cultural divides, offering inclusive environments where individuals from diverse backgrounds can engage in collective activities. Through regular training sessions, competitions, and community events, sports clubs contribute to the development of social networks and mutual trust among residents. This interconnectedness reinforces the stability and resilience of local communities, promoting a sense of unity and common purpose within the territory. Sports clubs (and football clubs in particular) are a very important element for the territories and their residents. Sports clubs often convey emotional and affective ties around historical and cultural values, even fostering feelings of "brand love" or "brand hate".

Participation in sports clubs significantly enhances residents' sense of belonging and attachment to their locality. The symbolic value of representing one's neighborhood or region in sporting events fosters pride and emotional connection to place. Moreover, the visibility and recognition of local athletes and teams can strengthen community identity and intergenerational ties. Sports clubs often act as custodians of local traditions and values, embedding themselves in the cultural fabric of the territory.

Sports clubs play a pivotal role in shaping intense emotional connections between individuals and brands, significantly influencing the phenomena of "brand love" and "brand hate." These affiliations often extend beyond mere team support, becoming integral to personal and collective identity, particularly in contexts marked by strong rivalries (Popp et al., 2016). Such emotional investment is frequently reinforced through symbolic representations, including animal mascots, which serve as accessible and emotionally resonant brand extensions (Velicia Martin, Toledo & Palos-Sanchez, 2020). Research in consumer psychology and sports marketing suggests that these mascots not only humanize the brand but also enhance emotional engagement, fostering loyalty among supporters while simultaneously intensifying antagonism toward rival entities. Sports clubs are also important in the context of territorial marketing and place marketing.

This dual dynamic underscores the capacity of sports branding to mobilize affective responses that shape consumer behavior, community cohesion, and intergroup perceptions. As such, they play a crucial role in cultivating place-based loyalty and reinforcing the social and emotional bonds that underpin sustainable local development. The use of culturally embedded animal figures contributes to the construction of local and regional identity, uniting residents and supporters under a common emblem. These symbols act as visual and emotional representations of collective memory and shared values, reinforcing social cohesion and civic pride. In this way, the dragon and the rooster transcend their zoological or mythical origins to become central elements in the emotional and cultural fabric of their respective communities. The case studies of FCPorto and Gil Vicente thus illustrate how animal symbolism in sport can serve as a strategic and affective mechanism for building identity, unity, and emotional resonance.

6. CONCLUSION

This chapter is exploratory in nature and is based solely on two cases illustrating the sporting context in northern Portugal. It is not possible to generalize the results obtained in this exploratory analysis and this highlights a strong limitation of the study. However, it seems to be clear that the use of animals in the sporting symbols of soccer clubs can provoke good feelings of affection, territorial identity (e.g. Galo de Barcelos) and local culture. Sports marketing is an aspect that should be strongly developed by sports clubs. The use of animals represents a differentiating element for sports clubs. There are many illustrative cases that can be highlighted in soccer in Portugal, soccer in Europe and soccer around the world. This chapter, being an exploratory study, only highlights two illustrative examples in the north of Portugal. From an interdisciplinary perspective, this chapter provides insights into sports marketing, territorial culture and the petfluencers and pet-powered branding literature. In the future, it will be important to develop the study with greater consistency and robustness. This will involve the authors initially developing some exploratory interviews to be carried out at sports clubs (communication directors) in order to understand the role that certain symbols (i.e. animals) play in the history and culture of the sports club. At a second stage, it will be essential to carry out focus groups with fans/participants of the sports clubs mentioned in the study and understand whether the "animal figure" has an important element of cohesion and identity among fans and in the culture of the local population and history of the city. Initial studies, and according to the embryonic perspective, show this relationship between the figure of an animal in the club's symbol and the values defended by the fans and the culture of the population. However, the study was initially only carried out with two sports clubs in the north of Portugal (i.e. F.C. Porto and Gil Vicente F.C.).

REFERENCES

Bailey, R., Hillman, C., Arent, S., & Petitpas, A. (2013). Physical activity: An underestimated investment in human capital? *Journal of Physical Activity & Health, 10*(3), 289–308. PMID: 23620387

Beetz, A., Uvnäs-Moberg, K., Julius, H., & Kotrschal, K. (2012). Psychosocial and psychophysiological effects of human-animal interactions: The possible role of oxytocin. *Frontiers in Psychology, 3*, 234. PMID: 22866043

Bühler, A., & Nufer, G. (2015). Relationship marketing in sports: Building and establishing longstanding relations in the business of sports. In *Routledge handbook of sports marketing* (pp. 207–221). Routledge.

Chen, K. K., & Zhang, J. J. (2011). Examining consumer attributes associated with collegiate athletic facility naming rights sponsorship: Development of a theoretical framework. *Sport Management Review, 14*(2), 103–116.

Cottingham, M. D. (2012). Interaction ritual theory and sports fans: Emotion, symbols, and solidarity. *Sociology of Sport Journal, 29*(2), 168–185.

da Silva, E. C., & Las Casas, A. L. (2020). Key elements of sports marketing activities for sports events. *International Journal of Business Administration, 11*(1), 11–21.

da Silva Pereira, I., & Sousa, B. B. (2020). Corporate social responsibility in the field of sports marketing: A study applied to SC Braga. In *Statistical Modelling and Sports Business Analytics* (pp. 108–118). Routledge.

Dashper, K. (2016). *Human-animal relationships in equestrian sport and leisure*. Routledge.

Dickson, G., & Zhang, J. J. (2021). Sports and urban development: An introduction. *International Journal of Sports Marketing & Sponsorship, 22*(1), 1–9.

Ferrand, A., & McCarthy, S. (2008). *Marketing the sports organisation: Building networks and relationships*. Routledge.

Gashi, A. (2025). Sports Marketing Strategies, Navigating the Intersection of Globalization and Internationalization. *Interdisciplinary Journal of Research and Development, 12*(1), 190–190.

Guo, C., Chen, F., & Wang, Y. (2025). The Psychological Impact of Competitive Sports Participation on Adolescent Athletes: An Analysis of Coping Mechanisms and Performance Outcomes. *Journal of Rational-Emotive & Cognitive-Behavior Therapy, 43*(2), 24.

Keen, S. (2011). Fast tracks to narrative empathy: Anthropomorphism and dehumanization in graphic narratives. *SubStance*, *40*(1), 135–155.

Kwak, D. H., Kim, Y. K., & Hirt, E. R. (2011). Exploring the role of emotions on sport consumers' behavioral and cognitive responses to marketing stimuli. *European Sport Management Quarterly*, *11*(3), 225–250.

Leite, E. T. (2025). The power of strategies in sports marketing sponsorship, licensing, and advertising in action. *Brazilian Journal of Development*, *11*(5), e79628–e79628.

Liang, L., & Cheong, C. Y. M. (2025). Brand identity construction through the heritage of Chinese destination logos. *Semiotica*, *2025*(263), 241–277.

Lloyd, S., & Woodside, A. G. (2013). Animals, archetypes, and advertising (A3): The theory and the practice of customer brand symbolism. *Journal of Marketing Management*, *29*(1-2), 5–25.

Marvin, S., Sorenson, K., & Stevens, J. R. (2022). Bringing human-animal interaction to sport: Potential impacts on athletic performance. *European Journal of Sport Science*, *22*(7), 955–963. PMID: 33840355

Omasta, M., & Chappell, D. (Eds.). (2015). *Play, performance, and identity: How institutions structure ludic spaces*. Routledge.

Popp, B., Germelmann, C. C., & Jung, B. (2016). We love to hate them! Social media-based anti-brand communities in professional football. *International Journal of Sports Marketing & Sponsorship*, *17*(4), 349–367.

Raso, G., & Cherubini, D. (2024). The sport tourism and regional economic development: A systematic review. *Scientific Journal of Sport and Performance*, *3*(1), 108–121.

Schultz, B., & Sheffer, M. L. (2018). The mascot that wouldn't die: A case study of fan identification and mascot loyalty. *Sport in Society*, *21*(3), 482–496.

Shank, M. D., & Lyberger, M. R. (2014). *Sports marketing: A strategic perspective*. Routledge.

Skinner, J., Zakus, D. H., & Cowell, J. (2008). Development through sport: Building social capital in disadvantaged communities. *Sport Management Review*, *11*(3), 253–275.

Smith, A. C., Stavros, C., & Westberg, K. (2017). *Brand Fans. Lessons from the Worlds Greatest Sporting Brands*. RMIT University.

Tymowsk, G. (2013). The virtue of compassion: Animals in sport, hunting as sport, and entertainment. In *Sport, animals, and society* (pp. 140–154). Routledge.

Velicia Martin, F., Toledo, L. D., & Palos-Sanchez, P. (2020). How deep is your love? Brand love analysis applied to football teams. *International Journal of Sports Marketing & Sponsorship*, *21*(4), 669–693.

Vieira, C. B., & Sousa, B. (2020). The brand attachment and consumer behaviour in sports marketing contexts: The case of football fans in Portugal. *International Journal of Sport Management and Marketing*, *20*(1-2), 29–46.

KEY TERMS AND DEFINITIONS

Competitive Advantage: Refers to the factors that allow a company to produce goods or services better or more cheaply than its rival

"Dragon" (or "dragão" in Portuguese): A symbol of the club and the city of Porto. It represents strength, fighting spirit, and invincibility. FC Porto is nicknamed "dragões" (dragons) because of the dragon featured on the club's crest, which is derived from the city's coat of arms. The dragon also appears in the name of the team's stadium, Estádio do Dragão, meaning "Dragon Stadium".

F. C. Porto: A Portuguese professional sports club, most famous for its football team, based in Porto. It's one of the "Big Three" Portuguese football clubs, along with Benfica and Sporting CP. The club is nicknamed "Dragões" (Dragons) and "Azuis e brancos" (Blue and whites).

Galo de Barcelos: It refers to a popular Portuguese symbol, often depicted as a brightly colored ceramic rooster, that is deeply rooted in a legend from the town of Barcelos. The legend tells of a pilgrim wrongly accused of a crime who, as proof of his innocence, declared a rooster would crow at his execution. The rooster did indeed crow, saving the pilgrim, and the story has since become a symbol of faith, justice, and good luck.

Gil Vicente F. C.: Gil Vicente Futebol Clube, often referred to simply as Gil Vicente, is a Portuguese professional football club based in Barcelos. The club's name honors Gil Vicente, a renowned Portuguese playwright and poet from the early 16th century, who is considered a foundational figure in Portuguese drama. The club was founded on May 3, 1924.

Pet-powered Branding: Also known as pet-centric marketing, leverages the strong emotional bond between people and their pets to build brand awareness, foster loyalty, and drive engagement. It involves using pets, whether real or stylized, in marketing campaigns, social media content, and even product design to connect with consumers on an emotional level.

Petfluencer: A pet, usually a domesticated animal like a cat or dog, that has gained a large following on social media and is used by their owner to promote brands and products. They are essentially social media influencers, but instead of humans, they are animals.

Place Marketing: A strategic approach to promoting a specific geographic location, such as a city, region, or even a country, to attract visitors, businesses, residents, or investors. It involves understanding the unique characteristics of a place and crafting targeted marketing messages to appeal to specific audiences. Ultimately, place marketing aims to enhance a location's image, boost its economy, and improve its overall appeal.

Sports Marketing: A specialized field of marketing focused on promoting sports events, teams, athletes, and related products or services using various marketing strategies and techniques. It involves promoting sports events, equipment, or products by leveraging athletes, teams, or sporting events as promotional tools. Essentially, it encompasses both the marketing of sports as an experience and the use of sports to market other products and services.

Chapter 4
Pet-Driven Branding and the Emotional Economy

Sandra Costa
https://orcid.org/0009-0007-4130-6523
Polytechnic University of Viseu, Portugal

ABSTRACT

This chapter places petfluencers in the context of the emotional economy of consumption and explores their function in modern branding. Through anthropomorphism, nostalgia, and parasocial interaction, it makes the case that animals are dynamic emotional agents rather than passive mascots that promote attachment, trust, and brand love. The chapter uses examples like Grumpy Cat, Nala Cat, and Doug the Pug to show how petfluencers are different from conventional animal symbols in that they co-create meaning with audiences and create commercial value through digital engagement, merchandising, and sponsorship. A conceptual model of pet-driven branding is proposed, integrating symbolic representation, identity mediation, emotional activation, and consumer outcomes. The chapter also discusses market saturation, ethical issues, and the growing popularity of AI-generated pets, pointing out both advantages and disadvantages. All things considered, it reinterprets animals as relational actors at the core of post-human branding.

1. INTRODUCTION

In a time when emotions, symbols, and identity are playing a bigger role in how people feel about brands, animals, both real and imagined, have become important tools in branding strategy (Kapferer, 2012; Zhang, 2015). The current rise of petfluencers and ads focused on pets has brought back interest in how animals can affect people's emotions in marketing. However, their symbolic function in branding has

DOI: 10.4018/979-8-3373-4342-6.ch004

a long history (Holt, 2004; Mark & Pearson, 2022). Animal iconography has long been a strategic way to show power, agility, exclusivity, and cultural capital. For example, the prancing horse of Ferrari, the crocodile of Lacoste, and the jumping jaguar of Jaguar (Kapferer, 2012; Mick, 1986).

The emotional and cultural framework in which these animal emblems work has changed. Today's consumers are more interested in building emotional connections with businesses than in getting things done (Fournier, 1998; Fournier & Alvarez, 2012; Thomson et al., 2005). In an emotional economy, brands that make people feel something tend to build stronger loyalty, perceived value, and brand connection (Batra et al., 2012; Pawle & Cooper, 2006). Animals are very important to this process because they are easy to relate to and can make people feel warm, trusting, empathetic, and familiar traits that are important to emotional branding (Aggarwal & McGill, 2007; Brown et al., 2003).

This chapter presents a conceptual framework for pet-driven branding, hypothesizing the role of animal symbolism in shaping brand identity to affect consumer emotions, perceptions, and behaviors. The model is based on ideas from several fields, such as emotional branding (Thomson et al., 2005), brand identity (Kapferer, 2012), symbolic consumption (McCracken, 1986), brand love (Batra et al., 2012), and anthropomorphism (Epley et al., 2007). The chapter presents a framework for comprehending the role of animal symbols, including actual pets, mascots, or symbolic creatures, in the development of emotional value, through a narrative literature review and illustrative brand examples.

Although there is increasing scholarly interest in brand emotion and meaning-making, the function of animals as symbolic and emotional assets in branding is still little explored. Some literature discusses anthropomorphism in advertising (Aggarwal & McGill, 2007) and the role of mascots in consumer trust (Reddy & Sathish, 2023), but there is a scarcity of studies that comprehensively investigate the function of animal symbolism within the overarching framework of brand identification and emotional branding. This chapter fills that gap by making both theoretical and managerial contributions to our knowledge of how animals serve as emotional and symbolic messengers in brand ecosystems (Fournier & Alvarez, 2012; Holt, 2004).

2. THEORETICAL FOUNDATIONS: EMOTION, IDENTITY, AND SYMBOLISM IN BRANDING

A foundation in a number of interconnected theoretical areas, including emotional branding, brand identity, symbolic consumption, anthropomorphism, and archetypal theory, is necessary to comprehend the function of animal symbolism in brand identity and consumer engagement. These viewpoints illuminate on how animals serve as psychologically significant, culturally charged, and emotionally resonance components in branding strategies.

2.1 Emotional Branding

The deliberate development of strong, emotional connections between customers and brands is known as emotional branding. In contrast to transactional or functional brand strategies, emotional branding aims to create long-term loyalty by arousing emotions like comfort, love, trust, and nostalgia (Pawle & Cooper, 2006; Thomson et al., 2005). In crowded markets, where emotional differentiation is crucial for relevance and memorability, emotional branding works especially well (Pawle & Cooper, 2006).

Because they inherently arouse feelings, particularly when anthropomorphized or positioned as companions, animals play a special role in this context. According to research, non-human agents (such as mascots or pets) that are perceived as friendly, reliable, or relatable elicit stronger emotional reactions to branding (Aggarwal & McGill, 2007; Epley et al., 2007; Reddy & Sathish, 2023). Higher levels of engagement, brand attachment, and word-of-mouth behaviors are all correlated with these emotional cues (Batra et al., 2012; Palusuk et al., 2019).

2.2 Brand Identity and Meaning Transfer

According to Kapferer (2012), brand identity is more than just visual design; it also includes the character, principles, and symbolic meaning that a brand communicates to its audience. According to Aaker (2012), brand identity is a multifaceted concept that encompasses self-expressive benefits, personality traits, and brand symbols. Animal symbols frequently function at the heart of this identity, giving brands with aspirational or human characteristics.

The meaning transfer model developed by McCracken (1986) states that cultural meanings are passed from the culturally embedded environment, which includes animal archetypes, to the brand or product and then to the customer. According to this framework, animals act as "cultural carriers," incorporating well-established symbolic meanings into the brand narrative (such as strength, loyalty, and elegance) (Holt, 2004). Customers can project or expand their identity through brand affiliation thanks to this symbolic dimension, which also improves the brand's perceived personality (Escalas & Bettman, 2005).

2.3 Symbolic Consumption and Brand Meaning

According to symbolic consumption theory, people purchase goods to express their identity, values, and sense of social belonging rather than just for practical purposes(Belk, 1988; Levy, 2014). Symbolic components like animals support the process of identity construction by giving brands a culturally relevant and emotionally charged meaning.

Animal branding often serves as a mirror for aspirational selves. For instance, a company like Ferrari uses its prancing horse to symbolically convey power, status, and elite masculinity in addition to speed (Kapferer, 2012; Mark & Pearson, 2022). Similar to this, Lacoste's crocodile serves as a metaphor for uniqueness and perseverance, connecting the buyer to a lifestyle story through symbolic alignment (Holt, 2004).

2.4 Anthropomorphism and Consumer Engagement

Customers' reactions to animal symbols in branding are largely influenced by anthropomorphism, which is the attribution of human traits to non-human entities (Epley et al., 2007). Consumers create relational bonds that mimic interpersonal relationships when they anthropomorphise animals (Fournier, 1998)(Fournier, 1998). Anthropomorphised brand characters or mascots have been found to increase perceived warmth, likeability, and trust (Aggarwal & McGill, 2007; Reddy & Sathish, 2023).

Additionally, consumers can give brands intentionality and emotion through anthropomorphism, which makes them seem more dependable, responsive, and trustworthy (Epley et al., 2007). This is especially important in pet-powered branding, where animals are seen as social actors in addition to being symbolic, particularly when it comes to petfluencers or animated mascots in online spaces (Giles, 2018).

While anthropomorphism highlights the projection of human traits onto animals, it often overlooks the social and relational context in which audiences interact with mediated figures. This limitation makes it insufficient on its own to explain the full appeal of petfluencers.

2.5 Animal Archetypes and Cultural Universality

Lastly, the use of animals in branding appeals to ingrained cultural and psychological stereotypes. According to Jung's theory of the collective unconscious (Jung, 2014), some symbols, including animals, have universal meaning structures that are relevant in all cultures and eras. Applying this to branding, Mark & Pearson (2022) propose that animal representations frequently represent brand archetypes like the Hero (e.g., lion, eagle), the Rebel (e.g., snake, bull), or the Innocent (e.g., dog, rabbit).

By serving as emotional shortcuts, these archetypes help brands establish an immediate connection and recognition. The bull in Lamborghini's logo, for example, represents unadulterated energy and defiance, associating the brand with strength and provocation (Kapferer, 2012). Animal symbols are especially effective at creating meaning and emotional branding because of these subconscious associations (Lafferty, 2001; Mick, 1986).

2.6 Parasocial Relationships and Media Psychology

The rise of petfluencers has reignited interest in parasocial interaction (PSI), a concept originally introduced by Horton & Richard Wohl (1956) to describe the illusion of intimacy audiences experience with media figures. Unlike traditional celebrities, petfluencers, because of their perceived innocence and apolitical status, create particularly strong parasocial bonds. These relationships are characterised by feelings of friendship, loyalty, and trust toward the influencer, despite the one-sided nature of the interaction (Dibble et al., 2016).

Pets as influencers heighten this effect. Consumers project emotions and personalities onto animals, perceiving them as authentic and trustworthy social actors (Giles, 2018). In marketing contexts, such parasocial relationships can translate into greater engagement, willingness to share content, and enhanced brand loyalty (Labrecque, 2014). This makes PSI theory especially relevant for understanding the unique effectiveness of animal-based branding in the digital era.

Parasocial interaction usefully explains mediated intimacy, but it does not account for symbolic and archetypal layers of meaning that animals embody in branding. This creates a gap that justifies integrating symbolic consumption and emotional branding perspectives.

2.7 Influencer Marketing and Digital Consumer Culture

The broader field of influencer marketing provides additional context. Research shows that social media influencers are effective because they combine perceived expertise, authenticity, and relatability (Lou & and Yuan, 2019). However, human influencers are also prone to skepticism due to over-commercialisation and reputational risks (Audrezet et al., 2020). Petfluencers, by contrast, benefit from the perception of purity and non-instrumentality—qualities rarely attributed to human influencers.

Studies indicate that consumers evaluate petfluencers as safer, less polarizing brand partners (Djafarova & Rushworth, 2017). This makes them valuable assets in industries where trust and emotional safety are paramount, such as food, wellness, and family-oriented products. Furthermore, petfluencers often generate higher engagement rates than human influencers, partly because they bypass identity politics and appeal across demographics (Chae, 2018; Marwick, 2015).

This intersection between influencer marketing and pet branding underscores the need to expand branding theory beyond traditional anthropomorphism and symbolism, integrating digital-era phenomena that reshape consumer-brand relationships.

2.8 Cross-Cultural Symbolism of Animals

Animal symbolism is not universally interpreted. While Jungian archetypes suggest some degree of collective unconscious resonance (Jung, 2014), cultural variation plays a significant role in shaping meaning. For instance, while dogs symbolize loyalty and companionship in Western contexts, in some Islamic traditions they may be perceived as unclean, altering their branding resonance (Foltz, 2014). Similarly, cows symbolize sacredness in Hindu-majority cultures (Bauer & Woodward, 2007), whereas in Western fast-food branding, cows often serve as symbols of humor or consumption (Mick, 1986).

The Chinese zodiac provides another illustration. Brands targeting East Asian markets often use animals like dragons, tigers, or rabbits to align with culturally specific beliefs about luck, power, or prosperity (Chevalier & Mazzalovo, 2008). African cultures, meanwhile, draw on animal symbolism linked to oral traditions and cosmologies, positioning animals as mediators between the human and spiritual worlds (Mbiti, 1990).

These examples highlight the importance of cultural sensitivity when adopting animal symbolism in branding. Misalignment can lead to backlash or rejection, whereas resonance can foster deep emotional and symbolic attachment. Cross-cultural branding research thus complements archetypal and symbolic consumption theories by emphasising diversity of meaning.

2.9 Posthumanism and Multispecies Perspectives

Recent scholarship in cultural studies and anthropology has called for a posthumanist perspective on branding. Posthumanism challenges anthropocentric assumptions, recognising animals as co-actors in cultural and economic systems (Haraway, 2008). In this view, pets are not passive symbols but active participants in meaning-making processes. Petfluencers exemplify this multispecies entanglement: their human handlers manage content, but the animal's presence drives engagement, affect, and symbolic resonance.

Multispecies ethnography further emphasizes the relational and interdependent character of human-animal interactions (Kirksey & Helmreich, 2010). Applied to branding, this approach invites us to consider not only what animals symbolize, but also how they actively shape consumer practices and communities. For example, followers of petfluencers often engage in "affective labor," sharing, commenting, and co-creating narratives around the pet's persona, effectively blurring the boundaries between consumer, producer, and animal subject.

Incorporating posthumanist perspectives into branding research expands the theoretical lens, framing petfluencers as more than anthropomorphic projections—they are nodes in complex human-animal-technological assemblages that structure consumer culture.

2.10 The Political Economy of Attention

Another emerging framework relevant to pet-driven branding is the political economy of attention. In digital environments saturated with content, attention has become a scarce commodity (Davenport, T. H., & Beck, 2021). Petfluencers thrive in this context because they capture attention efficiently through cuteness, humor, and emotional resonance. Nittono et al. (2012) describe the "power of kawaii," where exposure to cute animals narrows attentional focus and fosters careful, sustained engagement.

This aligns with research showing that consumers process emotionally salient stimuli more deeply, leading to better recall and stronger brand associations (Kronrod & Danziger, 2013). By functioning as attention magnets, petfluencers help brands break through the noise of digital clutter, embedding brand meaning in emotionally saturated encounters. The political economy of attention thus provides a macro-level frame for understanding why animals, especially in influencer form, remain highly effective in contemporary branding.

While emotional branding, anthropomorphism, and parasocial interaction are often treated separately in the literature, they intersect in important ways when analyzing petfluencers. Anthropomorphism emphasizes the projection of human qualities onto animals (Epley et al., 2007), while parasocial interaction highlights the mediated intimacy audiences experience with recurring figures (Labrecque, 2014). Emotional branding, in contrast, foregrounds the affective bonds that create loyalty and "brand love" (Batra et al., 2012). These frameworks are not contradictory but complementary: petfluencers succeed precisely because they simultaneously evoke anthropomorphic traits, encourage parasocial bonds, and generate emotional attachment. However, empirical studies applying these frameworks specifically to petfluencers remain scarce (C. Abidin, 2021; Djafarova & Rushworth, 2017). This gap justifies the need for a conceptual model that integrates these perspectives while also guiding future empirical inquiry.

The next section builds on this foundation by tracing the evolution of animals as emotional anchors, from their rabidiole in classic logos to their contemporary presence as digital petfluencers

3. ANIMALS AS EMOTIONAL ANCHORS: FROM CLASSIC LOGOS TO DIGITAL PETFLUENCERS

Animals have long been used as emotional anchors in brand strategy, acting as symbolic meaning-carrying objects as well as visual identity markers. Animals elicit a variety of emotional reactions, including affection, admiration, nostalgia, or trust, which are essential for solid consumer brand relationships, whether they are personified through digital content, incorporated into logos, or used as mascots (Pawle & Cooper, 2006; Thomson et al., 2005). Their appeal comes from a combination of emotional familiarity, archetypal resonance, and cultural symbolism, all of which strengthen a brand's personality and emotional connection.

3.1 Animals in Classic Brand Logos: Power, Prestige, and Archetype

Animals have long been incorporated into brand logos to convey prestige, power, heritage, and symbolic meaning. For instance, the emblem of a World War I fighter pilot served as the inspiration for Ferrari's famous Cavallino Rampante (prancing horse), which is associated with nobility, speed, and freedom (Kapferer, 2012). Similarly, Lamborghini's bull is a perfect fit for the brand's aggressive positioning because it represents the founder's zodiac sign as well as an image of brute force, masculinity, and challenge (Mark & Pearson, 2022).

These selections weren't just for show. They matched archetypal themes that have a subconscious resonance with brand identity. Animals like horses, lions, and snakes, which stand for qualities like strength, bravery, and skill, activate symbolic associations across cultures, according to Jungian theory (Jung, 2014). Because of this, companies that incorporate these animals into their visual identities are able to access deep psychological reserves that support symbolic and emotional meaning (Mark & Pearson, 2022).

Additionally, these animal symbols serve as nonverbal identity cues that help brands stand out in the marketplace right away. For example, the crocodile in Lacoste's logo represents perseverance and self-control, qualities linked to the brand's founder, René Lacoste, a French tennis icon known as "Le Crocodile." Humanizing the animal and fostering a sense of style and uniqueness were made possible by its symbolic link to the brand's history (Holt, 2004; Kapferer, 2012).

Even in the historically performance-focused automotive industry, animal logos have given functional features an emotional connotation. For instance, the jaguar embodies elegance and sensuality in addition to speed and agility. By using this symbolism, Jaguar elevated emotional value alongside engineering prowess, positioning itself as more than just a car but an experience (Aaker, 2012; McCracken, 1986).

3.2 Animals in Contemporary Branding: Soft Power, Warmth, and Relatability

Particularly in the context of emotional branding, brands have started using animals in more recent decades to convey empathy, innocence, humor, and reliability (Lafferty, 2001; Thomson et al., 2005). It has been demonstrated that animal mascots, like Tony the Tiger (Kellogg's), the Geico Gecko, or the Michelin Man (perhaps anthropomorphized), increase brand likeability, foster emotional warmth, and produce enduring customer memories (Aggarwal & McGill, 2007; Epley et al., 2007).

Crucially, animal mascots and logos are frequently employed as projective tools that allow customers to develop parasocial bonds with non-human entities (Brown et al., 2003). In industries where emotional safety and consistency are highly prized, like food, insurance, or children's products, these connections can increase brand trust and loyalty.

More subtly, companies like the British heritage fashion brand Barbour have made use of animal symbolism. Ads, seasonal campaigns, and user-generated content frequently feature dogs, reinforcing themes of family values, loyalty, and rural authenticity. The dog imagery serves as a narrative anchor, indicating values of tradition, companionship, and "slow living," even though it is not a part of its core logo (Beverland, 2006; Holt, 2004).

3.3 The Rise of Digital Petfluencers: Trust in a Post-Human World

In the current digital era, the symbolic and emotional power of animals has taken on new dimensions with the rise of petfluencers—pets with their own social media profiles, often curated by humans but perceived as authentic online personalities (Crystal Abidin, 2016). These accounts, such as *@jiffpom*, *@nala_cat*, or *@tunameltsmyheart*, attract millions of followers and are increasingly seen as safe, trustworthy brand ambassadors. Because animals are perceived as non-threatening and apolitical, they provide a low-risk, high-relatability platform for brand collaboration (Djafarova & Rushworth, 2017).

From a consumer psychology standpoint, petfluencers tap into the "cute-emotion" heuristic, where visually appealing stimuli (like baby animals) evoke rapid feelings of warmth, care, and attentiveness (Nittono et al., 2012) These emotional responses are often stronger than those elicited by human influencers, especially in younger or more emotionally fatigued audiences (Giles, 2018). For brands, this means higher engagement and more emotionally anchored interactions —especially when marketing wellness, fashion, home, or pet-related products.

Furthermore, petfluencers extend the tradition of emotional animal branding into interactive, community-driven experiences. Followers often attribute personalities, moods, and emotional states to the animals, demonstrating real-time anthropomorphism and projecting social meaning onto their actions (Epley et al., 2007; Giles, 2018). This creates a hybrid space where brands are no longer broadcasting symbolism but co-creating emotional meaning with consumers through animal figures (Audrezet et al., 2020)

The rise of petfluencers, or pets with their own social media profiles that are frequently curated by humans but are regarded as genuine online personalities, has given animals' symbolic and emotional power new dimensions in the current digital era (Crystal Abidin, 2016).

With millions of followers, these accounts, like @jiffpom, @nala_cat, or @ tunameltsmyheart, are becoming more and more regarded as reliable, secure brand representatives. Animals offer a low-risk, high-relatability platform for brand collaboration because they are seen as non-threatening and apolitical (Djafarova & Rushworth, 2017).

According to (Nittono et al., 2012), petfluencers use the "cute-emotion" heuristic, which states that visually appealing stimuli, such as infant animals, quickly arouse sentiments of warmth, care, and attentiveness. Particularly in audiences that are younger or more emotionally spent, these emotional reactions are frequently more powerful than those evoked by human influencers (Giles, 2018). Higher engagement and more emotionally charged interactions are what this means for brands, particularly when promoting wellness, fashion, home, or pet related goods.

Petfluencers also carry on the tradition of emotional animal branding by creating community driven, interactive experiences. Followers frequently project social meaning onto the animals' behaviors and exhibit real-time anthropomorphism by giving them personalities, moods, and emotional states (Epley et al., 2007; Giles, 2018). This results in a hybrid space where companies use animal figures to co-create emotional meaning with customers rather than broadcasting symbolism (Audrezet et al., 2020).

3.4 From Static Symbols to Dynamic Emotional Agents

These examples collectively demonstrate a move away from static animal logos that convey archetypal meaning and toward dynamic emotional agents (mascots, pets, and digital avatars) that engage in continuous relationships between brands and consumers (Crystal Abidin, 2016; de Brito Silva et al., 2022). These animal representations, whether real or symbolic, foster in the communication of emotion, identity, and intimacy for brands, especially in settings where there is an abundance of options and content (Jochen & Christopher, 2022).

Animal-based branding, whether traditional or digital, continues to offer brands a flexible, powerful tool for engaging consumers across product categories, cultures, and emotional touchpoints. Animals continue to be a universal language of trust, warmth, and aspiration in branding, from traditional emblems to Instagram-famous pets (Jochen & Christopher, 2022).

Table 1. Traditional versus Digital Animal Branding

Dimension	Traditional Animal Logos	Digital Pet Influencers/ Mascots
Medium	Static (logos, packaging)	Dynamic (social media, video)
Symbolic Function	Archetypal, timeless	Relational, playful, evolving
Consumer role	Passive observer	Active engager, co-creator
Cultural Universality	High (Jungian)	Variable (platform dependent)
Examples	Ferrari, Jaguar, Lacoste	@jiffpom, @nala_cat, Geico Gecko

3.4.1 Case Studies of Leading Petfluencers

The emergence of individual petfluencers demonstrates the variety of ways in which animals can function as emotional and symbolic agents in digital branding. Perhaps the most well-known example is Grumpy Cat (real name Tardar Sauce), whose unique facial expression went viral in 2012 and later spread to books, merchandise, and licensing agreements, bringing in an estimated $100 million in revenue over her lifetime (BBC, 2019; Marwick, 2015). Her journey shows how a pet can go from being a novelty on the internet to becoming a worldwide commercial property, with brand value that transcends the digital realm. Doug the Pug, on the other hand, has made a name for himself through relatability and comedy. With over 18 million followers on various platforms, Doug has collaborated with companies like American Greetings, Claire's, and Toyota. His lighthearted style allows him to connect with audiences of all ages (Crystal Abidin, 2016; Influencer Marketing Hub, 2024). Another aspect of petfluencer branding is the development of trust, cuteness, and everyday familiarity, as demonstrated by Nala Cat, who holds the Guinness World Record for having the most Instagram followers (4.4 million as of 2023) (Guinness World Records, 2023). Nala exemplifies how emotional resonance can be turned into a multi-million-dollar brand presence through partnerships with businesses like Fresh Step and PetSmart (Djafarova & Rushworth, 2017). With a huge following of 10 million on Instagram and over 20 million on TikTok, Jiffpom, a Pomeranian, thrives in the short-form video culture and collaborates with companies like Samsung and Target (Creator IQ Connect, 2025). Last but not least, Tuna the Dog (@tunameltsmyheart), who is renowned for his unusual overbite, epitomizes what academics have dubbed the "imperfectly cute" aesthetic, appealing to viewers weary of extremely polished human influencer content (Chae, 2018).

When combined, these examples demonstrate how petfluencers are different from static animal logos in that they are dynamic, ever-evolving entities that engage with audiences, co-create meaning, and establish brand connections in the context of daily digital life.

3.4.2 Commercialization and Monetization

As a component of the larger influencer marketing economy, the economic impact of petfluencers is becoming more widely acknowledged in academic and industry research. According to market research, the value of the global influencer market was estimated at $16.4 billion in 2022, with petfluencers constituting a rapidly expanding subset (Influencer Marketing Hub, 2024). Petfluencers' success is contingent upon the institutionalization of influencer culture as a monetized ecosystem backed by audiences, platforms, and brands, in addition to their symbolic appeal, according to scholars (Crystal Abidin, 2016; Khamis et al., 2017).

Opportunities for business go far beyond sporadic sponsorships. Because of the high levels of engagement that come with animal content, well-known petfluencer accounts can fetch between $10,000 and $20,000 per sponsored post (Creator IQ Connect, 2025). Petfluencers are particularly valuable for brand partnerships because, according to research on digital culture, "cute" aesthetics are particularly effective at maintaining attention and consumer interest (Nittono et al., 2012). Merchandising increases the brand value of these figures even more: calendars, children's books, stuffed animals, and clothing turn virtual identities into material goods, mirroring trends in the commodification of celebrity culture (Turner, 2014).

Cross-media franchising and licensing serve as examples of how resilient this type of commercialisation is. For instance, Grumpy Cat transformed from a viral meme to a worldwide brand that sells books, movies, and merchandise, bringing in an estimated $100 million in revenue (BBC, 2019; Marwick, 2015). Similar to this, @Jiffpom has made appearances in global marketing campaigns for Samsung and Target, establishing himself as a transmedia commercial asset in addition to an online celebrity (C. Abidin, 2021). Platform monetisation also generates ongoing income: the TikTok Creator Fund, Instagram monetisation initiatives, and YouTube ad revenue all work together to form a complex economy that supports petfluencer activity (Bishop, 2020).

The way petfluencers have evolved into dynamic, profitable entities sets them apart from conventional animal logos. Petfluencers represent symbolic and emotional value that is continuously converted into financial capital through platform economies, licensing, merchandising, and sponsorship, whereas logos serve as a symbolic anchor for brand identity. This intersection of monetisation and affect is a prime example of what academics refer to as the "attention economy," in which emotional investment is turned into quantifiable financial gains (Davenport, T. H., & Beck, 2021; Fuchs, 2014).

3.4.3 Risks, Ethics, and Market Challenges

Petfluencer success is not without its challenges. Similar to human influencers, these figures' quick commercialisation raises questions about their long-term viability, welfare, and authenticity. Scholars of marketing observe that excessive commercialisation frequently leads to "authenticity fatigue," in which viewers who at first appreciated an influencer's relatability feel that their content has lost its genuineness as a result of being over-sponsored (Audrezet et al., 2020; Khamis et al., 2017). When every post is linked to a business goal, petfluencers' effectiveness, innocence, playfulness, and perceived purity, can be compromised.

In this field, ethical issues are especially pressing. media and animal studies experts have long cautioned against the dangers of using animals for commercial purposes, emphasising that doing so could turn them into objects of consumption rather than sentient beings (Franklin, 1999). Problems like tense photo shoots, insufficient sleep, or putting appearance before welfare are echoed in larger discussions regarding the use of animals in human cultural industries (Malamud, 2012; Palmer, 2003). These issues touch on advertising regulations. Petfluencers are subject to the same disclosure laws as human influencers in a number of jurisdictions, such as the European Commission's transparency directives (Comission, 2024) and the Federal Trade Commission's (Federal Trade Comission, 2025) guidelines in the US. In addition to running the risk of legal action, non-compliance harms a brand's reputation with customers who place a higher value on transparency (Campbell & Grimm, 2018).

Ethical considerations extend beyond disclosure to include animal welfare, commercialization, and reputational risks. Overuse of sponsored content can trigger authenticity fatigue (Audrezet et al., 2020), while parody accounts or scandals surrounding mistreatment may undermine both influencer and brand credibility. Transparency remains central, with regulatory bodies such as the FTC requiring clear disclosure of sponsored posts (Federal Trade Comission, 2025). Brands should proactively communicate welfare standards and develop crisis protocols to safeguard against reputational damage (De Veirman & Hudders, 2020).

The market is saturated as a result of the growth in petfluencer accounts. Differentiation becomes more difficult as more pets are staged and advertised online. Digital culture scholars stress that only those who can develop unique stories, aesthetics, or communities stand a chance of surviving in crowded influencer markets (Crystal Abidin, 2016; Bishop, 2020). This frequently entails creating a distinctive symbolic identity for petfluencers that goes beyond simple cuteness, like Tuna's flaws or Grumpy Cat's grumpiness. When incorporating pets into branding strategies, this dynamic emphasizes the significance of ethical standards, narrative coherence, and strategic selectivity.

3.4.4. Segmentation and Consumer Variation

Consumer responses to petfluencers are shaped by demographic and cultural factors. Research shows that younger audiences often treat influencers as peers and are more likely to form parasocial bonds (Kim et al., 2024), whereas older consumers approach them with more skepticism. Cultural variation also plays a role: while Western audiences value transparency and disclosure, East Asian consumers often emphasise relational harmony and "cuteness aesthetics" (Ye, 2025). Moreover, pet ownership status influences receptivity, as owners of companion animals are more likely to project affection and trust onto petfluencers. These patterns highlight the importance of segmentation strategies when designing pet-driven campaigns.

3.4.5. Brand Risk Management

While petfluencers offer strong engagement, they also expose brands to reputational risks. Over-commercialisation can lead to authenticity fatigue (Audrezet et al., 2020), and scandals, including allegations of mistreatment, parody accounts, or backlash against excessive sponsorship which can damage credibility. Effective crisis communication is essential, requiring clear disclosure practices, welfare assurances, and rapid responses to reputational threats (De Veirman & Hudders, 2020). By anticipating these risks, managers can balance emotional appeal with responsible brand governance.

3.4.6 Comparisons with Human Influencers

Given that they both compete for consumers' attention and operate within the same digital ecosystems, comparisons between petfluencers and human influencers are inevitable. Influencer marketing research has repeatedly demonstrated that human influencers are assessed based on attributes like expertise, attractiveness, and trustworthiness (Ki et al., 2020; Lou & and Yuan, 2019). However, because audiences find petfluencers appealing due to their perceived innocence and authenticity rather than their expertise, they are mainly exempt from some of these evaluation criteria. The dynamics of persuasion are changed by this change. Online celebrity endorsements can have a significant impact on younger audiences' purchase decisions, as noted by Djafarova & Rushworth (2017). However, as commercialisation becomes more apparent, scepticism toward human influencers has increased. Because animals are seen as apolitical and free from selfish interests, petfluencers seem to escape most of this criticism.

This distinction is supported by industry analyses. According to Creator IQ Connect (2025) survey, petfluencers' Instagram posts receive 30–40% more engagement than those of human macro-influencers. This supports research in marketing that shows anthropomorphism and cuteness increase emotional reactions and memory (Nittono et al., 2012; Schroll et al., 2018). In this way, petfluencers are excellent at fostering emotional connections that go beyond logical assessment, or what Batra, Batra et al. (2012) refer to as "brand love."

However, human influencers continue to have significant advantages. In contrast to animals, they are able to converse with customers, explain products, and tell intricate stories (Casaló et al., 2020). Digital marketing experts observe that human influencers are frequently employed to represent social identities or aspirational lifestyles, which are challenging for pets to directly fulfil (Crystal Abidin, 2016; Khamis et al., 2017). This implies that choosing between human and pet influencers is not a simple binary decision but rather a strategic one, with humans being able to provide cognitive persuasion and symbolic identity work while pets may ensure emotional resonance and high engagement.

Hybrid strategies might be the best course of action from a managerial standpoint. Combining various endorser types can increase credibility and reach, according to studies on integrated influencer campaigns (Jin et al., 2019). When applied to petfluencers, this suggests that the narrative complexity of a human influencer can be used to enhance the emotional warmth produced by an animal account. These complementary tactics are a reflection of what Campbell & Grimm (2018) refer to as the "portfolio approach" to influencer marketing, which involves enlisting a variety of personalities to meet various customer demands within a single campaign.

3.4.6 Future Directions: Virtual Pets and AI Influencers

The development of petfluencers also suggests a new area of branding where it is becoming harder to distinguish between real animals, virtual personas, and artificially created things. Technological developments in computer-generated imagery (CGI), augmented reality (AR), and artificial intelligence (AI) have made it possible to create "synthetic influencers" that are just as popular and appealing to consumers as their human and animal counterparts. Lil Miquela, a computer-generated character with millions of Instagram followers who has worked with companies like Calvin Klein and Prada, is the most frequently mentioned example. According to academics, these characters represent the "post-human" shift in consumer culture, where identity and authenticity are created through aesthetically pleasing and algorithmic design rather than through lived experience (Cotter, 2018; de Brito Silva et al., 2022).

Despite not being an animal, Lil Miquela's success shows that virtual influencers can be profitable in general. In order to replicate the emotional impact of real animals without the uncertainty and welfare issues associated with working with live animals, brands have started experimenting with virtual pets. This is in line with what Fuchs (2014) refers to as the logic of digital capitalism, which substitutes programmable actors for organic ones in order to maximise control and minimise risk. Without the hassles of animal welfare, virtual pets can be infinitely customised, have personalities and looks that match brand values, and be guaranteed to be available.

These possibilities are further enhanced by emerging technologies in AR and VR environments. Immersion interaction boosts brand recall and emotional intensity, according to media innovation scholars (Casaló et al., 2020; Sundar et al., 2017). Customers could "play" with branded virtual pets in these settings, extending the concepts of parasocial interaction into interactive co-presence. This change would usher in a new era of "algorithmic intimacy," as defined by Jin et al. (2019), in which users develop emotional bonds with computationally created objects in addition to human or animal representations.

These developments have significant ramifications. On the one hand, by substituting digital simulations for actual animals, virtual pets address moral concerns regarding animal exploitation. On the other hand, they bring up fresh ontological and ethical issues regarding manipulation, transparency, and authenticity. Critical media studies scholars warn that if viewers learn that their emotional connections were created using algorithmic design, the growing popularity of fake influencers could undermine trust (Bishop, (Bishop, 2020; Cotter, 2018). The moral contract between the consumer, brand, and animal figure is complicated because, while the "cute-emotion heuristic" as defined by Nittono et al. (2012) may still be in effect, the object of affection is no longer a living being.

4. CONCEPTUAL MODEL: PET-DRIVEN BRANDING AND THE EMOTIONAL ECONOMY

Building on the theoretical foundations and brand cases discussed, this section introduces a conceptual model that explains the role of animals as emotional and symbolic assets within branding strategy. The model illustrates how animal symbolism, whether through logos, mascots, or petfluencer figures, functions within brand identity, activates emotional mechanisms, and leads to meaningful consumer outcomes.

This model positions animals not merely as decorative or attention-grabbing elements, but as strategic emotional anchors that foster connection, trust, and symbolic alignment between brands and consumers. It also shows how this process is influenced by contextual factors such as digital media, cultural symbolism, and consumer identity needs.

4.1 The Conceptual Model

An integrated perspective of pet-driven branding is provided by the conceptual model shown in Figure 1, which shows how animal symbolism, mediated through brand identity, triggers emotional processes that influence consumer outcomes. This process is influenced by contextual moderators like consumer characteristics, media channel, and culture.

It expands on the notion that animal representations, whether they be mascots, logos, or digital petfluencers, actively mediate brand identity and increase consumer engagement through emotionally compelling mechanisms, going beyond merely enhancing brand imagery. Four interconnected levels make up the model, which shows the relationship between symbolic representation and consumer outcomes while taking into account contextual factors that could influence this relationship.

The symbolic representation of animals forms the basis of the model. According to archetypal theory (Jung, 2014; Mark & Pearson, 2022), animals have intrinsic, universal meanings that cut across time and cultural boundaries. This dimension is based on this theory. Cultural narratives (McCracken, 1986) and the brand's historical identity (Kapferer, 2012) both influence and reshape these meanings, which are not static. For example, the prancing horse in Ferrari's identity or the bull in Lamborghini's logo are not arbitrary design choices; rather, they are potent symbols of strength, speed, and prestige that are ingrained in the cultural positioning of the brand. In this way, animals serve as cultural ambassadors, bringing symbolic meaning into the brand story in a way that is both emotionally stirring and intuitive.

The symbolic value of animals becomes strategically meaningful when it is mediated through the brand's identity system. This stage is grounded in brand identity theory (Aaker, 2012; Kapferer, 2012), which views identity as a multidimensional construct that includes personality, tone, values, and symbols. When an animal is integrated into this system, whether as a logo, a recurring mascot, or a relational figure such as a petfluencer, it serves to humanise the brand, communicate emotional tone, and reinforce narrative consistency. Through this mediation, the animal becomes a bridge between brand and consumer, translating abstract brand values into relatable emotional signals.

When the brand's identity system mediates the symbolic value of animals, it acquires strategic significance. According to brand identity theory (Aaker, 2012; Kapferer, 2012) identity is a multifaceted construct that encompasses personality, tone, values, and symbols. This stage is based on this theory. Whether an animal is used as a logo, a recurring mascot, or a relational figure like a petfluencer, its integration into this system humanises the brand, conveys an emotional tone, and strengthens narrative coherence. By converting impersonal brand values into relatable emotional cues, the animal serves as a conduit between the brand and its customers.

The emotional processes that are triggered when customers interact with animal-based branding are highlighted in the third layer of the model. This stage draws on concepts like anthropomorphism (Epley et al., 2007), warmth (Aggarwal & McGill, 2007), nostalgia (Holbrook & Schindler, 2003), and parasocial relationships (C. Abidin, 2021; Giles, 2018) from the literature on consumer psychology and emotional branding. According to research, when consumers believe that a brand (or its mascot) is familiar, human-like, or emotionally expressive, they are more likely to develop emotional attachments. This is particularly true in the context of petfluencers, where followers give the animals personalities, emotions, and even social identities, resulting in more profound emotional and symbolic engagement (de Brito Silva et al., 2022; Thomson et al., 2005). These emotional reactions are significant; they are associated with stronger memory encoding, greater trust, and more positive brand attitudes (Batra et al., 2012; Thomson et al., 2005).

The behavioural consequences that result from this symbolic emotional alignment are the focus of the model's last level. Effective use of animals in branding fosters loyalty, brand love, and emotional attachment. According to Hollebeek et al. (2014) and Dessart (2017), consumers are more likely to engage with these brands, share content related to them, and advocate for them. They also have a higher level of trust in these brands. In the end, animals aid consumers in creating or reaffirming their own identities through the brand, resulting in self-expression and symbolic consumption (Escalas & Bettman, 2005; Levy, 2014).

It's also critical to acknowledge that this process is neither static nor universal. The way animal symbolism functions in brand-consumer relationships can be influenced by a number of contextual and moderating factors. For instance, cultural variations may influence the symbolic meaning attached to particular animals (McCracken,

1986), and the medium of communication, such as packaging, advertisements, or social media, can alter the nature and course of the consumer's reaction (Colliander & Dahlén, 2011). The degree to which consumers emotionally connect with animal figures in branding may also be mediated by personal behaviours like pet ownership, nostalgia, or anthropomorphic tendencies (C. Abidin, 2021; Epley et al., 2007).

All things considered, the suggested conceptual model provides a methodical and theoretically based explanation of how animals work as emotionally intelligent brand assets. It combines knowledge from anthropomorphism, brand identity, emotional branding, and symbolic consumption to shed light on the symbolic channels via which animal representations affect the attitudes and actions of consumers. The model offers an analytical framework and a starting point for further empirical research by placing these processes within the larger emotional economy. Although the model provides a general framework, digital environments and emotionally charged consumer markets are where it is most useful. It is less relevant to B2B or utilitarian branding, where affective and symbolic elements play a smaller role. Animal symbolism may also be culturally specific and not always understood in the same way.

Figure 1. Conceptual Model of Pet-Driven Branding in the Emotional Economy

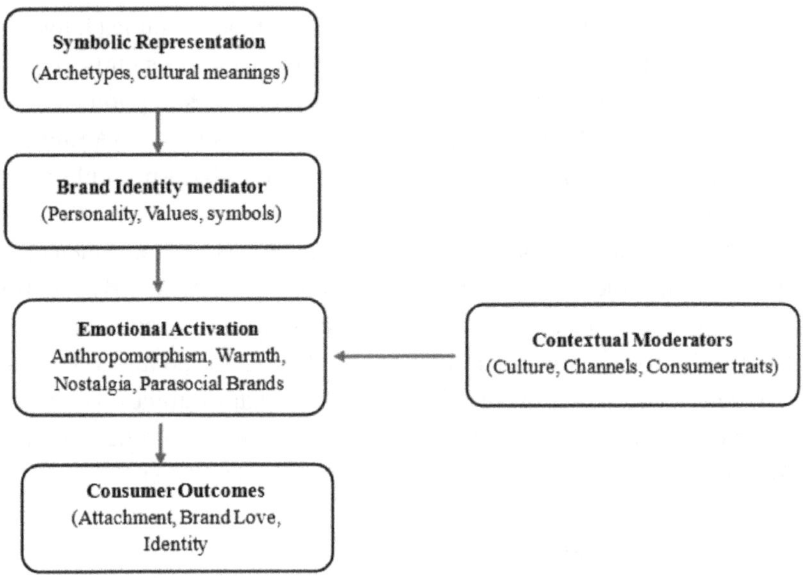

Figure 1. Conceptual Model of Pet-Driven Branding in the Emotional Economy

5. THEORETICAL AND PRACTICAL IMPLICATIONS

By providing a methodical explanation of how animal symbolism functions within the emotional economy of branding, the conceptual model put forth in this chapter advances both theory and practice. In order to present animals as emotionally intelligent agents of meaning rather than as immobile brand decorations, it integrates ideas from symbolic consumption, emotional branding, and brand identity theory. For academics who study consumer behavior, marketing communication, and brand strategy, this reinterpretation of animals' roles has consequences.

5.1. Theoretical Implications

By incorporating animal symbolism into pre-existing frameworks of brand identity and emotional engagement, the model theoretically closes a significant gap in the literature on branding. Few models specifically take into consideration how non-human figures, especially animals, mediate brand-consumer relationships across symbolic and emotional pathways, despite the fact that the emotional and symbolic aspects of branding have been extensively studied (Batra et al., 2012; Thomson et al., 2005). The model fills this gap by showing how animal representations serve as cultural carriers (McCracken, 1986), trigger anthropomorphic processing (Epley et al., 2007), and use archetypal resonance to reinforce brand meaning (Jung, 2014; Mark & Pearson, 2022). Additionally, it connects two rich but frequently disjointed theoretical traditions: emotional branding and symbolic consumption. By doing this, it provides a framework for upcoming empirical studies that may examine the relative effects of different animal representations across platforms, cultures, and product categories.

The model also presents animals as strategic brand assets that can enhance consumer identification, evoke strong feelings, and convey personality. By redefining animals as dynamic relational agents rather than just decorative components, this rethinking expands on conventional notions of brand mascots and logos. This viewpoint adds to a growing body of research in marketing that examines the affective, symbolic, and emotional aspects of consumption in addition to functional utility (Crystal Abidin, 2016; Fournier, 1998; Fournier & Alvarez, 2012).

5.2. Practical Implications

Practically speaking, the model provides brand managers with a framework for creating branding strategies that are both emotionally and symbolically compelling. It emphasises how crucial it is to select animal figures that complement the character, history, and narrative positioning of the brand. For example, archetypal symbols like bulls or eagles may work well for a brand that emphasises strength and boldness, but dogs or cats may work better for a brand that wants to evoke warmth and familiarity. The model also emphasises the significance of channel-specific adaptation: an animal logo on a product package has a very different symbolic impact than the emotional engagement a petfluencer on Instagram generates.

Additionally, the model encourages practitioners to view animals as anchors of emotional trust and relational depth in addition to being tools of attention. Brands that humanise themselves through emotionally charged animal symbols may have a higher chance of establishing enduring customer relationships in a time when consumers seek authenticity. In digital and social media contexts, where user engagement, co-creation, and community participation shape symbolic interaction, this is particularly pertinent (Jung, 2014).

In practical terms, managers can translate the conceptual model into actionable strategies. Campaign design should begin with clear segmentation, identifying whether the target audience values humor, authenticity, or luxury symbolism. Metrics of success must go beyond vanity measures such as follower counts and instead emphasize engagement rates, share-of-voice, and sentiment analysis (Colliander & Dahlén, 2011). Case evidence shows that petfluencers such as Nala Cat and Doug the Pug succeed when their symbolic persona aligns with brand values, reinforcing identity through consistent partnerships rather than one-off endorsements. Managers should also plan campaigns with a portfolio approach, combining petfluencers' emotional resonance with human influencers' narrative depth to achieve both affective impact and informational credibility (Campbell & Grimm, 2018). By adopting this structured approach, brands can maximize return on investment while safeguarding authenticity.

5.3. Ethical Considerations in Animal-Based Branding

The model emphasises significant ethical issues in addition to theoretical and practical ramifications. Animal symbolism is emotionally compelling, but it also raises moral questions. Particularly in digital contexts, the anthropomorphism of pets and mascots can blur the boundaries between fact and fiction, resulting in false authenticity or emotional dependence. Therefore, when it comes to human-managed petfluencers, consent and welfare concerns come up. Marketers need to exercise caution when navigating these areas, especially when aiming to reach audiences that are emotionally vulnerable or children. These ethical considerations ought to be specifically covered in future studies.

6. THEORETICAL PROPOSITIONS FOR FUTURE RESEARCH

To help empirical validation and theoretical refinement, we offer the following research propositions:

P1: Brands using animal symbolism that aligns with culturally resonant archetypes will stimulate higher consumer emotional attachment than those using abstract or non-archetypal imagery.

P2: The presence of anthropomorphised animal figures in branding will increase perceived brand warmth and trust, particularly in relational product categories.

P3: Petfluencers will generate stronger parasocial relationships than traditional mascots, leading to greater consumer engagement and brand loyalty in digital contexts.

P4: The symbolic value of animal branding will be moderated by cultural context, such that meanings attributed to specific animals will vary across regions.

P5: Consumers with higher tendencies toward anthropomorphism or pet affinity will exhibit stronger brand attachment to animal symbolic brands.

7. CONCLUSION

According to this chapter, animals are much more than just nostalgic elements or illustrations in brand communication; they are strong, emotionally charged, and culturally significant characters that actively contribute to the creation of brand identity. The chapter provides a structured lens through which to understand how animal figures participate in brand-consumer relationships, especially within the dynamics of the emotional economy, by putting forth a conceptual model that combines symbolic representation, identity mediation, emotional activation, and behavioural outcomes.

This model reframes animals as strategic brand assets that can elicit emotional engagement, promote symbolic alignment, and enhance brand meaning, as opposed to passive mascots or decorative designs. By doing this, the chapter advances the theoretical unification of ideas like anthropomorphism, symbolic consumption, and emotional branding that have, up until now, been discussed separately but rarely together.

Understanding the emotional and symbolic role of animals in branding is not only relevant but also essential in an era where consumers are increasingly influenced by affect, authenticity, and identity expression. Finally, the emotional and symbolic resonance of animals challenges us to reconsider branding as a relationship based on memory, meaning, and the timeless power of nonverbal connection, rather than merely as a means of communication. In addition to providing a conceptual framework for branding literature, this framework serves as a basis for critical analysis and empirical research into the moral and cultural ramifications of animal symbolism in branding. By investigating cross-cultural interpretations, animal-related brand failures, and the emergence of AI-generated petfluencers as a new area of post-human branding, future studies may expand on this model.

REFERENCES

Aaker, D. A. (2012). *Building strong brands*. Simon and schuster.

Abidin, C. (2016). "Aren't These Just Young, Rich Women Doing Vain Things Online?": Influencer Selfies as Subversive Frivolity. *Social Media + Society*, *2*(2), 2056305116641342. DOI: 10.1177/2056305116641342

Abidin, C. (2021). Mapping Internet Celebrity on TikTok: Exploring Attention Economies and Visibility Labours. *Cultura e Scuola*, *12*(1), 77–103. DOI: 10.5334/csci.140

Aggarwal, P., & McGill, A. L. (2007). Is That Car Smiling at Me? Schema Congruity as a Basis for Evaluating Anthropomorphized Products. *The Journal of Consumer Research*, *34*(4), 468–479. DOI: 10.1086/518544

Audrezet, A., de Kerviler, G., & Guidry Moulard, J. (2020). Authenticity under threat: When social media influencers need to go beyond self-presentation. *Journal of Business Research*, *117*, 557–569. DOI: 10.1016/j.jbusres.2018.07.008

Batra, R., Ahuvia, A., & Bagozzi, R. P. (2012). Brand Love. *Journal of Marketing*, *76*(2), 1–16. DOI: 10.1509/jm.09.0339

Bauer, A., & Woodward, L. (2007). People and Their Pets: A Relational Perspective on Interpersonal Complementarity and Attachment in Companion Animal Owners. *Society & Animals*, *15*(2), 169–189. https://doi.org/https://doi.org/10.1163/156853007X187117

BBC. (2019). *Grumpy Cat internet legend dies*. BBC NEWS. https://www.bbc.com/news/world-us-canada-48308638

Belk, R. W. (1988). Possessions and the Extended Self. *The Journal of Consumer Research*, *15*(2), 139–168. DOI: 10.1086/209154

Beverland, M. (2006). The 'real thing': Branding authenticity in the luxury wine trade. *Journal of Business Research*, *59*(2), 251–258. https://doi.org/https://doi.org/10.1016/j.jbusres.2005.04.007

Bishop, S. (2020). Algorithmic Experts: Selling Algorithmic Lore on YouTube. *Social Media + Society*, *6*(1), 2056305119897323. DOI: 10.1177/2056305119897323

Brown, Stephen, Kozinets, R. V, & SherryJr., John F. (2003). Teaching Old Brands New Tricks: Retro Branding and the Revival of Brand Meaning. *Journal of Marketing*, *67*(3), 19–33. DOI: 10.1509/jmkg.67.3.19.18657

Campbell, C., & Grimm, P. E. (2018). The Challenges Native Advertising Poses: Exploring Potential Federal Trade Commission Responses and Identifying Research Needs. *Journal of Public Policy & Marketing*, *38*(1), 110–123. DOI: 10.1177/0743915618818576

Casaló, L. V., Flavián, C., & Ibáñez-Sánchez, S. (2020). Influencers on Instagram: Antecedents and consequences of opinion leadership. *Journal of Business Research*, *117*, 510–519. https://doi.org/https://doi.org/10.1016/j.jbusres.2018.07.005

Chae, J. (2018). Explaining Females' Envy Toward Social Media Influencers. *Media Psychology*, *21*(2), 246–262. DOI: 10.1080/15213269.2017.1328312

Chevalier, M., & Mazzalovo, G. (2008). *Luxury brand management*. Franco Angeli.

Colliander, J., & Dahlén, M. (2011). Following the Fashionable Friend: The Power of Social Media. *Journal of Advertising Research*, *51*(1), 313–320. DOI: 10.2501/jar-51-1-313-320

Comission, E. (2024). *Influencer Legal Hub*. https://commission.europa.eu/live-work-travel-eu/consumer-rights-and-complaints/influencer-legal-hub_en

Cotter, K. (2018). Playing the visibility game: How digital influencers and algorithms negotiate influence on Instagram. *New Media & Society*, *21*(4), 895–913. DOI: 10.1177/1461444818815684

Creator, I. Q. Connect. (2025). *The State of Creator Marketing Report: Trends and Trajectory 2024-2025*. https://www.creatoriq.com/white-papers/state-of-creator-marketing-trends-2025?creative=721461056566&keyword=influencer marketing&matchtype=p&network=g&device=c&_bt=721461056566&_bk=influencer marketing&_bm=p&_bn=g&_bg=171923138873&utm_term=influencer mark

Davenport, T. H., & Beck, J. C. (2021). *The attention economy: Understanding the new currency of business*. Harvard Business Press. https://www.hbs.edu/faculty/Pages/item.aspx?num=

de Brito Silva, M. J., de Oliveira Ramos Delfino, L., Alves Cerqueira, K., & de Oliveira Campos, P. (2022). Avatar marketing: A study on the engagement and authenticity of virtual influencers on Instagram. *Social Network Analysis and Mining*, *12*(1), 130. DOI: 10.1007/s13278-022-00966-w

De Veirman, M., & Hudders, L. (2020). Disclosing sponsored Instagram posts: The role of material connection with the brand and message-sidedness when disclosing covert advertising. *International Journal of Advertising*, *39*(1), 94–130. DOI: 10.1080/02650487.2019.1575108

Dessart, L. (2017). Social media engagement: A model of antecedents and relational outcomes. *Journal of Marketing Management, 33*(5–6), 375–399. DOI: 10.1080/0267257X.2017.1302975

Dibble, J. L., Hartmann, T., & Rosaen, S. F. (2016). Parasocial Interaction and Parasocial Relationship: Conceptual Clarification and a Critical Assessment of Measures. *Human Communication Research, 42*(1), 21–44. DOI: 10.1111/hcre.12063

Djafarova, E., & Rushworth, C. (2017). Exploring the credibility of online celebrities' Instagram profiles in influencing the purchase decisions of young female users. *Computers in Human Behavior, 68*, 1–7. https://doi.org/https://doi.org/10.1016/j.chb.2016.11.009

Epley, N., Waytz, A., & Cacioppo, J. T. (2007). On seeing human: A three-factor theory of anthropomorphism. *Psychological Review, 114*(4), 864–886. DOI: 10.1037/0033-295X.114.4.864 PMID: 17907867

Escalas, J. E., & Bettman, J. R. (2005). Self-construal, reference groups, and brand meaning. *The Journal of Consumer Research, 32*(3), 378–389. DOI: 10.1086/497549

Federal Trade Comission. (2025). *Disclosures 101 for Social Media Influencers*. https://www.ftc.gov/business-guidance/resources/disclosures-101-social-media-influencers

Foltz, R. (2014). *Animals in Islamic tradition and Muslim cultures*. Simon and Schuster.

Fournier, S. (1998). Consumers and Their Brands: Developing Relationship Theory in Consumer Research. *The Journal of Consumer Research, 24*(4), 343–353. DOI: 10.1086/209515

Fournier, S., & Alvarez, C. (2012). Brands as relationship partners: Warmth, competence, and in-between. *Journal of Consumer Psychology, 22*(2), 177–185. DOI: 10.1016/j.jcps.2011.10.003

Franklin, A. (1999). *Animals and Modern Cultures: A Sociology of Human–Animal Relations in Modernity*. SAGE Publications Ltd., DOI: 10.4135/9781446217764

Fuchs, C. (2014). *Social Media: A Critical Introduction*. SAGE Publications Ltd., DOI: 10.4135/9781446270066

Giles, D. (2018). Twenty-First Century Celebrity: Fame In Digital Culture. In *Twenty-First Century Celebrity: Fame In Digital Culture* (pp. 207–235). Emerald Publishing Limited. https://doi.org/DOI: 10.1108/978-1-78743-708-120181018

Guinness World Records. (2023). *Most followers on Instagram for a cat.* Guiness World Records. https://www.guinnessworldrecords.com/world-records/465511-most-followers-for-a-cat-on-instagram

Haraway, D. (2008). *When species meet University of Minne.* sota Press, Minneapolis MN.

Holbrook, M. B., & Schindler, R. M. (2003). Nostalgic bonding: Exploring the role of nostalgia in the consumption experience. *Journal of Consumer Behaviour, 3*(2), 107–127. DOI: 10.1002/cb.127

Hollebeek, L. D., Glynn, M. S., & Brodie, R. J. (2014). Consumer Brand Engagement in Social Media: Conceptualization, Scale Development and Validation. *Journal of Interactive Marketing, 28*(2), 149–165. DOI: 10.1016/j.intmar.2013.12.002

Holt, D. B. (2004). *How brands become icons: The principles of cultural branding.* harvard business press.

Horton, D., & Richard Wohl, R. (1956). Mass Communication and Para-Social Interaction. *Psychiatry, 19*(3), 215–229. DOI: 10.1080/00332747.1956.11023049 PMID: 13359569

Influencer Marketing Hub. (2024). *The State of Influencer Marketing 2022: Benchmark Report.* Influencer Marketing Hub. https://influencermarketinghub.com/influencer-marketing-benchmark-report-2022/

Jin, S. V., Muqaddam, A., & Ryu, E. (2019). Instafamous and social media influencer marketing. *Marketing Intelligence & Planning, 37*(5), 567–579. DOI: 10.1108/MIP-09-2018-0375

Jochen, W., & Christopher, L. (2022). *Services marketing: People, technology, strategy.* World Scientific Publishing.

Jung, C. G. (2014). *The Archetypes and the Collective Unconscious.* Routledge., DOI: 10.4324/9781315725642

Kapferer, J.-N. (2012). *The new strategic brand management: Advanced insights and strategic thinking.* Kogan page publishers.

Khamis, S., Ang, L., & Welling, R. (2017). Self-branding, 'micro-celebrity' and the rise of Social Media Influencers. *Celebrity Studies, 8*(2), 191–208. DOI: 10.1080/19392397.2016.1218292

Ki, C.-W. (Chloe), Cuevas, L. M., Chong, S. M., & Lim, H. (2020). Influencer marketing: Social media influencers as human brands attaching to followers and yielding positive marketing results by fulfilling needs. *Journal of Retailing and Consumer Services, 55*, 102133. https://doi.org/https://doi.org/10.1016/j.jretconser.2020.102133

Kim, J.-Y., Ko, S.-H., & Choi, Y. (2024). Unveiling the power of social influencers in brand trust and brand identification. *South African Journal of Business Management, 55*(1), 4087.

KIRKSEY. S. E., & HELMREICH, S. (2010). THE EMERGENCE OF MULTISPECIES ETHNOGRAPHY. *Cultural Anthropology, 25*(4), 545–576. https://doi.org/https://doi.org/10.1111/j.1548-1360.2010.01069.x

Kronrod, A., & Danziger, S. (2013). "Wii Will Rock You!" The Use and Effect of Figurative Language in Consumer Reviews of Hedonic and Utilitarian Consumption. *The Journal of Consumer Research, 40*(4), 726–739. DOI: 10.1086/671998

Labrecque, L. I. (2014). Fostering Consumer–Brand Relationships in Social Media Environments: The Role of Parasocial Interaction. *Journal of Interactive Marketing, 28*(2), 134–148. DOI: 10.1016/j.intmar.2013.12.003

Lafferty, B. A. (2001). Emotional Branding: The New Paradigm for Connecting Brands to People20011Marc Gobé. Emotional Branding: The New Paradigm for Connecting Brands to People. New York, NY: Allworth Press 2001. iii + 319 pp., ISBN: ISBN: 1-58115-078-4 US $24.95. *Journal of Product and Brand Management, 10*(7), 466–469. DOI: 10.1108/jpbm.2001.10.7.466.1

Levy, S. J. (2014). How new, how dominant? In *The Service-Dominant Logic of Marketing* (pp. 57–64). Routledge.

Lou, C., & Yuan, S. (2019). Influencer Marketing: How Message Value and Credibility Affect Consumer Trust of Branded Content on Social Media. *Journal of Interactive Advertising, 19*(1), 58–73. DOI: 10.1080/15252019.2018.1533501

Malamud, R. (2012). *Animal movies guide*. Greenwood.

Mark, M., & Pearson, C. S. (2022). *The hero and the outlaw: Building extraordinary brands through the power of archetypes*. McGraw Hill-Ascent Audio.

Marwick, A. E. (2015). Instafame: Luxury Selfies in the Attention Economy. *Public Culture, 27*(1), 137–160. DOI: 10.1215/08992363-2798379

Mbiti, J. S. (1990). *African religions & philosophy*. Heinemann.

McCracken, G. (1986). Culture and Consumption: A Theoretical Account of the Structure and Movement of the Cultural Meaning of Consumer Goods. *The Journal of Consumer Research, 13*(1), 71–84. DOI: 10.1086/209048

Mick, D. G. (1986). Consumer research and semiotics: Exploring the morphology of signs, symbols, and significance. *The Journal of Consumer Research, 13*(2), 196–213.

Nittono, H., Fukushima, M., Yano, A., & Moriya, H. (2012). The Power of Kawaii: Viewing Cute Images Promotes a Careful Behavior and Narrows Attentional Focus. *PLoS One*, *7*(9), e46362. DOI: 10.1371/journal.pone.0046362 PMID: 23050022

Palmer, C. (2003). *Ethics and animals*. Oxford University Press.

Palusuk, N., Koles, B., & Hasan, R. (2019). 'All you need is brand love': A critical review and comprehensive conceptual framework for brand love. *Journal of Marketing Management, 35*(1–2), 97–129.

Pawle, J., & Cooper, P. (2006). Measuring Emotion—Lovemarks, The Future Beyond Brands. *Journal of Advertising Research, 46*(1), 38–48. DOI: 10.2501/S0021849906060053

Reddy, B. V. V., & Sathish, A. S. (2023). Creating Connections Through Characters: A Study of Brand Mascots and Their Influence on Consumer Purchase Intentions. *Advances in Decision Sciences, 27*(4), 1–17.

Schroll, R., Schnurr, B., & Grewal, D. (2018). Humanizing Products with Handwritten Typefaces. *The Journal of Consumer Research*. Advance online publication. DOI: 10.1093/jcr/ucy014

Sundar, S. S., Kang, J., & Oprean, D. (2017). Being There in the Midst of the Story: How Immersive Journalism Affects Our Perceptions and Cognitions. *Cyberpsychology, Behavior, and Social Networking, 20*(11), 672–682. DOI: 10.1089/cyber.2017.0271 PMID: 29125787

Thomson, M., MacInnis, D. J., & Whan Park, C. (2005). The Ties That Bind: Measuring the Strength of Consumers' Emotional Attachments to Brands. *Journal of Consumer Psychology, 15*(1), 77–91. DOI: 10.1207/s15327663jcp1501_10

Turner, G. (2014). *Understanding Celebrity*. SAGE Publications Ltd., DOI: 10.4135/9781473957855

Ye, C. (2025). Mapping out digital luxury marketing: A systematic review and future research agenda. *Marketing Intelligence & Planning*, •••, 1–24.

Zhang, Y. (2015). The impact of brand image on consumer behavior: A literature review. *Open Journal of Business and Management, 3*(1), 58–62.

Chapter 5
Petfluencers and Social Media Marketing

H. Lakshmi
https://orcid.org/0000-0003-3838-8787
NITTE Meenakshi Institute of Technology, NITTE University, India

Nilesh Anute
https://orcid.org/0000-0001-6599-813X
Sri Balaji University, India

Prashant Chordiya
https://orcid.org/0009-0005-6227-2583
Dr. D.Y. Patil Institute of Master of Computer Application and Management, India

Amruta Mahalle
https://orcid.org/0009-0001-4246-4060
Datta Meghe Institution of Management Studies, India

Tanmay Waghmare
Datta Meghe Institute of Management Studies, India

P. Selvakumar
https://orcid.org/0000-0002-3650-4548
Department of Science and Humanities, Nehru Institute of Technology, Coimbatore, India

T. C. Manjunath
https://orcid.org/0000-0003-2545-9160
Rajarajeswari College of Engineering, India

ABSTRACT

In the ever-evolving world of social media, new trends and influential personas emerge regularly, reshaping the way content is consumed and brands connect with audiences. Among these trends, one of the most intriguing and heartwarming phenomena is the rise of "petfluencers" — animals who have become online celebrities with massive followings across platforms like Instagram, TikTok, YouTube, and Facebook. These charismatic pets, often cats, dogs, rabbits, or even exotic animals, are more than just adorable faces; they are now powerful marketing tools,

DOI: 10.4018/979-8-3373-4342-6.ch005

brand ambassadors, and cultural icons in their own right.The concept of influencer marketing is not new. For over a decade, brands have collaborated with popular social media figures to promote products and services in a more authentic, relatable way. However, the evolution from human influencers to animal influencers signals a fascinating shift in consumer psychology and digital engagement. Unlike human influencers, petfluencers evoke a unique emotional appeal.

INTRODUCTION

In the ever-evolving world of social media, new trends and influential personas emerge regularly, reshaping the way content is consumed and brands connect with audiences. Among these trends, one of the most intriguing and heartwarming phenomena is the rise of "petfluencers" — animals who have become online celebrities with massive followings across platforms like Instagram, TikTok, YouTube, and Facebook. These charismatic pets, often cats, dogs, rabbits, or even exotic animals, are more than just adorable faces; they are now powerful marketing tools, brand ambassadors, and cultural icons in their own right. The concept of influencer marketing is not new. For over a decade, brands have collaborated with popular social media figures to promote products and services in a more authentic, relatable way. However, the evolution from human influencers to animal influencers signals a fascinating shift in consumer psychology and digital engagement. Unlike human influencers, petfluencers evoke a unique emotional appeal. (Alassani & Göretz, 2019) Their content often elicits feelings of joy, relaxation, and amusement — emotions that are universally appreciated and less likely to spark controversy or criticism. As a result, petfluencers enjoy a broad, diverse fan base that spans demographics, cultures, and continents.The emergence of petfluencers reflects broader changes in digital culture, where storytelling, emotional connection, and authenticity have become paramount. With millions of followers and sometimes even agents, merchandise lines, or book deals, pets like Grumpy Cat, Jiffpom, Doug the Pug, and Nala Cat have become household names. These animals, managed by their human owners or professional teams, are featured in advertisements, attend red-carpet events, and even collaborate with luxury brands. The phenomenon has given birth to a new breed of celebrity — one that wags its tail, purrs into the camera, and charms audiences without saying a single word. The appeal of petfluencers lies in their ability to cut through the noise of traditional advertising. In a world saturated with commercial content and sponsored posts, pet-centric content offers a refreshing and disarming alternative. Viewers are drawn to the simplicity, innocence, and humor that pets naturally exude. As a result, engagement rates on petfluencer content are often significantly higher than those of traditional influencers. Brands have recognized this potential and are increasingly allocating budgets to petfluencer campaigns, seeking to tap into their loyal and enthusiastic audiences. Moreover, petfluencers symbolize a cultural shift in how people perceive pets in modern society. No longer just household companions, pets are now integral members of the family and, in many cases, full-fledged media personalities. (Athavale et al., 2025)Their online personas often mirror the lifestyles and values of their owners, offering a glimpse into aspirational pet parenting, fashionable pet gear, organic diets, and wellness routines — all of which fuel consumer demand in the booming pet industry. In 2024, global pet care spending surpassed $250 billion, with a significant portion influenced by social media trends and petfluencer endorsements. Another key factor in the rise of petfluencers is the accessibility of content creation tools and platforms.

The Power of Pets on Social Media: Why They Matter

The dynamic landscape of digital advertising, petfluencer marketing has emerged as a vibrant and highly effective branch of influencer marketing, capitalizing on the universal appeal of animals and the emotional resonance they create. Petfluencer marketing refers to promotional activities and brand collaborations involving pets with substantial social media followings. (Bailey et al., 2009)With content ranging from adorable daily antics and quirky photoshoots to product placements and branded campaigns, petfluencers have become potent vehicles for brand storytelling, customer engagement, and product endorsement One of the core benefits of petfluencer marketing is its ability to foster authentic, non-threatening connections with audiences. Unlike traditional advertisements that can feel intrusive or overly polished, content from pet influencers is perceived as more organic, entertaining, and relatable. When a well-loved dog shows enthusiasm for a new chew toy or a cat lounge in a designer pet bed, the promotion feels more like a lifestyle recommendation than a hard sell. This subtle form of marketing often results in higher engagement rates, stronger brand recall, and increased consumer trust, making petfluencers an appealing choice for brands aiming to deepen their customer relationships. The opportunities in petfluencer marketing extend far beyond the pet industry itself. While pet food, toys, grooming products, and accessories remain the most obvious sectors to benefit from partnerships with petfluencers, other industries — including travel, fashion, wellness, tech, and even finance — (Bandura, 2002) have successfully incorporated petfluencers into their campaigns. For example, hotels and resorts have used pet influencers to promote pet-friendly accommodations, while insurance companies have launched campaigns featuring dogs and cats to humanize their brand messaging. The versatility of pet content allows marketers to creatively integrate animals into a wide range of narratives and product categories, making them powerful ambassadors across diverse markets Another advantage of petfluencer marketing is its inclusive and global appeal. People from all backgrounds and cultures share a common affection for animals, enabling petfluencers to transcend geographic and demographic boundaries. Unlike human influencers who might polarize audiences due to personal opinions, controversies, or lifestyle differences, petfluencers tend to maintain a universally positive image. (Bao et al., 2019) This characteristic reduces reputational risk for brands and allows for broader audience reach. Moreover, petfluencer content is often family-friendly and appropriate for all ages, adding to its accessibility and shareability on social media. The economics of petfluencer marketing also present compelling advantages. While celebrity-level pet influencers like Doug the Pug or Nala Cat can command premium rates for sponsored content, there are countless micro-petfluencers with loyal niche followings who offer excellent ROI for smaller brands. These micro-influencers, often with follower counts between 10,000 and 100,000, tend to have highly engaged audiences and are perceived as more approachable and trustworthy. Collaborating with several micro-petfluencers can be more cost-effective than partnering with a single macro-influencer and allows for diversified messaging across different audience segments. From a strategic perspective, petfluencer marketing also contributes to long-term brand building. Animals have the ability to embody brand values in a unique and memorable way. A playful puppy

Finding the Right Petfluencer: Criteria and Considerations

The age of digital connectivity and content overload, few subjects consistently capture attention and spark joy across global audiences like pets. Whether it's a clumsy puppy, a grumpy cat, a dancing bird, or a hedgehog enjoying a bubble bath, pets have carved out a unique and commanding presence on social media platforms. The power of pets on social media lies in their innate ability to elicit emotional responses, foster community, and provide moments of levity and authenticity in a space often dominated by curated perfection and commercial intent. (Chambers et al., 2018)Their presence is not just entertaining — it is deeply influential, shaping digital trends, consumer behavior, and even the way brands communicate with audiences At the heart of pets' appeal on social media is their universal relatability and emotional resonance. Pets do not judge, discriminate, or push agendas. They are spontaneous, sincere, and often hilarious — qualities that translate beautifully into content that feels real and unfiltered. This authenticity resonates deeply in an era when users are increasingly skeptical of over-produced and overly branded content. A dog's joyful reaction to a new toy or a cat's indifferent stare captures moments of genuine emotion, making them instantly shareable and highly engaging. The emotions pets evoke — love, laughter, warmth, comfort — are universally human, allowing pet content to transcend language and cultural barriers The metrics speak volumes: pet-related content consistently ranks among the most liked, shared, and commented-on across all major platforms. Instagram, TikTok, and YouTube are brimming with pet accounts that boast millions of followers, with some petfluencers rivalling — or even surpassing — human celebrities in reach and engagement. Hashtags such as #dogsofinstagram, #catsoftiktok, or #petlovers generate billions of views, reflecting a strong appetite for pet-centered media. (Cheung et al., 2009) This intense interest has not gone unnoticed by platforms themselves, which often highlight pet content in their discovery algorithms and trending sections to boost user interaction and platform retention.Beyond just viral videos and cute photos, pets on social media have become symbols of larger cultural and emotional phenomena. For many users, especially in urban or high-stress environments, consuming pet content offers a form of digital escapism and emotional therapy. Studies have shown that watching animal videos can reduce stress, lower blood pressure, and improve mood. This "feel-good" factor not only keeps users coming back for more but also positions pets as emotionally powerful content creators — a rarity in a landscape that often values performance over connection.Furthermore, pets have become digital conduits for identity expression and community building. Pet owners use social media to showcase their pets as extensions of their personalities and lifestyles. Whether it's a vegan cat, a skateboarding bulldog, or a fashion-forward bunny, these animals reflect their owners' values, humor, and creativity. Entire online communities have formed around pet content, connecting people with shared interests, challenges, or experiences — from training techniques and rescue stories to pet health tips and memorial tributes. (de Droog et al., 2012) (de Droog et al., 2011) These communities foster loyalty, trust, and engagement, making them fertile ground for brand collaborations, cause-driven campaigns, and advocacy work.

Collaborating with Petfluencers: Best Practices

As petfluencer marketing becomes a more strategic and mainstream component of brand promotion, selecting the right petfluencer has grown into a nuanced process that requires thoughtful analysis, alignment of values, and an understanding of audience dynamics. Not all petfluencers are created equal, and while a high follower count may seem appealing at first glance, it's far from the only — or most important — criterion. Brands seeking meaningful impact must carefully evaluate petfluencers based on a range of qualitative and quantitative factors that determine their suitability for a specific campaign, product, or message. The right match can drive engagement, foster loyalty, and generate authentic conversions, while a misalignment may result in wasted resources, diminished credibility, or even reputational damage. how closely that audience aligns with their target customer profile. (de Droog et al., 2011) A dog influencer with a predominantly North American, millennial audience might be an excellent partner for a premium pet food brand targeting health-conscious pet parents, whereas a rabbit influencer with a large European Gen Z following might be more suitable for a sustainable toy brand. Social media analytics tools — including native insights on Instagram and TikTok, as well as third-party influencer marketing platforms — can help brands assess follower location, age, gender, engagement behavior, and even interests. This data-driven approach ensures that marketing dollars are spent reaching not just a large audience, but the *right* one.by their follower count but by how actively and meaningfully their audience interacts with their content. High engagement rates — likes, shares, comments, and saves — indicate that the content resonates and inspires interaction. However, brands should look beyond surface metrics. Do followers leave genuine, thoughtful comments, or is the comment section filled with bots or spam? Is there evidence of an active community that returns regularly for content, or does engagement spike only during giveaways and promotions? Consistent, high-qualitycat in high-end fashion, or a talking parrot with sassy captions. (Evans et al., 2018). A minimalist, all-natural pet wellness brand, for instance, may not be the right fit for a loud, meme-heavy pet account, no matter how large the audience. Likewise, brands should examine the types of content the petfluencer usually posts (photos, videos, reels, stories), the frequency of posts, and whether their style can naturally incorporate branded content without feeling forced or inauthentic with their followers. Have they promoted similar products before? How did their audience respond? Do they disclose sponsored posts transparently and ethically? Audiences are far more likely to trust a petfluencer who maintains transparency, expresses honest opinions, and only partners with brands they truly believe in. Red flags include frequent product switches, excessive sponsorships, or a lack of personal engagement in comments and messages.workflows. Brands should assess the petfluencer's ability to meet deadlines, follow creative briefs, adhere to content guidelines, and provide performance metrics post-campaign. Previous collaborations, testimonials from other brands, and media kits can offer insight into a petfluencer's professionalism. The ability to communicate clearly, adapt content for specific goals, and represent a brand with integrity and enthusiasm is invaluable in maintaining campaign effectiveness. Cuddly, glamorous, sassy, or athletic. (Fair, 2019a). These personas should complement the tone and story the brand wants to tell. For example, an energetic, playful dog who loves the outdoors may be the perfect match for an outdoor gear brand launching a pet-friendly product line. In contrast, a relaxed, elegant cat may suit a high-end pet furniture brand. Choosing a petfluencer whose persona and lifestyle naturally reflect the brand narrative allows for smoother content integration and greater audience resonance.for longer-form storytelling, unboxings, and tutorials, while Facebook still has strong engagement among older demographics. Depending on campaign objectives, brands should consider where the petfluencer is most

CONTENT CREATION WITH PETFLUENCERS: TIPS AND IDEAS

Working with petfluencers requires brands to go beyond traditional advertising models and embrace the unique dynamics of influencer relationships — ones that involve not just human creators but their animal companions as central figures. From campaign planning to execution, there are several best practices that ensure fruitful, engaging, Before launching a campaign, both the brand and the petfluencer (or their handler or management team) must align on expectations, goals, messaging, and deliverables. This includes defining the scope of the partnership — whether it's a one-time post, a multi-platform campaign, product unboxing, video content, (Fair, 2019b) story takeovers, giveaways, or long-term ambassadorships. Clear communication around timelines, approval processes, content guidelines, and usage rights is essential to avoid misunderstandings. Written agreements or contracts are highly recommended to formalize the arrangement and establish accountability on both sides.pet and their storytelling style, overly scripted or branded posts may feel forced and reduce credibility. Trusting the creator to integrate the brand naturally into their narrative enhances relatability and boosts engagement. (Guttmann, 2019) For instance, a sponsored post featuring a dog exploring a new hiking trail with branded gear should feel like a natural extension of the petfluencer's lifestyle, not a staged advertisement. Style, and community. This demonstrates respect and interest in a genuine collaboration rather than a transactional deal. Over time, developing an ongoing relationship with the petfluencer can lead to deeper brand loyalty, more flexible collaboration opportunities, and better content outcomes. Repeat partnerships tend to generate stronger audience trust, as followers are more inclined to believe in products endorsed repeatedly over time by a trusted source. Nano petfluencers may accept gifted products in exchange for promotion, many — especially those with substantial followings and professional setups — (Hebden et al., 2011)expect financial compensation for their time, effort, and content creation. Brands should consider the value of the petfluencer's reach, engagement rates, content quality, and niche influence when negotiating rates. Offering fair pay, bonuses for performance, or added perks (such as exclusive product previews, affiliate links, or long-term contracts) fosters goodwill and incentivizes excellence. Their audience better than anyone else and can provide insights into what types of posts perform

Instagram for Petfluencers: Visual Storytelling and Hashtags

The charm of petfluencer content lies in its ability to delight viewers while seamlessly integrating brand messages, making it one of the most appealing formats in influencer marketing. However, crafting successful petfluencer content requires a careful blend of storytelling, audience alignment, brand integration, and an understanding of each pet's personality and platform strengths. Whether the campaign is a one-time sponsored post or a long-term brand ambassadorship, effective content creation begins with strategic planning and an appreciation for the unique dynamics of animal-centered media. energetic, making them ideal for dynamic videos or humorous reels, while others are calm and expressive, lending themselves to emotive storytelling or high-quality photography. The content must play to the pet's strengths rather than forcing unnatural actions or scenarios. (Hoffner, 2008) For example, if a dog naturally loves playing fetch, incorporating a branded ball into a playful video will feel authentic and entertaining. Conversely, trying to dress a cat in elaborate costumes for a fashion shoot might result in awkward content if the cat is clearly uncomfortable — and followers are quick to notice when a pet looks unhappy or stressed a narrative or moment that feels real and relatable. This could be a "day in the life" video where a dog uses a new harness on a morning walk, a tutorial-style clip demonstrating how to use a grooming tool, or a cozy scene where a cat snuggles in a branded pet bed. The more natural and story-driven the content feels, the more likely audiences are to engage with it. Brands and petfluencers can collaborate to develop creative storylines that highlight product benefits while maintaining entertainment value.. While authenticity is important, content should still be well-lit, visually appealing, and professionally composed whenever possible. High-resolution images, smooth video transitions, and thoughtful editing can elevate the look and feel of petfluencer posts, helping to reinforce brand professionalism. Many petfluencers use themed props, seasonal backgrounds, or coordinated color palettes to enhance their visual storytelling — tools that can be leveraged to match a brand's identity. However, the balance between polish and authenticity is key: overly stylized content may lose the casual charm that petfluencer audiences love. Content norms, audience preferences, and algorithmic tendencies. On Instagram, high-quality photos and carousel posts tend to perform well, while Reels offer opportunities for short, engaging videos with strong music or trend tie-ins. (Hoffner & Buchanan, 2005) TikTok favors fun, fast-paced, and humorous content — often benefiting from trending sounds or challenges. YouTube is ideal for longer-form content such as reviews, tutorials, or "a day in the life" vlogs. Facebook still offers strong community engagement, particularly for posts that evoke emotion or nostalgia. Understanding the platform's strengths and tailoring the content format accordingly ensures maximum reach and relevance. A post — whether through comments, polls, challenges, or contests — increases visibility and deepens audience involvement. For instance, a petfluencer might host a giveaway where followers tag friends or share photos of their own pets using a brand's product. This user-generated content not only boosts engagement

TikTok for Petfluencers: Short-Form Video Content

Instagram has established itself as the premier platform for petfluencers, offering a visually-driven space where cuteness, personality, and storytelling converge to capture the hearts of millions. With its emphasis on image and video content, Instagram allows petfluencers to showcase their animals in engaging, aesthetic, and emotionally resonant ways — making it a natural fit for brands seeking to connect with audiences through the charm and relatability of pets. At the core of successful Instagram marketing for petfluencers is the art of visual storytelling — the ability to craft narratives through images, captions, and reels that go beyond surface-level appeal to create emotional engagement, (Ismail, 2018) build a distinctive brand persona, and cultivate a loyal, interactive community Visual storytelling for petfluencers starts with consistent branding. A successful petfluencer account often features a cohesive aesthetic, including consistent lighting, color palettes, editing styles, and themes. Whether it's a pastel-toned profile focused on a cuddly kitten, a high-energy, vibrant feed starring an adventurous dog, or a luxurious, fashion-forward look for a pampered French bulldog, visual consistency helps followers quickly identify the petfluencer's identity and style. It also reinforces brand trust, making the page more appealing for partnerships. Instagram users typically decide within seconds whether to follow a profile, and a polished, visually harmonious grid is far more likely to convert casual viewers into loyal fans. But great visuals are only part of the equation. True storytelling on Instagram comes from combining imagery with thoughtful captions that provide context, personality, and emotional depth. Petfluencers often craft captions from the perspective of the animal — using humor, sass, affection, or wisdom to create a character that audiences grow to love. These captions can recount daily adventures, celebrate milestones, express relatable sentiments, or introduce branded content in a light-hearted, non-intrusive way. For example, a caption might read: (Jain et al., 2011) "Mom says I can't chew on the couch anymore… so I'm settling for this super-tough (and tasty) toy from @brandname instead. #CompromiseQueen." This kind of storytelling not only entertains but also humanizes the pet, encouraging followers to engage and share., allowing content to reach broader and more targeted audiences. Popular tags like #dogsofinstagram, #catsoftiktok (also trending on Instagram), #weeklyfluff, and #petstagram expose posts to millions of users searching or browsing similar content. Meanwhile, more niche hashtags like #adventuredog, #meowdel, or #rescuedismyfavoritebreed help petfluencers connect with specific communities that share particular interests or values. For brands, aligning with petfluencers who understand and leverage effective hashtag strategies ensures greater content visibility and enhances the likelihood of organic engagement and follower growth.

YouTube for Petfluencers: Long-Form Content and Monetization

TikTok has rapidly evolved into a dominant force in social media, redefining how content is created, consumed, and shared — and petfluencers have found an exceptionally strong foothold on the platform. Known for its fast-paced, trend-driven, and algorithmically personalized experience, TikTok offers petfluencers a unique stage to showcase their pets in ways that are not only entertaining but also deeply engaging and often viral. The platform's short-form video format — typically ranging from 15 seconds to 3 minutes — (Wong, 2019)is ideally suited for the quick, attention-grabbing antics of animals, from goofy dog tricks and quirky cat behaviors to inspirational rescue stories and pet fashion moments. For brands and creators alike, TikTok represents a powerful marketing channel where creativity and relatability outperform polish and production value, making it accessible to a broad spectrum of petfluencers, regardless of their follower count or budget. At the heart of TikTok's appeal for petfluencers is its highly responsive and discovery-focused algorithm, which gives even new or small accounts the potential to go viral with the right content. Unlike traditional platforms that often prioritize established creators, TikTok's "For You" page curates content based on user behavior and engagement rather than follower count, enabling a level playing field where a single post can attract millions of views overnight. This is especially valuable for petfluencers, whose content — naturally joyful, surprising, or funny — aligns perfectly with the platform's emphasis on shareability and emotional resonance. From a dog reacting hilariously to a new toy, to a parrot mimicking human speech, or a kitten "reviewing" snacks, the possibilities are nearly endless and tailor-made for short, loopable videos that captivate users quickly. Increase a video's reach. For example, syncing a pet's action to a trending song or creating a humorous twist on a viral meme can transform simple footage into a relatable, attention-grabbing post. Brands looking to partner with petfluencers on TikTok should consider how their products can be integrated into these trends in creative, non-intrusive ways. A chew toy might become part of a "zoomies" trend, a branded pet outfit might debut in a "catwalk challenge," or a nutritional product might feature in a "What I Eat in a Day" parody. (Wojdynski & Evans, 2016)The key is to match brand messaging with the organic, playful spirit of TikTok content. Unfiltered glimpses into their pet's personality — whether it's a dog's failed attempt at catching a treat or a cat knocking over a houseplant with regal indifference. This authenticity not only endears the pet to the audience but also builds trust, especially when sponsored content is presented in a transparent and entertaining way. For instance, rather than a polished product review, a petfluencer might film their dog's honest, hilarious first reaction to a new treat, complete with bloopers. This rawness is more engaging and believable to audiences

TRACKING ENGAGEMENT: METRICS FOR PETFLUENCER MARKETING

Unlike short-form platforms like TikTok and Instagram Reels, YouTube excels in immersive storytelling, making it an ideal space for petfluencers who want to share more than just fleeting moments. Whether it's through vlogs, tutorials, product reviews, training videos, or behind-the-scenes content, (Sugumaran et al., 2024) YouTube allows petfluencers to deliver richer, more informative, and emotionally compelling content that resonates on a deeper level with their audience. As petfluencer marketing continues to expand across digital platforms, YouTube stands out not only as a hub for creativity and authenticity but also as one of the most effective channels for long-term brand building and monetization. Video might capture a dog's funny sneeze, a 10-minute YouTube vlog can showcase an entire day in the life of a pet — from morning routines and mealtime rituals to playtime and evening wind-downs. This kind of content allows followers to feel more connected to the petfluencer, developing a sense of familiarity and emotional investment that's harder to achieve on fast-scroll platforms. Longer videos also enable petfluencers to include detailed explanations, demonstrate how products are used over time, or address complex topics such as pet health, behavior training, adoption journeys, or travel with pets. This positions YouTube petfluencers as both entertainers and educators, which significantly enhances their influence and authority within their niche. Sponsorships and affiliate deals, YouTube offers a built-in monetization system through the YouTube Partner Program (YPP). Once a creator meets the minimum threshold of 1,000 subscribers and 4,000 watch hours within a 12-month period, they can begin earning ad revenue from their videos. This passive income stream grows in proportion to the number of views, watch time, and engagement a channel receives. Petfluencers can monetize not only through pre-roll and mid-roll ads but also through channel memberships, Super Chat in live streams, (Sameer Babu et al., 2025) YouTube Premium revenue shares, and merch shelf integration. These monetization methods create sustainable income potential and incentivize creators to produce consistent, high-quality content for more meaningful and demonstrative product integration. Instead of a brief mention or visual placement, a petfluencer can dedicate an entire video to unboxing and reviewing a product, sharing their pet's genuine reactions, and offering thorough testimonials. This format is ideal for complex or

Measuring ROI: Evaluating the Effectiveness of Petfluencer Marketing

While the charm of a playful dog or a fashionable cat may generate likes and shares, effective influencer marketing requires data-driven analysis to determine whether those interactions translate into real impact. Engagement metrics serve as the heartbeat of any petfluencer campaign — indicators that show how well content resonates with audiences, how efficiently it drives brand awareness, and how effectively it influences consumer behavior. Understanding these metrics is critical for both brands and petfluencers to assess performance, identify opportunities for improvement, and measure return on investment (ROI).This percentage provides a snapshot of how actively a petfluencer's audience is interacting with their content. For instance, a petfluencer with 100,000 followers who receives an average of 5,000 likes and 300 comments per post has an engagement rate of approximately 5.3%, which is significantly higher than the average influencer rate across many industries. Engagement rate is particularly important because it often signals trust, relatability, and content quality — a high follower count without solid engagement may indicate a passive or artificially inflated audience.1,000 emojis or generic responses. Brands should analyze the nature of comments — (Shende et al., 2025) Are followers asking questions about the product? Are they tagging friends and starting conversations? Are they expressing purchase intent or sharing personal experiences? Additionally, sentiment analysis tools can evaluate whether the tone of engagement is positive, neutral, or negative. This qualitative layer is crucial for understanding how audiences perceive both the petfluencer and the sponsored content. Views by the same person). These metrics help brands understand how far their message is spreading. (Ranjitha et al., 2025) A post with high reach but low engagement may indicate weak content or misalignment with audience interests. Conversely, high impressions with modest reach may signal strong interest from a smaller, highly engaged community — often the case with niche petfluencers who foster deep loyalty within a targeted audience. Tracking reach and impressions across different types of content (static posts, videos, Reels, Stories, etc.) can also inform content strategy by highlighting which formats generate the most exposure.by dividing the number of clicks on a link by the number of impressions. For example, if a petfluencer's story with a swipe-up link garners 10,000 impressions and 500 clicks, the CTR is 5%, which is well above average. High CTRs suggest that the petfluencer's audience not only enjoys the content but is also motivated to take action — a strong indicator of influence. To further track conversions, brands often use unique URLs, UTM parameters, or affiliate codes specific to the petfluencer, allowing for precise attribution. Instagram Reels. These metrics reveal how compelling the content is: are viewers watching to the end, or dropping off after a few seconds? High retention indicates engaging storytelling and audience interest, while low watch time may suggest that content needs to be more dynamic or better aligned with viewer expectations. YouTube also provides insights into click-through rates on video thumbnails, traffic sources, and viewer demographics, which can be invaluable for campaign refinement. A post being saved often indicates high value — whether aesthetic, informative, or emotionally resonant. Shares reflect virality and peer-to-peer recommendation, one of the most powerful forms of organic

INFLUENCER MARKETING PLATFORMS: TOOLS FOR PET BRANDS

Measuring the Return on Investment (ROI) in petfluencer marketing can be a nuanced and multifaceted process, yet it is crucial for understanding whether the time, effort, and resources invested in influencer partnerships translate into tangible results. ROI is not a one-size-fits-all metric; it varies based on the specific goals of a campaign, th(Robehmed & Berg, 2018)e type of content produced, and the channels used. However, evaluating the effectiveness of a petfluencer campaign through a clear, data-driven lens helps brands gauge whether they are getting value from their partnerships and provides valuable insights into how to optimize future efforts. Whether the goal is to increase brand awareness, drive sales, boost engagement, or establish long-term brand loyalty, there are several methods and metrics to assess the effectiveness of petfluencer marketing.sign-ups, event registrations, or app downloads), tracking sales conversions is paramount. To effectively track conversions, brands often provide petfluencers with unique affiliate links or promo codes that can be used by their followers. These links can be tracked using UTM (Urchin Tracking Module) parameters, which allow brands to monitor which petfluencers or specific posts are driving traffic and conversions. When a petfluencer promotes a product with a discount code, the number of times that code is used serves as a direct indicator of the return generated from the collaboration. This form of tracking provides clear attribution to a particular petfluencer or content piece, enabling brands to calculate exactly how much revenue was generated as a result of the campaign(Pew Research Center, 2018). For example, if a petfluencer's promo code results in $5,000 in sales, and the petfluencer was compensated $1,000, the ROI for that collaboration is 400%., brands often monitor daily or weekly sales data to spot any increases in activity that coincide with the influencer's content going live.

Figure 1. The Power Of Social Media marketing

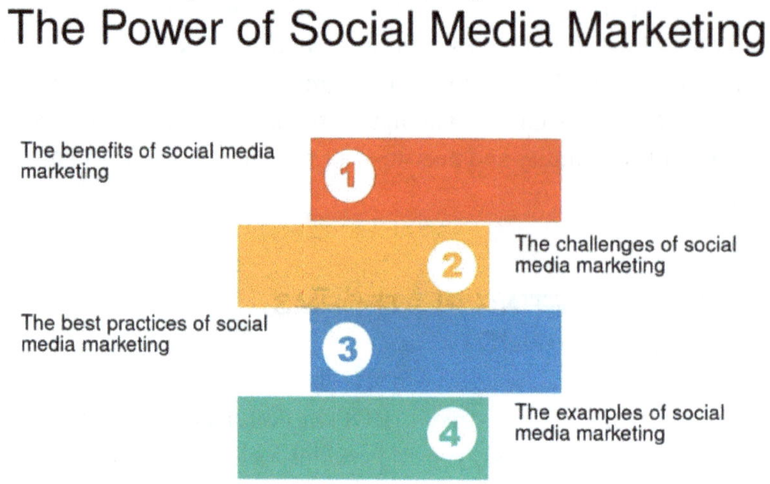

Analyzing sales spikes or drops during specific time frames can help brands determine whether petfluencer promotions are generating a measurable impact. It is essential, however, to account for external factors such as seasonality, other concurrent marketing efforts, or product availability that may influence sales trends., how actively they are engaging with the content, and how effectively the message is resonating. Calculating the cost-per-impression (CPI) or cost-per-engagement (CPE) allows brands to assess the efficiency of their marketing spend. By dividing the total cost of the campaign by the number of impressions or engagements generated, brands can determine whether they are achieving their brand awareness goals at an optimal cost. For instance, if a petfluencer campaign costs $5,000 and generates 500,000 impressions, the CPI would be $0.01, which is a relatively low cost to reach a large number of people. Similarly, the cost-per-engagement (CPE) metric evaluates the efficiency of driving meaningful interactions, such as likes, comments, shares, and saves, relative to the investment.used to assess the tone and emotional context of comments, shares, and mentions surrounding the petfluencer content. (Ogle et al., 2017)Are followers expressing excitement, curiosity, or positivity toward the brand and product being promoted? Positive sentiment can indicate successful brand alignment and a high level of trust between the petfluencer and their audience. Conversely, negative or neutral sentiment may signal misalignment between the brand's image and the petfluencer's personality or values. By measuring shifts in sentiment before, during, and after a campaign, brands can gauge how well the petfluencer's message is being received by their followers.influences overall brand visibility and audience growth over weeks or months, rather than just immediate results. Increased followers, social media mentions, and sustained engagement (such as ongoing discussions, shared posts, and return visits to the brand's website) are all indicators of long-term success. Additionally, repeat sales or customer lifetime value (CLV) metrics can provide insights into how well the brand has retained customers who were initially attracted by petfluencer campaigns. generates high-quality content, engages authentically with their audience, and drives sales over multiple campaigns will likely have a higher LTV compared to one-off collaborations with less engaged influencers. (Nairn & Fine, 2008)This approach underscores the value of building long-term, mutually beneficial relationships with petfluencers rather than focusing solely on short-term outcomes.brand perception, customer trust, and social media credibility — are equally valuable. These elements contribute to building a positive brand image, which can enhance future campaigns, foster customer loyalty, and create an enduring presence in the market. Brands must assess the combined impact of both hard and soft metrics to determinemetrics like sales conversions, engagement rates, sentiment analysis, and audience growth, brands can gain a clear understanding of the value petfluencers bring to their marketing strategy. With accurate measurement, brands can refine their approach, make data-driven decisions, and build stronger, more profitable relationships with both petfluencers and their audiences. Effective ROI tracking allows brands to allocate resources efficiently, improve future campaigns, and ultimately maximize the value of petfluencer marketing as a cornerstone of their digital marketing strategy.

Successful Petfluencer Marketing Campaigns: Case Studies

These platforms act as intermediaries, helping pet brands discover, vet, and manage relationships with the most suitable influencers for their campaigns, while offering both transparency and ease of use(Naderer et al., 2018). The sheer volume of influencers in the pet niche — ranging from micro-influencers with highly engaged local followings to macro-influencers with millions of followers — can make the process of finding the right fit daunting without the right tools. Influencer marketing platforms provide solutions for brands to find, collaborate with, and track the performance of petfluencers, streamlining the entire process from discovery to reporting. By leveraging these platforms, pet brands can save time, optimize their marketing spend, and ultimately improve the performance and ROI of their influencer marketing campaigns.across various social media channels (Instagram, TikTok, YouTube, and more) and present data-driven insights that help brands identify the right influencer partners based on specific criteria such as audience demographics, engagement rates, content style, and niche. Rather than relying on manual outreach, which can be time-consuming and inefficient, pet brands can use these platforms to streamline the search process by filtering influencers based on relevant characteristics,to find influencers who align with their values, product category, and target audience. Many platforms integrate sophisticated algorithms and artificial intelligence (AI) to analyze and evaluate influencers based on their content quality, engagement levels, and past collaborations. This ensures that brands can identify influencers who have genuine, engaged audiences, not just inflated follower counts. (Mehta et al., 2025) It's essential for pet brands to work with influencers who not only resonate with their brand values but also exhibit authentic relationships with their followers. By filtering influencers based on pre-defined criteria, brands can avoid ineffective partnerships and maximize the impact of back-and-forth via email or direct messages. Pet brands can create campaign briefs, outline expectations, and provide clear instructions for influencers to follow. This ensures that everyone involved is aligned on deliverables, timelines, and compensation, reducing the likelihood of misunderstandings. Many platforms also offer in-app communication tools that allow for real-time collaboration, enabling seamless coordination between pet brands and influencers throughout the campaign lifecycle.into the platform, pet brands can ensure that influencers are paid on time and according to pre-agreed terms, while influencers can focus on creating content rather than chasing payments. This integration not only streamlines the operational aspect of campaigns but also enhances trust between brands and influencers, as payments are handled transparently and efficiently.that provide brands with a comprehensive overview of how their petfluencer collaborations are performing. Key performance indicators (KPIs) such as impressions, reach, engagement rates, and click-through rates (CTR) are monitored and displayed on the platform's dashboard. This data allows brands to assess whether their campaigns are meeting their objectives, whether it's building brand awareness, generating leads, or driving sales.meaning brands can monitor the success of their campaigns not only on Instagram but also on TikTok, YouTube, Facebook, and more. By tracking these metrics, brands can adjust their strategies in real-time, identifying top-performing influencers or content types and optimizing their campaigns as needed. The ability to see all relevant data in one place allows for more informed decision-making, ensuring that pet brands can adjust their approach to maximize engagement and reach while staying on budget.sales, or leads directly to specific influencers or campaigns. By integrating affiliate links or promo codes into influencer posts, pet brands can track exactly how many purchases or sign-ups were driven by a specific influencer.

This level of accountability is essential for brands that are looking to measure the financial success of their campaigns and determine whether the investment in petfluencer partnerships is delivering the desired results. Platforms that integrate with eCommerce platforms, such as Shopify or WooCommerce, can provide even more precise insights into how influencer-driven traffic translates into direct sales.

This helps brands evaluate their campaign's effectiveness in a quantifiable manner.. These reports typically include metrics like engagement rates, total impressions, social shares, follower growth, and sales conversions. With detailed, easy-to-read reports, brands can quickly assess the performance of their influencer partnerships without having to manually compile data from multiple sources.For larger campaigns that involve numerous influencers, automated reporting can save substantial time and effort, especially when tracking the performance of multiple petfluencers across different platforms. These platforms can aggregate data into unified reports, making it easier to compare influencers' performance, identify trends, and determine which influencers are providing the best value. (Kelman, 2006)For larger campaigns, platforms often offer **bul**. This scalability is especially valuable for pet brands looking to expand their reach quickly and efficiently.Additionally, influencer marketing platforms often provide customization options that allow pet brands to tailor campaigns to their specific needs. For example, a pet brand may choose to run a product giveaway, create an affiliate program, or focus on generating video content. Platforms allow for this degree of customization by providing tools to create unique campaigns, define specific goals, and track progress toward those goals. This flexibility ensures that brands can run campaigns that align with their marketing objectives and resonate with their target audiences.with influencers. Rather than focusing solely on one-off collaborations, these platforms encourage brands to foster lasting relationships with petfluencers who align with their values and vision. This long-term approach allows brands to create more authentic content, as petfluencers who are genuinely invested in a brand's mission are more likely to produce high-quality, relatable content. Furthermore, ongoing collaborations with the same influencers can result in deeper audience engagement, greater trust, and more consistent brand messagingIn conclusion, influencer marketing platforms are indispensable tools for pet brands looking to harness the power of petfluencer marketing. These platforms simplify influencer discovery, streamline campaign management, and provide robust analytics to track performance and ROI. With the ability to connect with influencers, manage campaigns, track results, and optimize strategies, brands can maximize the effectiveness of their influencer partnerships. Furthermore, by offering scalability, customization, and long-term relationship-building opportunities, influencer marketing platforms allow pet brands to grow their presence, engage with targeted audiences, and create lasting impacts in the pet industry. Whether brands are new to influencer marketing or looking to scale existing efforts, these platforms provide the tools needed to succeed in the increasingly competitive petfluencer space.

THE FUTURE OF PETFLUENCER MARKETING: TRENDS AND OPPORTUNITIES

While petfluencer marketing has proven to be an incredibly effective tool for brands, it is not without its risks. As with any marketing strategy, there are numerous challenges and potential pitfalls that can lead to failed campaigns or less-than-ideal outcomes. In the fast-paced world of social media and influencer partnerships, mistakes can be costly, especially when petfluencers—often seen as "celebrities" in their own right—are involved. (Kamins, 2010)Understanding common errors in petfluencer marketing is crucial for ensuring that campaigns run smoothly, resonate with target audiences, and deliver a positive return on investment (ROI). By learning from past failures, pet brands can avoid these missteps and craft campaigns that not only succeed but also build long-term trust with their audience.One of the most significant mistakes that brands can make in petfluencer marketing is a lack of alignment between the brand's values and the petfluencer's image, audience, or content style. Petfluencers have highly engaged and loyal followers because they cultivate a specific type of content that resonates with their audience. If a brand selects a petfluencer whose values or personality do not align with the brand's message, the collaboration can come across as forced, inauthentic, or even disingenuous. This is particularly problematic in the pet industry, where authenticity and trust are key drivers of success.A famous example of a misaligned partnership occurred when a well-known petfluencer who typically promotes eco-friendly and sustainable pet products partnered with a brand that used plastic packaging and had questionable environmental practices. The backlash was swift, with followers expressing their dismay over the contradiction between the petfluencer's values and the brand they were promoting. This kind of misalignment can not only result in a failed campaign but can also damage the petfluencer's reputation and erode consumer trust. To avoid such mistakes, brands must carefully vet petfluencers to ensure that their content, values, and audience align with the brand's ethos and the quality of the audience. While it may seem logical to partner with a petfluencer who has millions of followers, a large following does not guarantee that the campaign will be successful. In fact, petfluencers with enormous followings often have lower engagement rates because their audience is less personal and more generic. On the other hand, micro-petfluencers, with a more niche and highly engaged audience, can drive more meaningful interactions and conversions, even if their follower count is relatively small.campaign resulted in disappointing sales and little engagement. Upon analyzing the campaign, it was found that the petfluencer's followers were largely uninterested in the brand's product, leading to a low click-through rate and minimal conversions. The brand failed to focus on engagement and relevance, which ultimately hurt the campaign's performance. Brands should prioritize engagement, niche targeting, and the authenticity of the petfluencer's community over sheer follower numbers to ensure that their message resonates with the right audience. areas for improvement. Brands must establish specific, measurable goals for their campaigns, whether it's raising brand awareness, increasing engagement, driving website traffic, or boosting sales. These goals should be communicated upfront to the petfluencer to ensure alignment and to give both parties a clear understanding of what success looks like.In one case, a pet brand launched a campaign with an influencer but failed to set clear objectiveeffectiveness.

As a result, the brand was left with little actionable data and could not optimize the campaign or justify the investment. To avoid this pitfall, brands should define specific goals, set measurable KPIs, and regularly communicate with petfluencers to track performance.excessive promotional language risk losing the natural charm and appeal that made the petfluencer successful in the first place.their messaging straightforward, allowing the petfluencer's personality and authenticity to shine through. Simplifying the message and focusing on one product at a time can help maintain the natural, fun tone that followers expectreputation. In some cases, brands launch a campaign without considering how their audience will react or without monitoring ongoing conversations during the campaign's rollout.A notable example of this occurred with a petfluencer who partnered with a controversial brand. While the petfluencer's content initially generated excitement, their followers began to voice concerns about the brand's practices, with some accusing the brand of poor animal welfare standards. The petfluencer, who had not properly vetted the brand's values, was caught in the middle of a social media firestorm. Despite having a large, engaged audience, the campaign was deemed a failure, as the petfluencer's audience felt betrayed by the partnership. This misstep highlights the importance of continuously monitoring audience sentiment and being responsive to any concerns that arise. Brands and petfluencers alike must remain agile, adjusting their messaging or even ending a partnership if necessary to maintain the trust and loyalty of their followers. When a petfluencer works with a brand over an extended period, they can create a more genuine connection with their audience, which often leads to higher engagement, loyalty, and conversions. significant failure in this area occurred when a major pet brand worked with a petfluencer for a one-time campaign without considering the potential for future collaborations. While the campaign saw initial success, the lack of ongoing partnerships meant that the brand could not maintain the momentum or build long-lasting brand recognition with the petfluencer's audience. In contrast, brands that build lasting partnerships with petfluencers create a sense of familiarity and trust, which results in more authentic content and better overall campaign performance.

CONCLUSION

The world of petfluencer marketing is poised for continued growth as more pet owners turn to social media platforms to share their pets' lives, creating massive online communities. These petfluencers, whether they are real animals or virtual avatars, have cultivated loyal followings that brands can tap into to promote products, services, and causes. However, to truly unlock the potential of petfluencer marketing, pet brands must adopt a strategic, thoughtful approach that goes beyond simply partnering with a well-known influencer. Instead, successful collaborations require careful planning, understanding of the petfluencer's audience, and alignment with brand values. The future of petfluencer marketing offers vast opportunities for pet brands that are willing to innovate and embrace the dynamic and rapidly changing landscape of social media. Here are some key tips for pet brands to unlock the full potential of petfluencer partnerships and ensure they stay ahead in this competitive field.can lead to more meaningful interactions and higher engagement rates. The primary benefit of working with micro-petfluencers is the authenticity they bring to their content, something that is often diluted in larger campaigns with major influencers.is already invested in the health and wellness of their pets. This strategy minimizes the risk of wasted impressions and maximizes the chances of generating meaningful conversions.Micro-petfluencers are also typically more affordable than high-profile influencers, making them an ideal option for smaller brands or those working within a limited marketing budget. By collaborating with several micro-petfluencers in a over time. This type of partnership also enables petfluencers to develop a deeper understanding of the brand's products and values, resulting in more natural, effective endorsementsniche, making them more likely to act on product recommendations.Additionally, long-term collaborations offer valuable insights into the petfluencer's audience. By working closely with an influencer over time, brands can gather data about what types of content perform best, allowing them to refine their marketing strategy and improve their return on investment (ROI). Over time, as petfluencers grow in popularity, brands that were early partners can benefit from the influencer's expanded reach, making long-term partnerships even more impactful.visually compelling content that authentically showcases their products in ways that resonate with the petfluencer's audience. Petfluencers are often chosen for their unique style and voice, so it's essential that brands allow petfluencers the creative freedom to craft content that feels authentic and true to their online persona. Instead of bombarding followers with repetitive product placements, brands should collaborate with petfluencers to create diverse and engaging content that aligns with their existing themes. For example, a petfluencer known for sharing funny pet videos might incorporate a product placement into a humorous skit, while a petfluencer focused on pet health might demonstrate how the brand's product contributes to a pet's overall well-being. By integrating the product naturally into the petfluencer's content, brands can create an emotional connection with the audience, making them more likely to trust the product and ultimately make a purchase.User-generated content (UGC) is an increasingly powerful tool in petfluencer marketing, as it leverages the power of a petfluencer's engaged community. In addition to working directly with petfluencers, pet brands can encourage their followers to create and share content that promotes the brand.

REFERENCES

Alassani, R., & Göretz, J. (2019). "Product placements by micro and macro influencers on Instagram" in *International conference on human-computer interaction* (Cham: Springer), 251–267

Athavale, V. A., Selvakumar, P., Poorani, S., Anand, T., & Rathore, D. S. (2025). Designing chatbots for educational leadership. In Musundire, A. (Ed.), *Chatbots in educational leadership and management* (pp. 181–204). IGI Global Scientific Publishing., DOI: 10.4018/979-8-3693-8734-4.ch008

Bailey, R., Wise, K., & Bolls, P. (2009). How avatar customizability affects children's arousal and subjective presence during junk food-sponsored online video games. *Cyberpsychology & Behavior*, *12*, 277–283. DOI: 10.1089/cpb.2008.0292 PMID: 19445632

Bandura, A. (2002). Social cognitive theory in cultural context. *Applied Psychology*, *51*, 269–290. DOI: 10.1111/1464-0597.0009

Bao, T., Chang, T.-L. S., Kim, A. J., & Moon, S. H. (2019). The characteristics and business impact of children's electronic word of mouth in marketing communications. *International Journal of Advertising*, *38*, 731–759. DOI: 10.1080/02650487.2018.1559558

Chambers, N., Kashefpakdel, E. T., Rehill, J., & Percy, C. (2018). *Drawing the future: Exploring the career aspirations of primary school children from around the world*. Education and Employers., Available at https://www.educationandemployers.org/wp-content/uploads/2018/01/Drawing-the-Future-FINAL-REPORT.pdf

Cheung, M. Y., Luo, C., Sia, C. L., & Chen, H. (2009). Credibility of electronic word-of-mouth: Informational and normative determinants of on-line consumer recommendations. *International Journal of Electronic Commerce*, *13*, 9–38. DOI: 10.2753/JEC1086-4415130402

de Droog, S. M., Buijzen, M., & Valkenburg, P. M. (2012). Use a rabbit or a rhino to sell a carrot? The effect of character–product congruence on children's liking of healthy foods. *Journal of Health Communication*, *17*, 1068–1080. DOI: 10.1080/10810730.2011.65083 PMID: 22650613

de Droog, S. M., Valkenburg, P. M., & Buijzen, M. (2011). Using brand characters to promote young children's liking of and purchase requests for fruit. *Journal of Health Communication*, *16*, 79–89. DOI: 10.1080/10810730.2010.529487 PMID: 21058143

Evans, N. J., Hoy, M. G., & Childers, C. C. (2018). Parenting "YouTube natives": The impact of pre-roll advertising and text disclosures on parental responses to sponsored child influencer videos. *Journal of Advertising*, *47*, 326–346. DOI: 10.1080/00913367.2018.1544952

Fair, L. (2019a). FTC-FDA warning letters: Influential to influencers and marketers. Available at: https://www.ftc.gov/news-events/blogs/business-blog/2019/06/ftc-fda-warning-letters-influential-influencers-marketers (Accessed November 21, 2019).

Fair, L. (2019b). Great American Fake-Off? FTC cases challenge bogus influencer metrics and fake reviews. Available at: https://www.ftc.gov/news-events/blogs/business-blog/2019/10/great-american-fake-ftc-cases-challenge-bogus-influencer (Accessed November 21, 2019).

Guttmann, A. (2019). Spending on advertising to children worldwide from 2012 to 2021, by format (in billion U.S. dollars). Available at: https://www.statista.com/statistics/750865/kids-advertising-spending-worldwide/ (Accessed November 21, 2019).

Hebden, L., King, L., & Kelly, B. (2011). Art of persuasion: An analysis of techniques used to market foods to children. *Journal of Paediatrics and Child Health*, *47*, 776–782. DOI: 10.1111/j.1440-1754.2011.02025.x PMID: 21707822

Hoffner, C. (2008). *"Parasocial and online social relationships" in The handbook of children, media and development* (Calvert, S. L., & Wilson, B. J., Eds.). Blackwell-Wiley.

Hoffner, C., & Buchanan, M. (2005). Young adults' wishful identification with television characters: The role of perceived similarity and character attributes. *Media Psychology*, *7*, 325–351. DOI: 10.1207/S1532785XMEP0704_2

Ismail, K. (2018). Social media influencers: mega, macro, micro or nano. Available at: https://www.cmswire.com/digital-marketing/social-media-influencers-mega-macro-micro-or-nano/ (Accessed November 21, 2019).

Jain, V., Roy, S., Daswani, A., & Sudha, M. (2011). What really works for teenagers: Human or fictional celebrity? *Young Consumers*, *12*, 171–183. DOI: 10.1108/17473611111141623

Kamins, M. A. (2010). An investigation into the "match-up" hypothesis in celebrity advertising: When beauty may be only skin deep. *Journal of Advertising*, *19*, 4–13. DOI: 10.1080/00913367.1990.10673175

Kelman, H. C. (2006). *"Interests, relationships, identities: three central issues for individuals and groups in negotiating their social environment" in Annual review of psychology* (Fiske, S. T., Kazdin, A. E., & Schacter, D. L., Eds.). Vol. 57). Annual Reviews.

Mehta, A. K., Yashoda, L., Selvakumar, P., Mishra, B. R., Das, A., & C. T. C., M. (2025). Teaching methods: Techniques for disadvantaged learners. In S. Hai-Jew (Ed.), Mitigating learner disadvantages in teaching and learning (pp. 181–206). IGI Global Scientific Publishing. https://doi.org/DOI: 10.4018/979-8-3693-8623-1.ch007

Naderer, B., Matthes, J., & Zeller, P. (2018). Placing snacks in children's movies: Cognitive, evaluative, and conative effects of product placements with character product interaction. *International Journal of Advertising*, *37*, 852–870. DOI: 10.1080/02650487.2017.1348034

Nairn, A., & Fine, C. (2008). Who's messing with my mind? *International Journal of Advertising*, *27*, 447–470. DOI: 10.2501/S0265048708080062

Ogle, A. D., Graham, D. J., Lucas-Thompson, R. G., & Roberto, C. A. (2017). Influence of cartoon media characters on children's attention to and preference for food and beverage products. *Journal of the Academy of Nutrition and Dietetics*, *117*, 265–270. DOI: 10.1016/j.jand.2016.08.01 PMID: 27793520

Pew Research Center. (2018). Many turn to YouTube for children's content, news, how-to lessons. Available at: https://www.pewinternet.org/2018/11/07/many-turn-to-youtube-for-childrens-content-news-how-to-lessons/ (Accessed November 21, 2019).

Ranjitha, P. K., Selvakumar, P., Anute, N., Manjunath, T., Sureshkrishna, G., & Pougajendy, S. (2025). Transportation challenges in islands tourism. In Hassan, V. (Ed.), *Navigating mass tourism to island destinations: Preservation and cultural heritage challenges* (pp. 287–312). IGI Global Scientific Publishing., DOI: 10.4018/979-8-3693-9107-5.ch01

Robehmed, N., & Berg, M. (2018). Highest-Paid YouTube Stars 2018: Markiplier, Jake Paul, PewDiePie and More. Available at: https://www.forbes.com/sites/natalierobehmed/2018/12/03/highest-paid-youtube-stars-2018-markiplier-jake-paul-pewdiepie-and-more/#563480c2909a (Accessed November 21, 2019).

Sameer Babu, M., Karunakaran, N. B., Selvakumar, P., Sethumadhavan, R., & Chandel, P. S. (2025). The role of chatbots in educational leadership. In Musundire, A. (Ed.), *Chatbots in educational leadership and management* (pp. 321–346). IGI Global Scientific Publishing., DOI: 10.4018/979-8-3693-8734-4.ch013

Shende, A. D., Tekade, S. A., Deshmukh, A. A., Tembhurkar, S. P., & Selvakumar, P. (2025). Water quality monitoring and control with AI. In Ruiz-Vanoye, J., & Díaz-Parra, O. (Eds.), *Smart water technology for sustainable management in modern cities* (pp. 51–80). IGI Global Scientific Publishing., DOI: 10.4018/979-8-3693-8074-1.ch003

Sugumaran, K. M. D., & Pandiyarajan, V. Y. B. S., Selvakumar, P., & M. S. (2024). Analysis of electromyography signals for control of mechanical prosthesis using machine learning techniques. In 2024 2nd International Conference on Intelligent Data Communication Technologies and Internet of Things (IDCIoT) (pp. 1059–1067). IEEE. https://doi.org/DOI: 10.1109/IDCIoT59759.2024.10467707

Wojdynski, B. W., & Evans, N. J. (2016). Going native: Effects of disclosure position and language on the recognition and evaluation of online native advertising. *Journal of Advertising*, *45*, 157–168. DOI: 10.1080/00913367.2015.1115380

Wong, J. C. (2019). 'It's not play if you're making money': how Instagram and YouTube disrupted child labor laws. Available at: https://www.theguardian.com/media/2019/apr/24/its-not-play-if-youre-making-money-how-instagram-and-youtube-disrupted-child-labor-laws (Accessed November 21, 2019)

Chapter 6
Sustainability on Stage: The Role of Pets in Legitimising Brands

Luzia Arantes
https://orcid.org/0000-0003-1179-9113
University of Aveiro, Portugal & Polytechnic University of Cávado and Ave, Portugal

Bruno Barbosa Sousa
https://orcid.org/0000-0002-8588-2422
Polytechnic University of Cávado and Ave, Portugal

ABSTRACT

This chapter explores how pet-powered branding intersects with sustainability in digital marketing, focusing on pets as symbolic mediators of trust, empathy, and ecological responsibility. As consumers demand authenticity, pets and petfluencers provide affective capital that supports imaginaries of care, adoption, and eco-friendly lifestyles. At the same time, their symbolic use can trivialise sustainability, enabling performative practices and masking weak commitments. Drawing on theories of performativity, affective capitalism, and ethical branding, the chapter proposes a framework showing how pets may both enhance authenticity and facilitate greenwashing or the commodification of animal welfare. The chapter contributes by integrating the affective role of pets into sustainable branding debates and offering recommendations for transparent, structurally aligned communication, stressing consumer literacy, regulation, and ethical coherence as conditions for substantive sustainability.

DOI: 10.4018/979-8-3373-4342-6.ch006

1. INTRODUCTION

At this pivotal moment in modern digital marketing, social and cultural values, like sustainability, have taken centre stage in brand communication (Effendy & Xiao, 2025). Customers are becoming more critical and knowledgeable, and they are no longer content with just goods or services (Tyagi et al., 2023). They want stories that portray sincerity, accountability, and moral dedication. The rise of petfluencers and the phenomenon of pet-powered branding have become more prominent in this context (Di Cioccio et al., 2024). Pets are now mediators of affection, trust, and symbolic legitimacy for brands rather than just being visual protagonists (Di Cioccio et al., 2024).

Despite the large body of research on sustainability in marketing, little is known about how animals fit into this process (Drury et al., 2023). Few studies have looked at how pets are used as symbols of care, well-being, and harmony with nature, especially in digital contexts (Jacobs et al., 2023). Recent studies have focused on sustainability as a value proposition and as a means of strategic differentiation (Yeboah et al., 2022). By examining critically how pets are used in sustainability narratives, this chapter aims to close this gap by pointing out the dangers of trivialization and superficial appropriation as well as the potential for building trust.

The following is an expression of the guiding research problem: how do pets, as affective and symbolic components, support the legitimacy of sustainable, or performatively sustainable, branding strategies in digital marketing? Because it highlights the conflicts between instrumentalization and authenticity at a time when the commodification of emotion and animal welfare collides with sustainability discourse, this question is both scientifically and socially pertinent.

Considering this, the primary goal of this research is to determine how the inclusion of pets in digital communication tactics affects consumers' perceptions of the sustainability of brands. To be more precise, it seeks to: (i) determine the primary ways that pets are linked to sustainable practices; (ii) examine how ethical commitment and performative sustainability are balanced; and (iii) talk about the process's implications for the creation of responsible branding. According to the underlying theory, pets can serve as emotional triggers that support the legitimacy of a sustainable value proposition, but they can also be used as props in flimsy narratives that cast doubt on sustainability.

By incorporating the symbolic role of animals into discussions on performativity and ethics in marketing, this research makes a theoretical contribution to the field of sustainable branding. It is also useful for professionals who want to create communication strategies that are more socially conscious, transparent, and responsible.

The chapter is organised as follows: the first part looks at how sustainability has developed as a brand value and strategic promise; the second part looks at petfluencers and the well-being imaginaries they support; the third part talks about performative sustainability and its moral implications; and the fourth part talks about the conflict between affective capitalism and ethics. The implications and difficulties for responsible branding are discussed in Section 5. The conceptual framework created to link pets, affective strategies, and sustainability narratives is introduced in Section 6. The major conclusions are finally presented in section seven, which also highlights the theoretical contributions, real-world applications, constraints, and directions for further study.

2. SUSTAINABILITY AS A BRAND VALUE: FROM ETHICS TO STRATEGY

As a marketing concept, sustainability emerged in the form of sustainability marketing and experienced a twisting evolution entangled with different understandings of ethics vs. strategy or another structural commitment vs. symbolic performance (Thu et al., 2023; Weder, 2023). Its modern roots go back to the concept of 'sustainable development' introduced in the Brundtland Report (WCED, 1987) that supports present needs without crushing future generations (Lopez, 2024). While sustainability was initially rooted in broader macro environmental and social dimensions, it has become a pillar of differentiation for corporations, leading to the theory of sustainable branding (green marketing).

In the 1990s and early 2000s, most marketing-based sustainability activities were peripheral; they tended toward reactive or reputational (Judijanto et al., 2024). Corporate attempts to "compensate" for the negative externalities with philanthropic initiatives, eco-labels, or reports on corporate social responsibility, in turn, without changing their business model and practices (Kassier, 2024). It will often be dominated by a compliance-based mentality, concerned with reputational risk and minimum-level legal or regulatory requirements (Reis et al., 2025).

The movement toward sustainability began to make more business sense with the advent of globalisation, digitisation, and higher environmental awareness among consumers (Štofejová et al., 2023). Brands like Patagonia, The Body Shop, and Ben & Jerry's openly started to define themselves around environmental or social issues, seeing that they could use sustainability as a positive factor within consumer decision-making, not the thing that caused negative differentiation, but rather positive brand loyalty (C. Singh et al., 2022; Sipos, 2024). This provided the matrix with a new theoretical and business justification, from which arose initiatives as diverse as shared value creation, in other words, integrating economic imperatives into the strategy of social museums (Möhrer, 2022).

Meanwhile, marketing studies started including sustainability as a moderator of the brand value proposition (Salinas & Abril, 2025). Societal marketing and conscious capitalism elucidated the fact that companies could, in addition to them being able to simply existing outside of a traditional profit-making realm (Dessart & Standaert, 2023; Kim & Yang, 2024). In this sense, sustainability stops being simply an ethical objective and becomes a source of symbolic, reputational and emotional value as an enabler to craft more engaging (and truthful) storytelling narratives. It's even higher performance in a digital environment & social media only consolidates the term (Bodie, 2022; Dessart & Standaert, 2023).

But the increasing incorporation of sustainability into marketing brings yet another challenge: with more brands using that tone, presumably for conscious or market-driven purposes alike, you run a higher risk of it all sounding like empty words (Dessart & Standaert, 2023). This leads to the idea of performative sustainability, where gestures co-opt community innovation. This can be seen as symptoms of a symbolic appropriation of sustainability, one that is geared more toward social legitimisation than actual transformation, like strategies as greenwashing, woke-washing and purpose washing (Williams, 2024).

Accordingly, the development of sustainability in marketing can be interpreted as an area of conflict between ethical and economic interests against communicational initiatives (Tolstoy et al., 2025). On the one hand, it is an opportunity to bring brands closer to new values with what society seeks; on the other hand, this transparent time demands more critical control and commitment so that sustainability does not remain a mere aesthetic or rhetorical code detached from practice (Kothari et al., 2025; Prihatiningrum et al., 2024).

In an environment of marketing message saturation and increasing consumer demands, as well as sustainability, it is now moving from an operational necessity to a broad strategic benefit in creating brand value propositions (Kharabsheh, 2024; Zheng, 2024). It is no longer only an ethical commitment or a reputational response, such as taking the right position on political issues: It constitutes something of its own, altering their brand positioning, in fact redefining itself for them; how they communicate and build symbolic currency among consumers (Odoom et al., 2025).

The value in what a marketer offers as tangible benefits and a sense of purpose that creates an emotional connection. Performance is more accurately described by the lens of purpose, so when this proposition includes sustainability, such as ecological practices or social justice (animal welfare and ethical trade), then it says something above performance alone (Kinnunen et al., 2022). This connection confers on the brand a collective purpose with the consumer, forming an indigenous bond that transcends product utility and price. It is about building meaning (Gowda, V. & H., 2024; Zürn et al., 2023).

In a market with more homogeneous products in terms of quality/performance, the different expectation is made by sustainability (Recabarren et al., 2024). Brands like Veja (ethical footwear), Too Good To Go (sustainable food) and BARK (eco-conscious pet products) show that they do not only compete on product but the narrative a certain brand tells, value it represents and role in which consumers can play as someone who made consciously, 'right' choices (Bonamigo et al., 2025; Dicu et al., 2025).

When it comes to markets motivated by ethics, social purpose or brand integrity differentiation through sustainability works particularly well (Simões-Coelho et al., 2023). Millennials and Generation Z are starting to see a shift that puts more pressure on companies to align their offering with the personal values of consumers, often asking for sustainable products, so they will accept paying more (Gomes et al., 2023; Sharma et al., 2025). In addition, brand value is increased by a symbolic side of reciprocity that reinforces identity: consuming "sustainable" as reaffirming individual positioning in the world (Nirupama et al., 2025).

Strategically, sustainable value cannot be reduced to ad campaigns or a green label. It calls for it from the purpose (stated) to practice and going back, beginning with sourcing raw materials until coming into supplier relations, working conditions (Allenbacher & Berg, 2023). Businesses thus need, more than ever before, not only to have consistent record keeping but also for that implicitly and de facto regulators no less strict on the accurate sales bill of materials found by consumers now embracing digital influencers and watchdogs who secondarily published access themselves via pressures on sustainability ranking public platforms (Jestratijevic et al., 2024a; Maghsoudi et al., 2025).

Additionally, in the current digitally led universe where perception and storytelling are paramount, sustainability helps brands to forge communities around themselves (Maghsoudi et al., 2025). Including the social or environmental causes surrounding any promise gives brands a language to mobilise consumers emotionally and turn them into co-creators of their positioning (Suo et al., 2025). This community, if established diligently, becomes a non-liquidation asset based on market volatility and immune to the noise of advertising.

That said, the viability of sustainability as a value proposition relies heavily on two factors: (1) how others see its genuineness (Suo et al., 2025) and (2) being able to bring that resonance into actual experiences for those consumers (Ta et al., 2022). The promise alone is insufficient. Unless backed by credible actions, it can be counterproductive and lead to doubt, scepticism, all the way up to outright brand rejection (Javed et al., 2024).

It's only natural that, as sustainability becomes an increasingly high-yield symbolic value within the realm of branding, so too does the risk of its trivialization (del Río et al., 2024). What had started as a difficult and transformative ethical sensibility designed to disrupt academic habits in the most deep-seated way imaginable turns out, all over today's ideological terrain, to have morphed into a cliché (Koch, 2025; Vienová & Mišík, 2025). The more popular the language of sustainability becomes, the easier it can be subsumed into brands that claim a sustainable pledge and simultaneously practice no changes in how clothes are conventionally produced than unless for advertisement (Adamkiewicz et al., 2022; Vienová & Mišík, 2025).

Nonetheless, the forms through which sustainability is strategically appropriated have become more fine-grained: they now function at a level of symbolic performance, aestheticised even (in terms of being performative) instead of one involving substantive commitment (Nejati & Shafaei, 2023). Language, visual codes (green, recycled, ethical, etc), emotional narratives and every label under the sun are there for brands to appropriate without verification or transparency; many just slap it on themselves (Adamkiewicz et al., 2022; Vienová & Mišík, 2025).

Illustrating an outline of a general logic where the true purpose has become "a good to sell" and where social, environmental causes are converted into communication resources (Diaz-Bustamante-Ventisca et al., 2025). The main danger is that this not only represents a departure between words and deeds but also leads to the symbolic emptying of sustainability as an idea in itself; it quickly becomes common parlance for anything, context or product without consideration (Kundi & Ernszt, 2024; Williams, 2024).

The very act of pressure could make brands want to "adopt" a cause so they do not get left behind, even if there is no real belief in it. Purpose, which should arise from the organisation having a clear identity, operates on yesteryear marketing trends and what sells well opportunistically (Chu et al., 2023). As such, the line drawn between true purpose and strategic appropriation becomes ever less clear, especially when viewed through a lens of an inundation with misinformation (Walter et al., 2024).

It's an ethical and reputational challenge when this happens. On the one hand, it clearly undermines trust in sustainable brands that are using transparency to build a better future (Tu et al., 2024). It is, however, also a driver of jadedness on the part of consumers, when all claims to responsibility ring hollow, then so will any attempt at marketing these positions (Tu et al., 2024). Trust, as social capital, becomes brittle, and its return is long-drawn-out (Tu et al., 2024).

The challenge for contemporary brands is therefore twofold: to resist the temptation of symbolic performativity and to demonstrate, in a clear and verifiable way, how their commitments to sustainability are reflected in concrete, structural, and continuous actions (Azazz et al., 2024; Tu et al., 2024). Purpose is only authentic when there is consistency between what the brand says, what it does, and what it allows the consumer to experience (Rosado-Pinto & Loureiro, 2024).

3. PETFLUENCERS AND THE IMAGINARY OF WELLBEING

The animals, and especially pets (in addition to the rest of horns and bells typical for animistic communication), become elements with an extraordinary symbolic power in a digital media saturated by visual impressions, ephemeral messages following attention algorithms (McGrane et al., 2024; Ubb Negotia et al., 2024). This is because their insertion into branded content creates anything but a neutral or decorative addition; rather, it performs constitutive affective and strategic work (Shamayleh & Arsel, 2025). Animals can bring so much empathy, positive emotion and trust to a brand, giving life to new stories written in language that is much more visceral with their audience (Fang, 2023).

Thus, animals assume a cultural and affective currency in contemporary societies that makes them powerful symbols within marketing (Kronenberg & Bocian, 2022). Pets sit at the emotional top table, as family members or faithful companions who can do no evil. As subjects of this being "at home" and as such emblematic of the condition or status that I am calling domestic other, they now become able to symbolize values in a way that people can relate with through their relationships not only mediated by their fellows but also via brands which talk about caring, authenticating originality, tender care/commitment (Huang & Hsieh, 2023). When a brand signs an animal, sofa or imaginary creature seeks to include part of that emotional and symbolic atmosphere for itself (Reddy B. & A. S., 2023).

Animals are agents of affective connection: they populate the logic of 'affective capitalism'. They do more than catch attention in marketing content; they emotionally validate the brand (Jacobson et al., 2022). A video with a rescued pup, a cat adopted by the company or another campaign where a petfluencer presents "choosing" this product sets up an emotional field, softening materials and making commercial relationships more human, relational, and consequently effective. People do not really "love a product," they love what it brings about in them, that is, status and romance, which are deep-seated instinctual programs; all these prompts were also activated by animals (Osmanova et al., 2023).

Animals are symbols of unconscious trust. They make us feel safe, secure and at home (Huang & Hsieh, 2023). In a landscape of deep mistrust for conventional advertising, pets serve as an illogical disruption to the logic of rational persuasion and point towards a more stripped-back, emotional, naked yet authentic realm (Myers et al., 2024). This phenomenon is perhaps most obvious in the realm of petfluencers, whereby animal accounts boasting tens (or even hundreds) of thousands of followers become unintentional brand ambassadors, simply by existing (Jacobson et al., 2022).

This form of symbolic mediation produces trust not only at the individual level but also at the social level. The local practices of care (Foucault's term) in the guardian's animal can give rise to communitas based on lifestyle choices that serve as a building block for virtual communities (Jacobson et al., 2022; Myers et al., 2024; Osmanova et al., 2023). Therefore, pets function as an emotional anchoring point in a digital tribe logic, perfect for symbol intimation and even loyalty/belonging generation.

But one must also resolutely contemplate the point of exhaustion to which this symbolic content can be brought: how far, in fact, does manipulation rely on a tenderness for animals' crumble from both sides into an ethicized de-trooping as well as fetishisation, if not cognitivism? Exploring important questions surrounding brand strategies and animal presence, these next sections will examine authenticity as well as agency & consent (Fennell, 2022).

The presence of pets in marketing content does not come solely from the emotional dimension but also integrates various broader visual and symbolic narratives that frequently refer to harmony with nature (or an ethically oriented "sustainable life") (Jacobs et al., 2023). These representations translate on social media, and in the digital environment shape this fantasy life where animal rights, ecology, respect, as well as a kind, not harmful way to your environment, would live together, feel good naturally through visualisations (Iqbal et al., 2025).

Animals are living happily ever after with humans in these tales of pet co-saviorship, investing pets as happy endings. Images of dogs on hiking trails, cats with vegan snacks or animals partaking in self-care activities (yoga, plant-based meals and home composting) all suggest a lifestyle rooted in sustainable values (Di Cioccio et al., 2024). The images do more than simply decorate; they sit within an ethical aesthetic in which looking after others (human and non-human) acts as a sign of moral worth.

This form of representation is an element in a logic which one may call the everyday life adulation, where decisions about consumption, food, place to live or recreation are not only aimed at responding to basic needs anymore but become investments towards building identity (Hochstein et al., 2025; Nirupama et al., 2025). Here, pets assume a distinct symbolic dimension: they are physical and emotional evidence that the subject/caregiver observes an ethical gaze of attentive behaviour (Tseng et al., 2024). This even extends to when people decide on sustainable animal products (biological nutrition, environmentally friendly toys and reusable accessories), that very decision becomes a performative gesture of these personal, but publicly communicable lifestyles (Provensi et al., 2024).

An algorithmic visual reward system further spreads these images via social media content, including pets regularly generate more impressions, engagement and shares (Myers et al., 2024). This increased visibility has a role in the creation of some visual stereotypes for sustainability: the minimalist plant-filled home, rescued dog with collar. Sunday walks and organic dinner routine all painstakingly documented, shared as "inspiration." Sustainability is not only an act or commitment, but something that can be consumed.

But these are surely not neutral narratives. By romanticising a sustainable animal experience often featured alongside preservation-oriented consumption practices, they risk fostering an elitist and normative understanding of sustainability, hard, replicate for people without the same resources or time or symbolic access. In addition, the incessant link between consumption and consciousness itself may generate a paradoxical effect: that of "sustainable being", meaning to consume more (though it is from an informed position), carrying on hierarchies of social distinction tuned with monetised care (Frig & Jaakkola, 2024; Mesiranta et al., 2024).

Consequently, this visual language represents a powerful tool for connecting to the emotions and shared identity of any community or tribe that is targeted by brands (Sha, 2024). But it also implies an inconvenience: sustainability on the back of animals, when they are reduced to a mere representation disconnected from both their systemic welfare and more holistic conceptions of sustainable practice, is at risk for banalization, which hints towards the next aspect performative sustainability will examine in detail (Kronenberg & Bocian, 2022).

Let alone, what used to be pet-keeping, eco-friendly adventures or a choice for wildlife preservation and sustainable ecosystem support are currently marketed above idealistic initiatives; they now direct toward an extra operating ground that exploits dignified symbolism in commonplace deeds (Lelo de Larrea & Smith, 2025). Businesses are aware of these, and therefore they use them to communicate actions that demonstrate their commitment, stand out from others in the market and even bring together emotional connections with consumers who increasingly adhere to precepts for other impacts beyond those related to animal welfare (environmental sustainability) (Gaiato et al., 2023).

4. PERFORMATIVE SUSTAINABILITY: BETWEEN VISIBILITY AND SUPERFICIALITY

Interpreting sustainability as a communicational matter demands more than an analysis of affirmatory statements per se and instead calls for scrutiny about how brands perform (or stage) their commitment to such an issue. This performativity, as a reiterated performance framework, is focused on a general performative model that produces what it seems to be doing (Singer, 2024). Viewed through a branding lens, this perspective enables the productive reimagining of sustainability not as having existed in some static and unchanging form or way but rather as being comprised of acts, signs and appearances that generate (or mimic) ethicality (Anantharaman, 2022).

There are no subjects before or outside of their performances; they are formed with them. In the same way, brands are not "sustainable" as an attribute intrinsic to their constitution but because they are reproduced in a series of gestures, discourses and signs, communicational rituals aimed at this meaning (Winit et al., 2023). This makes room for an interrogation of what we might call performative sustainability, the ability to enact and present as ethically committed without necessarily having a base in structures that can sustain it (Zaman et al., 2025).

In this context emerges the idea of greenwashing, which is defined as the practice of making an unsubstantiated or misleading claim about the environmental benefits of a product, service or technology (Williams, 2024). Yet, inside the world of performative theory, greenwashing is not so much a one-time lapse or crime but more properly recognised as part and parcel of the metacommunication rule according to which sustainability becomes hashed out on an aestheticised stage, producing only symbolic capital without any assurance for actual conversion (Vienová & Mišík, 2025; Williams, 2024).

This symbolic dimension is most evident in what we could call ethical aesthetics: an array of visual codes, narratives and sensory strategies that transmit a semblance of consciousness, empathy or accountability (Nassani et al., 2023). Cultural labels have been created about what is a «conscious» way of expression by using earth-tones in the packaging, hand-written typography nature nature-related photographs with animals, and an emotional language; everything accompanied hashtags like #sustainable or #ethicalcommitment (Kwon & Ha, 2023). Nevertheless, these indicators are not indicative of the coherence between discourse and practice. Morally, however, ethical aesthetics can still operate as an alibi, a shield that pretends to protect from the absence of structural (or binding) action if nothing else (Xie et al., 2024).

This aestheticisation of ethics aligns with the general logic of cultural capitalism, according to which brands not only compete for consumers' money through product marketing but also through market identity stories (Aman, 2024).

Therefore, it is necessary to differentiate between sustainability communication based on values, indicators, and effective actions, and the mere staging of this commitment through rhetoric (Oppong-Tawiah & Webster, 2023). This is a conceptual problem, as all brands are built through performance and performativity. It is, however, the disconnect between performance and practice, which can be seen in contrast to reality (Kumar et al., 2022). This contradiction remains at the heart of today's most pressing ethical and reputational dilemma regarding modern sustainable branding (Santos et al., 2024).

Pet-friendly brands are motivated to consistently convey sustainability. A new visual language, often confused with the language of love, will always bring references to affection, environmental responsibility, and social accountability (Almestarihi, 2024). This universe is accompanied by a standard set of recurring elements that serve as ethical values, even when they cannot be perpetuated structurally at the operational level (El-adaway & Jennings, 2022). These elements function as an easily recognisable brand image or iconography and are used countless times because they help build a highly consistent brand image and appeal to all of us (Wang, 2024). This aestheticisation of ethics aligns with the general logic of cultural capitalism, according to which brands not only compete for consumers' money through product marketing but also through market identity stories (Dagalp & Hartmann, 2022).

Therefore, it is necessary to differentiate between sustainability communication based on values, indicators, and effective actions, and the mere staging of this commitment through rhetoric (indices) (Golob et al., 2023). This is a conceptual problem, as all brands are built through performance and performativity. It is, however, the disconnect between performance and practice, which can be seen in contrast to reality (Onyas & Ryan, 2015). This contradiction remains at the heart of today's most pressing ethical and reputational dilemma regarding modern sustainable branding (Chowdhury, 2024).

Pet-friendly brands are motivated to consistently convey sustainability. A new visual language, often confused with the language of love, will always bring references to affection, environmental responsibility, and social accountability (Alves et al., 2022). This universe is accompanied by a standard set of recurring elements that serve as ethical values, even when they cannot be perpetuated structurally at the operational level (Abdulluh & Saud, 2025). These elements function as an easily recognisable brand image or iconography and are used countless times because they help build a highly consistent brand image and appeal to all of us (Jeffery et al., 2024).

Some of the most popular ways to pledge yourself to such causes as cruelty-free, vegan or eco-friendly are via stickers and seals (whether official ones or merely symbolic) (Jeffery et al., 2024). Others result from audits, but a lot is also coming about because brands are creating their own, functioning like "ethical cheat codes", allowing consumers to feel good without any further investigation (Agarwal et al., 2025; SIMION, 2024). These pseudo-sustainable labels mask a false change.

The plea on animals is another classic: it can be linked to a certain date (such as World Animal Day), there could be campaigns with shelters, and even stories of partnership that result in adoptions, creating the image that this company follows its objective offline too (Chamberlin & Plant, 2023; Stutey et al., 2022). But these are all acts of mere promotion without the long-term promise.

The sustainability of the product is also communicated through packaging design: green and brown are natural colours, leaf or paw print patterns create an image of nature, and hand-drawn typography implies simple genuineness (Ampuero-Canellas et al., 2023). Language like "plastic-free," "reusable", or even just the moralistic buzzword of our age, stealing chunks from religious rituals up and down ancient history: zero waste, only serves to reinforce this sense that all we need do is take control over individual use values when they are almost always covering industrial processes (Ajoykumar et al., 2022).

Outside of packaging and stickers, you will find an untold number of brands leveraging petfluencer endorsements as well as emotional storytelling that centres around the use of inclusive language (e.g., we animal lovers) (Gross et al., 2023). Still, these visual and discursive formulas often remain superficial (like kitschy) because they not seldom are often supplemented by no real actions. If valid practices are not part of the equation, sustainability becomes as much a charade and façade as it is where overuse prevails (Tu et al., 2024).

It is hard and only getting harder to differentiate between something that might be a genuine sustainability effort or a marketing façade, because there are so few qualified ways in which the industry knows how (let alone actually does) measure and validate whatever end they serve with time (Gleim et al., 2022; S. Singh & Singh, 2025). Words like eco-friendly, natural or similar ones are thrown around without defining what they mean in action and hence the increased dissonance between brand communication vs actual commitment (Javed, 2022). A lack of standardised nomenclature and scientific validation means that claims made in the absence of these robust categories may not resonate with consumers (Anisimova & Vrontis, 2024; Arayess & De Boer, 2022).

Very few established brands will ever go beyond general vague metrics (e.g. 'we planted' or 'reduced our footprint') and share real numbers on % recycled materials, reduced emissions, or the measured animal welfare impact of their relatively minuscule percentage of production twisted into sustainable marketing (Jestratijevic et al., 2024). That is, even in cases where they have such data, it is rarely audited or linked to durable structural objectives, adding to its lack of credibility (Amoako et al., 2023). No internal guidelines, no traceability in the supply chain and superficial external campaigns betray a lack of true dedication to sustainability, which then results only as a façade rather than a strategic keynote (Inês et al., 2023).

This is not a definitive indicator for valuing sustainable businesses, as true sustainability needs to be approached on a far more systemic level, an evaluation of production models along with supply chains and internal governance (Suoheimo et al., 2025). While cosmetic measures like planting trees or donating a percentage are needed, they will never be sufficient until deeper changes take place (Das & Albinsson, 2023). Therefore, critical literacy surrounding consumer culture is necessary to differentiate between genuine advancements and lipstick ethics (Hofverberg et al., 2023).

5. IMPLICATIONS AND PATHWAYS FOR RESPONSIBLE BRANDING

Companies and consumers alike still face challenges when it comes to building lasting ethical brands. Market pressure and public demand for sustainability communication soared, but tangible improvements to marketing practices were nowhere near as plentiful (Saputra & Asfiah, 2025). It means more than just lip service; eco-friendly catchphrases are needed here, and it requires their transformation into supply chains, production methods, and even business models, which may take time to accomplish, but not everyone can afford it (Ye & Lau, 2022).

But the nature of our society and its obsession with immediacy, as well as the popularity of social media trends, do not make ceremonial, aesthetic responses enough for true systemic change fighting back (Vladimirova, 2022). This tension emerges between a requirement for profound, systemic, and wide-reaching change on the one hand and the fact that companies are also lured to deliver superficial or symbolic gestures that have risks associated with creating brand detractors (Ahlström et al., 2025).

It remains a challenge for companies as well as consumers to build an ethically sustainable brand. Brands, despite increasing market pressure, are finding it challenging to align ethical sustainability with commercial competitiveness; these practices tend to be more costly and drive down margins (Choraria et al., 2020). Large numbers of consumers either refuse to pay the premium or do not recognise any extra value, given that a vocabulary hell-bent on meaningless promises and vague, unsubstantiated claims proliferates unchecked in multiple sectors with no standardised means for evaluation between genuine efforts from mere marketing (Choraria et al., 2020).

On the consumer side, we have not closed, or even begun to narrow, the intention-behaviour gap, as consumers with escalating levels of awareness and professed ethical concern make their purchase decisions primarily based on price, convenience, and aesthetics (Rausch & Kopplin, 2021). With contributions from information overload and symbolic gestures of (large) brands, the result is often confusion or cynicism, which weakens conscious demand. At the same time, responsibility is ever more placed on individual consumers, the finger is waved from industry and state, providing cover for those with real control to keep production unchanged (Savona et al., 2017).

The perversion of a new socio-economic ecosystem, in which the pressure to look good on social media plus feigned virtue-signalling plagues authentic sustainability projects from either side (Syahribulan et al., 2025). This war between drives and intentions signifies the kind of tension that will determine all branding in its future circumstances, requiring trust to be earned responsibly and (Borsa & Walls, 2022) respond with actions (Borsa & Walls, 2022).

Sustainability is a contestation of power, not an open field for campaigns and good intentions; it demands high ethical gatekeeping, enhanced media literacy, and well-facilitated regulation but foremost transpa (Vigneau & Adams, 2023) at can be verified (Vigneau & Adams, 2023). Rather than pivoting from greenwashing to data-driven communication, sharing real stats, for example, how product or supply chain impacts have changed because of material composition that is what consumers need information on to make educated decisions. For sustainable communication, it needs to become the reality, not just a line in your sustainability report (Sherfudeen, 2025).

Reliability of sustainability claims statements and the only possible way is external verification; open-access audits and reports from legitimised organisations are essential steps that guarantee items were independently certified (Bishop & Carlson, 2022). The key to preventing hypocrisy is transparency and consistency between public communication and internal practices (Ko et al., 2023). For these collaborations or campaigns to be effective, a brand's ethical narrative requires coherent action across functions (marketing, logistics & product sourcing), ensuring the credibility and internal alignment of all future propositions with corresponding strides in their supply chain practices as well (Ko et al., 2023).

Moreover, it needs to be transparent and use non-ambiguous language, staying clear of a patronising tone or minimising the structural injustices in place, which sometimes prevent consumers from living more sustainably (Duan et al., 2022). Essentially, ethical consumption is a sort of luxury; we need to work towards making ideal (Arman & Mark-Herbert, 2024) more people (Arman & Mark-Herbert, 2024).

Especially as regards sustainability communication, they need to adopt a more transparent and empathic view towards this process by not only reporting on achievements but also offering a behind-the-scenes look at the hurdles that need to be cleared and challenges still being tackled (Aggerholm & Thomsen, 2024). Some of this consumer scepticism can be neutralised by brands that are willing to openly discuss their merits and flaws (Putra Pratama & Koentoro Djati, 2021). We need education programs to help people better understand that marketing is not always grounded in truth and fact, so they can make smarter decisions on what products enable a more sustainable food system (Jurgena & Mikainis, 2011).

There is no script for authenticity, only constant truthful action derived from your own ethical principles. Yet excessive application of the symbolic can call into question our sincerity and accountability when it comes to actual consequences. Future work must address these inconsistencies, paying closer attention to brands' outcomes and effects of the regulatory frameworks, as well as answering questions regarding what program designs best advance meaningful change and how critical consumer literacy is in unlocking such planetary (Davies et al., 2020).

However, there is still much to learn about the real impact of sustainable branding strategies. Lots of brands talk the talk when it comes to humanity, animals & planet, but hard evidence and figures about how long those effects last are missing (Drury et al., 2023). Critical discourse analysis, performance indicators, value chain tracing and ethnographic audience reception studies are some examples of methodologies needed to answer questions such as: How effective are pet-friendly campaigns or eco-labels?

Regulation and verification mechanisms are necessary to safeguard against greenwashing, but existing standards can be ambiguous, resulting in penalising grassroots brands that may lack comprehensive documentation or favouring international conglomerates adept at sustainability jargon (Hassan, 2024). Another urgent space is consumer critical literacy, faced with information overload and conflicting messages, people require accessible means of weaving brand narratives to make sense before it lands on the shoulders of individual morality (Heidenstrøm, 2024).

We need to think of brands as cultural agents, not just economic entities, that also have a role in reimagining new worlds where true equality and sustainability thrive. In particular, the pet industry offers an under-explored context for theoretical and empirical inquiries to better understand consumer behaviours. Meeting these challenges will require constant questioning, public contestation and an unwillingness to allow sustainability to default as mere branding. It should be no less than accountability to one another and fundamental reform.

6. FRAMEWORK

The conceptual framework supporting this chapter is depicted in Figure 1, which combines the symbolic role of pets in modern branding with the dynamics of sustainability communication. The model illustrates how pet-driven affective strategies and sustainability intersect in digital spaces to create opportunities and risks for brands.

First, as a brand value, sustainability serves as both a strategic differentiator and an ethical requirement. It enables businesses to incorporate purpose into their value proposition by framing their identity around social justice, ecological responsibility, or animal welfare. Yet, the framework also recognises a crucial divide: sustainability serves as a genuine force behind responsible branding when it is ingrained structurally into supply chains and business operations; when it is reduced to superficial aesthetics or marketing gimmicks, it runs the risk of devolving into performative sustainability and greenwashing. The framework depicts this conflict as a crucial axis that determines whether sustainability narratives lead to real change or just serve as symbolic representations.

In parallel, the framework emphasises pets as affective and symbolic assets. Pets serve as intermediaries of trust, empathy, and emotional resonance in the logic of digital capitalism. In addition to humanising brands, their inclusion in influencer ecosystems and campaigns gives them a cultural currency closely linked to well-being, care, and authenticity. By mobilising the affective power of animals, brands can access what has been termed affective capitalism, where consumer engagement is secured less through rational persuasion and more through emotional attachment and lifestyle identification.

The realm of narratives and representations is where these two fields converge. Here, sustainability discourses and pet-driven symbolism come together in highly aestheticised communication formats, like digital storytelling (rescued pets, eco-conscious animal lifestyles) and visual codes (eco-friendly packaging, cruelty-free seals, pet adoption stories). Though they are presented as morally superior, these narratives have the potential to normalise a paradox in which "sustainable living" is associated with higher levels of consumption. Nevertheless, they also produce potent imaginaries of ethical consumption.

The conflict between affective commodification and ethical alignment is at the heart of the framework. By leveraging the ethical and sentimental connections between sustainability and pets, brands can create symbolic legitimacy. However, these symbolic resources run the risk of generating only rhetorical value if they are not accompanied by verifiable structural commitments. Accordingly, the framework views responsible branding as the result of communication, practice, and purpose alignment. According to this viewpoint, coherence is necessary for authenticity: there must be a convergence between the brand's claims, actions, and customer experiences.

In the end, Figure 1 implies that the way to responsible branding hinges on incorporating sustainability as a structural practice rather than a performative add-on while making sure that pet appeal deepens rather than trivialises commitments to ecological responsibility and animal welfare. The framework highlights the significance of ethical consistency, transparency, and consumer literacy as essential prerequisites for converting affective and symbolic capital into enduring cultural value by visualising this process.

Figure 1. Conceptual Framework: Pets, Sustainability and Responsible Branding

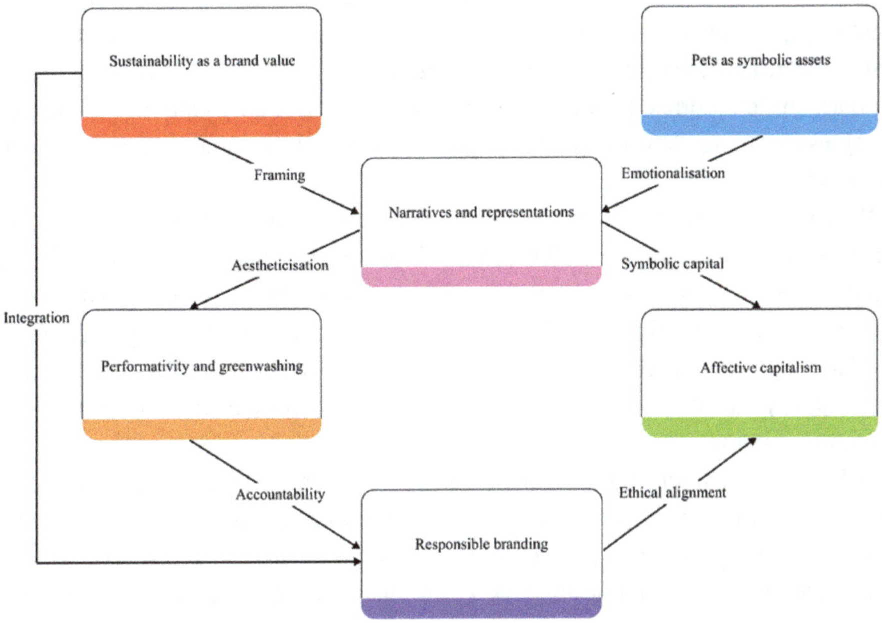

Source: Authors.

7. FINAL CONSIDERATIONS

The purpose of this chapter was to investigate how companion animals serve as symbolic mediators in the legitimisation of sustainability narratives in digital marketing through pet-powered branding and the emergence of petfluencers. Pets play two roles, according to the analysis: they can be used to foster trust and emotional resonance, but they can also be used as a tool in performative sustainability strategies. The conversation demonstrated that although animals can strengthen authenticity, there is a chance that they will be reduced to meaningless symbols, which would damage the credibility of a brand.

This study adds an understudied dimension that links affectivity, performativity, and symbolic legitimacy by integrating the role of animals into discussions on sustainable branding from a theoretical perspective. Practically speaking, it provides direction for marketing experts looking to develop communication plans that are more moral, dependable, and socially conscious, going beyond rhetoric or beauty to give brands structural value.

However, it is important to recognise certain limitations. Without exploring empirical measures or longitudinal data that could evaluate the persistence of sustainability perceptions associated with pets, the analysis mainly concentrated on communicational and symbolic dynamics. Future studies could examine cross-sector comparisons, examine consumer reaction more closely, and create methodological strategies that more clearly differentiate between staged sustainability and structural commitment.

When framed by the Sustainable Development Goals (SDGs), this reflection becomes even more pertinent. SDG 15 - Life on Land, emphasises the significance of preserving ecosystems and animal welfare, while SDG 12 - Responsible Consumption and Production, highlights the necessity of minimising greenwashing practices and encouraging knowledgeable consumer choices. Pet ownership in sustainability narratives will only be acceptable if it advances these objectives and maintains consistency between policy and practice.

All things considered, the nexus of digital marketing, affectivity, and sustainability offers worthwhile prospects but necessitates ongoing critical examination. Converting the symbolic capital connected to animals into structural pledges that bring brands closer to genuine and significant sustainability is still the main obstacle.

REFERENCES

Abdulluh, M. N. A., & Saud, Z. Y. (2025). Branding and its Relationship with Ethical Marketing: An Empirical Study on Iraqi Delivery Companies. *International Journal of Research and Innovation in Social Science, IX*(IV), 5354–5363. DOI: 10.47772/IJRISS.2025.90400384

Adamkiewicz, J., Kochańska, E., Adamkiewicz, I., & Łukasik, R. M. (2022). Greenwashing and sustainable fashion industry. *Current Opinion in Green and Sustainable Chemistry, 38*. Advance online publication. DOI: 10.1016/J.COGSC.2022.100710

Agarwal, P., Tikkha, V., & Rajwanshi, R. (2025). A Study to Explore the Effect of Brand Label Vs. Information Label in the Food and Beverage Industry Towards Greenwashing Practices. *International Journal of Agriculture and Environmental Research, 11*(1), 1–15. DOI: 10.51193/IJAER.2025.11101

Aggerholm, H. K., & Thomsen, C. (2024). Strategic communication in contexts of high sustainability pressure: Balancing purposefulness, transparency and participation in pursuit of organizational legitimacy. *Journal of Communication Management (London), 28*(1), 58–73. DOI: 10.1108/JCOM-12-2022-0131

Ahlström, H., Williams, A., Wassénius, E., & Downing, A. S. (2025). Deepening the Conversation on Systemic Sustainability Risks: A Social-Ecological Systems Approach. *Journal of Business Ethics, 199*(3), 495–506. DOI: 10.1007/S10551-024-05860-3/FIGURES/1

Ajoykumar, K. N., Singh, G., & Shackira, A. M. (2022). Corporate Social Accountability in Waste Production and Management. *Utilization of Waste Biomass in Energy, Environment and Catalysis*, 305–334. https://doi.org/DOI: 10.1201/9781003196358-15

Allenbacher, J., & Berg, N. (2023). How assessment and cooperation practices influence suppliers' adoption of sustainable supply chain practices: An inter-organizational learning perspective. *Journal of Cleaner Production, 403*, 136852. DOI: 10.1016/J.JCLEPRO.2023.136852

Almestarihi, R. (2024). Eco friendly branding and digital marketing strategies in Jordanian assessment. *Journal of Infrastructure. Policy and Development, 8*(7). Advance online publication. DOI: 10.24294/JIPD.V8I7.4843

Alves, H. M., Sousa, B., Carvalho, A., Santos, V., Dias, Á. L., & Valeri, M. (2022). Encouraging brand attachment on consumer behaviour: Pet-friendly tourism segment. *Journal of Tourism. Heritage and Services Marketing, 8*(2), 16–24. DOI: 10.5281/ZENODO.7357978

Aman, H. M. (2024). Cultural identities in Marketing and Branding: Appreciation vs. Appropriation. *Proceedings of the 8th International Visual Methods Conference*, 170–177. https://doi.org/DOI: 10.21467/PROCEEDINGS.168.19

Amoako, G. K., Bawuah, J., Asafo-Adjei, E., & Ayimbire, C. (2023). Internal audit functions and sustainability audits: Insights from manufacturing firms. *Cogent Business & Management*, *10*(1). Advance online publication. DOI: 10.1080/23311975.2023.2192313

Ampuero-Canellas, O., González-Del-Río, J., & Tarazona-Belenguer, N. (2023). Communicating Sustainability through Packaging Graphic Design: Associated Sociodemographic Factors. *Design Principles & Practices*, *17*(1), 1–21. DOI: 10.18848/1833-1874/CGP/V17I01/1-21

Anantharaman, M. (2022). Is it sustainable consumption or performative environmentalism? *Consumption and Society*, *1*(1), 120–143. DOI: 10.1332/LTTT8626

Anisimova, T., & Vrontis, D. (2024). The food you can trust: The moderating role of age in the relationship between consumer values and organic food trust. *Journal of Business Research*, *182*. Advance online publication. DOI: 10.1016/J.JBUSRES.2024.114803

Arayess, S., & De Boer, A. (2022). How to Navigate the Tricky Landscape of Sustainability Claims in the Food Sector. *European Journal of Risk Regulation*, *13*(4), 643–664. DOI: 10.1017/ERR.2022.6

Arman, S. M., & Mark-Herbert, C. (2024). Ethical Consumption: A Review and Research Agenda. *International Journal of Consumer Studies*, *48*(5). Advance online publication. DOI: 10.1111/IJCS.13079

Azazz, A. M. S., Elshaer, I. A., Al Thani, A., Algezawy, M., Mahrous, A. A., Mansour, M. A., Abdel Moneim, A., & Fayyad, S. (2024). The Influence of Green Demarketing on Brand Credibility, Green Authenticity, and Greenwashing in the Food Industry. *Sustainability*, *16*(21), 1–17. DOI: 10.3390/SU16219215

Bishop, K. J., & Carlson, K. M. (2022). The role of third-party audits in ensuring producer compliance with the Roundtable on Sustainable Palm Oil (RSPO) certification system. *Environmental Research Letters*, *17*(9). Advance online publication. DOI: 10.1088/1748-9326/AC8B96

Bodie, M. T. (2022). Labor Relations at the Woke Corporation. SSRN *Electronic Journal*, 1–30. https://doi.org/DOI: 10.2139/SSRN.4298588

Bonamigo, A., Makhija, H., Theocharis, D., & Tsekouropoulos, G. (2025). Sustainable Consumption and Branding for Gen Z: How Brand Dimensions Influence Consumer Behavior and Adoption of Newly Launched Technological Products. *Sustainability*, *17*(9), 1–40. DOI: 10.3390/SU17094124

Borsa, Z., & Walls, J. L. (2022). Sustainability Branding: Challenges with Building and Maintaining Stakeholder Trust. Https://Doi.Org/10.5465/AMBPP.2022.16111abstract, *2022*(1). https://doi.org/DOI: 10.5465/AMBPP.2022.16111ABSTRACT

Chamberlin, K. G., & Plant, E. A. (2023). Systemic sexism recognition and antisexism encourage gender equality activism: An adaptation of bystander intervention theory. *Journal of Applied Social Psychology*, *53*(10), 911–924. DOI: 10.1111/JASP.12976

Choraria, C. A. R., Jain, M., & Goel, C. A. P. (2020). Global Fashion Brands: Does Sustainability Make Business Sense? [IJRTE]. *International Journal of Recent Technology and Engineering*, *9*(1), 895–903. DOI: 10.35940/IJRTE.A1476.059120

Chowdhury, R. H. (2024). Sustainability Marketing and Ethical Branding in the Digital Space. *Journal of Trends in Applied Science and Advanced Technologies*, *1*(1), 18–27. DOI: 10.61784/ASAT3002

Chu, S. C., Kim, H., & Kim, Y. (2023). When brands get real: The role of authenticity and electronic word-of-mouth in shaping consumer response to brands taking a stand. *International Journal of Advertising*, *42*(6), 1037–1064. DOI: 10.1080/02650487.2022.2138057

Dagalp, I., & Hartmann, B. J. (2022). From "aesthetic" to aestheticization: A multilayered cultural approach. *Consumption Markets & Culture*, *25*(1), 1–20. DOI: 10.1080/10253866.2021.1935900

Das, A., & Albinsson, P. A. (2023). Consumption Culture and Critical Sustainability Discourses: Voices from the Global South. *Sustainability*, *15*(9), 1–19. DOI: 10.3390/SU15097719

Davies, I., Oates, C. J., Tynan, C., Carrigan, M., Casey, K., Heath, T., Henninger, C. E., Lichrou, M., McDonagh, P., McDonald, S., McKechnie, S., McLeay, F., O'Malley, L., & Wells, V. (2020). Seeking sustainable futures in marketing and consumer research. *European Journal of Marketing*, *54*(11), 2911–2939. DOI: 10.1108/EJM-02-2019-0144 del Río, C., González-Álvarez, K., & López-Arceiz, F. J. (2024). Examining greenwashing and SDG-washing: An analysis of corporate engagement with the SDGs. *Sustainability Accounting. Management and Policy Journal, 15*(2), 412–456. DOI: 10.1108/SAMPJ-02-2023-0080

Dessart, L., & Standaert, W. (2023). Strategic storytelling in the age of sustainability. *Business Horizons, 66*(3), 371–385. DOI: 10.1016/J.BUSHOR.2023.01.005

Di Cioccio, M., Pozharliev, R., & De Angelis, M. (2024). Pawsitively powerful: Why and when pet influencers boost social media effectiveness. *Psychology and Marketing, 41*(7), 1614–1628. DOI: 10.1002/MAR.22000

Diaz-Bustamante-Ventisca, M., Carcelén-García, S., Díaz-Soloaga, P., & Kolotouchkina, O. (2025). Greenwashing perception in Spanish fast-fashion brands' communication: Modelling sustainable behaviours and attitudes. *International Journal of Fashion Design, Technology and Education, 18*(2), 179–189. DOI: 10.1080/17543266.2024.2343934

Dicu, A. M., Rad, D., Barbu, F., Cuc, L. D., Feher, A., Roman, D., Mazuru, L., Sanda, G., & Pîrvulescu, L. (2025). From Attachment to Action: Consumer Identification and the Sustainable Buying of Rural Brand Products Like "Pită de Pecica.". *Sustainability, 17*(9), 1–19. DOI: 10.3390/SU17094133

Drury, M., Fuller, J., & Hoeks, J. (2023). Embedding animals within a definition of sustainability. *Sustainability Science, 18*(4), 1925–1938. DOI: 10.1007/S11625-023-01310-7/FIGURES/1

Duan, Y., Aloysius, J. A., & Mollenkopf, D. A. (2022). Communicating supply chain sustainability: Transparency and framing effects. *International Journal of Physical Distribution & Logistics Management, 52*(1), 68–87. DOI: 10.1108/IJPDLM-04-2020-0107

Effendy, V., & Xiao, Z. (2025). How Does Cultural Sustainability Promote Fashion Consumers' Purchase Intention? *Sustainability, 17*(5), 1–7. DOI: 10.3390/SU17052034

El-adaway, I. H., & Jennings, M. (2022). Professional and Organizational Leadership Role in Ethics Management: Avoiding Reliance on Ethical Codification and Nurturing Ethical Culture. *Science and Engineering Ethics, 28*(4), 1–30. DOI: 10.1007/S11948-022-00385-2/METRICS PMID: 35939145

Fang, Z. (2023). Ananlysing the Effectiveness of Anime-like Virtual Influencer. *Advances in Economics. Management and Political Sciences, 33*(1), 232–239. DOI: 10.54254/2754-1169/33/20231660

Fennell, D. A. (2022). Animal-informed consent: Sled dog tours as asymmetric agential events. *Tourism Management, 93*. Advance online publication. DOI: 10.1016/J.TOURMAN.2022.104584

Frig, M. M., & Jaakkola, M. (2024). Between conspicuous and conscious consumption: The sustainability paradox in the intermediary promotional work of an online lifestyle site. *Journal of Consumer Culture, 24*(1), 3–23. DOI: 10.1177/14695405231170684/ASSET/0F8CA3F7-8E6F-4422-9A41-0AE9DA59A5C4/ASSETS/IMAGES/LARGE/10.1177_14695405231170684-FIG1.JPG

Gaiato, G., Ardigó, C. M., & Limberger, P. F. (2023). Animal Welfare Certification Seal and the Effect on Brand Equity: Consumer Perspective of Chicken Commodity. *Journal of Food Products Marketing, 29*(6), 197–218. DOI: 10.1080/10454446.2023.2227583

Gleim, M., Sreen, N., & Pant, L. (2022). Is Doing Right All that Matters in Sustainability Marketing? The Role of Fit in Sustainable Marketing Strategies. SSRN *Electronic Journal*. https://doi.org/DOI: 10.2139/SSRN.4093796

Golob, U., Podnar, K., & Zabkar, V. (2023). Sustainability communication. *International Journal of Advertising, 42*(1), 42–51. DOI: 10.1080/02650487.2022.2144035

Gomes, S., Lopes, J. M., & Nogueira, S. (2023). Willingness to pay more for green products: A critical challenge for Gen Z. *Journal of Cleaner Production, 390*. Advance online publication. DOI: 10.1016/J.JCLEPRO.2023.136092

Gowda.V, S., & H., A. (2024). The role of brand storytelling in creating emotional connections. *ShodhKosh: Journal of Visual and Performing Arts, 5*(1), 1843–1848. https://doi.org/DOI: 10.29121/SHODHKOSH.V5.I1.2024.4576

Gross, J., Cui, Z., & von Wangenheim, F. (2023). How to Make Influencer Advertising Engaging on Instagram: Emotional Storytelling in Sponsored Posts. *Journal of Interactive Advertising, 23*(4), 388–408. DOI: 10.1080/15252019.2023.2211579

Hassan, S. M. (2024). Greenwashing in ESG: Identifying and Addressing False Claims of Sustainability. *Journal of Business and Strategic Management, 9*(8), 90–105. DOI: 10.47941/JBSM.2390

Heidenstrøm, N. (2024). Green marketing in the fashion industry: A critical analysis of sustainability narratives. *Consumption Markets & Culture, 27*(5), 488–504. DOI: 10.1080/10253866.2024.2440557

Hochstein, R. E., Veresiu, E., & Harmeling, C. M. (2025). Moralizing Everyday Consumption: The Case of Self-Care. *The Journal of Consumer Research, 52*(1), 219–242. DOI: 10.1093/JCR/UCAE056

Hofverberg, H., Franzén, J., & Maivorsdotter, N. (2023). Education for sustainable clothing consumerism?: A critical examination of educational material for design and craft education. *FormAkademisk, 16*(5), 1–21. DOI: 10.7577/FORMAKADEMISK.5234

Huang, W. H., & Hsieh, S. Y. (2023). The impact of animal metaphors on consumer response to courtesy advertising. *Journal of Retailing and Consumer Services, 75.* Advance online publication. DOI: 10.1016/J.JRETCONSER.2023.103485

Inês, A., Diniz, A., & Moreira, A. C. (2023). A review of greenwashing and supply chain management: Challenges ahead. *Cleaner Environmental Systems, 11.* Advance online publication. DOI: 10.1016/J.CESYS.2023.100136

Iqbal, N., Arif, M., Abbas, Q., Mahmood, Q., Naseem Anwar, M., Mansoor, M., & Khan, D. (2025). Green Influencers. *The Power of Social Media in Shaping Eco-Conscious Communities., 3*(02), 402–412. DOI: 10.55966/assaj.2025.3.2.001

Jacobs, T. P., Humphrey, B. T., & McConnell, A. R. (2023). Nature's Best Friend: Viewing Pets as Having Greater Emotional Experience Increases Ecological Concern. *Anthrozoos, 36*(4), 625–639. DOI: 10.1080/08927936.2023.2200647

Jacobson, J., Hodson, J., & Mittelman, R. (2022). Pup-ularity contest: The advertising practices of popular animal influencers on Instagram. *Technological Forecasting and Social Change, 174.* Advance online publication. DOI: 10.1016/J.TECHFORE.2021.121226

Javed, U. (2022). Linking Perceived Greenwashing with Brand Credibility: An Empirical Evidence from Pakistan. *International Journal of Business and Economic Affairs, 7*(3), 1–10. DOI: 10.24088/IJBEA-2022-73001

Javed, U., Rashid, M. A., Hussain, G., & Shafique, S. (2024). Consumers' perception of green brand attributes and its outcomes: A sustainable perspective. *Journal of Environmental Planning and Management, 67*(8), 1655–1677. DOI: 10.1080/09640568.2023.2178882

Jeffery, T., Hirche, M., Faulkner, M., Page, B., Trinh, G., Bruwer, J., & Lockshin, L. (2024). Branding consistency across product portfolios in the wine industry. *International Journal of Wine Business Research, 36*(4), 473–488. DOI: 10.1108/IJWBR-11-2023-0067

Jestratijevic, I., Uanhoro, J. O., & Rana, M. R. I. (2024). Transparency of sustainability disclosures among luxury and mass-market fashion brands: Longitudinal approach. *Journal of Cleaner Production, 436.* https://doi.org/ https://doi.org/DOI: 10.1016/J.JCLEPRO.2023.140481

Judijanto, L., Suroso, A., & Choerudin, A. (2024). The Evolution of Sustainable Business Practices: A Bibliometric Study on Corporate Social Responsibility and Green Marketing. *Sciences Du Nord Economics and Business*, *1*(02), 83–91. DOI: 10.58812/SNEB.V1I2.33

Jurgena, I., & Mikainis, Z. (2011). Consumer Citizenship Education for Sustainable Development in Higher Education in Latvia. *The China Business Review*, *10*(12). Advance online publication. DOI: 10.17265/1537-1506/2011.12.011

Kassier, L. (2024). Identifying transitions in corporate sustainability reporting: a content analysis of JSE/FTSE multinational sustainability reports from 2016 to 2021. *International Journal of Corporate Social Responsibility 2024 9:1*, *9*(1), 1–23. https://doi.org/DOI: 10.1186/S40991-024-00099-7

Kharabsheh, R. (2024). Strategic Green Marketing: Exploring Consumer Perceptions and Preferences for Sustainable Products. *International Journal of Green Management and Business Studies*, *4*(1). Advance online publication. DOI: 10.56830/IJGMBS06202405

Kim, C. G., & Yang, O. S. (2024). Global Companies' Dynamic Response to Business Environment Uncertainty through Digital Transformation: Sustainable Digital Quality–Customer Value–Market Performance Relationships. *Sustainability*, *16*(15), 1–32. DOI: 10.3390/SU16156541

Kinnunen, J., Saunila, M., Ukko, J., & Rantanen, H. (2022). Strategic sustainability in the construction industry: Impacts on sustainability performance and brand. *Journal of Cleaner Production*, *368*, 133063. DOI: 10.1016/J.JCLEPRO.2022.133063

Ko, T., Lee, J., Park, D., & Ryu, D. (2023). Supply chain transparency as a signal of ethical production. *Managerial and Decision Economics*, *44*(3), 1565–1573. DOI: 10.1002/MDE.3765

Koch, N. (2025). The symbolic power of sustainability: Gulf megaprojects and the case of Expo City Dubai. *Cambridge Journal of Regions, Economy and Society*, *18*(2), 279–292. DOI: 10.1093/CJRES/RSAE046

Kothari, H., Choudhary, A., Jain, A., Singh, S., Prasad, K. D. V., & Vani, U. K. (2025). Impact of social media advertising on consumer behavior: Role of credibility, perceived authenticity, and sustainability. *Frontiers in Communication*, *10*. Advance online publication. DOI: 10.3389/FCOMM.2025.1595796/BIBTEX

Kronenberg, J., & Bocian, M. (2022). Animal and plant images in corporate marketing communications are ecosystem services that should be paid for. *Ecosystem Services*, *56*. Advance online publication. DOI: 10.1016/J.ECOSER.2022.101464

Kundi, V., & Ernszt, I. (2024). The Phenomenon of Greenwashing: An Analysis of the Hungarian Regulation. *Journal of Sustainability Research, 6*(4). Advance online publication. DOI: 10.20900/JSR.20240066

Kwon, S., & Ha, S. (2023). Examining identity- and bond-based hashtag community identification: The moderating role of self-brand connections. *Journal of Research in Interactive Marketing, 17*(1), 78–93. DOI: 10.1108/JRIM-07-2021-0183

Lelo de Larrea, G., & Smith, S. J. (2025). Bear E. Drooley: Achieving Business Growth With the Help of Pets-In-Residence and Resort Mascots. *Journal of Hospitality & Tourism Cases, 13*(1), 3–11. DOI: 10.1177/21649987231221484

Lopez, D. V. (2024). Well-being and Sustainable Development: An Exploratory Approach from a Marketing Perspective. *European Journal of Sustainable Development, 13*(1), 205–205. DOI: 10.14207/EJSD.2024.V13N1P205

Maghsoudi, M., Shokouhyar, S., Sanaee, N., & Shokoohyar, S. (2025). Enhancing sustainability reporting practices in the notebook manufacturing industry: A multi-faceted analysis integrating traditional reports and social media data. *Annals of Operations Research, 345*(1), 317–349. DOI: 10.1007/S10479-024-06343-4/METRICS

McGrane, C., Hjorth, L., & Murray, P. (2024). "We Make Them Our Kin": Australian Older Adult's Playful Kinship Practices Through Sharing Animal Images on Social Media. *Social Media + Society, 10*(4). Advance online publication. DOI: 10.1177/20563051241306540/ASSET/B3196695-E21C-4311-93DC-D567875D3A0D/ASSETS/IMAGES/LARGE/10.1177_20563051241306540-FIG5.JPG

Mesiranta, N., Mattila, M., Koskinen, O., & Närvänen, E. (2024). Circular Consumption Practices as Matters of Care. *Journal of Business Ethics, 200*(1), 13–30. DOI: 10.1007/S10551-024-05888-5/TABLES/1

Möhrer, M. (2022). *Shared Value Statement: New Perspectives on Measuring Business Value Creation*. 111–131. https://doi.org/DOI: 10.1007/978-3-030-86526-9_7

Myers, S., Sen, S., Syrdal, H., & Woodroof, P. (2024). The impact of Persuasion knowledge cues on social media engagement: A look at pet influencer marketing. *Journal of Marketing Theory and Practice, 32*(1), 43–60. DOI: 10.1080/10696679.2022.2093224

Nassani, A. A., Yousaf, Z., Grigorescu, A., & Popa, A. (2023). Green and Environmental Marketing Strategies and Ethical Consumption: Evidence from the Tourism Sector. *Sustainability, 15*(16), 1–13. DOI: 10.3390/SU151612199

Nejati, M., & Shafaei, A. (2023). Why do employees respond differently to corporate social responsibility? A study of substantive and symbolic corporate social responsibility. *Corporate Social Responsibility and Environmental Management, 30*(4), 2066–2080. DOI: 10.1002/CSR.2474

Nirupama, M. I., Galdolage, B. S., Al-Daoud, K., Vasudevan, A., Mohammad, S., Vasumathi, A., & Qin, P. (2025). The effect of conspicuous consumption on social identity formation in the branded clothing sector: The mediating effect of product symbolism. *Uncertain Supply Chain Management, 13*, 395–408. DOI: 10.5267/j.uscm.2024.9.013

Odoom, R., Odoom, P. T., Amu, P. Y., & Adams, M. (2025). Sustainable digital marketing practices and consumer brand engagement – a brand reputation mediation investigation. *Journal of Strategic Marketing, 33*(2), 254–270. DOI: 10.1080/0965254X.2025.2453690

Onyas, W. I., & Ryan, A. (2015). Exploring the brand's world-as-assemblage: The brand as a market shaping device. *Journal of Marketing Management, 31*, 141–166. DOI: 10.1080/0267257X.2014.977333

Oppong-Tawiah, D., & Webster, J. (2023). Corporate Sustainability Communication as 'Fake News': Firms' Greenwashing on Twitter. *Sustainability, 15*(8), 1–26. DOI: 10.3390/SU15086683/S1

Osmanova, I., Ozerden, S., Dalal, B., & Ibrahim, B. (2023). Examining the Relationship between Brand Symbolism and Brand Evangelism through Consumer Brand Identification: Evidence from Starbucks Coffee Brand. *Sustainability, 15*(2), 1–15. DOI: 10.3390/SU15021684

Prihatiningrum, R. R. Y., Supraptiningsih, J. D., Lutfi, L., Imron, A., & Fithoni, A. (2024). Sustainable Marketing Strategies: Aligning Brand Values with Consumer Demand for Environmental Responsibility. *Global International Journal of Innovative Research, 2*(9), 2271–2283. DOI: 10.59613/GLOBAL.V2I9.304

Provensi, T., Marcon, M. L., Schmidt, J. L., Rodrigues, C. de O., & Sehnem, S. (2024). Sustainability and Innovation in the Pet Industry: An Analysis from the Perspective of Ecological Modernization Theory. *Revista de Administração de Empresas, 64*(3), e2023-0247. https://doi.org/DOI: 10.1590/S0034-759020240301

Putra Pratama, A., & Koentoro Djati, D. (2021). Balanced messaging for experienced laptop consumers. *Jurnal Sosioteknologi, 20*(3), 299–311. DOI: 10.5614/SOSTEK.ITBJ.2021.20.3.2

Rausch, T. M., & Kopplin, C. S. (2021). Bridge the gap: Consumers' purchase intention and behavior regarding sustainable clothing. *Journal of Cleaner Production, 278*. Advance online publication. DOI: 10.1016/J.JCLEPRO.2020.123882

Recabarren, J. I., Castillo, E., García, A., & Cantallopts, J. (2024). Product differentiation in mineral commodities based on sustainability indicators: The case of copper mining. *Journal of Cleaner Production*, *476*, 143786. DOI: 10.1016/J.JCLEPRO.2024.143786

Reddy, B. V. V., & A. S., S. (2023). Delineation on Celebrity Endorsement and Brand Mascot Towards Attitudes, Beliefs, Purchase Intention and Behaviour of the Consumers. SSRN *Electronic Journal*. https://doi.org/DOI: 10.2139/SSRN.4330745

Reis, T. dos S. M., Drumond, M. V. G., Gomes, P. R., Tonacio, C. M. S. de P., & Junior, P. C. T. (2025). Environmental Compliance, ESG Practices, and Stakeholder Capitalism: Challenges For Sustainable Corporate Management. *Revista de Gestão - RGSA, 19*(3). https://doi.org/DOI: 10.24857/rgsa.v19n3-071

Rosado-Pinto, F., & Loureiro, S. M. C. (2024). Authenticity: Shedding light on the branding context. *EuroMed Journal of Business*, *19*(3), 544–570. DOI: 10.1108/EMJB-08-2021-0115

Salinas, G., & Abril, C. (2025). Integrating sustainability into brand valuation models: an integrative literature review. *European Journal of Management and Business Economics*. https://doi.org/DOI: 10.1108/EJMBE-03-2024-0104/1249822/INTEGRATING-SUSTAINABILITY-INTO-BRAND-VALUATION

Santos, C., Coelho, A., & Marques, A. (2024). The greenwashing effects on corporate reputation and brand hate, through environmental performance and green perceived risk. *Asia-Pacific Journal of Business Administration, 16*(3), 655–676. DOI: 10.1108/APJBA-05-2022-0216

Saputra, A. I., & Asfiah, N. (2025). Bibliometric Analysis of Green Marketing Strategies: Innovative Approaches to Improve Sustainability. *Jurnal Ekuisci*, *2*(3), 158–170. DOI: 10.62885/EKUISCI.V2I3.589

Savona, N., Thompson, C., Smith, D., & Cummins, S. (2017). Proportional responsibility versus individual responsibility for healthy eating: A complex systems analysis. *Lancet*, *390*. Advance online publication. DOI: 10.1016/s0140-6736(17)33015-5

Sha, L. (2024). Design of a Brand Emotional Connection System Based on Visual Communication. *Proceedings - 2024 International Conference on Computers, Information Processing and Advanced Education, CIPAE 2024*, 430–435. https://doi.org/DOI: 10.1109/CIPAE64326.2024.00084

Shamayleh, G., & Arsel, Z. (2025). Digital Affective Encounters: The Relational Role of Content Circulation on Social Media. *The Journal of Consumer Research.* Advance online publication. DOI: 10.1093/JCR/UCAF023

Sharma, A., Kumar, K., & Dwesar, R. (2025). "Keenly aware of environmental issues, yet wavering in conviction": Understanding the factors influencing the consumers' willingness to pay for green energy. *Sustainable Futures : An Applied Journal of Technology, Environment and Society*, *9*. Advance online publication. DOI: 10.1016/J.SFTR.2024.100427

Sherfudeen, N. (2025). Sustainable Supply Chain Management: Assessing Environmental Impact Using Data Analytics. *Journal of Information Systems Engineering & Management*, *10*(12s), 313–323. DOI: 10.52783/JISEM.V10I12S.1813

SIMION, R. (2024). Eco-Frauds: The Ethics and Impact of Corporate Greenwashing. *Studia Universitatis Babe -Bolyai Philosophia*, *69*, 7–26. DOI: 10.24193/SUBBPHIL.2024.2.01

Simões-Coelho, M., Figueira, A. R., & Russo, E. (2023). Motivations for a sustainable ethos: Evidence from the globally present Brazilian multinational Natura &Co. *Environment Systems & Decisions*, *43*(3), 321–336. DOI: 10.1007/S10669-022-09890-Y/METRICS PMID: 36628130

Singer, A. E. (2024). Marketing objects as talking machines: The performative capacity of product packages. *Marketing Theory*, *24*(3), 481–497. DOI: 10.1177/14705931231207319

Singh, C., Park, H., & Joyner Martinez, C. M. (2022). Love letters to Patagonia: Fostering sustainable consumption via consumer–brand relationships. *International Journal of Sustainable Fashion & Textiles*, *1*(1), 41–62. DOI: 10.1386/SFT/0003_1

Singh, S., & Singh, A. K. (2025). Regulations and Prevention – "Green Washing and Green Marketing. *IJFMR - International. Journal of Multidisciplinary Research*, *7*(3). Advance online publication. DOI: 10.36948/IJFMR.2025.V07I03.41968

Sipos, D. (2024). The Role of Social Media in Promoting Sustainable Brands: Influencing Consumer Perceptions and Behavior Towards Sustainable Products. *Technium Sustainability*, *8*, 1–11. DOI: 10.47577/SUSTAINABILITY.V8I.11741

Štofejová, L., Král', Š., Fedorko, R., Bačík, R., & Tomášová, M. (2023). Sustainability and Consumer Behavior in Electronic Commerce. *Sustainability*, *15*(22), 1–16. DOI: 10.3390/SU152215902

Stutey, D. M., Solis, A. E., Notestine, L., & Wehrman, J. (2022). The Impact of Therapy Dogs on Graduate-Level, Military-Affiliated Students. *Society & Animals, 32*(3), 309–327. DOI: 10.1163/15685306-BJA10106

Suo, D., Dai, J., & Gong, S. (2025). Doing good with flow: Unlocking brand passion through virtual CSR co-creation participation and immersive experiences. *Corporate Social Responsibility and Environmental Management, 32*(1), 1309–1324. DOI: 10.1002/CSR.3023

Suoheimo, M., Walter, S., Backer, H., Kotaniemi, S., & Pyykkö, H. (2025). Service Designing Transitions to More Sustainable Supply Chains: A Systematic Literature Review through the Lens of Systemic Design Approach. *Journal of Sustainability Research, 7*(2). Advance online publication. DOI: 10.20900/JSR20250020

Syahribulan, S., Elliyana, E., & Rosmiati, R. (2025). The Role of Social Media Influencers in Shaping Sustainable Purchasing Behavior: Genuine Consumer Interest or Impulsive Trends? *Journal of Production. Operations Management and Economics, 5*(1), 63–77. DOI: 10.55529/JPOME.51.63.77

Ta, A. H., Aarikka-Stenroos, L., & Litovuo, L. (2022). Customer Experience in Circular Economy: Experiential Dimensions among Consumers of Reused and Recycled Clothes. *Sustainability, 14*(1), 1–18. DOI: 10.3390/SU14010509

Thu, N. N. Q., Kadirov, D., Fam, K. S., & Tho, N. D. (2023). Firms' Sustainability Marketing Commitment: The Roles of Chief Marketing Officers' Future Focus and Prosocial Motivation. *Journal of Macromarketing, 43*(3), 306–321. DOI: 10.1177/02761467231174027

Tolstoy, D., Melén Hånell, S., & Ghauri, P. N. (2025). Unpacking the Role of Ethical Leadership in the Era of Sustainable Development Goals and Values-Based Marketing. *Journal of International Marketing, 33*(2), 19–38. DOI: 10.1177/1069031X241296468/ASSET/5755ECDA-2A24-4226-84CA-04F927A9F496/ASSETS/IMAGES/LARGE/10.1177_1069031X241296468-FIG2.JPG

Tseng, T. A., Fang, H. Y., Shen, C. C., & Chang, Y. C. (2024). Peer bonds and nature's embrace: Exploring the influence of pet caregiving on social well-being and nature connection among Taiwanese children. *Frontiers in Public Health, 12*. Advance online publication. DOI: 10.3389/FPUBH.2024.1431939/BIBTEX PMID: 39498111

Tu, J. C., Cui, Y., Liu, L., & Yang, C. (2024). Perceived Greenwashing and Its Impact on the Green Image of Brands. *Sustainability, 16*(20), 1–17. DOI: 10.3390/SU16209009

Tyagi, V. K., Kumar, S., Gulyani, M., & Gahlawat, R. (2023). E-SERV-EX: A Multi-item Scale for Measuring Customer Expectations from the Online Retail Services. *NMIMS Management Review, 31*(2), 131–144. DOI: 10.1177/09711023231197795

Ubb Negotia, S., Lxix; E, & Harmati, A. (2024). Pets In Advertising or How to Influence Consumers? *Studia Universitatis Babe -Bolyai Negotia, 69*(1), 55–68. DOI: 10.24193/SUBBNEGOTIA.2024.1.03

Vienová, R., & Mišík, M. (2025). *Far-right greenwashing: the twisting of sustainability*. Sustainability Accounting, Management and Policy Journal., DOI: 10.1108/SAMPJ-10-2024-1184/1256108/FAR-RIGHT-GREENWASHING-THE-TWISTING-OF

Vigneau, L., & Adams, C. A. (2023). The failure of transparency as self-regulation. *Sustainability Accounting. Management and Policy Journal, 14*(4), 852–876. DOI: 10.1108/SAMPJ-01-2022-0051

Vladimirova, K. (2022). Behind 11 million likes: Sustainable fashion on Instagram – A critical analysis of actors and discourses on fashion, sustainability and social change. *International Journal of Sustainable Fashion & Textiles, 1*(1), 107–148. DOI: 10.1386/SFT/0006_1

Walter, N., Föhl, U., Sander, F., & Nies, A. (2024). Act as you preach! Authentic brand purpose versus "woke washing's" impact on brand credibility: The moderating role of cause involvement and consumer skepticism. *Journal of Business Research, 184*. Advance online publication. DOI: 10.1016/J.JBUSRES.2024.114868

Wang, X. (2024). Visual Communication and Branding: The Role of Graphic Design in Building Brand Image and Recognition. *Highlights in Art and Design, 8*(2), 19–22. DOI: 10.54097/QWY32G44

Weder, F. (2023). The Evolution of the Sustainability Story: Strategic Sustainability Communication as Niche Construction. *International Journal of Strategic Communication, 17*(3), 228–244. DOI: 10.1080/1553118X.2023.2229304

Williams, J. (2024). Greenwashing: Appearance, illusion and the future of 'green' capitalism. *Geography Compass, 18*(1), e12736. DOI: 10.1111/GEC3.12736

Winit, W., Kantabutra, S., & Kantabutra, S. (2023). Toward a Sustainability Brand Model: An Integrative Review. *Sustainability, 15*(6), 1–25. DOI: 10.3390/SU15065212

Xie, Z., Liu, Y., Liu, Y., & Xu, L. (2024). Unveiling greenwashing dynamics: Exploring the nexus between transparent corporate practices, employee perspectives, and ethical leadership impact. *Environment, Development and Sustainability, 2024*, 1–25. DOI: 10.1007/S10668-024-04665-8

Ye, Y., & Lau, K. H. (2022). Competitive Green Supply Chain Transformation with Dynamic Capabilities—An Exploratory Case Study of Chinese Electronics Industry. *Sustainability*, *14*(14), 1–23. DOI: 10.3390/SU14148640

Yeboah, A. Y. O., Jibril, A. B., & Novak, P. (2022). A strategic framework for developing sustainable value propositions. *Problems and Perspectives in Management*, *20*(4), 407–421. DOI: 10.21511/PPM.20(4).2022.31

Zaman, S. U., Asif, H., & Alam, S. H. (2025). Beyond Influence: The Behavioral Blueprint of Ethical and Sustainable Consumer Decision-Making. *Journal of Social and Organizational Matters*, *4*(2), 254–279. DOI: 10.56976/JSOM.V4I2.219

Zheng, Y. (2024). The Impact of Brand Loyalty on Consumer Purchase Decisions and Analysis of Sustainable Consumption Strategies. *Frontiers in Business, Economics and Management*, *15*(2), 219–222. DOI: 10.54097/PS4YA869

Zürn, M., Buder, F., & Unfried, M. (2023). Brand Purpose and Brand Success. *NIM Marketing Intelligence Review*, *15*(1), 54–59. DOI: 10.2478/NIMMIR-2023-0008

Chapter 7
Paws and Influence:
The Power of Petfluencers in Modern Branding

Anjel Raj Y.
https://orcid.org/0000-0003-3591-0672
GNA University, India

J. Hemalatha
Crescent School of Business, B.S. Abdur Rahman Crescent Institute of Science and Technology, Chennai, India

ABSTRACT

In today's fast-changing digital marketing world, a fresh wave of influencers pet-fluencers has taken centre stage, becoming surprisingly powerful players in brand promotion and connecting with consumers. This chapter dives into the rise of pet-fluencers, those lovable domesticated animals whose social media followings often outshine even human celebrities, and explores how they're reshaping the way brands connect with people. Through real-world examples, trends in influencer marketing, and the emotional pull of these furry stars, we'll see how pets use their charm, relatability, and heart-tugging appeal to bring brands and their audiences closer together. We'll look at what makes their influence tick, who's following them, and the clever partnerships that boost their reach. The chapter also tackles the ethical side of things and how pet content is turning into big business. By unpacking the mix of adorable animals, engaging posts, and smart marketing, this chapter shows just how much untapped potential petfluencers have and why they're leaving a lasting mark on today's branding scene.

DOI: 10.4018/979-8-3373-4342-6.ch007

1. INTRODUCTION

In the ever-evolving and dynamic world of social media, influencer marketing has firmly established itself as one of the most powerful and innovative strategies for brands eager to build authentic and meaningful connections with their audiences (Kádeková and Holienčinová, 2018). The traditional methods of marketing long dominated by television commercials, print advertisements, and billboards have gradually lost their dominance. Consumers today live in an environment saturated with information and advertisements, making it increasingly difficult for brands to cut through the noise. Social media platforms such as Instagram, TikTok, YouTube, and Facebook have fundamentally transformed the way consumers discover, interact with, and respond to brands and products (Gil, 2021). These platforms have turned marketing from a monologue into a dialogue, encouraging engagement, conversation, and community building in ways that were unimaginable a few decades ago.

At the core of this transformation are the influencers individuals who have harnessed their creativity, personality, and relatability to cultivate large, devoted followings. These influencers range from everyday people to experts and celebrities, but what sets them apart is their ability to build trust and rapport with their audiences (Micle, 2020). Unlike conventional advertising, which can often feel impersonal or intrusive, influencers share aspects of their personal lives, product experiences, and opinions in a manner that resonates deeply with followers. Their content often feels less like a sales pitch and more like a conversation with a trusted friend, which fosters strong emotional connections. Followers tend to view influencers not just as entertainers or opinion leaders but as friends, mentors, or role models, despite never having met them face-to-face (Kim and Kim, 2020). This perceived intimacy and trust make influencer marketing an incredibly effective strategy for brands seeking to humanize their messaging and increase consumer loyalty.

Traditionally, influencer marketing centered around celebrities, fashion models, and industry specialists, who used their popularity or credibility to promote products and way of life. Of late, though, the environment has expanded considerably, welcoming a broader array of creators and niches targeting special interests and communities (Campbell and Farrell, 2020). Among these new niches, one of the most interesting and fastest-growing is the domain of petfluencers animal-only social media accounts, be they dogs, cats, birds, or more unusual pets such as hedgehogs or reptiles. What sets petfluencers apart and makes them so popular is not just their inbuilt cuteness but the individual personalities, quirky antics, and interesting content that they provide which keeps their users hooked (Spee et al., 2019).

Petfluencers illustrate the way individuals in the influencer arena have branched out, moving away from human-centric stories towards those involving furrier, feathered, or even scaly characters that win hearts across the globe. Take the classic case of Grumpy Cat, whose perpetually grumpy-looking face turned her tail up online since 2012. Here are some characteristics that petfluencers share:. Grumpy Cat's face was everywhere memes, products, books, and even a Lifetime TV movie showcasing the massive business potential for animal influencers. This internet sensation was a turning point moment illustrating how pets could transform from transient web sensations into influential marketing characters with real clout and widespread appeal (Holbrook, 2008).

Likewise, Jiffpom, that small Pomeranian who is widely recognized for his exquisite sense of style and quick wit, has emerged as a popular influencer, gathering millions of followers and working with big brands on different campaigns. And here's Nala Cat, who marries cute content with a broader purpose, acting as a brand ambassador for pet goods as well as working for charitable causes related to animal welfare. These petfluencers have graduated from mere social media stardom to recognized authority in the marketing and brand space, generating considerable attention and consumer trust.

What essentially sets petfluencers apart from other influencers is that they can relate to people on a much more emotional and instinctual basis (Shamayleh and Arsel, 2025). In an era where many consumers have become skeptical of traditional marketing approaches, particularly overt and aggressive advertisements, petfluencers offer a refreshing alternative. Their content is universally appealing, wholesome, and heart-warming. Pets evoke a range of positive emotions joy, amusement, comfort, nostalgia, and that special "aww" factor that are difficult to manufacture artificially but extremely valuable to brands (Weber, 2016; Hasson, 2017). This emotional resonance drives significant engagement, as posts featuring petfluencers typically generate more likes, comments, shares, and most importantly, foster a deeper sense of trust between the brand and its audience. Trust, in the digital realm, is arguably the most critical currency, and petfluencers have mastered the art of earning it.

However, behind the adorable photos and viral videos lies a sophisticated industry supported by professional human teams that manage and maximize the marketing potential of these animal stars. Petfluencers often have dedicated managers and marketing experts who carefully plan and execute campaigns, ensuring that sponsored content, product placements, merchandising opportunities, and even participation in large-scale advertising campaigns are seamlessly integrated into the petfluencer's brand (Jacobson, 2019). This professionalism has elevated petfluencers from casual hobbyists to major players in the marketing world.

Many petfluencers have broken into mainstream advertising with notable success. Some have featured prominently in Super Bowl commercials arguably the pinnacle of marketing exposure partnered with corporate giants like Amazon or Mercedes-Benz, or launched exclusive pet product lines that capitalize on their social media fame. These developments underscore the fact that petfluencers are much more than cute internet phenomena; they are economic powerhouses with real influence and substantial earning potential (Chase, 2020). In fact, top petfluencers can earn thousands of dollars for a single sponsored post, showcasing the lucrative possibilities of this niche (Lindimore, 2020).

This chapter offers an in-depth exploration of the enchanting world of petfluencers, examining why these four-legged or sometimes feathered or scaled stars command such magnetic appeal. It illuminates how petfluencers have been able to occupy a distinctive and compelling niche within the larger influencer marketing environment. By drawing on engaging real-life evidence and case studies, this chapter shows how brands use petfluencers to attain a range of marketing outcomes ranging from driving brand awareness and creating emotional relationships to long-term customer loyalty.

Just as crucial, this chapter is not afraid to consider the issues and ethical dilemmas that come with this growing discipline. These include protecting the humane treatment and well-being of animals used in marketing, being transparent and honest regarding sponsored content to ensure consumer trust, and addressing the intricate legal and regulatory frameworks that control influencer marketing practices. These are important considerations for the maintenance of the credibility and viability of petfluencer marketing.

Through the juxtaposition of evocative storytelling and astute analysis, this chapter seeks to offer readers a comprehensive, engaging, and balanced view of how petfluencers are transforming the marketing strategies of our times. Not a fleeting fashion trend or novelty alone, petfluencers are a powerful force that reconfigures our comprehension of influence, authenticity, and emotional connection in the age of the digital. Their authentic charm, human appeal, and narrative potential remind us that sometimes the best marketing is not the most boisterous or flashy but the humblest and truest.

1.1 Objectives and Scope of the Chapter

This chapter takes an engaging and approachable journey into the captivating realm of petfluencers, a niche that has rapidly become one of the most intriguing and effective corners of modern digital marketing. Rather than just skimming the surface, it offers a comprehensive look at the subject from a grounded, accessible perspective making complex concepts easy to grasp and relatable to anyone, whether you're a marketer, a pet lover, or simply curious about social media trends.

We start with building a solid foundation with the fundamentals of influencer marketing. This involves investigating how influencer marketing works in our digital age, when social media influencers have incredible influence in deciding opinions and buying habits. One of the major areas of emphasis here is how central emotions are to this process—why individuals are attracted to influencers, how emotional relationships fuel interaction, and what precisely accounts for online communities becoming so intensely connected to the personalities they are following. This is important to understand because it is why influencer marketing is not simply about product promotion; it's about establishing trust and inducing real, genuine interactions that are both personal and genuine.

From that foundation, the chapter turns its attention to the stunning ascendancy of petfluencers those cute and cuddly creatures who have swept social media off its feet. We trace their key moments and cultural transformations that elevated pets from simple companions to full-fledged digital icons. This chapter breaks down how viral pet videos, memes, and platforms' visual-first nature produced the perfect storm for animals to amass huge followings. By showcasing examples of popular petfluencers, we demonstrate how the right mix of cuteness, humor, and relatability in these animals' content has engaged international audiences. It also looks at how petfluencers are part of larger social media trends and consumer aspirations, creating a unique niche space that human influencers may be unable to match.

The chapter then deconstructs the real-world mechanics involved in effective petfluencer campaigns. Brands are not simply sitting idly waiting for their sponsored animals to become viral sensations; there's a careful, planned process at work. This chapter describes how marketers find and engage the best audiences for petfluencer posts usually enthusiastic pet owners and animal enthusiasts and also how they capitalize on pets' natural emotional draw to increase brand engagement. We examine the skill of creating standout posts from the visual narrative tricks to the placement of products that comes across as organic and authentic. Monitoring and quantifying the performance of these campaigns are also addressed, illustrating how data and analytics shape what is most effective and how to further hone strategies in the future.

Peeking over the horizon, the chapter explores the thrilling future of petfluencers, with a nod to new trends such as virtual petfluencers—computer-generated creatures brought to the fore using AI and animation. These virtual pets present brands with new creative possibilities and the means to connect people in new ways, while balancing ethical questions regarding actual animals. We also explore how AI is being leveraged more and more to drive content creation, personalize engagement, and further the dynamics of petfluencer marketing. This vision of the future enables readers to envision how this trend may progress and what new opportunities may emerge. Along the way, broad themes are interwoven with compelling, real-life examples, which serve to shed light on the revolutionary effect pets are having on the marketing landscape. Through exploring the influence of petfluencers on remaking concepts of influence, authenticity, and engagement, the chapter invites readers to rethink what it really means to be influential today. Finally, it illustrates the ways in which brands are thinking up innovative and heart-warming ways to connect with audiences and how sometimes the best marketing tools have paws, whiskers, or feathers.

2. REVIEW OF LITERATURE

2.1 Definition of Petfluencers

Petfluencers those irresistibly cute animals lighting up social media feeds represent a unique fusion of "pet" and "influencer." From playful puppies and grumpy cats to stylish hedgehogs and talkative birds, these furry (or feathered) stars capture the hearts of millions with their quirky antics and picture-perfect charm. But they're far more than just adorable companions they are miniature celebrities, curating content that ranges from humorous skits and candid moments to sponsored brand endorsements. Through photos, videos, and even meme-worthy expressions, petfluencers evoke joy, laughter, and emotional connection, transforming casual scrolling into an uplifting experience.

Unlike their human counterparts, petfluencers thrive on authenticity and natural charisma. They don't need curated personas or expert opinions to win attention their appeal is rooted in their unfiltered innocence and relatability. This purity makes them incredibly trustworthy in the eyes of followers, enabling them to build loyal communities that often engage more actively than those of traditional influencers. Well-known petfluencers like *Doug the Pug*, famous for his expressive face and silly costumes, *Tuna the Chiweenie*, whose endearing overbite charmed millions, and *Nala Cat*, who's gentle demeanor turned her into a feline phenomenon, exemplify this charm (White, 2020).

These animal stars aren't just internet darlings they are serious marketing assets. Brands such as Google, Netflix, Petco, and others have partnered with petfluencers to tap into their massive reach and deep audience trust. What makes petfluencers particularly effective is their ability to humanize brands through emotional storytelling and visual appeal. Their content often humorous, cute, or heart-warming resonates across age groups and demographics, giving campaigns a universal touch that's hard to replicate with human influencers alone.

What began as a light-hearted trend has rapidly evolved into a commercially powerful movement within the broader influencer marketing industry. According to Hartama (2021), some petfluencers now command high earnings through brand deals, merchandise, appearances, and sponsored content. Studies have shown that petfluencer posts frequently outperform those of human influencers in terms of engagement likes, shares, and comments largely due to the genuine and feel-good nature of their content.

In a digital world oversaturated with polished personas and aggressive promotions, petfluencers offer a refreshing, emotionally driven alternative. Their content cuts through the noise with authenticity and charm, allowing brands to connect with audiences in a more heartfelt and approachable way. As social media continues to evolve, petfluencers are poised to remain a vital part of digital marketing strategies blending entertainment, trust, and emotional resonance in a way that few others can match.

2.2 Theoretical Foundations

Petfluencers' magnetic pull has its roots in the psychology of parasocial relationships, which are one-sided emotional connections individuals establish with media personalities, initially recognized by Horton and Wohl in 1956. Initially applied to explaining relationships with celebrities, news readers, or fictional personalities, parasocial relationships have found plentiful soil in the social media era, particularly around petfluencers (Lotun, 2022). What distinguishes petfluencers is the way they naturally and compellingly trigger feelings of love, empathy, and companionship. Their perceived innocence, sense of humor, and threat-free presence render them even more emotionally intimate than other human influencers (Maddox, 2022). Fans don't merely look up to these pets from a distance they experience a real sense of emotional proximity, as they bestow affection, loyalty, and even friendship onto them (Kim & Kim, 2020).

This emotional closeness directly carries over into trust and perceived authenticity, two of the most under-supplied and underserved in digital marketing. Research has indicated that the emotional connections made with petfluencers not only extend engagement but also impact purchasing behavior and brand loyalty (Di Cioccio et al., 2024). In contrast to human influencers, who can find themselves at the center of scandals, share polarizing views, or appear excessively polished, animal influencers are relatively scandal-free. Their "squeaky clean" public persona creates them perfect messengers of brand campaigns in need of a wholesome, scandal-free presence (Hu, 2024).

This trend aligns with the emotional branding strategy of brands attempting to create strong emotional bonds with consumers, not to sell products but to create experience-oriented, memorable experiences. In a digital market saturated with homogenous ads, emotional appeal is a strong differentiator. Petfluencers are particularly good at this, as their energetic play, expressive eyes, and affectionate interactions induce laughter, smiles, joy, nostalgia, or relaxation—all which form good connections with the brands that they endorse (Kansara, 2024).

What's so interesting is the way petfluencers incorporate products into their work in a manner that's both seamless and organic. Instead of employing hard-sell strategies, they organically feature products within realistic, ordinary situations such as a dog unboxing a treat with excitement or a cat relaxed on a branded blanket. They don't sit awkwardly or uncomfortably; they bring the audience into a lifestyle that's desirable but attainable.

Visual narrative is central to this emotional connection, particularly on visually-oriented platforms such as Instagram, TikTok, and YouTube Shorts. Petfluencers excel at this medium, with engaging, bite-sized narratives conveyed through short videos, images, and gifs. A fleeting frame of a puppy rolling over or a cat providing a spot-on side-eye can be humorous, personable, and endearing in an instant leaving a lasting impression far more impactful than copy-dense advertising (Margaron, 2024; Podhovnik, 2023). As argued by semiotic theorist Roland Barthes, images carry meaning that is both symbolic and emotive that goes beyond language (Oxman, 2010). In an acceleration-scrolling, attention-constrained digital environment, the capacity to bring viewers to a halt with one photograph or brief video is a significant competitive edge (Shamayleh, 2019).

Effectively, petfluencers occupy the nexus of emotional psychology, visual media, and online commerce. They provide brands a way to engage with audiences in terms that are honest, emotionally connected, and visually engaging. Through the exploitation of the profound parasocial attachments humans have for animals, and the potential of image-driven narrative, petfluencers continue to redefine what successful, heartfelt, and ethical marketing can be in the digital space.

2.3 Relevance in Digital Marketing and Consumer Psychology

Petfluencers are a strategic treasure trove for companies facing the challenges of contemporary digital marketing and consumer psychology (Kansara, 2024). Amidst a backdrop characterized by ad saturation, algorithmic white noise, and growing consumer cynicism, petfluencers represent a welcome respite that combines authenticity with emotive tenor. From a marketing point of view, they provide remarkable return on investment. Their content naturally reaches wide audiences, often going viral due to its feel-good nature, and consistently garners high levels of engagement (Ashtiani, 2012). This organic reach makes petfluencer campaigns cost-effective and efficient, especially in comparison to traditional advertising, which is frequently blocked, ignored, or distrusted by today's digitally-savvy consumers (Lee, 2023).

Unlike aggressive promotion copy, petfluencer posts come across as intimate and non-intrusive tending to look like a friend posting a sweet moment instead of a business promoting something. That “soft-sell” strategy is not only more appealing but also psychologically influential. Key to their success is affective conditioning a psychological process by which repeated viewing of a pleasant stimulus, such as a cute pet video, influences positive feelings toward an unrelated brand or product

(Pilley & Hinzmann, 2014). For example, when viewers are regularly shown a smiling golden retriever with a branded toy, the warmth and happiness with which they regard the dog become transferred to the brand itself. Gradually, this creates an unconscious preference what marketers like to call "brand warmth."

Another applicable notion is cognitive dissonance, which is a state in which individuals experience distress when their attitudes, beliefs, or behaviors are at odds (Eidelson & Eidelson, 2003). Traditional advertising tends to cause this tension by showing forceful sales messages that could be incongruent with a consumer's sense of self or values. On the other hand, petfluencer content alleviates this distress through the congruence of what viewers see with their emotional worlds. Instead of interrupting their social media experience, these posts augment it. Fans might unconsciously think, "I care about animals, and so does this brand, so it should be a brand I can trust." This congruence between content and customer values lowers friction and strengthens brand love.

Trust is a currency that cannot be neglected in the online world, and petfluencers are masters at creating it. Their appeal lies in seeming authenticity audiences feel that their material is authentic since it is about animals that are naturally pure and innocent. This emotional draw builds trust faster than traditional influencer marketing, which is why petfluencers are particularly effective in businesses where credibility and loyalty are key like pet care, lifestyle, well-being, and even travel (McEwen, 2005). A travel company, for instance, working with popular adventure dog account can place itself both as pet-friendly and emotionally compelling, generating interest among consumers who crave experiences over transactions.

Finally, petfluencers combine marketing science and emotional intelligence. By accessing behavior psychology through affective conditioning, reducing cognitive dissonance, and establishing trust they enable brands to create deeper, more engaged relationships with consumers. As the online space becomes even more populous and consumer attention increasingly difficult to secure, petfluencers are a remarkably effective and emotionally compelling marketing solution.

3. EVOLUTION OF PETFLUENCING

The rise of petfluencers didn't happen overnight it grew slowly as social media and our online habits evolved. Back in the early 2000s, the internet was a playground for quirky, user-made content, and pets quickly stole the spotlight. From Reddit and Tumblr's meme-driven corners to YouTube's funny and heart-warming animal videos, pets became accidental stars. These platforms showed how much people craved light-hearted, feel-good content that everyone could relate to. It wasn't just about news or information anymore people were online for connection, fun, and a quick emotional pick-me-up.

When Instagram launched in 2010 and TikTok followed in 2016, things really took off. These platforms, with their focus on visuals and short videos, were perfect for turning pets into digital icons. Take Grumpy Cat, whose real name was Tardar Sauce. She became a global sensation in 2012, all thanks to her perpetually unimpressed face. Her fame wasn't just a viral moment it was a game-changer. Grumpy Cat sparked memes, merchandise, media appearances, and even a Lifetime movie, showing that pets could be more than fleeting internet stars. They could be full-on brands with loyal fans and real marketing power.

Since then, petfluencing has grown into a polished industry. Apps like Pawbo, Petzbe, and Dogster let pet owners share curated content and build communities around their animals' lifestyles. Meanwhile, platforms like Instagram and TikTok added pet-themed filters, hashtags, and challenges that made pet content spread faster and wider. Today, petfluencing isn't just a hobby—it's a professional operation. Specialized agencies now manage petfluencers, handling everything from branding and sponsorships to content planning and monetization, much like they do for human influencers. These agencies help pets maintain consistent online personalities and land big partnerships.

What started as casual pet photos has turned into a powerful, emotionally engaging, and culturally significant corner of influencer marketing. Petfluencers bridge the gap between brands and people, using their authenticity, charm, and viral appeal to grab attention and build trust. As our online world keeps leaning into visuals and curated emotions, petfluencers aren't just sticking around they're reshaping how brands connect with us in the digital age.

4. PETFLUENCERS AND BRANDING STRATEGY

In today's digital marketing world, petfluencers have become powerful storytellers, weaving emotional connections, sparking consumer engagement, and crossing industry lines with ease. Unlike human influencers who often lean on polished lifestyles, expert knowledge, or aspirational vibes, petfluencers win hearts through a unique blend of authenticity, emotional pull, and universal charm. Their magic lies not in slick talk or celebrity clout but in their natural knack for spreading joy, comfort, and warmth through what seems like simple content. Picture a dog happily chewing on a branded toy, a cat lounging on a stylish pet bed, or a playful "unboxing" of gourmet treats these moments may look casual, but they're carefully crafted stories that weave products into everyday life in a way that feels effortless.

This subtlety is what makes them stand out. Petfluencer posts don't scream "ad" they feel like stories, which makes them more inviting and trustworthy. Instead of jarring viewers with obvious sales pitches, their content pulls people in with fun, eye-catching moments that just happen to feature a brand. This authenticity, whether it's genuine or carefully curated, builds consumer trust and keeps people engaged. That's why brands are teaming up with petfluencers not just to reach pet owners but to tap into diverse, emotionally invested communities, from wellness buffs to tech geeks and even fashion-forward folks.

At the core of petfluencer magic is the emotional bond they create. Years of research in consumer psychology show that emotions shape how we see brands, remember them, and stay loyal. Feelings like joy, amusement, or nostalgia can make a brand stick in our minds. Petfluencers deliver these warm, fuzzy emotions effortlessly. Their content sparks relatable, heart warming moments that, when tied to a brand, forge deeper, lasting connections with customers. This turns casual scrollers into devoted fans and one-time viewers into loyal brand champions.

What's truly remarkable is how versatile petfluencers are across industries. Sure, they shine in pet-related spaces like food, grooming, accessories, and vet care, but their influence stretches far beyond. They're strutting into fashion, modeling everything from high-end couture to streetwear; diving into tech, showcasing smart feeders, pet trackers, and AI-powered cameras; and even popping up in lifestyle areas like home décor, wellness, travel, and automotive brands. In these varied settings, petfluencers become symbols of comfort, companionship, and aspirational living, making the products they promote feel more human and relatable.

This ability to cross industries shows why petfluencers are more than a passing fad—they're a flexible, powerful branding tool that adapts to what today's consumers want. As people grow wary of traditional ads and crave authentic, emotionally rich content, petfluencers offer a fresh solution. Their mix of innocence, relatability, and storytelling charm lets brands connect in a way that feels real and meaningful.

In essence, petfluencers are the perfect blend of emotional influence, visual storytelling, and digital savvy, bridging the gap between commerce and connection in a way few other influencers can. As long as they keep evolving with tech and consumer moods, these four-legged (or feathered) stars will remain some of the most captivating ambassadors in the marketing world.

5. AUDIENCE AND CONSUMER BEHAVIOUR

Pet content monetization in the form of videos, images, or commercially branded pet merchandise poses significant ethical questions regarding the fate of the animals themselves. With increasing growth in petfluencer marketing comes increasing concern that these pets are not being treated ethically and with the respect they deserve in the race for interaction and dollars (Brockman et al., 2008). Most importantly, content creators and collaborating brands should be committed to ensuring that the animals involved are not only physically healthy but also emotionally sound never overworked, stressed, or subjected to hazardous or unnatural positions just for the sake of going viral (Farquer, 2015). Animal welfare should always be a major concern if this platform is to be ethical and sustainable (Sirgy & Lee, 2008).

Correspondingly, transparency in advertising is more and more a necessity. With increasing regulatory pressures, honesty and lawfulness in influencer marketing actions are in greater demand (Hartama, 2021). Among the important aspects of this is accurate disclosure properly identifying sponsored content such that audiences are not confused regarding the type of post (Shen et al., 2022). This openness not only maintains lawfulness but also contributes to upholding the confidence that is fundamental in petfluencer-audience relationships.

Another intricate issue is intellectual property and ownership rights. Since petfluencer content brings money in the form of merchandise, media licensing, and brand endorsements, the question of whether the creator, agency, or brand owns the content can result in disputes if not defined clearly beforehand (Carvalho et al., 2023). Terms of use and ownership must be clearly stated in contracts and agreements to prevent possible disputes.

Ultimately, upholding authenticity and social responsibility isn't merely a moral imperative it's a strategic imperative. Petfluencer marketing centered on honest storytelling, upholding animal dignity, and seeking to make a positive impact on audiences can foster richer, more significant relationships with followers (Di Cioccio et al., 2024). By doing so, it also protects the long-term integrity and credibility of the industry.

6. ETHICAL AND LEGAL CONSIDERATIONS

Monetizing pet content whether through videos, photos, or branded merchandise raises important ethical questions, particularly concerning the welfare of the animals involved. As petfluencer marketing grows, so too does concern over whether these pets are being treated ethically and humanely in the pursuit of engagement and profit (Brockman et al., 2008). Above all, content creators and partnering brands have a responsibility to ensure that the animals featured are not only physically healthy but also emotionally well never overworked, stressed, or placed in unsafe or unnatural situations merely for the sake of virality (Farquer, 2015). Respecting animal welfare must remain a top priority if this space is to operate ethically and sustainably (Sirgy & Lee, 2008).

At the same time, transparency in advertising is becoming increasingly important. As regulatory scrutiny intensifies, there is a growing demand for honesty and legal compliance in influencer marketing practices (Hartama, 2021). One crucial element of this is proper disclosure clearly labeling sponsored content so that audiences are not misled about the nature of the post (Shen et al., 2022). This transparency not only ensures legal compliance but also helps preserve the trust that is essential in petfluencer-audience relationships.

Another complex issue is intellectual property and ownership rights. As petfluencer content generates revenue through merchandise, media licensing, and brand deals, the question of who owns the content the creator, the agency, or the brand can lead to legal disputes if not clearly outlined in advance (Carvalho et al., 2023). Contracts and agreements must explicitly define ownership and usage rights to avoid potential conflicts.

Ultimately, maintaining authenticity and social responsibility is not just a moral obligation it's a strategic imperative. Petfluencer marketing that emphasizes genuine storytelling, respects animal dignity, and aims to positively influence audiences can build deeper, more meaningful relationships with followers (Di Cioccio et al., 2024). In doing so, it also safeguards the long-term credibility and integrity of the industry.

While popular and emotionally resonant, petfluencer marketing is already encountering major challenges with the online space growing more crowded. With the burst of content from both independent creators and large corporations, the novelty of pet-based campaigns grows less unique. As the space grows congested, it is increasingly difficult for any given campaign to really reach beyond that or hold viewers' attention. This saturation compels marketers to strive for greater levels of creativity and innovativeness, continually searching for new, unique perspectives to maintain content relevance and competitiveness.

Compounding the complexity is the unstable nature of social media algorithms. Sites regularly modify their feed-ranking protocols, shifting when, where, and how petfluencer posts appear in users' feeds. The changes can suddenly cutoff a campaign's visibility and activity, no matter its quality or popularity. For marketers, this translates to techniques that need to stay nimble and adaptable constantly evolving in response to platform changes in order to remain visible and effective.

Additionally, one of the biggest ongoing struggles in petfluencer marketing is illustrating long-term return on investment (ROI). Although figures such as likes, comments, shares, and followers are readily available, they provide only superficial information. Showing that a campaign translates into long-term brand affinity, customer retention, or boosted sales is considerably more complicated (and less quantifiable). This absence of transparent, long-term performance metrics can complicate it to justify marketing expenditure or to optimize approaches for subsequent campaigns.

Overall, as petfluencer marketing matures, brands need to contend with congested content landscapes, algorithmic uncertainty, and more stringent criteria for success beyond vanity metrics. Overcoming these obstacles is crucial not merely to ensuring the quality of individual campaigns, but to the credibility and sustainability of petfluencer marketing as a strategic tactic.

6. FUTURE TRENDS AND OPPORTUNITIES

The petfluencer space is on the cusp of an exciting new phase, fueled by accelerating technological innovation that's reshaping how brands interact with consumers. One of the most revolutionary trends is the emergence of AI-created and virtual petfluencers. These virtual personalities enable marketers to build perfect, always-on brand representatives without the ethical complications of working with real pets. Unencumbered by limitations such as fatigue, health issues, or unpredictability, virtual pets provide unlimited creative freedom, with the ability to deliver consistent, well-curated content that aligns beautifully with brand messaging. AI petfluencers also bring novelty and innovation to the table, allowing campaigns to cut through an increasingly competitive market. With their appearance fresh from scratch and ability to be programmed with desired behavior, they enable creative storytelling, brand mascots, and engaging campaigns that engage audiences particularly younger, digitally native audiences.

At the same time, increasing power from augmented reality (AR) and the metaverse is opening up new frontiers of involvement. AR experiences enable consumers to engage with virtual pets in real-time using their smartphones or AR-enabled devices, turning passive viewing of content into active, interactive experiences. These interactive experiences not only increase memorability but create enhanced emotional bonds with brands. The metaverse goes even further than this evolution, providing interactive digital worlds where petfluencers may "exist," engage, and form communities. Within these virtual worlds, fans can participate in events, experience live interactions, and even buy branded virtual products, ushering in completely new styles of brand loyalty and monetization without the constraints of existing platforms.

Simultaneously, developments in data analytics and personalization are propelling petfluencer marketing to a new era of accuracy and timeliness. Leveraging behaviour data and audience knowledge allows brands to provide highly personalized content and product suggestions that cater to specific tastes. This hyper-personalization not only increases user experience but also solidifies brand loyalty and propels long-term consumer engagement. In short, the convergence of AI, AR, and immersive virtual worlds is transforming petfluencer marketing into a more ethical, interactive, and data-driven space. These technologies provide brands with potent new tools to build emotional connections, create brand communities, and drive sustainable growth in an increasingly digital-first world.

7. TAKEAWAYS

Petfluencers have cut a special and powerful niche in today's marketing space by riding the strong emotional bonds humans share with animals. These online personalities real or imagined speak profoundly to fans who are attracted to genuine, heart-warming, and humor-filled content. Unlike regular influencers, petfluencers create a wholesome perception of innocence and genuineness that strongly builds trust and connectivity. Consequently, their audiences are more likely to be open to brand communications and to actively engage with or buy the products and services being promoted. For pet owners and animal lovers, petfluencers offer a strategic and emotionally resonant marketing opportunity.

But with power comes duty. Moral issues particularly about the handling of actual animals should be at the top of every campaign. Keeping pets safe, healthy, and free from being used for financial purposes is key to upholding the credibility of the petfluencer ecosystem. Being in compliance with legal regulations, such as clear disclosure of sponsorships and ad regulations compliance, is also paramount to sustaining trust and authenticity. Marketers have to balance art and authenticity and be agile enough to adapt in an ever-changing digital world. Social media channels constantly modify their algorithms, changing what is featured and consumed. To continue being effective, marketers have to continuously adjust their approach, maintain content freshness, and react to changes in audience behavior and platform trends.

In addition, creating honest, ethical partnerships with petfluencers based on respect and shared values can promote richer, longer-term brand affinity. Consumers today appreciate brands showing social responsibility, particularly in specialized groups such as pet owners. Here, petfluencer marketing focused on authentic storytelling and emotional connections makes an impact. New technologies also create new possibilities in the arena. AI-created petfluencers and augmented reality (AR) are creating new avenues for brands to experiment. These technologies enable brands to produce interactive, immersive content and connect with consumers in new, compelling ways without some of the ethics issues around genuine animal influencers.

Finally, what makes petfluencers so long-lasting is the fact that they humanize brands. By means of authentic, sentimental content that speaks to the masses, they create emotional connections that are difficult for standard advertising to emulate. As the virtual world continues to change, petfluencers are going to be a treasure in brand planning as long as innovation is sought out considerately, morally, and with ongoing emphasis on genuine connection.

8. CASE STUDY

Grumpy Cat, also known as Tardar Sauce, is perhaps the most legendary case of how a petfluencer can be developed from a mere internet meme to become a full-fledged marketing giant. She initially became popular in 2012 when pictures of her peculiarly "grumpy" face were being shared online on Reddit and won the hearts of millions of people everywhere. What started as a grassroots viral phenomenon soon became a strategic branding phenomenon. Grumpy Cat's owners rode the success by getting brand endorsements, licensing her face for just about every item of merchandise from calendars to mugs to clothing and even having a Lifetime movie made based on her called Grumpy Cat's Worst Christmas Ever. Grumpy Cat's success in marketing was rooted primarily in the emotional appeal she had for her audience; her unique appearance and offbeat personality invoked humour and identification that resonated well, building a loyal following. Brands that partnered with her were able to leverage this emotional connection, enabling them to acquire consumer trust and interest without using conventional, frequently intrusive, advertising techniques. At the height of her fame, Grumpy Cat earned millions of dollars from endorsements, merchandise, and licensing, illustrating the potent economic clout petfluencers can exert. This introduces of concept entertainment and marketing, which will help marketers. Her tale teaches several important lessons for marketers: authenticity must be paramount, emotional connection fuels fan devotion, branching out from social media into merchandise and media can supercharge influence, and expert management is essential to maximizing commercial benefit while keeping the pet healthy. Generally, Grumpy Cat illustrates how petfluencers are not so much a passing online trend but can turn into enduring, powerful players in the branding game.

Case Study 1: Jiffpom X Banana Republic – Fashion With a Furry Twist

Campaign Objective

To attract younger, digitally-native shoppers and boost brand engagement for Banana Republic's pet-friendly apparel.

Petfluencer Overview

Jiffpom, a Pomeranian with over **9 million followers on Instagram**, is known for his adorable outfits and high-energy videos.

Execution

- Custom-designed outfits for Jiffpom in Banana Republic's seasonal styles.
- A series of Instagram Reels and Story takeovers.
- Behind-the-scenes "Barkstage" content on TikTok.

Performance Metrics

- **Engagement Rate:** 7.8% (industry average is 1.22% for fashion)
- **Impressions:** Over **4.5 million** in the first week
- **Click-Through Rate (CTR):** 3.4% (compared to standard 0.8% for fashion ads)
- **Sales Impact:** 12% increase in traffic to Banana Republic's pet accessory section within 10 days of campaign launch.

Takeaway

The campaign was a hit because it blended visual storytelling with soft-sell aesthetics, leveraging Jiffpom's brand-safe persona to drive meaningful engagement.

Case Study 2: Nala Cat X Fresh Step – Pet Wellness With Purr-Sonality

Campaign Objective

To reposition Fresh Step's kitty litter brand as both fun and functional by reaching millennial pet owners.

Petfluencer Overview

Nala Cat, one of the most followed cats on Instagram with **4.5 million+ followers**, advocates for pet welfare and humane adoption.

Execution

- Co-branded "Litter with Love" campaign promoting Nala's rescue story.
- Monthly giveaways with Fresh Step merchandise.
- Short videos of Nala engaging with the product (walking in the litter, playful moments).

Performance Metrics

- **Video Views:** 3.2 million across platforms
- **Brand Sentiment:** +24% improvement in positive mentions (measured via Brandwatch)
- **User-Generated Content (UGC):** Over 18,000 posts under #LitterWithLove
- **Ad Recall:** 31% increase, compared to typical CPG campaigns (average is 18%)

Takeaway

Nala's authenticity and charitable image aligned well with Fresh Step's social responsibility strategy, making it a feel-good campaign with commercial and ethical wins.

Case Study 3: Doug the Pug X Netflix – Entertainment Meets Emotion

Campaign Objective

To promote the release of a Netflix family film using light-hearted, shareable pet content.

Petfluencer Overview

Doug the Pug, a social media celebrity with **over 13 million followers across platforms**, is known for comedic and highly relatable content.

Execution

- Doug "starring" in mini parody trailers of the movie.
- Instagram carousel posts featuring Doug dressed as various movie characters.
- Behind-the-scenes YouTube shorts with Doug on a movie set.

Performance Metrics

- **Engagement (likes, comments, shares):** 1.6 million within 72 hours
- **Hashtag Reach (#DougOnNetflix):** 9.3 million
- **Watch Time Lift (on Netflix landing page):** 18% increase over baseline
- **Cost-Per-Engagement (CPE):** $0.03 (vs. $0.14 for standard entertainment campaigns)

Takeaway

By creating emotional resonance through humor and nostalgia, Doug helped make the Netflix release a more personal and viral experience.

9. IMPLEMENTING ETHICAL GUIDELINES FOR ANIMAL WELFARE

Ensuring animal welfare in petfluencer marketing isn't just a moral obligation it's a reputational safeguard. Brands and content creators must move beyond vague principles and establish clear operational standards. Here are practical steps and policies:

1. DEVELOP AN ANIMAL WELFARE COMPLIANCE PROTOCOL (AWCP)
    - **VETERINARY OVERSIGHT:** Regular health check-ups for all featured animals, documented and reviewed by certified vets.
    - **PERFORMANCE LIMITS:** Set a maximum number of hours per day/week animals can participate in shoots or public appearances.
    - **CONSENT & SUPERVISION:** Require that all petfluencer content be created under the pet owner's direct supervision, with stress signals monitored.
    - **BANS ON CERTAIN PRACTICES:** Prohibit restrictive costumes, bright lights, loud environments, or use of behavior-altering substances.
2. ADOPT A CODE OF CONDUCT OR ETHICS CHARTER
    - Partner with organizations like the **American Humane Association** or **PETA** to align campaign standards with accepted animal rights practices.
    - Use the "No Harm, No Stress" pledge: content must be fun, natural, and stress-free for the animal.
3. THIRD-PARTY AUDITS & TRANSPARENCY
    - Employ third-party animal welfare consultants to review campaign concepts and footage.
    - Create a public-facing "Welfare Compliance Badge" on campaign materials to signal ethical standards.

10. MAINTAINING AUTHENTICITY AMIDST INCREASING COMMERCIALIZATION

Commercial partnerships risk eroding the charm that makes petfluencers so effective. To preserve authenticity:

1. CO-CREATION, NOT COMMAND
    - Empower petfluencers (and their owners) to shape creative direction. Campaigns should match the pet's personality and tone.
    - Example: Let a playful dog be goofy, not glamorous, if that's what their audience expects.
2. LIMIT SPONSORED CONTENT RATIO
    - Maintain a **70/30 balance**: No more than 30% of content should be branded. This sustains trust and keeps the feed authentic.
    - Use a "Brand Fit Matrix" to vet partnerships: Does the brand align with the pet's existing lifestyle?
3. STORY-DRIVEN, NOT PRODUCT-DRIVEN POSTS

- Embed the product in a relatable narrative:

Instead of "Here's our new dog shampoo," show the pet enjoying a playful bath with natural reactions, then casually highlight the product.

4. DISCLOSE TRANSPARENTLY, YET NATURALLY
    - Use intuitive and platform-native labels: "Partnered with @brand" or "Our favourite toy from @brand" rather than jarring legal disclaimers.
    - Integrate disclosures visually on-screen or in speech especially for video platforms like TikTok or YouTube Shorts.
5. COMMUNITY ENGAGEMENT > VIRALITY
    - Encourage UGC (User-Generated Content): Run campaigns where followers share their own pets using the same product.
    - Respond to comments, share follower stories, and repost tagged content to deepen emotional bonds.

Table 1. Real-world best practices & brand examples

Brand	Practice Adopted	Outcome
Petco	Hired certified animal behaviorists for campaigns	Increased campaign trust & reach
BarkBox	90% non-sponsored pet content policy	Built 2M+ strong organic community
Chewy	Features real customer pets, not actors	3x higher engagement rates
Blue Buffalo	Highlighted rescue pet stories, not just products	Improved brand sentiment by 18%

11. CONCLUSION

- Does the campaign respect the pet's natural behavior and wellbeing?
- Has the content been co-developed with the petfluencer's human handler?
- Are branded messages seamlessly embedded within the pet's daily context?
- Are you limiting ad density and maximizing organic storytelling?
- Is there transparent disclosure of sponsorships without disrupting the user experience?
- Are audience interactions being acknowledged, reposted, or rewarded?

As petfluencer marketing continues to scale, its sustainability depends on maintaining its original emotional truth. Ethical rigor and emotional integrity are not

REFERENCES

Ashtiani, J. (2012). Social Media Marketing for an Artist: Using Engagement to Build a Loyal Fan Base.https://www.theseus.fi/bitstream/handle/10024/55945/Thesis?sequence=1

Campbell, C., & Farrell, J. R. (2020). More than meets the eye: The functional components underlying influencer marketing. *Business Horizons*, *63*(4), 469–479. DOI: 10.1016/j.bushor.2020.03.003

Chase, B. (2020). *Strategy First: How Businesses Win Big*. Greenleaf Book Group. https://books.google.co.in/books?hl=en&lr=&id=Pcv1DwAAQBAJ&oi=fnd&pg=PT12&dq=Some+have+popped+up+in+Super+Bowl+ads,+teamed+up+with+giants+like+Amazon+or+Mercedes-Benz,+or+launched+their+own+pet+accessory+lines&ots=h71RdIDTAC&sig=Bko2YT3XW1fDlbWtDG8RlxHso_4&redir_esc=y#v=onepage&q&f=false

Di Cioccio, M., Pozharliev, R., & De Angelis, M. (2024). Pawsitively powerful: Why and when pet influencers boost social media effectiveness. *Psychology and Marketing*, *41*(7), 1614–1628. DOI: 10.1002/mar.22000

Eidelson, R. J., & Eidelson, J. I. (2003). Dangerous ideas: Five beliefs that propel groups toward conflict. *The American Psychologist*, *58*(3), 182. DOI: 10.1037/0003-066X.58.3.182 PMID: 12772423

Gil, C. (2021). *The end of marketing: Humanizing your brand in the age of social media*. Kogan Page Publishers. https://scholar.google.com/scholar?hl=en&as_sdt=0%2C5&q=Platforms+like+Instagram%2C+TikTok%2C+YouTube%2C+and+Facebook+have+changed+the+game%2C+moving+away+from+old-school+ads+to+something+more+personal%2C+genuine%2C+and+engaging&btnG=

Hartama, E. (2021). Possibilities of influencer marketing through pet Instagram accounts: a fast lane to a pet owner's pocket? https://urn.fi/URN:NBN:fi-fe2021072241653

Hasson, G. (2017). *Emotional intelligence pocketbook: Little exercises for an intuitive life*. John Wiley & Sons. url: https://books.google.co.in/books?hl=en&lr=&id=o-jFDQAAQBAJ&oi=fnd&pg=PA1&dq=Pets+spark+universal+emotions+joy,+laughter,+maybe+a+little+%E2%80%9Caww%E2%80%9D+that+brands+love+to+link+to+their+image&ots=NfyEew17BW&sig=S_Ue-ILEvxXlGx9CwDU3BAYlv5E&redir_esc=y#v=onepage&q&f=false

Holbrook, M. B. (2008). Pets and people: Companions in commerce? *Journal of Business Research*, *61*(5), 546–552. DOI: 10.1016/j.jbusres.2007.07.010

Hu, X. (2024). Presenting Global Brands with Celebrity Endorsement through Impression Management and Storytelling Techniques: A Case Study of 12 Brand Archetypes in Personal Care Product Category (Doctoral dissertation, Bangkok University). http://dspace.bu.ac.th/jspui/handle/123456789/5767

Jacobson, M. (2019). *Marketing madness: A survival guide for a consumer society*. Routledge., DOI: 10.4324/9780429038938

Kádeková, Z., & Holienčinová, M. (2018). Influencer marketing as a modern phenomenon creating a new frontier of virtual opportunities. *Communication Today, 9*(2). url: https://www.ceeol.com/search/article-detail?id=715881

Kansara, T. (2024). *Awwvertising strategy: exploring how cuteness impacts influencer marketing* (Doctoral dissertation, Concordia University). https://spectrum.library.concordia.ca/id/eprint/994095/1/Kansara_MSc_F2024.pdf

Kim, M., & Kim, J. (2020). How does a celebrity make fans happy? Interaction between celebrities and fans in the social media context. *Computers in Human Behavior, 111*, 106419. DOI: 10.1016/j.chb.2020.106419

Lee, H. H. (2023). *How Do Ad-Blockers Affect Various Stakeholders? Perspectives from Consumers, Marketers, and Legal Professionals*. Indiana University. https://www.proquest.com/openview/f2b2946ccf14ad8e4ad9f8766f20246b/1?pq-origsite=gscholar&cbl=18750&diss=y

Lindimore, J. (2020). People, Property, Or Pet-Influencers? *J. Animal & Env't L., 12*, 44. https://heinonline.org/HOL/LandingPage?handle=hein.journals/jael12&div=7&id=&page=

Lotun, S. (2022). *Social media for social good: Understanding, creating, and harnessing the strength of parasocial relationships* (Doctoral dissertation, University of Essex). https://repository.essex.ac.uk/33077/

Maddox, J. (2022). *The Internet is for cats: How animal images shape our digital lives*. Rutgers University Press., https://books.google.co.in/books?hl=en&lr=&id=zsaHEAAAQBAJ&oi=fnd&pg=PP1&dq=When+it+comes+to+petfluencers,+these+connections+hit+harder+because+animals+come+off+as+sweet,+harmless,+and+funny&ots=EGdl6LFK5p&sig=W2z7bpuaATZEihKzhpRuRftuBH4&redir_esc=y#v=onepage&q&f=false

Margaron, A. (2024). *The Eye, the Heart, and the Network: the Humanistic Blogging of Tumblr's Webweaving Community* (Doctoral dissertation, Concordia University). Margaron_MA_F2024.pdf

McEwen, W. J. (2005). *Married to the brand: Why consumers bond with some brands for life*. Simon and Schuster. https://books.google.co.in/books?hl=en&lr=&id=ydpDCwAAQBAJ&oi=fnd&pg=PA1&dq=That+makes+them+perfect+for+industries+like+pet+care,+lifestyle,+wellness,+or+even+travel,+where+their+authentic+appeal+turns+fans+into+loyal+customers.&ots=TKYWITQ3iY&sig=KQNUrs96UdRVyM9hzW79yEKUFUs&redir_esc=y#v=onepage&q&f=false

Micle, B. G. (2020). The Influencer Role of Charismatic Renewal in the Spirituality of Post-Covid Society. *Dialogo, 7*(2), 247-259. https://www.ceeol.com/search/article-detail?id=964351

Oxman, E. (2010). Sensing the image: Roland Barthes and the affect of the visual. *SubStance*, *39*(2), 71–90. DOI: 10.1353/sub.0.0083

Pilley, J. W., & Hinzmann, H. (2014). *Chaser: Unlocking the genius of the dog who knows 1000 words*. Simon and Schuster. https://books.google.co.in/books?hl=en&lr=&id=Cve7DwAAQBAJ&oi=fnd&pg=PT10&dq=%E2%80%A2%09Pilley,+J.+W.,+%26+Hinzmann,+H.+(2014).+Chaser:+Unlocking+the+genius+of+the+dog+who+knows+1000+words.+Simon+and+Schuster.&ots=ve7kZg5lKl&sig=HMAdj40B31hRcF0C7ZG26trylYE&redir_esc=y#v=onepage&q&f=false

Podhovnik, E. (2023). *Purrieties of Language*. Cambridge University Press., https://books.google.co.in/books?hl=en&lr=&id=womzEAAAQBAJ&oi=fnd&pg=PR12&dq=Petfluencers+shine+at+spinning+short,+captivating+tales+through+photos,+videos,+or+gifs&ots=ineT4xT5vO&sig=98Pxxl08o6-qCp-ZT7ioxa9C8ys&redir_esc=y#v=onepage&q&f=false

Shamayleh, G. (2019). *Engagement and Monetization on Instagram Pet Influencer Communities* (Doctoral dissertation, Concordia University). Shamayleh_MSc_F2019.pdf

Shamayleh, G., & Arsel, Z. (2025). Digital Affective Encounters: The Relational Role of Content Circulation on Social Media. *The Journal of Consumer Research*, , ucaf023. Advance online publication. DOI: 10.1093/jcr/ucaf023

Spee, L. B., Hazel, S. J., Dal Grande, E., Boardman, W. S., & Chaber, A. L. (2019). Endangered exotic pets on social media in the Middle East: Presence and impact. *Animals (Basel)*, *9*(8), 480. PMID: 31344918

Weaver, H. (2013). Becoming in Kind": Race, Class, Gender, and Nation in Cultures of Dog Rescue and Dogfighting. *American Quarterly*, *65*(3), 689–709. DOI: 10.1353/aq.2013.0034

Weber, D. (2016). *Brand seduction: How neuroscience can help marketers build memorable brands.* Red url: Wheel/Weiser.https://books.google.co.in/books?hl=en&lr=&id=sd9EDwAAQBAJ&oi=fnd&pg=PT10&dq=Their+posts+are+wholesome,+fun,+and+tug+at+your+heartstrings,+making+them+perfect+for+brands+wanting+to+create+warm,+fuzzy+feelings&ots=Gn_gnnzzz0&sig=zDuYQwKqyv8YFwWLdC1E6MkA4eA&redir_esc=y#v=onepage&q&f=false

White, E. J. (2020). *A unified theory of cats on the internet.* Stanford University Press., https://books.google.co.in/books?hl=en&lr=&id=fuD5DwAAQBAJ&oi=fnd&pg=PA1934&dq=Doug+the+Pug,+rocking+goofy+outfits+with+his+squishy+face,+Tuna+the+Chiweenie,+whose+quirky+looks+became+an+internet+sensation,+or+Nala+Cat,+a+fluffy+feline+with+a+talent+for+melting+hearts&ots=ax0W5X3MSl&sig=fKYVPNP3Ykwx6d2OssomIFYfB7g&redir_esc=y#v=onepage&q&f=false

KEY TERMS AND DEFINITIONS

Petfluencer: A blend of "pet" and "influencer," petfluencers are animals typically cats, dogs, or other domestic or exotic pets that have large followings on social media platforms. They generate high engagement through content such as images, videos, and memes, and often participate in brand collaborations or sponsored campaigns. Their charm lies in natural authenticity and emotional appeal.

Influencer Marketing: A form of social media marketing involving endorsements and product placements from individuals or entities who have a dedicated social following and are viewed as experts or trusted figures within their niche. In this context, petfluencers serve as unique influencer personas.

Parasocial Relationship: A one-sided emotional bond where an individual feels a deep connection to a media figure or character (in this case, a petfluencer) despite no direct interaction. This helps drive trust and loyalty in marketing contexts.

Affective Conditioning: A psychological process where repeated exposure to a pleasant stimulus (e.g., cute pet videos) results in positive feelings being associated with unrelated products shown in that context. This principle is key to understanding why petfluencer marketing is effective.

Soft-Sell Strategy: A subtle approach to advertising that avoids hard-selling tactics. Petfluencers naturally integrate products into everyday content, making promotions appear more genuine and trustworthy.

Authenticity: In influencer marketing, authenticity refers to the perceived genuineness of content. Petfluencers are considered highly authentic due to their non-verbal, emotion-evoking presence, unfiltered behaviors, and the innocence associated with animals.

Emotional Branding: A marketing approach that builds brands by evoking emotions such as joy, nostalgia, or affection. Petfluencers excel at emotional branding due to their ability to trigger heartfelt responses from followers.

Visual Narrative: Storytelling through images or short-form videos. Petfluencer content leverages visual narratives to capture attention quickly and elicit emotional engagement on platforms like Instagram and TikTok.

Trust Currency: Refers to the value of consumer trust in a digital marketing ecosystem. Petfluencers often hold high levels of trust due to their perceived innocence, which can translate into increased brand loyalty and credibility.

Virtual Petfluencer: Digitally created animal avatars or characters powered by artificial intelligence and animation, used for branding or entertainment purposes. They eliminate ethical concerns related to real animal welfare and offer limitless creative potential.

Brand Fit Matrix: A tool or method used by marketers to evaluate whether a specific petfluencer aligns with a brand's identity, values, and audience expectations. Ensures authenticity and consistency in collaborations.

User-Generated Content (UGC): Content created and shared by fans or consumers rather than brands. Petfluencers often encourage UGC through challenges, campaigns, or reposts, which deepens community engagement and broadens brand visibility.

Ad Disclosure: A transparent labeling practice that indicates when a piece of content is sponsored or paid for. This is crucial in maintaining ethical standards and audience trust in petfluencer marketing.

Cognitive Dissonance: The discomfort experienced when behavior or information conflicts with beliefs or values. Petfluencer content often reduces this tension by aligning emotionally with viewers' values, thus easing brand communication.

Ethical Petfluencing: A practice of ensuring animals involved in influencer campaigns are treated with respect, safety, and care. It includes compliance with welfare standards, transparency in advertising, and authenticity in storytelling.

Chapter 8

Traveling Tails: Exploring Airline Innovations in International Pet-Onboard Services

Jagjit Singh
https://orcid.org/0009-0001-3680-3556
Chandigarh University, India

Aman Kumar
Chandigarh University, India

Manish Kumar Sharma
Chandigarh University, India

Shikha Sharma
Chandigarh University, India

ABSTRACT

As pet ownership increases globally and the human-animal bond strengthens, consumer demand for pet-inclusive travel experiences is rising. This study investigates innovations in international airline services that accommodate pets onboard, reflecting shifting customer expectations and a growing pet travel market. Focusing on a case study of selected international airlines that allow pets in the cabin—such as Lufthansa, Air France, Turkish Airlines, and American Airlines—this research explores policy frameworks, service models, and customer satisfaction related to pet-onboard travel. Through content analysis of airline policies, passenger reviews, and expert interviews, the study highlights best practices, logistical challenges, and

DOI: 10.4018/979-8-3373-4342-6.ch008

regulatory considerations associated with traveling with pets across borders. It further examines how pet-friendly services contribute to airline brand positioning, customer loyalty, and revenue diversification.

1. INTRODUCTION

The growth in the number of people who own pets worldwide, in conjunction with the growing emotional bond that individuals and families have with their pets, has resulted in a substantial shift in the way consumers travel. The perception of pets as part of the family has shifted from that of animals to that of family members, resulting in an increased demand for pet-friendly air travel options. The airline industry has responded by adopting laws that permit pets, particularly dogs, to travel in the cabin of the aircraft. The cost, weight constraints, breed restrictions, paperwork requirements, and route availability of these policies, on the other hand, vary significantly from one airline to the next. As a result of this inconsistency, travellers are left feeling confused, the quality of service they get is diminished, and animal welfare regulations are put to the test. Because of this, it is not only relevant but also important to conduct a comprehensive comparison of regulations regarding the transportation of pets in the cabin. This will help improve transparency, provide consumers with information, and potentially promote regulatory consistency. Because of the rising trend of pet companionship extending to travel, airlines have progressively altered their services to accept dogs in the passenger cabin. This trend is expected to continue developing (Santos & Murça, 2025). The purpose of this research study is to provide a comparative examination of the rules regarding the transportation of dogs inside the cabins of 10 major airlines. These airlines are Aegean Airlines, Air Canada, Air Europa, Alaska Air, American Airlines, Air France, Delta, French Bee, JetBlue, and Lufthansa. By examining major policy parameters, such as limits on weight and carrier size, travel expenses, age and breed constraints, and authorization for foreign travel, the research intends to provide information to pet owners worldwide (Yue et al., 2025). This article aims to assist travelers in making educated choices about the safe and compliant transportation of their pets over the air by highlighting variances and similarities across airline rules (Albert et al., 2025).As a result of the widespread perception that dogs are members of the family, the practice of traveling with our four-legged friends has grown more common. To meet this demand, a few airlines have begun allowing dogs to travel in their aircraft cabin under certain circumstances. On the other hand, these regulations differ significantly from one carrier to another, which impacts the travel experience for both the owners of pets and the creatures themselves. A few semi-private airlines may provide choices for bigger breeds of dogs. Still, most commercial airlines restrict in-cabin travel to small dogs within a certain weight and size capacity restriction. If pet owners want to travel with their dogs without experiencing any needless stress or problems, they must thoroughly understand the complexities related to these laws (Zhang et al., 2025).

The purpose of this article is to give a comprehensive examination of the in-cabin dog travel regulations established by 10 notable airlines. By analyzing essential aspects such as weight and carrier size constraints, travel prices, breed and age restrictions, and foreign travel authorization, this research provides pet owners with a helpful resource that may assist them in navigating the needs of airlines. By using this comparison approach, our objective is to determine which airlines are the most accommodating to canine travelers, therefore contributing to the development of a travel sector that is more pet-friendly (Wandelt et al., 2025).

Figure 1. Documents by type

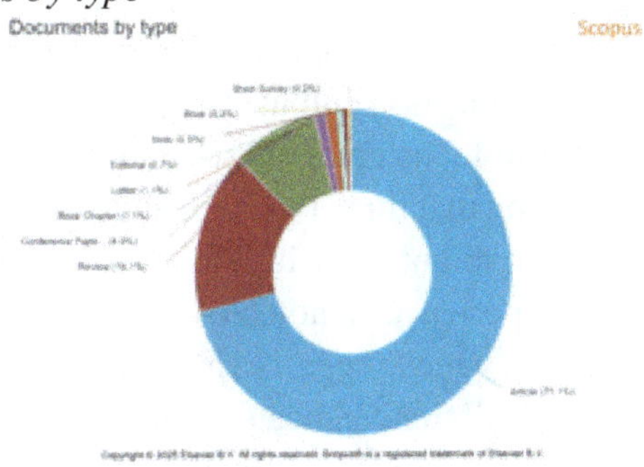

(source https://www.scopus.com/)

Figure 1 shows the chart presents the distribution of document types indexed in Scopus, emphasizing the dominance of research articles within the realm of academic publishing. Articles comprise the most significant portion at 71.1%, highlighting their role as the primary channel for sharing original research findings. Subsequently, review articles account for 16.1%, serving a vital role in synthesizing existing knowledge. Conference papers represent 8.9%, highlighting the significance of academic conferences in disseminating preliminary research findings. Other document types contribute relatively more minor proportions: book chapters and letters each represent 1.1%, editorials account for 0.7%, notes make up 0.5%, while books and short surveys are the least common, each comprising only 0.2%. The chart clearly illustrates that journal articles hold the position of being the most utilized and impactful format within the academic community.

Figure 2. Documents per year

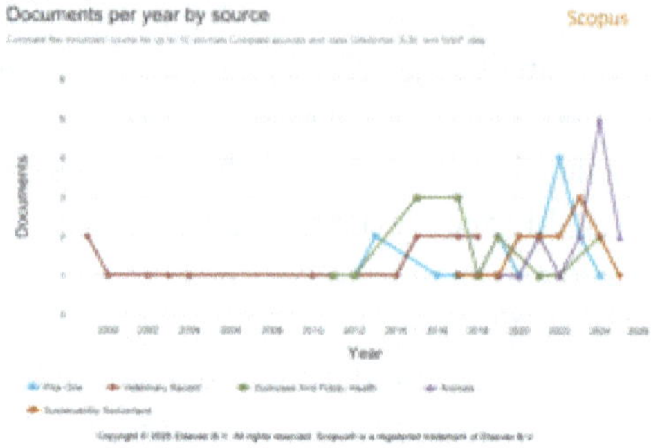

(source https://www.scopus.com/)

Figure 2 shows the line graph illustrates the yearly publication trends from diverse sources indexed in Scopus concerning pet and animal studies, covering the period from 2000 to 2025. Throughout the timeline, the Veterinary Record demonstrates a steady yet modest level of publication output. The period from 2013 to 2016 witnessed a significant increase in focus on zoonoses and public health, indicating a surge in scholarly inquiry during that time. Plos One and Sustainability Switzerland exhibit inconsistent yet moderate output, with Plos One reaching its peak around 2022. The journal Animals experienced a notable increase in publications in 2024, reaching a peak of 5 documents, which suggests a marked growth in significance and research engagement. This overall trend indicates an increasing variety and quantity of academic examinations of animal-related subjects in numerous esteemed journals.

Figure 3. Document by year

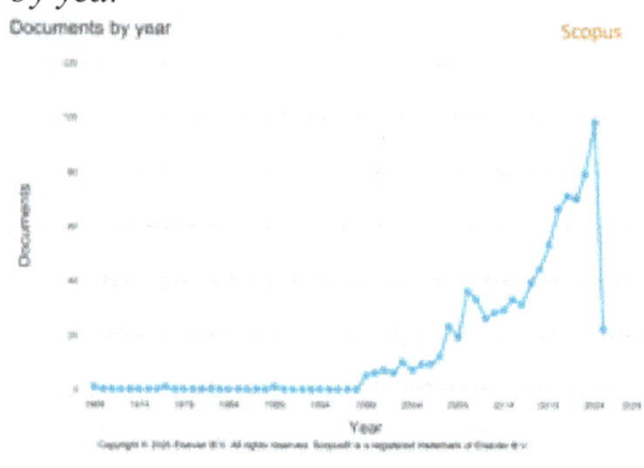

(source https://www.scopus.com/)

Figure 3 shows the publication trend from 1969 to 2025, as depicted in the Scopus data, reveals a significant evolution in scholarly interest over time. For several decades, from 1969 to the late 1990s, the volume of documents remained minimal, indicating limited research activity in the field. However, starting around the year 2000, there was a gradual rise in publications, which accelerated considerably after 2008. This upward trajectory continued steadily, with notable peaks post-2015, indicating a surge in academic engagement and an expansion of research dimensions. The year 2024 marked the highest output, with over 100 documents published—reflecting peak interest and possibly increased funding or relevance of the topic. A sudden drop in 2025 is likely due to incomplete indexing rather than an actual decline. Overall, the trend highlights a growing and sustained academic focus that has matured significantly in the last two decades.

Figure 4. Document by subject area

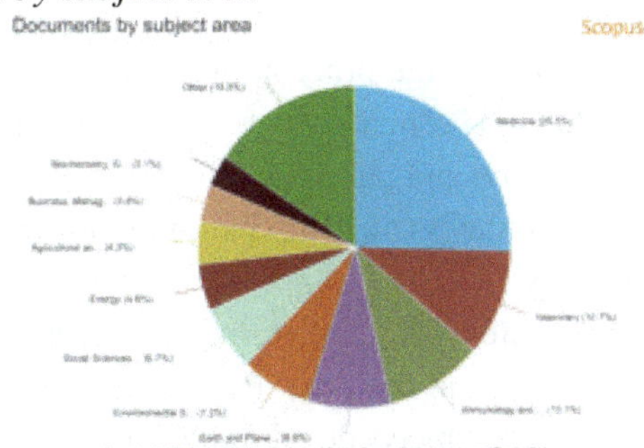

(source https://www.scopus.com/)

Figure 4 labeled "Documents per year by source" illustrates the trends in publications from various academic journals over time, highlighting the shifting interests among sources. Between 2000 and approximately 2010, various sources, including Veterinary Record, Zoonoses and Public Health, and PLOS ONE, exhibited a consistent and modest output, generally fluctuating between one and two documents per year. Following 2010, there is a clear expansion and rise in engagement. The journal Zoonoses and Public Health experienced a notable increase in activity from 2013 to 2016, whereas Plos One exhibited intermittent spikes, reaching its highest point in 2022. The journal Animals exhibited a significant rise in 2024, with five documents marking the highest individual contribution from any source in a single year. The observed fluctuations suggest an increase in academic focus on topics related to animal and public health, particularly over the past decade, driven by global challenges such as zoonotic diseases, sustainability, and the ethical treatment of animals.

2. BACKGROUND

Segmentation of the Pet Travel Services Market

The worldwide pet travel services market has experienced considerable growth since 2018 and is projected to continue its expansion until 2030, driven by increasing pet ownership, stronger emotional bonds with companion animals, and a rising demand for pet-friendly travel facilities. The market is categorized by travel type into domestic and international pet travel, reflecting customers' varied mobility choices for both short-haul and long-haul routes. The market is segmented by application into transportation, which pertains to ordinary travel logistics, and relocation, including the long-term or permanent movement of pets, usually associated with migration or job changes. The segmentation by pet type indicates a pronounced predominance of dogs and cats, while other animals, including rabbits and birds, constitute a minor percentage. The market has adopted digital transformation in booking modes, including online and phone bookings, in addition to conventional offline channels; nevertheless, the former is expanding more rapidly because of its ease and real-time availability.

North America predominates the market in service maturity and customer awareness, followed by Europe and the Asia-Pacific area. In North America, the U.S. market has experienced advanced development in all categories, exhibiting steady demand for both domestic and international travel. Meanwhile, Canada and Mexico are also witnessing significant growth, particularly in relocation services. Likewise, Europe boasts robust marketplaces in countries such as Germany, the United Kingdom, France, Italy, Spain, and the Nordic countries (Denmark, Sweden, and Norway), featuring organized services designed for both short- and long-distance pet transportation. The Asia-Pacific market, comprising prominent nations such as China, Japan, India, Australia, South Korea, and Thailand, is experiencing robust growth due to rising pet adoption rates and increasing middle-class incomes. Latin America, especially Brazil and Argentina, is witnessing a gradual acceptance, while the Middle East and Africa—featuring countries such as the UAE, Saudi Arabia, South Africa, and Kuwait—are emerging as new growth areas for luxury pet services and foreign relocations.

The research includes comprehensive qualitative and quantitative analysis, with geographical and application-based segmentation, providing insights into industry trends, market drivers and constraints, and development prospects. It integrates Porter's Five Forces and PESTEL research to assess the competitive and regulatory landscapes. The market is evaluated quantitatively by revenue (in USD million) from 2018 to 2030, including predictions for each sector and region. The research includes a company-level analysis, encompassing financial performance, strategic developments, product benchmarking, and competitive positioning, thereby providing a comprehensive overview of the key entities in the pet travel services industry. This segmentation framework enables a detailed understanding of customer behaviour, service deficiencies, and opportunities for innovation across various regions and service categories.

Figure 5. Pet Travel Service Market

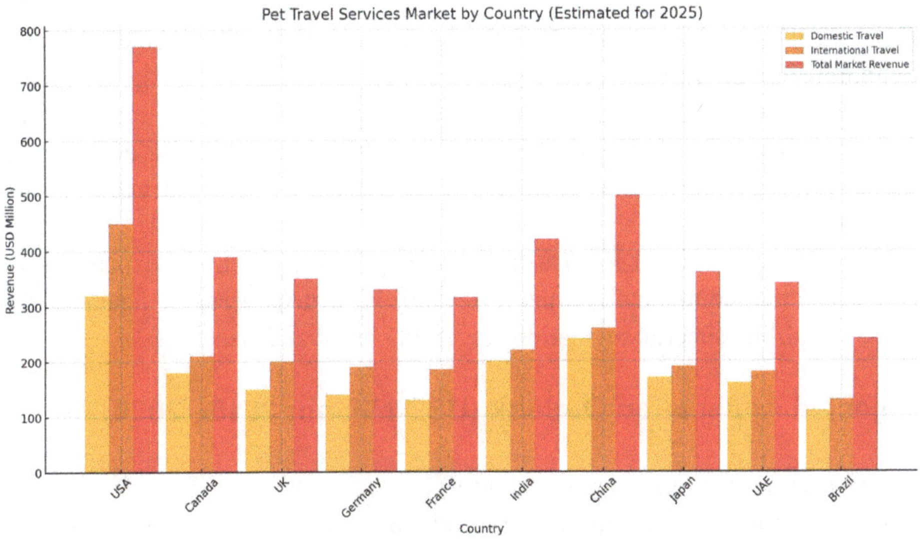

Here is a bar chart comparing estimated **pet travel services market revenue** across major countries for 2025. It shows:

- **Domestic travel revenue**
- **International travel revenue**
- **Total market revenue**

The USA and China lead in total revenue, with India, Canada, and Germany also showing significant market activity. This chart illustrates the regional strength and scale of the pet travel(Underwood, 2000).

Market Segmentation: Global Pet Travel Services Market (2018-2030)

OverviewThe worldwide pet travel services industry has seen considerable transformation in the last ten years. The significant rise in pet ownership, especially among millennials and Gen Z, has transformed the perception of pets as essential family members, hence altering travel dynamics. Pet travel has evolved from a recreational activity to a significant sector in both domestic and international flight travel. This segmentation examines trip type, application, pet kind, booking methods, and regional insights, offering a comprehensive market analysis.

Travel Category Forecast (USD Million; 2018 - 2030)

The pet travel industry is divided into two primary categories: Domestic Travel and International Travel.

Domestic Travel: The rise in inter-city relocations, vacations, and weekend excursions has made domestic pet travel more desirable. Airlines and ground transportation providers offer cabin and freight services designed explicitly for short-haul journeys.

International pet travel is influenced by long-term relocations, expatriate pet owners, and transcontinental journeys. It entails intricate paperwork, health certificates, and airline-specific regulations regarding breed and size.

Projected Application Outlook (USD Million; 2018 - 2030)

Pet travel services are categorized into:

Transportation: Pertains to routine travel plans for recreation, tourism, or brief visits.

Move: Entails the permanent or semi-permanent migration of pets resulting from the owner's move. Services include comprehensive pet relocation, quarantine administration, and international compliance.

Forecast for Pet Types (USD Million; 2018 - 2030)

Market segmentation by pet categories comprises:

Dogs constitute the predominant sector due to elevated ownership rates and sociability, particularly when travelling.

Cats: The second-largest sector; need specific servicing methods owing to anxiety and crate compatibility.

Others: Comprises rabbits, birds, guinea pigs, and exotic pets—experiencing modest growth due to increasing urban interest.

Projected Booking Outlook (USD Millions; 2018 - 2030)

Online and phone bookings are the predominant booking methods due to their digital accessibility, seamless connectivity with airline systems, and ease of use.

Offline Bookings: Conventional travel agencies, relocation firms, and physical airline counters continue to cater to specific sectors, especially in areas without digital infrastructure.

Regional Forecast (USD Million; 2018 - 2030)

North America

North America continues to dominate the global pet travel services sector, characterized by well-structured airline regulations and robust regulatory oversight. The United States generates the most revenue, followed by Canada and Mexico.

In terms of travel type, domestic travel predominates in the U.S., while Mexico and Canada demonstrate an increase in international pet relocation services.

By Application: Transportation prevails in the U.S., whereas relocation is gaining momentum.

By Pet Type: Dogs are the most predominant, followed by cats and other unusual animals.

Online reservations are widespread due to the widespread use of smartphones and airline connectivity.

Europe

Europe has a meticulously organized pet travel framework shaped by EU-wide travel and quarantine regulations.

Germany, France, the United Kingdom, Italy, and the Nordic countries excel in pet-friendly services.

Significant demand for domestic leisure and foreign relocations.

Booking continues to be a hybrid approach—digital for younger pet owners and traditional for older demographics.

Asia-Pacific

This area represents the most rapidly expanding market, with China, India, Japan, and Australia seeing a significant increase in both domestic and international pet travel.

Growth is driven by urbanization, the humanization of pets, and rising disposable incomes.

India and China are emerging as significant centres for relocation due to expatriate migration.

Latin America

Countries such as Brazil and Argentina have begun formalizing the pet travel marketplaces.

Domestic travel is increasing owing to enhanced airline coverage.

Infrastructure is constrained, creating opportunities for emerging service providers.

Middle East and Africa

This area, spearheaded by the UAE, Saudi Arabia, and South Africa, is evolving to meet the needs of expatriates.

Luxury and premium travel services prevail in this domain, particularly for overseas relocations.

Offline booking remains a substantial priority.

Qualitative Assessment

Industry Overview: The pet travel service industry has evolved from specialized relocation services to a comprehensive consumer market.

Emerging trends include AI-driven crate monitoring, digital pet passports, stress-reduction technologies, and customized in-flight meals for pets.

Factors: Urban pet ownership, normalization of travel, millennial demand, dual-income families.

Constraints Include Regulatory impediments, a lack of standards, variability across airlines, and elevated expenses.

Strategic Insights

Porter's Five Forces: Moderate competitive rivalry; significant hurdles to entry stemming from licensing and compliance; moderate consumer bargaining power.

PESTEL Examination:

Political: Affected by transnational regulations.

Economic: Closely linked to middle-class affordability.

Social: Increasing acceptance of pets in public areas.

Technological advancements: Improved crate design, biochips, and digital pet health data.

Environmental: Issues with carbon emissions and sustainability in pet freight transportation.

Legal: Adherence to IATA, USDA, DEFRA, and customs regulations.

Market Competition

Prominent global entities include PetRelocation, Airpets International, Blue Collar, and Jet-A-Pet.

Strategies include partnerships with airlines, cellphone tracking, pet concierge services, and tiered pricing structures.

Quantitative Analysis

Projection Interval: 2018 to 2030

Essential Metrics:

Annual sales increase by category of travel and pet

Projected Compound Annual Growth Rate by area

Market penetration of booking modalities

Comparative revenue analysis for leading airlines providing pet-friendly accommodations

This segmentation illustrates a dynamic market that corresponds with changing consumer lifestyles and mobility requirements. The pet travel services sector is expected to grow in both scope and geographical reach worldwide by 2030, driven by a heightened focus on comfort, transparency, and safety.

The global pet travel services market has experienced significant evolution over the past decade. With a marked increase in pet ownership, particularly among millennial and Gen Z demographics, the notion of pets as integral family members has redefined travel dynamics. From leisure to relocation, pet travel is no longer a niche but a growing segment across both domestic and international air corridors. The following segmentation explores travel type, application, pet type, booking methods, and regional insights, providing a detailed market outlook.

Travel Type Outlook (USD Million; 2018 - 2030)

The market for pet travel is segmented into two core categories: **Domestic Travel** and **International Travel**.

- **Domestic Travel**: The increasing popularity of inter-city relocations, vacations, and weekend getaways has made domestic pet travel highly sought after. Airlines and ground transport operators offer cabin and cargo services tailored for short-haul trips.
- **International Travel**: International pet travel is driven by long-term relocations, expatriate pet owners, and transcontinental travel. It involves complex documentation, health certifications, and airline-specific policies regarding breed and size.

Application Outlook (USD Million; 2018 - 2030)

Pet travel services bifurcate into:

- **Transportation**: Refers to regular travel arrangements for leisure, tourism, or short-term visits.
- **Relocation** involves the permanent or semi-permanent migration of pets due to owner relocation. Services include end-to-end pet relocation, quarantine management, and compliance with cross-border regulations.

Pet Type Outlook (USD Million; 2018 - 2030)

Market distribution by pet type includes:

- **Dogs** represent the largest segment due to higher ownership rates and their sociability during travel.
- **Cats**: Second-largest segment; require distinct service protocols due to anxiety and crate compatibility.
- **Others** include rabbits, birds, guinea pigs, and exotic pets—categories that are growing gradually in response to rising urban interest.

Booking Outlook (USD Million; 2018 - 2030)

- **Online & Phone Bookings**: Dominates the booking mode due to digital access, integration with airline systems, and convenience.

- **Offline Bookings**: Traditional travel agents, relocation companies, and walk-in airline counters continue to serve niche segments, particularly in regions that have not yet been digitized.

Regional Outlook (USD Million; 2018 - 2030)

North America

North America remains the global leader in pet travel services, characterized by highly organized airline policies and robust regulatory oversight. The United States drives the most significant revenue, followed by Canada and Mexico.

- **By travel type, domestic** travel is more prominent in the U.S., whereas Mexico and Canada exhibit rising international pet relocation services.
- **By Application**: Transportation dominates in the U.S., with relocation gaining traction.
- **By Pet Type**: Dogs remain dominant, followed by cats and exotic pets.
- **By Booking**: Online bookings are prevalent due to high smartphone penetration and airline integration.

Europe

Europe showcases a highly structured pet travel ecosystem influenced by EU-wide travel and quarantine policies.

- Countries such as Germany, France, the U.K., Italy, and the Nordics lead in terms of pet-friendly services.
- High demand for both domestic leisure and international relocations.
- Booking remains hybrid—online for younger pet parents and offline for elder populations.

Asia Pacific

This region is the fastest-growing market, with China, India, Japan, and Australia witnessing a surge in both domestic and international pet travel.

- Urbanisation, pet humanisation trends, and rising disposable incomes are driving the growth of the pet care industry.
- India and China are emerging hubs for relocation due to expatriate movement.

Latin America

Countries like Brazil and Argentina have begun formalizing pet travel markets.

- Domestic travel is rising due to better airline coverage.
- Infrastructure remains limited, presenting opportunities for new service providers to emerge.

Middle East & Africa

Led by UAE, Saudi Arabia, and South Africa, this region is developing in response to expat demands.

- Luxury and premium travel services are particularly prominent in this area, especially for international relocations.
- Offline booking still plays a significant role.

Qualitative Analysis

- **Industry Overview**: The pet travel service sector has evolved from niche relocation services to a full-fledged consumer market.
- **Trends**: AI-based crate monitoring, digital pet passports, stress-reducing technology, and personalized in-flight pet meals are gaining popularity.
- **Drivers**: Urban pet ownership, travel normalization, millennial demand, dual-income households.
- **Restraints** Include Regulatory barriers, a lack of standardization, airline inconsistency, and high costs.

Strategic Insights

- **Porter's Five Forces**: Medium competitive rivalry; high barriers to entry due to licensing and compliance; moderate bargaining power of consumers.
- **PESTEL Analysis**:
- Political: Influenced by cross-border regulations.
- Economic: Strongly tied to middle-class affordability.
- Social: Rising acceptance of pets in public spaces.
- Technological: Enhanced crate design, bio-chips, and online pet health records.
- Environmental: Concerns about carbon footprints and sustainability in pet cargo logistics.

- Legal: Compliance with IATA, USDA, DEFRA, and customs.

Competitive Landscape

- Global players include PetRelocation, Airpets International, Blue Collar, and Jet-A-Pet.
- Strategies include forming alliances with airlines, utilizing mobile tracking, offering pet concierge services, and implementing tiered pricing models.

Quantitative Analysis

- **Forecast Period**: 2018 to 2030
- **Key Metrics**:
- Year-on-year revenue growth by travel and pet type
- Forecasted CAGR by Region
- Market penetration for booking modes
- Comparative revenue performance for major carriers offering pet-friendly cabins

This segmentation reflects a dynamic market that aligns with evolving consumer lifestyles and mobility needs. With an increasing emphasis on comfort, transparency, and safety, the pet travel services industry is poised to expand both in terms of depth and geographic reach globally by 2030.

3. LITERATURE REVIEWS

Despite the subject's growing importance, academic research in this field remains fragmented. Despite numerous studies on topics such as animal welfare in transit, discussions about emotional support animals (ESA), and general concerns regarding pet transportation, there is a lack of comprehensive comparative research that focuses explicitly on in-cabin travel rules among major international airlines. Through the compilation, analysis, and interpretation of airline-specific data in a manner that is both consumer-friendly and academically rigorous, this study fills a critical need in the existing literature. Those responsible for developing airline policies may use this document as a strategic benchmarking tool in addition to serving as a reference guide for passengers.

Additionally, the reasoning is based on the fact that the post-pandemic airline policy overhaul, particularly about ESAs, has led to uncertainty. In 2020, for example, the United States Department of Transportation made significant changes by allowing airlines to ban ESAs. This development prompted airlines worldwide to reassess their regulations regarding the transportation of pets in the cabin. In this context, the report describes a critical period of change in the airline sector, characterised by the process of standardising, revising, or introducing new laws related to animal flight.

In addition to this, the research makes a contribution to the field of consumer behaviour by incorporating models such as the Theory of Consumer Decision-Making, as well as service quality and quantity. This theoretical foundation enables the study to extend beyond a basic comparison of rules and investigate how pet-related regulations influence traveller choices, perceptions of service quality, and overall satisfaction. Through this approach, the study establishes a connection between the operational practices of airlines and the psychology and expectations of passengers. This subject is often overlooked in the literature on aviation and hospitality.

From a practical standpoint, the study helps passengers navigate the numerous airline regulations and make informed decisions that prioritise their pet's safety and convenience. In addition to this, it offers airlines and regulatory bodies insights supported by data, which can be used to enhance policy formulation, standardise essential features (such as carrier size and price structure), and address service gaps. The findings of this research may, from a policy perspective, lead to long-term changes in the sector. These improvements may include the establishment of guidelines for international pet travel or the implementation of minimum service requirements.

Lastly, the use of current data (2023–2025), real-world airline websites, insights from the International Air Transport Association (IATA), and academic literature from a variety of fields, including veterinary science, tourism, transportation, and law, lends legitimacy to the research and ensures that it is of interdisciplinary significance. Not only does the article establish its significance to passengers and airlines, but it also proves its relevance to legislators, animal welfare groups, and hospitality experts. This is because the research draws on such a broad domain.

Current Practices in International Pet Travel

Airline pet travel policies have historically classified animals as either cargo or cabin passengers, taking into account weight and breed restrictions. Nonetheless, investigations such as those conducted by Landers et al. (2025) have identified a notable policy shift, especially following the pandemic, influenced by a rise in demand for in-cabin animal services, alterations in emotional support animal (ESA) classifications, and changing passenger expectations (Amer et al., 2023).

Animal Welfare and Health Management Onboard

Lambert et al. (2025) and Rideout et al. (2025) highlighted the difficulties associated with ensuring animal welfare in confined, high-stress environments, such as aeroplane cabins. Challenges include confinement stress, temperature fluctuations, and hydration issues. The acceptance of CBD oils and various welfare-enhancing treatments is on the rise, although inconsistencies in regulations remain evident (Edwards, 2007).

Zoonotic Disease Risks in Companion Animal Travel

Erol et al. (2025) and Tao et al. (2025) provided insights into the transmission risks of zoonotic diseases and the challenges of monitoring during flights, emphasizing the need for real-time health sensors and digital veterinary records to enhance pet care on board (Sah et al., 2022).

Emotional well-being and affective experiences

Shi (2025) posited that animals undergo affective states that impact their behaviour and stress reactions in environments managed by humans. This finding underpins advancements in the airline industry, such as virtual reality pet training tools (Omran et al., 2025) and designated relaxation areas for pets in airports, which aim to alleviate pre-flight anxiety (Bennetts et al., 2022).

Expectations of Pet Owners and Innovations in Services

Nguyen et al. (2025) illustrated that the psychological ownership that pet owners feel significantly influences the demand for services akin to those available for human travellers — including customized pet meals, digital pet passports, and onboard pet attendants. Bostenaru Dan et al. (2025) investigated disaster evacuation strategies for pets, providing valuable insights applicable to emergency protocols on flights (Ying et al., 2021).

Innovative Approaches for Improved Safety and User Experience

Omran et al. (2025) and Rideout et al. (2025) have identified emerging technological innovations, including wearable pet health trackers, AI-based distress monitors, and mobile applications for live pet tracking. These developments reflect broader trends in the integration of pet technology within airline service frameworks. Trade in Wildlife and the Transportation of Companion Animals .Lambert et al. (2025)

investigated the impact of the global wildlife trade on animal welfare, emphasizing the logistical, health, and ethical challenges associated with long-distance animal transport. The findings indicate similarities in the management of stress, safety, and welfare for domesticated pets during international air travel (Abdukayumov et al., 2023).

Risks of Zoonotic Diseases Associated with Travelling with Companion Animals

Erol et al. (2025) analysedanalyzed zoonotic disease risks in domestic cats, emphasisingemphasizing the importance of molecular detection methods, which are crucial for preventing cross-species transmission. The insights provided are crucial for maintaining health compliance and safety standards in the protocols governing international pet transportation (Donmez et al., 2022).

Innovative Diagnostics for Canine Air Travellers

Tao et al. (2025) conducted a comparative analysis of ultrasonographic diagnostics in wild and domestic canines, emphasizing the need for portable diagnostic solutions during transit. The findings advocate for the incorporation of health assessment tools within airline services for pets, especially during long-haul flights (Menon et al., 2020).

Development of Protocols for Therapy Animals and Service Use

Gabel et al. (2025) examined contemporary methodologies in animal-assisted therapy programs, emphasizing the importance of structured handling and welfare monitoring standards. These protocols provide valuable insights into optimal practices for managing pets and service animals within the cabin environment of aviation (Visnes et al., 2021).

Emotional Bonds and Anticipated Service Outcomes

Nguyen et al. (2025) investigated the impact of psychological ownership of pets on consumer expectations regarding service quality and personalization. Their efforts align with the increasing need for customized, welfare-focused pet travel experiences (Malancus et al., 2024).

Changes in Airline Policies Regarding Service Animals

Landers et al. (2025) performed a retrospective analysis of policy changes related to in-flight service animals following the pandemic. The findings indicate a growing focus on regulatory oversight and the necessity for humane, efficient protocols for pet travellers (Liao et al., 2024).

Insights on Disaster Resilience for the Evacuation of Airborne Pets

Bostenaru Dan et al. (2025) examined digital disaster resilience tools specifically for pet evacuations, providing valuable insights that can be applied to emergency response strategies in airline contexts, including flight rerouting and contingency pet-care systems (Rafique et al., 2025).

Emotional Conditions of Animals During Transportation

Shi (2025) examined the emotional states and affective performance in animals, highlighting the need to alleviate fear and distress during travel. These findings support the implementation of welfare-focused innovations such as relaxation zones and in-flight pet companionship services (Clément et al., 2020).

Identifying Deficiencies in Pet Health Record Keeping

Numerous investigations have highlighted deficiencies in standardized standardizedinternational pet health documentation, which frequently result in stress and procedural delays (e.g., Lambert et al., 2025; Erol et al., 2025). Implementing integrated digital pet passports has the potential to optimize services and improve welfare outcomes (Stavleu et al., 2024).

Exploring the Dynamics of Owner-Pet Separation Anxiety During Travel

Gabel et al. (2025) highlighted separation anxiety in therapy animals as a significant welfare concern, reflecting similar dynamics in pet-owner relationships during flights. This underscores the necessity for advancements such as onboard pet viewing systems and provisions for owner-pet interaction during transit (Donmez et al., 2022).

4. RESEARCH METHODOLOGY

This study employs a qualitative-comparative research methodology to examine and interpret the in-cabin pet travel policies of various global airlines. The aim is to provide a detailed comparison using publicly accessible policy information, highlighting aspects such as cost, convenience, service quality, and accessibility for travelers accompanied by dogs. Comparative Analysis of In-Cabin Pet Travel Regulations Among Selected International Airlines

As the number of pet owners who desire to travel with their animals increases, the airline industry has adapted by establishing pet travel regulations. Nonetheless, these regulations differ significantly among airlines in terms of service quality, cost, and accessibility. This research seeks to do a comparative examination of in-cabin canine travel regulations among 10 prominent international airlines: Aegean Airlines, Air Canada, Air Europa, Air France, Alaska Airlines, American Airlines, Delta, French Bee, JetBlue, and Lufthansa. The objective is to help pet owners choose the most suitable airline based on several practical considerations.

This research has three objectives: first, to assess the scope and clarity of in-cabin pet policies of each airline; second, to compare related costs and logistical requirements; and third, to evaluate the airlines' geographical coverage and distinctive customer services that improve the travel experience for pet owners.This research utilizes a comparative descriptive technique. Airlines were chosen based on their publicly accessible rules that specifically permit dogs to ride in the cabin. Essential characteristics for comparison include allowed pet species, weight and carrier constraints, pet travel charges, international route availability, and significant policy attributes or limitations. Data were primarily collected from airline websites, customer service information pages, and industry sources, including the rules of the International Air Transport Association (IATA).The results are presented in a comparison table, which outlines the key data points. This includes designated weight limits (often between 8–10 kg), carrier dimensions stipulations, pricing brackets (commonly $50 to $125 each journey), and limitations such as breed prohibitions or disqualification from premium aircraft seats. Alaska Airlines and JetBlue distinguished themselves by providing economical and adaptable policies, whilst Lufthansa and Air France offered comprehensive international networks and well-established pet assistance services.Analysis reveals that while the majority of airlines offer comparable services, notable disparities exist in cost structures, pet capacity restrictions, and booking protocols. Certain airlines, such as JetBlue and Delta, offer loyalty or support programs, like JetPaws, that enhance the consumer experience. Conversely, inexpensive or leisure airlines, such as French Bee, may provide fewer services and impose higher weight limitations. In summary, Alaska Airlines, JetBlue, and Lufthansa distinguished themselves as frontrunners in harmonizing cost-effectiveness, convenience, and pet safety. The research highlights the need for uniformity in pet travel regulations, including the definition of carrier dimensions and the streamlining of reservation processes. It also advises visitors to investigate the criteria of each airline beforehand and to assess their pet's temperament and comfort before choosing in-cabin travel.

In the future, airlines are encouraged to refine their pet policies by enhancing transparency, offering tiered services based on pet size or breed, and ensuring greater international alignment with global aviation safety standards. Regulatory authorities may consider establishing common norms to reconcile the disparities among airlines. The study's results may serve as a valuable resource for passengers, airline personnel, and policymakers seeking to improve pet travel services within the aviation sector.

Research Design

The study employs an exploratory and descriptive approach. The study employs a cross-sectional comparative methodology, focusing on ten airlines that permit dogs to travel in the cabin. The design facilitates the recognition of both similarities and differences among various policy parameters, including weight limits, carrier dimensions, pet fees, route coverage, and service flexibility. The study framework does not incorporate fieldwork or experimental methods; instead, it utilizes secondary data sources, allowing for an extensive geographical and organizational range.

Population and Sample

The study encompasses all international airlines that allow in-cabin travel for pets, specifically dogs. A purposive sample of ten airlines was chosen from this population, focusing on the clarity, availability, and completeness of their in-cabin pet policy documentation. The airlines included in the sample are:

The following airlines allow flying with dogs in-cabin:

1. Aegean Airlines
2. Air Canada
3. Air Europa
4. Air France
5. Alaska Air
6. American Airlines
7. Delta
8. French Bee
9. JetBlue

10. Lufthansa

The selection of these carriers is based on their operational diversity, global reach, and significance to passengers traveling with pets.

Statement of the Problem

The increasing trend of pet ownership has prompted the airline industry to implement pet-friendly policies, particularly for in-cabin travel. Nonetheless, there are notable differences among airlines in these policies regarding expenses, route availability, weight limitations, and the quality of service provided. The absence of clear, consistent, and user-friendly guidelines leads to uncertainty and restricts consumer options. This study seeks to fill the existing gap by analyzing the in-cabin dog travel policies of various international airlines to identify which carriers provide the most dependable and economical services for pet owners.

Objectives of the Study

- The objective is to analyze the in-cabin pet travel policies of ten airlines
- The objective is to examine airline services with a focus on the structure of pet fees, limitations on carrier sizes, and weight allowances.

Research Questions

- What are the primary distinctions in in-cabin dog travel policies across various airlines?
- What is the influence of fees, carrier requirements, and weight restrictions on passenger decision-making?

Hypotheses

H1: A notable disparity exists in the costs associated with pet travel among the chosen airlines.

H2: Airlines that provide extensive international route options tend to have more accommodating pet travel policies.

Significance of the Study

This study offers valuable insights for individuals who frequently travel by air and wish to bring their dogs with them. This provides them with distinct, comparative insights into airline policies, enabling them to make well-informed decisions. Furthermore, the findings can assist airlines in establishing more uniform and clear pet policies while also serving as a resource for policymakers and tourism stakeholders who are promoting improved travel conditions for companion animals. Through the identification of optimal practices, this study enhances the inclusivity and traveler-friendliness of the aviation ecosystem.

Scope and Limitations

This study compares the in-cabin dog travel policies of ten international airlines. The study does not assess cargo pet transport, service animal regulations, or policies for other species unless allowed in-cabin. Information was collected from official airline websites and publicly accessible sources as of 2025; any policy changes occurring mid-year may not be included. Furthermore, the analysis did not include a quantitative examination of user experience data, such as customer reviews, which could have limited the understanding of passenger satisfaction beyond the declared policies.

5. DATA ANALYSIS AND FINDINGS

The investigation is based solely on secondary data sources. Information regarding the policy was gathered from: Websites of official airlines and documentation for customer support

Guidelines for pet travel by IATA, Announcements from airlines and frequently asked questions

Publications from the aviation sector and credible pet travel blogs In instances where clarification was necessary, customer service representatives were engaged through email or chat to verify ambiguous policy details. Data collection occurred from April to June 2025.

Data Analysis Techniques

The analysis involved a comparative content approach, with the findings systematically organized into a tabular format utilizing Microsoft Excel. All airlines underwent evaluation based on standardized criteria that included:

- Permitted species of pets
- Weight and carrier restrictions
- In-cabin pet fee (adjusted to a similar currency scale)

- Access to routes and services

Table 1. Regulations Policies (Source: Airlines official sites)

Airline	Max Weight (kg)	Max Carrier Size (cm)	Cost (USD)	International Allowed	Min Age (weeks)	Carrier Type	Notes
Aegean Airlines	8	55 x 40 x 23	35-65 EUR	Yes	12	Leak-proof, ventilated	Breed restrictions; one dog per passenger
Air Canada	10	27x40x55 (soft), 23x40x55 (hard)	50-118 CAD	Yes	12	Leak-proof, ventilated	Size limits vary by aircraft
Air Europa	10	55 x 35 x 25	27-165 USD	Yes	12	Leak-proof, ventilated	Up to 3 dogs per carrier
Alaska Air	9	43x28x24 (soft), 43x28x19 (hard)	100 USD	Yes	8	Leak-proof, ventilated	Max 2 carriers if buying adjacent seat
American Airlines	9	Varies	125 USD	Yes (restrictions apply)	Not stated	Leak-proof, ventilated	Flight length and breed restrictions
Air France	8	46 x 28 x 24	40-125 EUR	Yes (restrictions apply)	10-15	Leak-proof, ventilated	No intercontinental Business Class cabin pets
Delta	N/A	Varies	75-200 USD	Yes	10-16	Leak-proof, ventilated	Many breed, seat, and destination restrictions
French Bee	8	43 x 35 x 20	50 EUR	Yes	Not stated	Leak-proof, ventilated	Only 4 pets per flight
JetBlue	9	43 x 31 x 21	125 USD	Yes	Not stated	Leak-proof, ventilated	Some destination restrictions
Lufthansa	8	55 x 40 x 23	50-110 EUR	Yes	12-16	Soft-sided, leak-proof	Multiple pets allowed if under 8kg total

Table 1 depicts Many international airlines allow pets to travel in the cabin under specific conditions. Most require leak-proof, ventilated carriers with size and weight restrictions, typically between 8-10 kg. Carrier dimensions vary by airline, with soft and hard options available. Minimum pet age ranges from 8 to 16 weeks. Costs differ widely, from 27 USD to 200 USD depending on the airline, destination, and aircraft type. Some airlines permit multiple pets per carrier or per flight, while others enforce strict breed, seat, and route limitations. Notably, policies on Business Class travel, intercontinental flights, and adjacent seat bookings also vary significantly.

Table 2. Airlines Pet Charges (Source: Airlines official sites)

Airline	Pet In-Cabin Fee
1. Aegean Airlines	€35 (domestic) / €65 (international; may vary by season)
2. Air Canada	CAD $50–$59 (Canada/USA) / CAD $100–$118 (international)
3. Air Europa	USD $27–$55 (within Europe) / USD $165 (long-haul)
4. Air France	€40 (domestic) / €30–€125 (international)
5. Alaska Air	USD $100 each way
6. American Airlines	USD $125 each way
7. Delta	USD $125 (within North America) / USD $200 (international) / USD $75 (to Brazil)
8. French Bee	€50 each way
9. JetBlue	USD $125 each way
10. Lufthansa	€50 (domestic) / €60 (within Europe) / €80–€110 (intercontinental)

Table 2 shows Airlines charge varying fees for in-cabin pet travel, depending on route and destination. Domestic fees typically range from €35 to USD $125, while international and long-haul rates can reach up to USD $200. Some carriers, like Aegean Airlines and Lufthansa, adjust prices seasonally or by region, while others maintain flat fees. Delta, for example, charges differently for Brazil-bound flights. Fees are usually charged each way and vary by currency based on the airline's country. French Bee, Alaska Air, and JetBlue offer simple, one-way rates, while Air France, Air Canada, and Air Europa apply flexible pricing depending on flight distance and region.

6. CONCLUSION

Preparation for Traveling with Pets

Instructions Tailored to Each Airline:

- Passengers flying with Aegean Airlines are responsible for ensuring that their dogs have sufficient food and water throughout the journey, including any transfer periods (Sun et al., 2025).
- Although specialized pet food services are not specified, customers are recommended to carry the required supplies for their dogs whenever they travel with Air Canada (Varenna et al., 2025).

- Air Europa does not mention pet feeding services specifically; travellers should make appropriate preparations (Bakir et al., 2025). 1 Air France India (Indian) +1 for AA Cargo
- Air France's website does not mention pet food services; travellers should make preparations at their own discretion.
- Pet food services are not explicitly mentioned, so travelers should prepare accordingly.
- Four hours before the scheduled departure time, it is advised that dogs be fed by American Airlines. A small bag of dry food may be taped to the top of the kennel by passengers so that they can utilize it if there are delays. Cargo from AA
- Pet feeding services are not mentioned on the Delta website; travelers should adequately prepare themselves.
- Pet food services are not explicitly mentioned, but travelers should prepare according to the situation.
- There is no particular mention of pet food services on JetBlue; travelers are expected to make appropriate preparations.
- However, the Lufthansa website does not mention pet food services; customers should make appropriate preparations.
- Feeding Schedule: To avoid any pain, you should feed your pet a few hours before the journey. Cargo from AA
- You should bring a small quantity of dry food with you on the flight and ensure that your pet has access to water. +1 for AA Cargo Support for the French Bees +1
- Comfort objects, such as a favorite blanket or toy, may help relieve stress and provide a sense of familiarity. Cargo from AA
- The carrier's requirements include ensuring that it has enough ventilation, is not prone to leaks, and is comfortable for your cat.

Documentation and Legal Requirements

Necessary Documentation for In-Cabin Canine Travel

Traveling with dogs in the cabin requires meticulous planning, particularly regarding paperwork. The particular criteria differ significantly according to the airline and the nations of departure and destination. Although many local airlines may not need paperwork, most overseas flights impose rigorous standards to safeguard animal welfare and mitigate the transmission of zoonotic illnesses (Greger, 2007).

1. ***Requirements for Domestic and International Travel***: Documentation requirements for domestic flights are often modest. For example, Southwest Airlines does not need documentation for in-cabin dogs; nonetheless, possessing your pet's health documents is often prudent. Conversely, several airlines, like Aegean Airlines, mandate a health booklet even for domestic flights (Buenavista et al., 2021). For overseas travel, the paperwork gets more extensive. Typically, the accompanying papers are necessary:Microchip Certification Rabies Vaccination Certification Animal Health Certification Supplementary Vaccination Records Rabies Titer Test Results (if applicable) Parasite Treatment Certification (Martins & Cró, 2022)

   2 Microchip Certification: A microchip is a small electrical device embedded under the pet's skin, usually in the neck region. It has a distinctive identifying number that vets or shelters may scan to access the owner's contact details (Rose, 2016).Numerous airlines and nations require that dogs be microchipped before travel, particularly for overseas flights. Even when not obligatory, microchipping is strongly advised as a precautionary step. It significantly enhances the likelihood of recovery if a dog becomes lost while traveling (Theaker, 2020).Location for Acquisition: Your local veterinarian or animal welfare organization, such as the RSPCA, may execute the microchipping process and provide the necessary certification (Masilamani & Ganapathy, 2020).

   3 Certificate of Rabies Vaccination: Rabies is a lethal illness that presents considerable public health hazards. Consequently, most nations and airlines require evidence of rabies vaccination for your dog.The rabies vaccine must be provided at least 30 days before and no more than 12 months before the trip date. A registered veterinarian must provide the certificate, which must include information about the vaccination manufacturer, batch number, and administration date (Crozet et al., 2021).

   4 Animal Health Certificate (AHC): An Animal Health Certificate (AHC) is an essential document a licensed veterinarian provides. It verifies that your pet is sufficiently healthy for air travel and without infectious illnesses (Dadhich et al., 2021).For foreign travel, the certificate often requires endorsement by the appropriate national authorities, such as: USDA (United States Department of Agriculture) for travelers from the U.S. CFIA (Canadian Food Inspection Agency) for travelers from Canada. The certificate is generally valid for 10 days from issuance and must include all transit and arrival locations (Kumar, 2019).

   5 Supplementary Vaccination Certificates: Depending on your location, your dog may require immunizations in addition to rabies. For instance: Turkey requires vaccinations for parainfluenza, leptospirosis, parvovirus, bordetella, hepatitis, and distemper.Other nations may mandate vaccines for canine influenza or kennel cough.These immunizations safeguard your dog from contracting or transmitting illnesses endemic to the destination area (Haghani, 2022).

6 Rabies Titer Examination: Certain nations, especially those with rigorous biosecurity protocols, mandate a rabies titer test. This test evaluates the concentration of rabies antibodies in your dog's blood to verify whether the vaccination has conferred sufficient protection (Suijkerbuijk et al., 2020).

7 Titer test procedure:

Your veterinarian collects a blood sample no sooner than 30 days after rabies vaccination.

The specimen is sent to a certified laboratory.

Results must demonstrate an antibody concentration of no less than 0.5 IU/ml.

You must wait three months from the day the sample was collected before traveling.

Your veterinarian will provide a certificate verifying successful outcomes (Wolf et al., 2024).Countries often needing a titer test include those in the European Union, Australia, Japan, and New Zealand.

8 Certificate of Parasite Treatment:

To secure entry into several nations, dogs must undergo treatment for internal and external parasites. The therapy must be delivered within a designated time range (often 24 to 120 hours) before entrance.

Frequently needed therapies comprise: Cestodes (e.g., Echinococcus) Fleas and ticks Nematodes and cestodes

Before reserving a flight, pet owners have to:

Contact the airline to enquire about their unique regulations regarding pet travel. Confer with a veterinarian to establish a vaccine and documentation timetable. Initiate the procedure well ahead of time—certain documentation and tests, like the rabies titer test, require months of preparation.Maintain all original papers and copies in a systematically arranged folder throughout travel.Proactively comprehending and organizing the necessary documentation will guarantee adherence to airline and national rules, enhancing safety and reducing the stress of the voyage for both you and your pet (Giannitrapani, 2018).

Table 3. Airlines Pet Charges

Airline	Allowed Pets	Breed Restrictions
Aegean Airlines	Small dogs and cats (combined weight with carrier ≤ 8 kg)	Certain breeds may be restricted; specific details not publicly listed.
Air Canada	Small dogs and cats (combined weight with carrier ≤ 10 kg)	No specific breed restrictions mentioned for in-cabin travel.
Air Europa	Small dogs and cats (combined weight with carrier ≤ 8 kg)	Certain breeds may be restricted; specific details not publicly listed.
Air France	Small dogs and cats (combined weight with carrier ≤ 8 kg)	Brachycephalic breeds (e.g., Boxers, Pekingese, Shih Tzus, Persian, Burmese cats) allowed but may face health risks; consult a vet before travel.
Alaska Airlines	Small dogs and cats; domesticated rabbits and household birds (excluding Hawaii and international flights)	Brachycephalic breeds may travel in the cabin but are prohibited in the cargo hold.
American Airlines	Small dogs and cats (combined weight with carrier ≤ 9 kg)	Brachycephalic breeds are prohibited in the cargo hold; no specific restrictions for in-cabin travel.
Delta Air Lines	Small dogs, cats, and household birds (on domestic flights)	Brachycephalic breeds may travel in the cabin; restrictions apply for cargo transport.
French Bee	Small dogs and cats (combined weight with carrier ≤ 8 kg)	No specific breed restrictions mentioned.
JetBlue	Small dogs and cats (combined weight with carrier ≤ 9 kg)	No specific breed restrictions mentioned.
Lufthansa	Small dogs and cats (combined weight with carrier ≤ 8 kg)	Brachycephalic breeds may travel in the cabin; restrictions apply for cargo transport.

(Source: Airlines official sites)

Table 3 shows Most airlines allow small dogs and cats to travel in-cabin, typically with a combined pet and carrier weight limit between 8–10 kg. Some, like Alaska Airlines and Delta, also permit rabbits and household birds on certain routes. Breed restrictions vary: while several airlines like Air Canada, French Bee, and JetBlue don't publicly list specific in-cabin breed bans, others caution against brachycephalic (short-nosed) breeds like Boxers, Pekingese, and Persians due to health risks during flight. Cargo transport for these breeds is often restricted. Alaska, American, Delta, and Lufthansa allow such breeds in-cabin but with advisories or restrictions for cargo travel.

Table 4. Airlines Routes (Source: Airlines official sites)

Airline	Continents Flown
Aegean Airlines	Europe, Asia, Africa
Air Canada	North America, Europe, Asia, Oceania
Air Europa	Europe, North America, South America
Air France	Europe, Africa, Asia, North America, South America
Alaska Air	North America, Central America
American Airlines	North America, South America, Europe, Asia, Caribbean
Delta	North America, Europe, Asia, South America, Oceania
French Bee	Europe, North America, Oceania
JetBlue	North America, Central America, South America, Caribbean
Lufthansa	Europe, North America, Asia, Africa, South America

Table 4 shows Airlines offering in-cabin pet travel serve a wide range of global destinations. Aegean Airlines covers Europe, Asia, and Africa, while Air Canada's routes extend across North America, Europe, Asia, and Oceania. Major carriers like Air France, American Airlines, Delta, and Lufthansa operate on multiple continents, including Europe, Asia, Africa, North and South America, with Delta and Air France also reaching Oceania. JetBlue and Alaska Air primarily serve North America, Central America, and the Caribbean. French Bee connects Europe, North America, and Oceania, while Air Europa's network includes Europe, North America, and South America, offering varied international pet travel options.

Table 5. Airlines official booking sites (Source: Airlines official sites)

Airline	Official Pet Travel Website
Aegean Airlines	www.aegeanair.com/en/travel-info/pet-travel
Air Canada	www.aircanada.com/ca/en/aco/home/plan/pet-travel.html
Air Europa	www.aireuropa.com/us/en/aea/travel-information/passengers/pets.html
Air France	www.airfrance.com/US/en/common/guidevoyageur/pets.htm
Alaska Airlines	www.alaskaair.com/content/travel-info/pets
American Airlines	www.aa.com/i18n/travel-info/special-assistance/pets.jsp
Delta	www.delta.com/us/en/pet-travel/overview
French Bee	www.frenchbee.com/en/travel-with-pets
JetBlue	www.jetblue.com/pets
Lufthansa	www.lufthansa.com/us/en/pets

Table 5 shows how customer can book their pets if they full fill condition and book their seats via above official websites which is just one click away.

Table 6. Airlines details related Pets

Airline	Allowed Pets	Weight Limit (Pet + Carrier)	Carrier Dimensions (L x W x H)	Pet Fee (One-Way)	Notable Restrictions	Route Coverage
Aegean Airlines	Dogs and cats	8 kg (17.6 lbs)	Not specified	Varies by route	One pet per passenger; pets must be familiar if sharing a carrier; advance booking required	Europe, Middle East
Air Canada	Small dogs and cats	Must fit comfortably in carrier	55 x 40 x 27 cm (21.5 x 15.5 x 10.5 in)	\$50–\$118 CAD/ USD	Not allowed in Premium Economy; one pet per passenger; advance notice required	Canada, U.S., International
Air Europa	Dogs, cats, small birds	10 kg (22 lbs)	55 x 35 x 25 cm (22 x 14 x 10 in)	€25–€100	Max 5 pets per flight; pets must be at least 3 months old; advance booking required	Europe, Americas
Air France	Dogs and cats	8 kg (17.6 lbs)	Not specified	€30–€400	Pets over 8 kg must travel in hold; advance booking at least 24 hours before departure	Europe, Africa, Americas, Asia
Alaska Airlines	Dogs, cats, rabbits, birds	Must fit comfortably in carrier	43 x 28 x 20 cm (17 x 11 x 8 in)	\$100	Max 2 pets per carrier; pets must remain in carrier under seat; advance booking recommended	U.S., Mexico, Canada
American Airlines	Dogs and cats	Must fit comfortably in carrier	48 x 33 x 22 cm (19 x 13 x 9 in)	\$125	Pets must remain in carrier under seat; not allowed in certain seating areas; advance booking required	U.S., International
Delta Air Lines	Dogs, cats, small birds	Must fit comfortably in carrier	Not specified	\$95–\$125	Pets must remain in carrier under seat; advance booking recommended	U.S., International
French Bee	Dogs and cats	8 kg (17.6 lbs)	43 x 35 x 20 cm (17 x 13.8 x 7.9 in)	€50–€100	Only one pet per passenger; snub-nosed breeds not allowed; advance booking required	France, U.S., Caribbean
JetBlue Airways	Dogs and cats	Must fit comfortably in carrier	43 x 31 x 21 cm (17 x 12.5 x 8.5 in)	\$125	One pet per carrier; max 2 pets per passenger with purchase of additional seat; advance booking required	U.S., Caribbean, Latin America
Lufthansa	Dogs and cats	8 kg (17.6 lbs)	55 x 40 x 23 cm (21.5 x 15.5 x 9 in)	€55–€100	Pets over 8 kg must travel in hold; advance booking required	Europe, Asia, Americas, Africa

(Source: Airlines official sites)

Table 7 shows airlines weight limit and dimensions and routes

Table 7. Airlines Rating (Source: Airlines official sites)

Airline	Pet Fee (20%)	Weight Limit (20%)	Carrier Size Flexibility (20%)	Route Coverage (20%)	Pet Services/Extras (20%)	Total Score (100%)	
JetBlue	8	7	8	7	9	**7.8**	1
Alaska Airlines	9	8	7	6	7	**7.4**	2
Air Canada	7	7	8	8	6	**7.2**	3
Delta	7	7	7	8	6	**7.0**	4
American Airlines	6	7	7	7	6	**6.6**	5
Lufthansa	5	8	6	8	5	**6.4**	6
Air France	5	7	6	7	5	**6.0**	7
Air Europa	6	8	5	6	4	**5.8**	8
French Bee	7	6	5	5	4	**5.4**	9
Aegean Airlines	6	6	5	5	3	**5.0**	10

Table 7 the comparative analysis of airlines that allow in-cabin pet travel ranks **JetBlue** as the most pet-friendly airline, with a top score of **7.8/10**, due to its flexible pet policy and exceptional pet services. **Alaska Airlines** follows closely with a **7.4**, offering affordable fees and generous weight limits. **Air Canada** and **Delta** also perform well, scoring **7.2** and **7.0**, respectively, mainly because of broad route coverage and decent in-cabin policies. **American Airlines** and **Lufthansa** offer moderate services with scores above **6.0**, whereas **Air France**, **Air Europa**, **French Bee**, and **Aegean Airlines** rank lower, primarily due to limited extras and stricter restrictions. Overall, the study highlights that while many airlines accommodate pets, there is significant variation in the level of comfort, cost, and flexibility offered to pet owners.

An Analysis of the Market for Pet Travel Services

The global market for pet travel services was estimated to be $ 2.4 billion in 2024, and it is anticipated to reach $ 3.9 billion by 2030, growing at a compound annual growth rate (CAGR) of 8.9% from 2025 to 2030. The expansion of the market is being driven by a variety of reasons, including the increasing adoption and humanization of pets, the growing number of tourists who are travelling with their companion animals, the availability of travel services and hotels that are pet-friendly, and the increased interest among individuals in travelling after the implementation of pandemic lockdowns.

Key Insights and Trends in the Market

The North American market for pet travel services had the most significant revenue share of 36.9% in 2024, making it the dominant market in the sector.

In 2024, the United States had the largest market share for pet travel services.

In 2024, the domestic travel sector had the most significant revenue share, accounting for 77.2% of the total market. This segment was the most dominant in terms of travel type.

According to the application, the transportation sector had the highest revenue share in the year 2024.

In terms of pet types, the category that accounted for the largest revenue share in 2024 was the dogs section.

Size and Forecast of the Market in 2024. The market size is projected to be 2.4 billion USD by 2030. The projected market size is $ 3.9 billion, and the compound annual growth rate (CAGR) for the period 2025-2030 is 8.9%.

The Asia-Pacific region is projected to have the highest growth rate in 2024.

In 2024, the largest market is expected to be in North America.

For example, in 2021, Condor Ferries, a passenger and freight ferry service provider in the United Kingdom, claimed that more than 53 per cent of people who own dogs worldwide take their animals on vacation. Currently, 3 per cent of families include their pets on vacations that are considered part of complete family vacations. This rate has seen a considerable 19% rise over the previous decade.

REFERENCES

Abdukayumov, A., Maturazov, I. S., & Yaronova, N. V. (2023). Improvement of the Aircraft Aviation Equipment Diagnostic System after Flight. In S. S. & S. P. Saint Petersburg Electrotechnical University LETI Prof. Popov Str. 5 (Eds.), *Proceedings of the Seminar on Information Systems Theory and Practice, ISTP 2023* (pp. 9 – 13). Institute of Electrical and Electronics Engineers Inc. https://doi.org/DOI: 10.1109/ISTP60767.2023.10427496

Albert, J.-F., Gómez-Fernández, N., & Boto-García, D. (2025). Up in the air: How do carbon policy shocks affect air travel? *Transport Policy*, *168*, 54–68. DOI: 10.1016/j.tranpol.2025.04.003

Amer, F., Khalifa, H. E. S., Elahmady, M., ElBadawy, N. E., Zahran, W. A., Abdelnasser, M., Rodríguez-Morales, A. J., Wegdan, A. A., & Tash, R. M. E. (2023). Mpox: Risks and approaches to prevention. *Journal of Infection and Public Health*, *16*(6), 901–910. DOI: 10.1016/j.jiph.2023.04.001 PMID: 37062165

Bakir, N., El Nemar, S., Gehchan, F. B., Samrouth, K., & Vrontis, D. (2025). Optimizing airline services: Leveraging data-driven strategies for enhanced customer satisfaction and engagement. *Journal of Asia Business Studies*, *19*(2), 487–510. DOI: 10.1108/JABS-09-2024-0559

Bennetts, S. K., Crawford, S. B., Howell, T. J., Burgemeister, F., Chamberlain, C., Burke, K., & Nicholson, J. M. (2022). Parent and child mental health during COVID-19 in Australia: The role of pet attachment. *PLoS ONE, 17*(7 July). https://doi.org/DOI: 10.1371/journal.pone.0271687

Buenavista, D. P., Dinopol, N. M. A., Mollee, E., & McDonald, M. (2021). From poison to food: On the molecular identity and indigenous peoples' utilisation of poisonous "Lab-o" (Wild Yam, Dioscoreaceae) in Bukidnon, Philippines. *Cogent Food & Agriculture*, *7*(1). Advance online publication. DOI: 10.1080/23311932.2020.1870306

Clément, G. R., Boyle, R. D., George, K. A., Nelson, G. A., Reschke, M. F., Williams, T. J., & Paloski, W. H. (2020). Challenges to the central nervous system during human spaceflight missions to Mars. *Journal of Neurophysiology*, *123*(5), 2037–2063. DOI: 10.1152/JN.00476.2019 PMID: 32292116

Crozet, G., Lacoste, M.-L., Rivière, J., Robardet, E., Cliquet, F., & Dufour, B. (2021). Management practices of dog and cat owners in France (pet traveling, animal contact rates and medical monitoring): Impacts on the introduction and the spread of directly transmitted infectious pet diseases. *Transboundary and Emerging Diseases*. Advance online publication. DOI: 10.1111/tbed.14088 PMID: 33787076

Dadhich, J. P., Smith, J. P., Iellamo, A., & Suleiman, A. (2021). Climate Change and Infant Nutrition: Estimates of Greenhouse Gas Emissions From Milk Formula Sold in Selected Asia Pacific Countries. *Journal of Human Lactation*, *37*(2), 314–322. DOI: 10.1177/0890334421994769 PMID: 33586512

Donmez, K., Kaplan, Z., Cetek, F. A., Rogošic, T., Juricic, B., & Francetic, I. (2022). Service Quality and Efficiency-Oriented Training Design in Air Traffic Management. In P. M., D. I., & C. A.L. (Eds.), *Transportation Research Procedia* (Vol. 64, Issue C, pp. 345 – 355). Elsevier B.V. https://doi.org/DOI: 10.1016/j.trpro.2022.09.038

dos Santos, R. M., & Murça, M. C. R. (2025). Airport capacity prediction and optimal allocation for strategic air traffic flow management at Sao Paulo/Guarulhos International Airport. *Case Studies on Transport Policy*, *20*. Advance online publication. DOI: 10.1016/j.cstp.2025.101414

Edwards, S. (2007). Role of organic agriculture in preventing and reversing land degradation. *Environmental Science and Engineering*, 523–536. https://www.scopus.com/inward/record.uri?eid=2-s2.0-85108904023&partnerID=40&md5=127c3fb4c7afdf38c7ae715f361592d7

Giannitrapani, A. (2018). Cat Cafes and Dog Restaurants. In Marrone, G., & Mangano, D. (Eds.), *SEMIOTICS OF ANIMALS IN CULTURE: ZOOSEMIOTICS 2.0* (Vol. 17, pp. 91–102)., DOI: 10.1007/978-3-319-72992-3_7

Greger, M. (2007). The long haul risks associated with livestock transport. *Biosecurity and Bioterrorism*, *5*(4), 301–312. DOI: 10.1089/bsp.2007.0028 PMID: 18081490

Haghani, M. (2022). Crowd dynamics research in the era of Covid-19 pandemic: Challenges and opportunities. *Safety Science*, *153*. Advance online publication. DOI: 10.1016/j.ssci.2022.105818 PMID: 35582429

Kumar, K. (2019). A study of Veterinary Scholars' Perception of MOOCs. *Information and Learning Science*, *120*(11–12), 743–757. DOI: 10.1108/ILS-04-2019-0031

Liao, H., Lyon, C. J., Ying, B., & Hu, T. (2024). Climate change, its impact on emerging infectious diseases and new technologies to combat the challenge. *Emerging Microbes & Infections*, *13*(1). Advance online publication. DOI: 10.1080/22221751.2024.2356143 PMID: 38767202

Malancus, R. N., Arsenoaia, V. N., & Ghita, M. (2024). Comparative analysis of stress responses in dogs and cats during the covid-19 pandemic: A focus on cortisol, total leukocytes, eosinophils, and behavioral changes; [Análise comparativa das respostas ao estresse em cães e gatos durante a pandemia de covid-. *Arquivo Brasileiro de Medicina Veterinária e Zootecnia*, *76*(3). Advance online publication. DOI: 10.1590/1678-4162-13153

Martins, A. M., & Cró, S. (2022). Airline stock markets reaction to the COVID-19 outbreak and vaccines: An event study. *Journal of Air Transport Management*, *105*. Advance online publication. DOI: 10.1016/j.jairtraman.2022.102281 PMID: 36034526

Masilamani, N., & Ganapathy, D. (2020). Knowledge and awareness about MERS-CoV among the dental students in Chennai. *International Journal of Research in Pharmaceutical Sciences, 11*(Special Issue 1), 847–851. https://doi.org/DOI: 10.26452/ijrps.v11iSPL1.3091

Menon, J., Shanmugam, N., Patel, K., Hakeem, A., Reddy, M. S., & Rela, M. (2020). Awareness and concerns about novel coronavirus disease 2019 (COVID-19) among parents of pediatric liver transplant recipients. *Pediatric Transplantation*, *24*(8). Advance online publication. DOI: 10.1111/petr.13805 PMID: 32663351

Rafique, N., Hassan, I., & Adil, M. (2025). *Flight PK8303 crash: a disastrous failure of human factors*. CASE Journal., DOI: 10.1108/TCJ-08-2024-0234

Rose, P. (2016). A lifetime in airline revenue management. *Journal of Revenue and Pricing Management*, *15*(3–4), 197–202. DOI: 10.1057/rpm.2016.21

Sah, R., Hada, V., Mohanty, A., Alshahrani, N. Z., Chakraborty, S., Bhattacharya, M., Chakraborty, C., & Dhama, K. (2022). Recent first report of human-to-dog transmission of Monkeypox virus emphasizes an urgent need of enhancing surveillance and strengthen further explorative research to reveal its real magnitude of reverse zoonosis from other animals including pets as like. *International Journal of Surgery*, *106*. Advance online publication. DOI: 10.1016/j.ijsu.2022.106949 PMID: 36174830

Stavleu, D. C., Mulder, R. L., Kruimer, D. M., Kremer, L. C. M., Tissing, W. J. E., & Loeffen, E. A. H. (2024). Less restrictions in daily life: A clinical practice guideline for children with cancer. *Supportive Care in Cancer*, *32*(7). Advance online publication. DOI: 10.1007/s00520-024-08537-9 PMID: 38850341

Suijkerbuijk, A. W. M., Mangen, M.-J. J., Haverkate, M. R., Luppino, F. S., Bantjes, S. E., Visser, L. G., Swaan, C. M., Ruijs, W. L. M., & Over, E. A. B. (2020). Rabies vaccination strategies in the Netherlands in 2018: A cost evaluation. *Eurosurveillance, 25*(38). Advance online publication. DOI: 10.2807/1560-7917.ES.2020.25.38.1900716 PMID: 32975187

Sun, B., Xu, Z., Wei, M., & Wang, X. (2025). A study on the strategic behavior of players participating in air-rail intermodal transportation based on evolutionary games. *Journal of Air Transport Management, 126*. Advance online publication. DOI: 10.1016/j.jairtraman.2025.102793

Theaker, A. (2020). The public relations handbook. In *The Public Relations Handbook*. Taylor and Francis., DOI: 10.4324/9780429298578

Underwood, P. J. (2000). Pet Travel Scheme. *The Veterinary Record, 146*(9), 263. https://www.scopus.com/inward/record.uri?eid=2-s2.0-0034716454&partnerID=40&md5=aabe276cb445522ab465e806e2977857 PMID: 10737301

Varenna, S., Li, H., Ribeiro, M., & Santos, B. F. (2025). Stochastic discrete event simulation of airline network and maintenance operations. *Journal of Air Transport Management, 125*. Advance online publication. DOI: 10.1016/j.jairtraman.2025.102789

Visnes, T., Benítez-Buelga, C., Cázares-Körner, A., Sanjiv, K., Hanna, B. M. F., Mortusewicz, O., Rajagopal, V., Albers, J. J., Hagey, D. W., Bekkhus, T., Eshtad, S., Baquero, J. M., Masuyer, G., Wallner, O., Müller, S., Pham, T., Göktürk, C., Rasti, A., Suman, S., & Helleday, T. (2021). Targeting OGG1 arrests cancer cell proliferation by inducing replication stress. *Nucleic Acids Research, 48*(21), 12234–12251. DOI: 10.1093/nar/gkaa1048 PMID: 33211885

Wandelt, S., Wang, S., Chen, X., Zheng, C., Chang, S., & Sun, X. (2025). Network structures in air transportation: A comprehensive review of applications and challenges. *Journal of Air Transport Management, 126*. Advance online publication. DOI: 10.1016/j.jairtraman.2025.102794

Wolf, S. M., Pruett, T. L., McVan, C. C., Brister, E., Callier, S. L., Capron, A. M., Childress, J. F., Goodwin, M. B., Hyun, I., Isasi, R., Maynard, A. D., Oye, K. A., Thompson, P. B., & Tiersch, T. R. (2024). Anticipating Biopreservation Technologies that Pause Biological Time: Building Governance & Coordination Across Applications. *The Journal of Law, Medicine & Ethics, 52*(3), 534–552. DOI: 10.1017/jme.2024.129 PMID: 39676361

Ying, T., Tang, J., Wen, J., Ye, S., Zhou, Y., & Li, F. (Sam). (2021). Traveling with pets: Constraints, negotiation, and learned helplessness. *Tourism Management, 82*. Advance online publication. DOI: 10.1016/j.tourman.2020.104183

Yue, S., Liao, W., Ji, Q., & Wang, C. (2025). The effect of financial performance on aviation carbon emissions. *Journal of Air Transport Management, 126*. Advance online publication. DOI: 10.1016/j.jairtraman.2025.102800

Zhang, L., Yang, H., & Bian, L. (2025). Complex network analysis of China's domestic air cargo network based on actual flight data. *Transport Policy, 168*, 133–156. DOI: 10.1016/j.tranpol.2025.04.015

Chapter 9
Pet Influencer's Power and Effective Social Media Marketing

Geetha Manoharan
https://orcid.org/0000-0002-8644-8871
SR University, India

ABSTRACT

The power of pet influencers in social media marketing is growing. Their vast appeal and real involvement are driving appealing marketing efforts. Petfluencers are reliable and emotive, unlike human influencers. This combination resonates with many customers and boosts conversions. The expanding impact of pet influencers across a number of industries is highlighted in this chapter, as their "paw of approval" expands beyond pet products to other product categories. Using Nala the Cat and Doug the Pug as examples, it shows how clever pet influencer partnerships can boost brand exposure, customer loyalty, and revenue. The study also examines platform selection, content strategy, and audience targeting in pet influencer marketing. Marketers are investing more in this niche to create engaging campaigns, eliminate influencer fatigue, and boost social media effectiveness as pet ownership and spending rise worldwide.

INTRODUCTION

In recent years, the social media spectrum appreciably altered from certainly one of many avenues for private expression during periods of solitude into an existent cash-making hub for promotions and brand engagement. The extension of social media to marketing and marketing strategies has through now become a should for

DOI: 10.4018/979-8-3373-4342-6.ch009

companies wishing to get admission to offshore markets and create meaningful bonds with their consumers ("Have A study The effect Of Social Media On advertising and marketing A emblem," 2023). In that ever-evolving surroundings, Influencer marketing has emerged as a fierce competitor by means of harnessing the credibility and attain of individual influencers with substantial followership to sway the evaluations and behaviours in their audience (Rani et al., 2022). The upward push of puppy influencers is an exciting and rare nook of influencer advertising, specially leveraging the prevalent attraction of an animal to attain an impossible audience (Ingale, 2024). Puppy influencer territories encompass a few well-known dog and tom cat personalities, likewise, extending their impact to exotic pets so that they certainly exist within a third zone in the digital market that has done excessive followership and engagement ranges as compared to their human counterparts. The phenomenon of puppy influencers gained fantastic popularity during the recent past and can alternatively be viewed considering this cultural ethos that increasingly glorifies animals as worthy constituents of our lives (Ilieva et al., 2024). That is the method that harnesses online influencers in advocating products to their target audience by leveraging on their specific influence (Łaszkiewicz, 2023).

According to Waltenrath (2024), the success of influencer marketing depends on the network agreement that exists between the influencer and his/her fans. Authenticity is a requirement in influencer marketing, by which the influencers must sincerely believe in the products they recommend. puppy influencers have turn out to be increasingly popular, revolutionizing the advertising panorama with their specific capability to connect to audiences' manufacturers are engaging social media influencers to attain their target audience (Ao et al., 2023). Influencer advertising and marketing capitalizes on social have an impact on at the client stage and on phrase-of-mouth guidelines within the virtual age, thru which brands can goal consumers to prompt them to adopt precise customer actions. Those influencers who have that enticing content alongside actual enthusiasts create an opportunity for brands to connect to customers on a private degree and attain meaningful engagement. The idea of influencer advertising is now prepared for growing logo identification and boosting sales. Puppy influencers are synonymous with changing how and what advertising and marketing strategies can be used to keep up with purchaser conduct. They showcase the power of authenticity and relatability within the basically emotional connection people have on this virtual age. Traditional online marketing practices face challenges with respect to audiences, who are becoming increasingly averse to such strategies (Gu & Duan, 2024).

As a result, this chapter seeks to provide an in-depth investigation of the size and the effectiveness of the pet influencers for that matter in social media marketing, reconciling their precise appeal, impact on patron behaviour, and strategic implications for manufacturers. The focus of modern marketing is on the velocity with which changes in advertising and marketing procedure can be taken up. This bankruptcy seeks to present the top pet influencer tactics and their star ingredients to help brands use their educational blanket in pet influencer campaigns. The modern marketing conditions differ largely from the previous ones, and every company needs an understanding of the effectiveness, ethical concerns, social repercussions, and prospects of influencer marketing, as stated by Aw and Agnihotri.

The research proceeds to examining successful pet influencer campaigns while analysing the metrics that would determine their effectiveness and talking to ethical considerations that marketers ought to bear in mind while engaging with pet influencers. Those kinds of explorations intention to offer entrepreneurs with actionable insights and strategic guidance in the direction of harnessing the strength of pup influencers in boosting their social media advertising efforts. It therefore places entrepreneurs in a function to formulate consumer-particular techniques; enhance brand credibility; and align with the values of clients. This takes a look at appears at the social media surroundings about the way it impacts customer purchasing for conduct across special product instructions. The contemporary-day studies goals at locating the influencer advertising effect on patron conduct and electronic buying alternatives.

Social Media Marketing Overview

But social media advertising opens large possibilities, rightly regarding it as a possibility within the advertising horizon for appealing target audiences, constructing emblem recognition, and in the end enhancing sales. The multitude of techniques and equipment that social media advertising and marketing and marketing can provide-from content fabric introduction and network engagement to paid marketing and influencer collaboration-is overwhelming. It is located that social media advertising is exceptional desirable for strengthening emotional relationships with customers, compared with any traditional digital medium. Electronic mail marketing and role search engine optimization (Migkos et al., 2025). Via developing brand visibility, consumer loyalty, or genuinely boosting income on their very own, social media advertising mechanisms have made their manner slowly however certainly into the minds of potential purchasers (Salhab, 2024). Therefore, social media represents a fertile ground for influencers, wherein enormous behavioural modifications of customers are introduced approximately in phrases of purchasing intentions (Chen et al., 2024).

Types of Influencers in the Pet Industry

- **Petfluencers**

Those are pets having their social media profiles frequently maintained with the aid of the use of their owners. Maximum of the famous puppies, cats, or even parrots on Instagram are followed via many people. Such reels create huge engagements as it comes from a unique angle or is very funny, and people just simply love cute pets with product usage.

- **Pet Experts & Veterinarians**

Some of the noteworthy influencers are touted for their behavioural history. Clear advice on pet care, exercise, and beneficial products for varied needs can be given by veterinarians and trainers.

- **Pet Owners & Bloggers**

While these influencers may not have the same fame as movie stars, they are relatable; they share relevant content with their audience. Owners of pets with involved and engaged followings provide real product reviews, advice, and experience.

- **Celebrity Pet Owners**

When giving up their pets, the public figures can reach a far larger target market. While there may be a bigger reach, the messages will be much less focused and hence, alignment of the target audience with the area of interest for puppies is very important.

Reasons for Influencer Marketing Works in the Pet Industry

- Pet Lovers Trust Recommendations

Pet owners treat their pets like family and are often very picky about what products they will purchase for their beloved animals. Influencers develop strong relationships with their followers over extended periods of time, and their word carries great weight. Therefore, puppy parents are more likely to trust the recommendations of an influencer who shares the same passion for pets and can give a fair evaluation of the product or actual-day-to-day usage.

- Strong Emotional Connection

Almost everyone will feel a strong connection with pets, and so influencers use this to show pets and how they engage in fine products in their everyday lives. In puppy owners, this magic is always more intense because they tend to relate with other puppy owners and find them straightforward and relatable in the end.

- Niche Audiences

At least one necessary consideration in choosing a pet influencer as a channel partner is the proven dedication of their followers. Most pet lovers comprise the focal point audience, hardly ever found anywhere else. Whether it is a dog, a cat, a breed, or an exotic pet channel, the audiences are generally involved and sincerely willing to learn about products. Above all, these audiences are readily prone to spending money on things that make their lives easier or pamper their beloved pets.

- Social Proof

Social proof influences decisions by clients. When followers see an influencer using and endorsing something, they become more likely to try it for themselves. Humans hate feeling left out and love being part of new trends.

Recent Studies

Lavertu et al. (2025) stated that research on social media influencers (SMIs) is of interest to advertisers and researchers alike. This is the major reason why much research up to date is focusing on human influencers. However, there is a trend as more advertising agencies or brands are now turning towards animal influencers for brand promotion. In view of petfluencers' increasing attraction, the authors become interested in evaluating the possible factors that would enable pets to be more persuasive than humans and the reasons for the persuasive power. Four studies, consisting of one field study and one laboratory experiment, have been put forward as evidence supporting the idea that pet influencers are more persuasive as such effects stem from greater perceptions of sincerity associated with being petfluencers. The authors also claim that petfluencers are more persuasive when the petfluencer's message is congruent with the consumer's mindset being present-oriented.

Di Cioccio et al. (2024), influencer marketing is a potent tool for brands aimed at creating connections with their audiences. Just like any other business market, many have leveraged human influencers; however, rising popularity of pet influencers like (dogs, cats) opened a new avenue for these businesses to market themselves. The present research poses the question: Why and when are pet influencers better than their human counterparts to increase engagement and purchase intentions? They provided six experimental studies (N = 1166), by which they demonstrated that pet influencers will lead them to higher engagement with promoted content and willingness to buy advertised products because they are viewed as more credible than human influencers. Pet influencers are seen as cuter, which positively impacts their credibility. Specifically, whimsicality is the cuteness dimension that explains their greater credibility. These effects are all the stronger when the product promoted is pet-related, and they apply whether a person owns a pet. Lastly, a clear cuteness manipulation supports the causal relation of cuteness to credibility. This affirms that pet influencers shape the way individuals react to promotional social media posts, increase the understanding of the mechanisms underlying effectiveness in influencer marketing, and clarify how to implement more influential social media campaigns.

Zhang et al. in 2023 asserted that power pet influencers are becoming increasingly popular to practitioners in hospitality and tourism owing to the shift in visit patterns of human beings, having favoured traveling these days with pets. Pet influencers are social media influencers who mostly focused on pets. A successful social media advertisement by pet influencers can massively affect the buying decision of pet owners when it comes to accommodation, restaurants, and tourism destinations. The current research was designed under a 2×2 experimental design to determine the interactional effect of message appeal and narrative on hotel customers' attitudes and booking intentions. Results indicate that when the social media post is written from a pet's point of view, consumers respond better to rational appeal (vs. emotional appeal). In terms of the post written from the owner's perspective, it makes no difference in terms of consumers' attitudes and booking intentions irrespective of message appeal. Meanwhile, the mediator in terms of interaction effect includes consumer curiosity and the perceived helpfulness of the post.

Jacobson et al. (2022), this research examines not only human social media influencers but the emergence of online influencers in the study of non-human animal celebrities. Via qualitative in-depth content analysis of Instagram images and captions, we examine the social presence strategies—affective, interactive, and cohesive—and advertising strategies of the top animal influencers. All three social presence strategies were used, although animal influencers most often employed affective and cohesive strategies, thus suggesting emotions and community rather than being interactive for animal influencers. Most influencers engaged in social media advertising by brand-related posts, yet their social media feeds do not overly bear advertising messages. The main implication of this research is that it shows how animal influencers build parasocial relationships with their followers benefitting brands.

Yoo et al. (2024) referred to that creating dedicated bills for posting pet content material with the aid of users on Instagram appears to be a flourishing trend these days. While the concerned account proprietors may delight of their sports, they also do face some grievance and demanding situations through doing so. Nonetheless, there arises a expertise hole as to how pet account proprietors manipulate their pets' online presence efficiently and triumph over those obstacles. From 21 interviews with Instagram puppy account proprietors, we discover motivations for establishing puppy bills ranging from private, altruistic, and to business-degree ones. They then discover approximately their strategies for crafting the online identification and personality in their pets in addition to the demanding situations in implementing such techniques for the proprietors and their pets alike in their digital identification control. This is also a discussion in which the rapidly shifting members of the family among human and puppy are conversely seen as a collaborative endeavour within the co-creation of puppy identities, which represents a type of 0.33 shift, pointing to the need for intervention design to help this peculiar identity control journey.

The Rise of Influencer Marketing

In this crowded area, brands will try finding out innovative approaches to market them to ability clients, in which most of the ways to acquire this is thru influencer advertising. Influencer marketing is about using someone with an audience who has been able to capture their attention through a social media platform so that you can use that platform to sell your company's services or products. The pet industry is especially powerful in this way because most pet owners will take the advice of someone, they follow on social media, most often a pet lover. Through association with influencers, pet brands can target a highly curated and passionate audience and increase visibility and sales.

Advertising zones now have seismic shifts in social media that opened floodgates re-counting influencer marketing to connect with the target industry by businesses (Kumar et al. 2023). Influencer marketing has now taken position as one of the most efficient gears for online engagement, performing better than traditional forms in terms of consumer trust and ROI (Migkos et al., 2025). Influencer marketing has emerged as one of the ways modern businesses present themselves and engage prospective consumers, hoping to be seen as more authentic and appealing ways of reaching customers than what traditional advertisement methods portray (Joshi et al., 2023). The clearer meanings of Influencer Marketing contest the relationships or interactions between brands and customers, which have been established as a practice with much more credibility over the years. Influencer marketing is also one of the systems through which the brands link up to the customers and build up customer actions through social influence and word-of-mouth feelers digital platform (Iqbal et al., 2023).

THEORETICAL PERSPECTIVES

The emergent trend of pet influencers or "petfluencers" can be understood through various communication and marketing theories that highlight the fields of audience engagement and persuasion.

Apart from being owned by people, pets can also build a one-sided yet emotionally rewarding relationship with favourite media personalities (including animals) through a parasocial interaction theory. Pets on network sites create warmth and trust among users who engage on a personal level, hence credibility and loyalty as a result of this phenomenon (Jacobson et al., 2022).

Apart from that, Source Credibility Theory suggests that positive views towards trustworthiness, attractiveness, and expertise result in increased appeal. Pets are not only considered to have specialist knowledge, but also their cuteness and innocent character are associated with an increased authenticity, which audiences internalize to mean sincerity for better marketing results (Lavertu et al., 2025).

Even after providing much needed insights into use petfluencers with customers, very few research studies exist on petfluencers. Most research understand petfluencers through the meaningful 'pet' constructs.

The theory of cue utilization further elaborates on how consumers use basic cues such as cuteness, friendliness, or relatability to judge endorsements. Pet influencers are low-involvement yet potent cues for lifestyle and hedonic products (Di Cioccio et al., 2024).

The fourth proposition of the elaboration likelihood model speaks of a situation when consumers are not particularly motivated to pay attention to the advertisement and thus adopt the peripheral route to persuasion. This is where pet influencers act as a very strong peripheral cue (great visuals, cute captions) to develop consumers' favourable attitudes and purchase intentions (Petty & Cacioppo, 2012; Zhang et al., 2023).

The Social Presence idea offers with the seeming personal and real experience of digital communications. The potential of storytelling, network interaction, and anthropomorphism in addition heightens emotional presence from the facet of the petfluencers and nurtures very strong parasocial relationships (Jacobson et al., 2022).

Pet influencers owe their achievement now not to rational persuasion but to affective acceptance as true with, cuteness, and emotional relatability. They kill client skepticism through creating parasocial closeness and peripheral effective cues, which makes them robust gamers inside the virtual advertising and marketing palms in recent times.

Pup possession has changed enter dramatically in modern years, and the twin connection among human and animal has now strengthened (Dzreke & Dzreke, 2025). Pet ownership and social media participation have merged to create a colourful internet community of animal fans who percent their lives, studies, and products with their furry opposite numbers. With the aid of the usage of web hosting energetic puppy-related content material fabric on social media pages, agencies can leverage them to interact with doggy owners alike. Within this community are the pup influencers who have been diagnosed as a crucial voice through capitalizing on the pets' superstar popularity and unique content to acquire large followership and collaborate with manufacturers. This permits the manufacturers to tap into a splendid manner of connecting with clients as puppy influencers. The capacity of companies to leverage pet influencers affords an possibility to attain a gap market, foster emblem agrees with and capitalize at the emotional bond proprietors share with their pets. The growth in the employment of social media influencers for advertising has proved to be a strong tool for the promotion and sales growth of brands (Ilieva et al., 2024).

Consumer Behaviour and Pet-Related Content

How customers behave has changed by the increase of pet-related contents in social media; owners of puppies are turning to social media for information, recommendation, and ideas concerning their pet friends (Andika et al., 2024). They often tend to use social media systems to get input from other customers of the product before making a buying decision (Martini et al., 2022). Patters of consumer behaviour are greatly influenced by the contents related to pet influencers, such that they inform brand perception and purchasing choices as well as levels of engagement. Those influencers are usually cautioned with reference to products and services for pets, and those are more likely to simply accept the ones hints. Consequently, the advancement of technology and facts analysis is essential to enhance operation efficiency and customer enjoy in a fast-converting environment of e-buying and selling, especially in sectors as specialised as puppy zones (Liu, 2024). Social media provides the principal foundation for consumers' influence over their shopping behaviour and emblem interplay. For instance, product suggestions can be made in a customised way to clients whilst exceptional customer support interacts with the entire buying enjoy of the consumer (Liu, 2024).

Evolving Consumer Expectations

Consumer expectancies alter unendingly interior social media's age, inviting the target market to a brand-new degree requiring greater authenticity, transparency, and relevance from their manufacturers and influencers in following them. While authenticity and transparency in influencer marketing create predominant concerns, customers are more disturbing genuine and sincere endorsements. Consumers are getting greater sophisticated and crucial of advertising messages, making it extra critical to get the statistics from social media sites (Rani et al., 2022). Audiences look for influencers like them with similar values and who realize their needs as well as providing valuable content material cloth that fertilizes their lives (Guerra-Tamez et al., 2024). Consequently, manufacturers are required to prioritize establishing true members of the family with influencers owning similar values to grow to be relatable to the audience being focused. That could call for a motion far away from traditional advertising and marketing techniques into a much greater cooperative and network-orientated method to advertising. purchasers need manufacturers to talk with them in customized and applicable approaches relating to their desires and possibilities (Yoo, 2024).

Ethical Considerations in Pet Influencer Marketing

The modern-day social networks that preserve changing the buyers' expectations and stressing these audiences at the extra authenticity, transparency, and relevance they look for in brands and the affects they are following. Certainly, an influential marketing architect for transparent and authentic client value draws customers, who are growing in numbers, attempting to find actual and honest suggestions. The customers grow to be an awful lot extra knowledgeable and essential of advertising and marketing communications, and advertising these days requires information that is to be had from social media sites (Rani et al., 2022).

Humans are seeking out influencers who percentage their values, recognize their needs, and provide them treasured content material that adds something to their lives (Guerra-Tamez et al., 2024). It consequently method that manufacturers will need to shift their attention toward making actual contacts with the influencers whose values resonate with theirs and who will connect to their audiences. The change is going to return from a shift faraway from advertising right into a greater collaborative grassroots participatory marketing approach. The expectation customers have from manufacturers is that the latter will talk with them in approaches that carry logo messages which are customized to their precise wants and needs (Yoo, 2024). Entrepreneurs that can supply personalised stories individualized to options are higher located to capture interest, generate loyalty, and power conversions.

THE POWER OF PET INFLUENCERS

Building Brand Awareness

The puppy shop is expanding internationally, especially in developing countries such as China, due to the rising numbers of puppies and changing consumer attitudes (Xu, 2024). Puppy influencers can assist brands in increasing awareness by drawing upon the fame of their pets and relatable content material to expose products, services, and campaigns to a much wider audience. Puppy influencers generally work with agencies to create backed content, run contests, and market products and this may significantly enhance logo exposure and engagement (Zniva et al., 2023).

Driving Consumer Engagement

A few factors of rivalry in which includes folks that are frequently taken into consideration doggy influencers underneath the one's definitions could probably comprise precisely what is taken into consideration puppy-influencer-authorized imagery. Others may additionally consist of a few counts, on the grounds that many pup influencers commonly move past simply supplying puppies. They have been diagnosed to engender emblem loyalty and advocacy by means of damn their followers on sharing reviews, movies, and pictures of their pets underneath branded tags and social media campaigns. By way of virtue of constructing actual relationships with their target marketplace, the influencers may enhance the engagement that manifests itself in earnings and retention. in this age of interactive and dynamic commercial enterprise environments, consumer engagement is critical for boosting the patron cost and amusement if it must capture extra eyeballs (Kumar et al., 2023).

Creating Authentic Connections

It is on this pillar of authenticity that influencer marketing stands, and pet influencers do a great job at being authentic through building connections with their audience in a relatable yet obvious manner about sharing their lives, experiences, and opinions (Hardey, 2024). They help in establishing consideration and credibility as they indulge in showing love for their pets, sharing their plight and victories, and giving frank reviews and suggestions. Consumers with respect to advertising are more inclined to pay attention to and support those influencers who are candid and transparent. Brands can consequently harness the power of human connection and develop a long-lasting bond with the audience by associating with pet influencers who are genuine (Ünalmış et al., 2024).

Impact on Purchase Decisions

The instantaneous effect of influencer advertising on customer purchase decisions is one of its key advantages. Puppy influencer's function specialists to customers for recommendations, evaluations, or even endorsements in the purchase of products for their bushy pals. The purchase-in-to-their-fans transfer of believe is what an influencer performs on; those influencers transform the marketing message into valid endorsements that connect with the target market's appeal. Informative product reviews and demonstrations and comparisons will result in clients into making smart purchases, to be able to increase conversions and income for their companies.

EFFECTIVE SOCIAL MEDIA MARKETING STRATEGIES

Platform Selection and Optimization

The maximum essential social media channels for successful implementation of campaigns about puppy influencers due to the fact every has its specific niche in insurance, composition, and strategies through special varieties of audiences. Brands must study their target audiences regarding demographic and engagement-style characteristics before choosing any medium for their campaigns. Therefore, Instagram would mainly have been suitable for those kinds of image content-oriented pet lifestyle, whereas Facebook might have been more for community engagement and education via articles and videos.

Thus, brands can maximize their reach, engagement, and ROI by optimizing the presence they choose through creating compelling profiles, using relevant hashtags, and facilitating engaging interactions with their audience on the daily basis. There is no means by which social media is less flexible or cheaper than enabling marketers to talk to existing customers and find new ones. There should be harmony between the marketing goals of the brand and the strategies that they adopt in social media since not all platforms suit each brand ("A take a look at the impact of Social Media on advertising and marketing an emblem," 2023). A poorly imagined approach can severely damage the image of a brand (Brambilla et al., 2022).

Content Creation and Storytelling

In the digital space, content indeed reigns supreme, and puppy influencers create excellent content that mesmerizes their audience while promoting interaction. By using storytelling techniques in their content, brands evoke puppy owners' emotions and persuade them to act. The tales may be anything from some relatable antics and heartwarming little tips to behind-the-scenes glimpses into the lives of puppy influencers and their furry companions. The capability of the influencers to create relatable and worth content material also engenders real interplay with their audience, even growing a network within the technique.

Proficiently attractive with an audience in social media allows producers show conversations regarding their recognition and place of interest to reveal consumer ache factors and sentiment whilst refining their marketing techniques (Shevchenko, 2023). Content fabric needs to consequently be amusing, innovative, and something but stupid; multimedia, emotional customization, and decided on endorsers can do more to pull up the engagement stage (Drossos et al., 2023).

Audience Targeting and Segmentation

The first point of touch in this example explains that the social media advertising approach can work if market segmentation and goal definition are as it should be described, which means that first-rate messages can be healthful with numerous demographics relying on a tough and rapid of pursuits, behaviours, and demographics surpassed over to them. With effective targeting, brands can be certain that their messages are reaching only the people that usually show some interest in their products or services. Puppy owners can technically be split into consumer segments based on further variables, such as the types of pets, age, breed, geographic area, and lifestyle preferences. Further, such a type of strong insight allows them to alter their content, offer, and marketing with the differing needs and opportunities created by each segment.

Engagement Tactics and Community Building

Engaging in an array of networks surrounding the products and their values is the creation of a lively and engagement strategy using deafness to respond to comments as well as messages by hosting contests and giveaways, soliciting for consumer-generated content, and encouraging discussions among the followers. Thus, the endurance of its use by organizations has forged a closer relationship with the customers ("A study of the impact of social media on advertising and marketing a brand," 2023; Setyawati & Anindita, 2022).

Examples of Successful Pet Influencer Campaigns

Campaign 1: Brand Collaboration Example

A pair of those pup dog fashions breathe the air of novelty with healing collaborations and creative campaigns. to present an example, a well-known famous pet meals brand utilized the abilities of a dog influencer in large call for as the spokesperson for its new line of desirable dog meals. The collection of posts and testimonies become all approximately the influencer's pooch consuming the food, stressing its fitness blessings and giving personal reviews. Going out with a bash, the vending created quite a sharp noise, in the long run ensuing in big income increase - the excellent argument there can be for proper endorsements and relatable content material.

Campaign 2: Product Launch Example

An example of its miles a toy employer that focuses on doggie playthings. It has released a brand-new line of interactive toys in association with a tom cat influencer. The influencer created a series of exciting videos of her cats playing with the toys and displaying their sturdiness, safety, and enjoyment price. The marketing campaign stirred quite a few interest and right evaluations, which brought about a spike in on-line and retail sales (Maulidian et al., 2023).

Campaign 3: Social Cause Advocacy Example

Also, a doggy adoption enterprise receives the most powerful endorsement for elevating consciousness about pet adoption and accountable pet possession from star animal rights propose. Due to that heartwarming memory shared via the influencer, which additionally offers some suggestions on puppy care and public adoption on a local refuge, adoption inquiries accelerated extensively, along inspiring a greater intimate connection with puppy fans Influencer marketing is when manufacturers group up with famous or even famous social media personalities to sell their product or offerings (Hardey, 2024). Qualifying, in element, what makes influencer advertising artwork is the influencer's capability to engage an target market honestly, and that's what creates engagement and drives conversion (Yang et al., 2024).

Analysis of Key Success Factors

Here are predominant factors contributing to the fulfilment of pet influencer advertising: authenticity, relevance, creativity, and strategic alignment. Authenticity is the largest winner due to the fact influencers ought to say “sure” to the products or offerings they promote it after which deliver their target market the enthusiastic upswing and genuinely “into” the enjoy (Ünalmış et al., 2024). It is also applicable-for this reason the alignment among the influencer and their audience for the messaging to resonate with the proper people (Harst & Angelopoulos, 2024). In a comparable vein, creativity performs a huge role in catching hobby and generating memorable paintings to be remembered above the whole lot else in an already crowded our on-line world. Campaigns ought to additionally be hitch to strategic alignment so that influencer campaigns are in line with overall advertising targets and supply measurable outputs to the brand. when entrepreneurs seek advice from those experts, they name them impacts in income, boosting upswing unexpectedly (Doshi et al., 2022).

CHALLENGES AND CONSIDERATIONS

Authenticity and Transparency

Marketers have obtained lots of suitable with the influencer marketing approach, but it brings alongside constraints and worries that marketers will face so that sustainable and moral packages may be accomplished. Therefore, it is far vital for marketers to make certain that influencers declare the partnership and do not have interaction in deceptive and unsubstantiated claims about services or products.

Regulatory Compliance

Regulatory compliance, furthermore, is by using far the most critical of all because influencer advertising is difficulty to distinctive legal guidelines and pointers concerning marketing supposed to shield clients in opposition to fraud or deception (Antoniou, 2024). All these influencer rules should be found on an character foundation to avoid unethical practices which include undisclosed endorsements, fake critiques, or misleading advertisements.

Measuring ROI and Campaign Effectiveness

Measuring the go back of funding of investor-centric advertisement campaigns can at instances be tough because of the intangible nature of logo impact and engagement (Gracias et al., 2024). However quantitative metrics including likes, feedback, and stocks supply a few perceptions into campaign performance however do no longer seize absolutely the qualitative input of influencer advertisement on logo keep in mind, customer loyalty, and buy rationale.

Managing Negative Feedback and Crisis Communication

A marketer must have a proactive plan to monitor social media channels, counter terrible feedback, and cope with crises as it should be. This will require a mixture of energetic listening, empathy, and obvious conversation to soften the blow from negative commentaries and maintain consider with customers. Superior analytics which include device studying techniques can do wonders in execution of a hit influencer advertising and advertising marketing campaign specially within the floor of the choice of influencers (Ilieva et al., 2024).

Future Trends in Pet Influencer Marketing and Emerging Platforms and Technologies

Everyday puppy influencer advertising is an ever-evolving affair wherein more modern structures and technologies are increasingly coming to play within the disruptions on how manufacturers and influencers relate to their audiences. New systems-vintage and new-at the side of TikTok, Snapchat, and Twitch-are supplying a plethora of opportunities to engage with and obtain extra youthful audiences even as growing immersive emblem stories. In recent times, tendencies are set thru collaborative efforts of many social media influencers, video content, and user-generated content fabric (Jiang, 2023). Augmented fact and digital reality are giving rise to potentials for yet any other wave of innovations inside the influencer advertising international wherein manufacturers offer customers interactive and personalised stories that maintain interest and force engagement. The exponential boom of influencer advertising equates to the huge call for influencer-led content material introduction, therefore proving it an powerful weapon with the resource of far in trendy digital arena (SanMiguel & Sádaba, 2024). Trends on social media shall always keep evolving, and brands should always think to change their strategies and look for new opportunities to collaborate with influencers. In the future, social media marketing may witness strong tech integration plus artificial intelligence, plus machine learning.

However, consumers may not comprehend that AI-powered digital influencers already emerge as a cost-effective, efficient and even more viable substitute for human influencers in terms of attracting brands towards comprehensive control over content and audience engagement, say the authors (Allal-Chérif et al., 2023). Low profile virtual influencers offer amplified management over content and behaviour, thereby reducing the risks of human error, as they are online avatars, remaining ageless, thereby avoiding compromising their ego online (Kim & Wang, 2023). As AI technology progresses, digital influencers will certainly be more intelligent and realistic to blur the lines between fact and fiction (Looi & Kahlor, 2024). These digital personas have gained huge followings and are gradually being taken over by brands from which to promote products and lifestyles (Dondapati & Dehury, 2024).

The Role of AI and Automation

The position of artificial intelligence and automation is becoming increasingly important in pet influencer marketing, as it allows brands to streamline content creation, customize target audience research, and optimize performance of their campaigns (Babadoğan, 2024). AI-powered tools can analyse copious volumes of data, detect patterns and trends, and develop insights that inform influencer selection, content strategy, as well as campaign optimization (Ziakis and Vlachopoulou, 2023). AI helps evaluate large datasets, thus allowing pattern and trend identifications to influence the procedures of picking influencers, content methods, and campaign optimization (Hicham et al., 2023). AI-based gear may want to greatly speed up content material technology and make it more relevant the use of sophisticated vocabulary, stylistics, or visuals (Murár and Kubovics, 2023). Today, it is an overwhelming phenomenon created by speedy advancements in technology, state-of-the-art computing capabilities, complex algorithms, and enormous datasets (Park et al., 2024; Ziakis & Vlachopoulou, 2023). Though AI-powered personalization would possibly growth target audience engagement and loyalty, massive use of it raises ethical issues such as privacy, bias, manipulation, and societal affects.

Opportunities for Innovation

Suitable commercial opportunities are given with the aid of the puppy influencer fashion; businesses can meddle with formats for exciting content, information-driven marketing campaign metrics, and many more modern advances towards social media marketing. Upgrades in advertising also entered as digital interactions with clients and statistics-oriented selection-making (Yoo, 2024). They will additionally test with new interactive content styles like motion pictures, AR tales, and person-generated content material campaigns to have interaction audiences greater holistically. With information analytics and machine gaining knowledge of, target audience behaviour also can be found, campaigns overall performance measured, and strategies of influencer advertising and marketing optimized for maximum effect (SINGH, 2024). Micro-influencers are a great road for manufacturers to narrowcast to unique patron segments to have actual, meaningful engagements. Further to this, pet influence is a manner that an organization can market its animal welfare causes to the public, successfully demonstrating social stewardship while improving don't forget. Obviously, the way to cultivate brand allegiance is through influencer marketing based on the endorsements of those very credible personalities (Ilieva et al., 2024). Thus, brands are empowered to use animal agents in promoting adoption events, creating awareness about animal cruelty, and enhancing the support available to pet shelters and rescues.

In fact, Influencer advertising extends every form of traditional advertising and has exceptional benefits in establishing the brand-union connection with the end-user (Ingale, 2024). The other above merger of social media, pets, and the advertising world creates a lively landscape breeding grounds by which brands can reach consumers in novel and exciting ways (Łaszkiewicz, 2023). Influencer marketing is modernized, innovatively typed digital advertisement through involving influencers who have a wide but loyal follower base who could market for products, services, and brands. This industry has continued to develop at an astoundingly fast rate and is expected to grow to $16.4 billion by 2023. Influencer marketing works on these credibility, authenticity, and social standing that an influencer has under their followers, thereby manipulating the behavioural preference of the latter into the consumer. After picking only those who conform with the values and goals of the brand as well as applying transparency and ethics, then the power of social influence with word-of-mouth recommendations can be infused into the digitalized world. Emerging trends in consumer purchasing behaviour toward discovering, researching, and ultimately purchasing goods and services have formed a significant shift with the advent of influencer marketing.

CONCLUSION

Puppy influencers are quickly becoming the most effective and compelling form of advertising on social media, making people laugh and, in turns, other people form real connections with the pups themselves. Animals learn to make more noise in channels other than social media, which lets the brands target them for other forms of possible interaction with their desired consumers (Ao et al., 2023). It is miles the joining of pets with social media and the classified ads and advertising, giving advantage blessings and alternatives to producers on how to maximize the energy of influencer marketing. Via information key fulfilment motivators in navigating ethical troubles and in embracing innovation, brands will efficaciously make use of domestic dog influencer energy to force their emblem reputation and loyalty before advertising achievements. The evolution of influencer advertising need to, therefore, be reflected in a logo's approach so that it also stays applicable, genuine, and impactful amongst this ever-changing social media landscape. Further, manufacturers need to evolve with those converting client preferences the usage of statistics analytics with a purpose to supply centred personalized stories, for that reason enticing and maintaining logo loyalty (Salhab, 2024). As Migkos et al. (2025) put it, this comes from the trust and confidence constructed by the influencer with the target market.

Endorsements have shifted from mass media to extra slim-capturing scopes; yet influencer advertising and marketing is bendy and has a more fee within the subjective nature of the channel itself (Waltenrath, 2024). As a matter of fact, sometimes by virtue of market evolution with the great emphasis that is now put on social influencers within marketing, this becomes even imperative from a marketing and corporate perspective (Ayob et al., 2023). They are people or "celebrities" who "influence" the decision-making of their followers-the youth who mostly comprise a large percentage of social media users (Ayob et al., 2023). They have great influence on consumers; thus, marketers have started to recognize the value of social media influencers (Afzal et al., 2024; Chen et al., 2024; Gu & Duan, 2024).

Influencer advertising and marketing were suddenly established as dominant forces in today's marketing trends, and it currently plays the role of a channel through which clients are reached in a more proper and effective way than in the past (Migkos et al., 2025). Engagement rates are certainly higher than those of traditional virtual advertising and marketing. The largest shift that has took place in patron conduct about product discovery, assessment, and eventual purchasing is through influencer marketing (Migkos et al, 2025). Therefore, information analytics, gadget gaining knowledge of, and measurement might go very a whole lot deeper to glean insights into target market behaviour, monitor how the campaigns carried out, and optimize influencer techniques for maximum effectiveness (Ilieva et al. 2024). It would act as an intermediary among brands and all followers for direct communication and was intended to convert and deliver message advertising to them (Ismail & Mohamed, 2024). Influencer advertising and marketing is an amazing phenomenon in actual content material marketing. Influencer advertising now movements a few ways beyond traditional advertising and marketing well described. This interface of interplay now opens between the brand and its customers. Combining social media with pets and advertising and marketing creates completely unique surroundings for brands to the touch base with clients in a vibrant and effective way. Then credibility and authenticity are the lifeblood of pet influencers internal their operation (Andika et al., 2024).

A few different great assignments are to make certain that transparency, disclosure, and ethics are maintained in influencer advertising and marketing campaigns if they may be to advantage client consent and emblem popularity. The modern-day social-media structures, which encompass Instagram and TikTok, now provide those pet influencers new avenues to exhibit their animals and reap a target marketplace (Peng, 2023). With the rise of domestic dog influencers, an entire new economic device of doggy-associated merchandise, services, and stories have come into being. Influencer advertising permits income, complements brand photo, and builds consumer loyalty, thereby reinforcing its relevance in present day marketing and advertising strategies. Marketers need to assess functionality puppy influencers very carefully to align with values and types of goal market (Aw & Agnihotri, 2023). Influencer advertising works because influencers create remember and credibility with their fans (Li, 2025). Transparency, disclosure, and ethical issues are essential in influencer commercial campaigns for maintaining client believe and emblem popularity (Zhang, 2023).

Influencer marketing and advertising is rapid growing right into a cornerstone of higher level of advertising, presenting manufacturers with the potential to assemble deeper connections on a private and relatable degree. The efficacy of influencer advertising and marketing arises from trust and credibility that the influencers create with their follower base (Ünalmış et al., 2024). Inside the very fast development of influencer marketing, it has emerged as one of the pillars on which modern-day advertising requirements stand, permitting marketers to forge deep bonds with consumers on a private and relatable diploma (Salhab, 2024).

REFERENCES

Afzal, B., Xiao, W., Nazir, A., Junaid, D., & Silva, L. J. O. (2024). Analyzing the Impact of Social Media Influencers on Consumer Shopping Behavior: Empirical Evidence from Pakistan. *Sustainability, 16*(14), 6079. DOI: 10.3390/su16146079

Allal-Chérif, O., Puertas, R., & Carracedo, P. (2023). Intelligent influencer marketing: How AI-powered virtual influencers outperform human influencers. *Technological Forecasting and Social Change, 200*, 123113. DOI: 10.1016/j.techfore.2023.123113

Andika, A. D. P., Lestari, E. I. P., & Wiliam, A. (2024). Analyzing the Role of Influencers in Digital Marketing Strategy: A Case Study in the Online Fashion Industry. *Ilomata International Journal of Social Science, 5*(2), 444. DOI: 10.61194/ijss.v5i2.1166

Antoniou, A. (2024). When likes go rogue: Advertising standards and the malpractice of unruly social media influencers. *Journal of Medicine and Law, 16*(1), 74. DOI: 10.1080/17577632.2024.2361517

Ao, L., Bansal, R., Pruthi, N., & Khaskheli, M. B. (2023). Impact of Social Media Influencers on Customer Engagement and Purchase Intention: A Meta-Analysis. *Sustainability, 15*(3), 2744. DOI: 10.3390/su15032744

Aw, E. C., & Agnihotri, R. (2023). Influencer marketing research: Review and future research agenda. *Journal of Marketing Theory and Practice, 32*(4), 435. DOI: 10.1080/10696679.2023.2235883

Ayob, N. A., Kamaruddin, N. A., & Zaidi, M. Z. H. M. (2023). Social Influencer Factors that Affect Young Adult Buying Behaviour. *International Journal of Academic Research in Business & Social Sciences, 13*(1). Advance online publication. DOI: 10.6007/ijarbss/v13-i1/14610

Babadoğan, B. (2024). Exploring the Role of AI in Automating Content Marketing: Unlocking Opportunities and Navigating Challenges. *Next Frontier., 8*(1), 67. DOI: 10.62802/gkj6f352

Brambilla, M., Badrizadeh, H., Mohammadi, N. M., & Sabet, A. J. (2022). Analyzing Brand Awareness Strategies on Social Media in the Luxury Market: The Case of Italian Fashion on Instagram. *Digital, 3*(1), 1. DOI: 10.3390/digital3010001

Chen, Y., Qin, Z., Yan, Y., & Yi, H. (2024). The Power of Influencers: How Does Influencer Marketing Shape Consumers' Purchase Intentions? *Sustainability, 16*(13), 5471. DOI: 10.3390/su16135471

Di Cioccio, M., Pozharliev, R., & De Angelis, M. (2024). Pawsitively powerful: Why and when pet influencers boost social media effectiveness. *Psychology and Marketing*, *41*(7), 1614–1628.

Dondapati, A., & Dehury, R. K. (2024). Virtual vs. Human influencers: The battle for consumer hearts and minds. *Computers in Human Behavior Artificial Humans*, *2*(1), 100059. DOI: 10.1016/j.chbah.2024.100059

Doshi, R., Ramesh, A., & Rao, S. (2022). Modeling Influencer Marketing Campaigns in Social Networks. *IEEE Transactions on Computational Social Systems*, *10*(1), 322. DOI: 10.1109/tcss.2022.3140779

Drossos, D., Coursaris, C. K., & Kagiouli, E. (2023). Social media marketing content strategy: A comprehensive framework and empirically supported guidelines for brand posts on Facebook pages. *Journal of Consumer Behaviour*, *23*(3), 1175. DOI: 10.1002/cb.2269

Dzreke, S. S., & Dzreke, S. E. (2025). Influence of Social Media on Consumer Behavior: Investigating How Social Media Platforms Shape Consumer Purchasing Decisions and Loyalty. *Open Journal of Business and Management*, *13*(2), 1154. DOI: 10.4236/ojbm.2025.132061

Gracias, A., Olukemi, A., & Bell, C. (2024). Influencer Marketing ROI: Measurement Techniques and Optimization Strategies. SSRN Electronic Journal. DOI: 10.2139/ssrn.4907402

Gu, C., & Duan, Q.-T. (2024). Exploring the dynamics of consumer engagement in social media influencer marketing: From the self-determination theory perspective. *Humanities & Social Sciences Communications*, *11*(1). Advance online publication. DOI: 10.1057/s41599-024-03127-w

Guerra-Tamez, C. R., Flores, K. K., Serna-Mendiburu, G. M., Robles, D. C., & Cortés, J. I. (2024). Decoding Gen Z: AI's influence on brand trust and purchasing behavior. *Frontiers in Artificial Intelligence*, *7*. Advance online publication. DOI: 10.3389/frai.2024.1323512 PMID: 38500672

Hardey, M. (2024). What Is Influencer Marketing? DOI: 10.4135/9781071959664

Hicham, N., Nassera, H., & Karim, S. (2023). Strategic Framework for Leveraging Artificial Intelligence in Future Marketing Decision-Making. *Journal of Intelligent Management Decision*, *2*(3), 139. DOI: 10.56578/jimd020304

Ilieva, G., Yankova, T., Ruseva, M., Dzhabarova, Y., Klisarova-Belcheva, S., & Bratkov, M. (2024). Social Media Influencers: Customer Attitudes and Impact on Purchase Behaviour. *Information (Basel)*, *15*(6), 359. DOI: 10.3390/info15060359

Ingale, A. (2024). The Role of Influencer Marketing in Brand Building. SSRN Electronic Journal. DOI: 10.2139/ssrn.4972626

Iqbal, A., Aslam, S., Jalali, W. U. B., Saboor, A., & Haider, W. (2023). Unveiling the Power of Influencer Marketing: A Systematic review of Influencer Marketing Antecedents, Outcomes, Theoretical Framework and the Future Research Directions [Review of Unveiling the Power of Influencer Marketing: A Systematic review of Influencer Marketing Antecedents, Outcomes, Theoretical Framework and the Future Research Directions]. *Research Journal for Societal Issues*, *5*(2), 362. DOI: 10.56976/rjsi.v5i2.119

Ismail, S. A., & Mohamed, M. (2024). Analyzing the effects of influencer marketing on consumer behavior: Insights from social influence theory in TikTok Campaigns. *World Journal of Advanced Research and Reviews*, *24*(3), 2116. DOI: 10.30574/wjarr.2024.24.3.3926

Jacobson, J., Hodson, J., & Mittelman, R. (2022). Pup-ularity contest: The advertising practices of popular animal influencers on Instagram. *Technological Forecasting and Social Change*, *174*, 121226.

Jiang, Y. (2023). The Research on the Current Situation and Trends of Social Media Marketing. In Advances in Social Science, Education and Humanities Research/ Advances in social science, education and humanities research (p. 348). DOI: 10.2991/978-2-38476-062-6_44

Joshi, Y., Lim, W. M., Jagani, K., & Kumar, S. (2023). Social media influencer marketing: Foundations, trends, and ways forward. *Electronic Commerce Research*. Advance online publication. DOI: 10.1007/s10660-023-09719-z

Kim, D.-G., & Wang, Z. (2023). The ethics of virtuality: Navigating the complexities of human-like virtual influencers in the social media marketing realm. *Frontiers in Communication*, *8*. Advance online publication. DOI: 10.3389/fcomm.2023.1205610

Kumar, P., Oberoi, S., & Jaitly, R. C. (2023). Impact of Social Media Influencers on Consumer Engagement and Its Consequences in the Emerging Environment of Metaverse. In *Advances in marketing, customer relationship management, and e-services book series* (p. 225). IGI Global., DOI: 10.4018/978-1-6684-8898-0.ch014

Łaszkiewicz, A. (2023). THE USE OF INFLUENCER MARKETING IN MARKETING COMMUNICATION OF PLACES. *Scientific Papers of Silesian University of Technology Organization and Management Series*, *2023*(173), 445. DOI: 10.29119/1641-3466.2023.173.29

Lavertu, L., Kulow, K., Cowan, K., & Marder, B. (2025). Petfluencers, the fur-mula for sincere endorsements: Examining how and when pets exhibit greater persuasion as influencers. *Journal of Advertising Research*, •••, 1–16.

Li, R. K. (2025). The Impact of Social Media Influencers on Gen Z's Online Purchase Decisions. *Advances in Economics Management and Political Sciences*, *150*(1), 178. DOI: 10.54254/2754-1169/2024.19299

Liu, P. (2024). Optimizing E-commerce Operational Efficiency and Customer Experience Through Data Analytics and Technological Innovation. *Advances in Economics Management and Political Sciences*, *100*(1), 14. DOI: 10.54254/2754-1169/100/20241121

Looi, J., & Kahlor, L. A. (2024). Artificial Intelligence in Influencer Marketing: A Mixed-Method Comparison of Human and Virtual Influencers on Instagram. *Journal of Interactive Advertising*, *24*(2), 107. DOI: 10.1080/15252019.2024.2313721

Martini, E., Shidqi, M. N., Hurriyati, R., & Widjajanta, B. (2022). *The Impact of Brand Experience on Consumer Engagement*. Advances in Economics, Business and Management Research/Advances in Economics, Business and Management Research., DOI: 10.2991/aebmr.k.220701.062

Maulidian, M., Zahra, S. F., Nadela, A. T., & Fitriani, A. (2023). Content categories on Instagram: From promotional to interactivity for business development. *Journal of Enterprise and Development*, *5*(1), 15. DOI: 10.20414/jed.v5i1.6774

Migkos, S. P., Giannakopoulos, N. T., & Σακάς, Δ. Π. (2025). Impact of Influencer Marketing on Consumer Behavior and Online Shopping Preferences. DOI: 10.20944/preprints202504.0787.v1

Murár, P., & Kubovics, M. (2023). Using AI to Create Content Designed for Marketing Communications. European Conference on Innovation and Entrepreneurship, 18(1), 660. DOI: 10.34190/ecie.18.1.1638

Park, H. W., Lim, C. V., Zhu, Y. P., & Omar, M. (2024). Decoding the Relationship of Artificial Intelligence, Advertising, and Generative Models. DOI: 10.20944/preprints202401.0373.v1

Peng, C. (2023). Influencer Marketing: Statistics and Skepticism. *Open Journal of Business and Management*, *11*(2), 744. DOI: 10.4236/ojbm.2023.112040

Petty, R. E., & Cacioppo, J. T. (2012). *Communication and persuasion: Central and peripheral routes to attitude change*. Springer Science & Business Media.

Rani, A., Roy, A., Boaler, M., & Itam, U. J. (2022). Determinants of Influencer Credibility and Platform Credibility to Understand the Effectiveness of Indian Fashion Influencers. *International Journal of Online Marketing, 12*(1), 1. DOI: 10.4018/ijom.299399

Salhab, H. A. (2024). Social media marketing—Rise of social media influencer marketing and Instagram. *Journal of Infrastructure Policy and Development, 8*(8), 3783. DOI: 10.24294/jipd.v8i8.3783

SanMiguel, P., & Sádaba, T. (2024). Who is Accountable for the Negative Effects of Influencer Marketing? Voices of the Influencer Ecosystem. Revista ICONO14, 22(1). DOI: 10.7195/ri14.v22i1.2103

Setyawati, R. L., & Anindita, R. (2022). Developing Customer Engagement Through Instagram Social Media on Local Coffee Shop. *Majalah Ilmiah Bijak, 19*(2), 168. DOI: 10.31334/bijak.v19i2.2539

SINGH, P. K. (2024). The Role of Artificial Intelligence in Personalized Marketing Strategies of AMAZON. INTERANTIONAL JOURNAL OF SCIENTIFIC RESEARCH IN ENGINEERING AND MANAGEMENT, 8(4), 1. DOI: 10.55041/ijsrem32818

Ünalmış, E., Dirsehan, T., & Erdoğmuş, İ. E. (2024). Consequences of influencer-created content on influencers' authenticity in the beauty and personal care industry. *Journal of Marketing Communications, 1*. Advance online publication. DOI: 10.1080/13527266.2024.2371833

van der Harst, J. P., & Angelopoulos, S. (2024). Less is more: Engagement with the content of social media influencers. *Journal of Business Research, 181*, 114746. DOI: 10.1016/j.jbusres.2024.114746

Waltenrath, A. (2024). Consumers' ambiguous perceptions of advertising disclosures in influencer marketing: Disentangling the effects on current and future social media engagement. *Electronic Markets, 34*(1). Advance online publication. DOI: 10.1007/s12525-023-00679-8

Xu, S. (2024). Research on marketing strategies in the pet food industry: A case study based on existing brands. SHS Web of Conferences, 207, 1002. DOI: 10.1051/shsconf/202420701002

Yang, J., Zhang, J., & Zhang, Y. (2024). Engagement That Sells: Influencer Video Advertising on TikTok. *Marketing Science*. Advance online publication. DOI: 10.1287/mksc.2021.0107

Yoo, S., Pu, K., & Truong, K. N. (2024, May). Behind the Pup-ularity Curtain: Understanding the Motivations, Challenges, and Work Performed in Creating and Managing Pet Influencer Accounts. In *Proceedings of the 2024 CHI Conference on Human Factors in Computing Systems* (pp. 1-17).

Yoo, W.-S. (2024). The Impact of Artificial Intelligence on Marketing Strategies. *International Journal of Science and Research Archive*, *13*(1), 3211. DOI: 10.30574/ijsra.2024.13.1.2042

Zhang, L., Wei, W., Rathjens, B., & Zheng, Y. (2023). Pet influencers on social media: The joint effect of message appeal and narrator. *International Journal of Hospitality Management*, *110*, 103453.

Zhang, X. (2023). Influencer Marketing: Assessing Effectiveness and Exploring Potential Drawbacks in Advertising Strategies. *Highlights in Business Economics and Management*, *23*, 171. DOI: 10.54097/t83twa35

Ziakis, C., & Vlachopoulou, M. (2023). Artificial Intelligence in Digital Marketing: Insights from a Comprehensive Review [Review of Artificial Intelligence in Digital Marketing: Insights from a Comprehensive Review]. Information, 14(12), 664. Multidisciplinary Digital Publishing Institute. DOI: 10.3390/info14120664

Zniva, R., Weitzl, W., & Lindmoser, C. (2023). Be constantly different! How to manage influencer authenticity. *Electronic Commerce Research*, *23*(3), 1485. DOI: 10.1007/s10660-022-09653-6

Chapter 10
The Role of Bees in Food Security and Honey Tourism:
The Case of Bee Nectar at Reserva Andirá, Lima Duarte, MG- Brazil

Annaelise Fritz Machado
https://orcid.org/0000-0003-3849-7350
Universidade Federal de Viçosa, Brazil

Marcelo Leles Romarco de Oliveira
Universidade Federal de Viçosa, Brazil

André Luiz Lopes de Faria
Universidade Federal de Viçosa, Brazil

Renata Falcão Rabello da Costa
Universidade Federal Fluminense, Brazil, Brazil

Sérgio Nogueira Pereira
https://orcid.org/0000-0002-9459-2531
Universidade Federal Rural do Rio de Janeiro, Brazil

Janderson Damaceno dos Reis
https://orcid.org/0000-0002-7175-0496
Universidade Federal de Viçosa, Brazil

ABSTRACT

The chapter presents a case study on Bee Nectar, located at Reserva Andirá, in Lima Duarte (MG), Brazil, integrating beekeeping, stingless beekeeping, and honey tourism. Its objective is to assess the role of bees in food security, income generation, and environmental education. The methodology combined bibliographic and documentary research, interviews, and direct observation, allowing for an understanding of both declared practices and aspects of daily life on the property. The central research question investigated was: How can the preservation of bees, through the Bee Nectar initiative at Reserva Andirá, simultaneously contribute to food security,

DOI: 10.4018/979-8-3373-4342-6.ch010

income generation, and the strengthening of honey tourism? The results indicate that bee management promotes the preservation of the Atlantic Forest biodiversity, generates high value-added products, strengthens honey tourism, and contributes to the environmental education of visitors and the local community.

INTRODUCTION

Bees play a fundamental ecological role as essential agents in the pollination of various plant species, directly impacting food security and the maintenance of biodiversity. Beyond their environmental value, beekeeping and bee management present significant potential, enabling the production of high value-added foods and artisanal cosmetics aligned with socially and environmentally responsible practices.

In the context of rural and environmental tourism, initiatives that integrate beekeeping, meliponiculture, and educational experiences have proven promising in generating income and strengthening ecological awareness among visitors and local communities. Within this framework lies Bee Nectar, developed in Reserva Andirá, a rural property located in Lima Duarte (MG), Brazil. Created as a space for conservation and environmental education, it combines the keeping of sting and stingless bees, the production of high-quality honeys and by-products, and honey tourism activities, demonstrating how the relationship between conservation, production, and tourism can be articulated in a sustainable manner.

The objective of this work is to assess the role of bees in food security, income generation, and environmental education. For this purpose, the chapter is structured into five sections: The first addresses sting and stingless bees, highlighting their role in pollination, biodiversity maintenance, ecosystem balance, and food security, with emphasis on the relationship between native species, flora, and fauna in Brazilian biomes. The second section discusses the importance of bees for food production and agriculture, including public policies aimed at conservation and the promotion of sustainable production. The third explores bee management as a strategy for generating high value-added products, fostering innovation, enhancing biodiversity, and strengthening the local economy.

The fourth section introduces Honey Tourism (Apiecotourism) as a diversification strategy for rural producers, emphasizing how educational experiences, tastings of different types of honey, and hands-on activities with bees can add value to beekeeping and meliponiculture, strengthen the local economy, and raise awareness among tourists about the importance of environmental conservation. Finally, the fifth section presents the case study of Bee Nectar at Reserva Andirá, in Lima Duarte (MG), integrating beekeeping, meliponiculture, and honey tourism, based on interviews, direct observation, and the analysis of socio-environmental impacts.

METHODOLOGY

This study adopted a qualitative approach, aimed at understanding the practices, experiences, and innovations of Bee Nectar at Reserva Andirá, in Lima Duarte (MG). The theoretical framework and contextualization were built upon bibliographic research, IBGE data, and the analysis of institutional documents from the *Entre Serras – Rural Tourism Association*. Founded in 2016, this association brings together 11 rural properties committed to valuing the territory and offering authentic experiences, promoting activities that go beyond traditional lodging, such as agricultural practices, typical gastronomy, contact with nature, cultural hospitality, and social innovations focused on sustainability (Statute, 2021; Entre Serras, 2018; Machado et al., 2025).

In the empirical scope, field research was conducted at Reserva Andirá, one of the associated properties, through semi-structured interviews with its owners, a couple identified as Associate A and Associate B. Field activities, carried out between 2023 and 2025, focused on observing the daily management of hives and bees, as well as the tourism practices linked to the project. Impressions, reflections, and observation notes were systematically recorded in a field notebook, forming the empirical material for this research.

In this chapter, the researchers contributed in a multidisciplinary manner to the understanding of bee diversity and ecological function, as well as to the analysis of the beekeeping sector in its socioeconomic and environmental context, each emphasizing their specific field of expertise. The perspective of Tourism and Rural Extension enabled the exploration of the potential of honey tourism, demonstrating how beekeeping can be integrated into sustainable tourism practices, environmental education, and rural development. The field of Social Sciences and Anthropology offered an analysis of the historical and cultural relationships between human communities and bees, highlighting how traditional and contemporary practices influence species conservation and management. Training in Geography and Soils contributed technical knowledge about sustainable habitat management and the influence of environmental conditions on hive productivity. Biology deepened the understanding of bee behavior, diversity, and species adaptation, which are essential for the pollination of endemic plants. Veterinary Medicine added knowledge on bee health, hygiene, and honey quality, emphasizing the interdependence between animal health, beekeeping, meliponiculture, and human consumption. Finally, Zootechnics and Economics enabled the evaluation of productivity, management, and economic viability of beekeeping, considering its role in income generation and the strengthening of the local market.

1. STING AND STINGLESS BEES: DIVERSITY, ECOLOGICAL FUNCTION, AND IMPORTANCE FOR BIOMES

Bees have played a central role in the history and culture of many civilizations, from prehistory to the Middle Ages. Sumerians, Egyptians, Greeks, and Romans attributed sacred and symbolic meanings to them, associating bees with deities, fertility, power, and victory. Archaeological evidence, such as horizontal and vertical ceramic hives, paintings, murals, and coins, demonstrates that beekeeping was a common practice in regions such as the Mediterranean, the Middle East, and southern Urals, with methods adapted to local conditions, such as hollow logs used for predator protection. In addition, honey and beeswax were associated with religious and cultural rituals, reinforcing the importance of bees to ancient societies (Kristsky, 2017; Eroğlu, 2020; Topal et al., 2021).

In contemporary contexts, bees continue to be cultural and educational symbols, represented in postage stamps, apiculture museums, and ethnographic exhibitions in countries such as Italy, Turkey, and Slovenia. Museums dedicated to apiculture preserve local traditions, promote knowledge about native species, and highlight the relevance of bees to the environment and food security. The history of bees reflects both their practical role in honey production and their symbolic, artistic, and educational value, demonstrating the enduring relationship between humans, nature, and culture throughout the centuries (Eroğlu, 2020; Fontana & Fontana, 2020; Chirsanova et al., 2021; Kösoğlu, 2021; Topal et al., 2021).

Bees are among the most vital insect groups for the balance of terrestrial ecosystems, going beyond honey production to perform an irreplaceable ecological function: pollination. With more than 20,000 species catalogued worldwide (Faita et al., 2022; National Geographic, 2022), these pollinators form the foundation of both natural ecosystems and agricultural systems.

Brazil, known for its immense biodiversity, is home to more than 2,500 bee species essential for pollination and ecosystem maintenance. Beekeeping in the country began in 1839 with the introduction of *Apis mellifera* by Father Antônio Carneiro and was consolidated during the 20th century with the arrival of the African subspecies *Apis mellifera scutellata*. Crossbreeding with European subspecies gave rise to the Africanized bee, more defensive and challenging to manage. However, the development of proper techniques in the 1970s allowed the expansion of the activity and the strengthening of honey and by-product production (Pegoraro et al., 2017; Marcelino et al., 2022; Sousa Júnior et al., 2024).

The quality of honey, regulated by the Ministry of Agriculture, Livestock, and Food Supply (MAPA), depends on factors such as floral sources, climate, and region, as well as chemical composition, hygiene, and management practices, requiring attention to avoid primary and secondary contaminations, including pesticide residues (Carvalho et al., 2019; Ribeiro et al., 2023).

Among the most relevant species are the stinging bees, such as *Apis mellifera*, and the native stingless bees (Meliponini), including genera such as *Melipona*, *Scaptotrigona*, and *Tetragonisca* (see Table 1). The latter, with more than 250 species adapted to different Brazilian biomes, maintain a close relationship with native flora, playing a central role in the pollination of endemic species and the conservation of biodiversity (Nogueira et al., 2023; Melo, 2020; Pegoraro et al., 2017; Sousa Júnior, 2024).

Table 1. Comparison between stinging bees (Apis mellifera) and stingless bees (Tribe Meliponini), highlighting ecological functions, agricultural importance, and specific threats observed in some parts of the world.

Aspect	**Stinging bees** (*Apis mellifera*)	**Stingless bees (Tribe Meliponini; e.g.,** *Melipona quadrifasciata, Tetragonisca angustula, Scaptotrigona xanthotricha*)
Distribution & diversity	Present in nearly all biomes (except Antarctica). Widely managed.	Predominantly in tropical/subtropical regions of the Americas, Africa, Oceania, and Asia; high diversity of native species.
Sociability & nests	Eusocial[1]; large colonies (tens of thousands). Nests in cavities with wax combs; standardized management (Langstroth hives).	Eusocial; generally smaller colonies. Nests in tree/soil cavities; built with cerumen (wax + resin) and geopropolis; management varies by species.
Defense	Functional sting; defense through stinging and alarm pheromones.	Atrophied sting; defense through biting, resins/propolis, and entrance-blocking behavior.
Ecological functions	Generalist pollinators with large foraging range; connect fragmented landscapes and increase gene flow.	Keystone pollinators in tropical forests; high floral fidelity in many species, supporting native pollination networks.
Agricultural importance	High economic impact: commercial pollination of almonds, apples, canola, sunflower, citrus, stone fruits.	Increasing local/urban use in greenhouses and tropical orchards (e.g., strawberry, pepper, blueberry/guava depending on species/system).
Products	Large volumes of honey, wax, propolis, pollen, royal jelly, venom.	"Native bee honey" (higher moisture), cerumen/geopropolis, pollen; high gastronomic/medicinal demand.
Main threats	Specific: Varroa mite, American foulbrood, viruses, small hive beetle (in some regions). General: habitat loss, monocultures, pesticides (neonicotinoids), transhumance stress, extreme climate.	Specific: Phorid flies, ants, robber bees (*Lestrimelitta*), illegal nest extraction/trade. General: deforestation (loss of cavities), urbanization without green areas, pesticides, heatwaves/drought.

continued on following page

Table 1. Continued

Aspect	Stinging bees (*Apis mellifera*)	Stingless bees (Tribe Meliponini; e.g., *Melipona quadrifasciata, Tetragonisca angustula, Scaptotrigona xanthotricha*)
Conservation status	*Apis mellifera* is widely managed.	Many species have restricted distribution and are at higher risk due to habitat loss; several taxa listed as threatened.
Best management practices	Sanitary control (Varroa/foulbroods), floral diversification, ecological corridors, pesticide reduction, continuous flowering.	Protection of cavities/native vegetation, installation of pollinator hotels/rational hives, anti-phorid management, native tree planting.

Source: Produced by the researchers (2025).

The comparative table highlights functional and ecological differences between stinging and stingless bees, emphasizing their complementarity. While *Apis mellifera* has high agricultural relevance as a generalist pollinator across multiple crops, stingless bees specialize in pollinating native species, many of them endemic and threatened, particularly in biomes such as the Atlantic Forest. This distinction reinforces the need for conservation strategies that address not only insects but also the habitats sustaining their interactions with flora, ensuring biodiversity maintenance and ecosystem stability (Nogueira et al., 2023).

The complementary functions of these groups are directly related to the morphological and behavioral adaptations developed throughout evolution. Specialized structures such as corbiculae (Michener, 2007; Faita et al., 2022) and plumose hairs (Neff & Simpson, 1993) enable efficient pollen transport, consolidating their irreplaceable role in pollination within both natural and agricultural ecosystems. Thus, the functional diversity of bees contributes not only to agricultural productivity but also to the reproduction of native plants and the maintenance of complex ecological networks (Faita et al., 2022; Caetano et al., 2024).

This ecological and economic relevance is closely tied to Earth's history, marked by billions of years of climatic and biological transformations. Natural changes shaped the evolution of species, including bees and flowering plants, but in recent decades, human activities such as deforestation, agricultural expansion, pollution, and intensive fossil fuel use have accelerated climate change, generating unprecedented and severe impacts on ecosystems and their interactions (Santos et al., 2022).

Within this context, bees (Hymenoptera: Apoidea) are among the most affected groups, playing a key role in biodiversity maintenance and food production, since about 90% of wild flowering plants and 70% of global crops depend on pollinators (Imperatriz-Fonseca et al., 2012; Yasmi, 2025).

Bees ensure the reproduction of a large portion of agricultural crops, covering 87 of the 115 main species cultivated for human consumption. This contribution extends far beyond food production: it directly influences dietary diversity and quality, ensures ecological balance, and sustains the livelihoods of approximately 1.4 billion people, particularly small farmers in Africa, Asia, and Latin America (Yasmi, 2025).

The ecosystem services provided by these insects transcend ecology, reaching significant economic and cultural impacts. It is estimated that bee pollination contributes about US$ 54 billion annually to the global economy (UN, 2025), being particularly relevant for Brazilian crops such as coffee, soybeans, and fruit species (Nogueira-Couto, 1998). At the same time, various traditional communities maintain ancestral relationships with bees, using their products not only as food but also in rituals and medicinal practices (Cortopassi-Laurino et al., 2006; Faita et al., 2022), corroborated by scientific research that has identified antibacterial and anti-inflammatory properties (Pires et al., 2020; Rao et al., 2016).

However, pollinator population declines threaten the stability of both natural and agricultural systems. Reduced pollination compromises crop productivity, lowers nutritional diversity, and weakens rural economies, increasing food insecurity and favoring the emergence of diet-related diseases, especially in vulnerable regions (Yasmi, 2025).

The situation is worsened by climate change, which imposes additional challenges on pollinators. Rising temperatures may exceed species' physiological tolerance, irregular rainfall reduces nectar and pollen availability, and mismatches between flowering and colony activity disrupt ecological interactions consolidated over millions of years (Santos et al., 2022). Consequently, the decline of bee populations directly impacts agriculture, with pollination in Brazil estimated to be worth more than US$ 12 billion annually, in addition to affecting food chains, nutritional diversity, and global food security (Yasmi, 2025).

This crisis is intensified by habitat loss. Deforestation, particularly in the Atlantic Forest, fragments essential areas for the nesting and feeding of native bees, especially stingless species specialized in pollinating endemic plants (Kerr et al., 2010; Nogueira et al., 2023). Urban expansion and intensive agriculture aggravate this situation, eliminating natural vegetation and introducing neonicotinoid pesticides that cause neurological disorders and contribute to Colony Collapse Disorder (Higes et al., 2009; Sanchez-Bayo & Goka, 2014).

In this context, stingless bees, critical for pollination, are also impacted by pesticides such as the fungicide difenoconazole, which affects behavior, survival, and physiology differently depending on species and exposure pathways (Araujo et al., 2025). Complementarily, studies indicate that ingestion of TiO_2 nanoparticles by *Partamona helleri* alters hemocytes, enzymatic activity, and movement patterns, even without affecting survival or food intake, highlighting additional risks to pollinator health and the need for further research on the impacts of emerging pollutants (Viana et al., 2025).

Additionally, biological and climatic factors combine to heighten risks. Changes in flowering cycles and reduced food resources during critical periods jeopardize bee survival (Ogilvie, 2017; Maia-Silva et al., 2020), while exotic pests such as the *Varroa* mite and the small hive beetle (*Aethina tumida*) proliferate in weakened colonies, amplifying population losses (Martel et al., 2007; Pereira et al., 2021). The economic impact is direct: it is estimated that pollinator decline could reduce Brazil's agricultural GDP by 19% (Novais et al., 2016) and compromise the reproduction of plants essential for human food (Rodgers et al., 2021).

Given this complex scenario, bee conservation requires integrated actions. Strict regulation of pesticides, particularly neonicotinoids, is crucial to reducing insect mortality (Barbosa et al., 2017; Beringer, Maciel & Tramontina, 2019). At the same time, the preservation and restoration of natural habitats, including ecological corridors, are essential measures to ensure the availability of floral resources and nesting sites (Kevan & Imperatriz-Fonseca, 2002).

Meliponiculture emerges as a sustainable practice capable of reconciling environmental preservation and community development (Carvalho, Martins & Mourão, 2014), simultaneously promoting bee protection and income generation for local communities (Rodrigues, 2015; Barbosa et al., 2017; Beringer, Maciel & Tramontina, 2019). This integration establishes the foundation for reflecting on the role of bees in food security and public policies, the theme addressed in the following section.

2. BEES, FOOD SECURITY, AND PUBLIC POLICIES

Food security, according to the United Nations Food and Agriculture Organization (FAO), consists of regular physical, social, and economic access to safe, nutritious, and sufficient food to meet the dietary needs and cultural preferences of populations (FAO, 2023; FAO, 2025). This concept goes beyond mere food availability; it involves stability in supply, sustainability in production, and effective distribution policies. However, in 2025, various interconnected factors profoundly threaten this basic right, putting the food supply of millions of people worldwide at risk.

First, armed conflicts remain one of the greatest threats to global food security. The ongoing war between Russia and Ukraine continues to drastically affect the global supply of grains and fertilizers. Moreover, intense conflicts persist in regions such as Sudan, Yemen, Syria, Palestine, Myanmar, and more recently, tensions have increased in parts of Sub-Saharan Africa and the Sahel, where climate change and ethnic rivalries exacerbate disputes over natural resources (Nhemachena et al., 2022; European Commission, 2022; Leal Filho et al., 2023; Statista, 2025). These wars compromise not only local production but also international trade flows, causing shortages and rising prices.

The situation is further aggravated by health crises. Although the COVID-19 pandemic has largely been controlled, new viral variants and regional outbreaks of zoonotic diseases, such as monkeypox and avian influenza, continue to affect production chains and public health. These events expose the fragility of global food systems, highlighting the need for greater sanitary surveillance and biosecurity (Morens & Fauci, 2020; Ribeiro-Silva, 2020; Knowledge Policy, 2021; Leal Filho et al., 2023).

The environmental scenario is also alarming. Accelerated deforestation, especially in the Amazon, the Brazilian Cerrado, African forests, and Southeast Asian forests, contributes to biodiversity loss, alters rainfall patterns, and degrades soils, directly impacting agriculture (Nobre et al., 2016; IPCC, 2022). The indiscriminate use of chemical pesticides, in turn, contaminates soils, water, and food while affecting essential pollinators such as bees. The drastic reduction of bee populations, caused by pesticides, diseases, and climate change, compromises the pollination of more than 75% of global crops, including fruits, vegetables, and oilseeds (Potts, 2016; Pignati et al., 2017; Jornal USP, 2019; Santos, 2024).

Bees play a central role in food security and ecosystem health. According to the UN, approximately 90% of wild flowering plants and more than 75% of global food crops depend on animal pollination, with bees being essential for foods such as coffee, chocolate, blueberries, and cucumbers (UN, 2025). Additionally, they act as environmental sentinels, indicating the health of local ecosystems.

In Brazil, beekeeping and meliponiculture are essential for biodiversity conservation and food production but face growing threats such as climate change, habitat loss, and pollution (Embrapa, 2025). To ensure sector resilience and the continuity of ecosystem services provided by bees, measures are needed, including proper colony management, beekeeper training, and public policies for protection.

These actions align with broader food security strategies, which should include agroecological practices, support for family farming, pollinator protection, sustainable land management, deforestation reduction, and investment in green technologies. Strengthening local supply networks and international cooperation, aligned with the Sustainable Development Goals, especially SDG 2, is crucial to ensure equitable access to food, safeguarding the right to life, dignity, and the future of coming generations.

Public policies aimed at protecting pollinators, such as bees and other insects, have proven essential at both national and international levels. In Brazil, the National Pollinator Conservation Plan (PNCP) establishes guidelines for preserving pollinator species, promoting the integration of agricultural, environmental, and scientific research policies (Pignati et al., 2017; Brazil, 2022). Additionally, several Brazilian states have implemented specific laws encouraging meliponiculture, recognizing the rearing of native stingless bees as a strategy for environmental conservation and income generation for rural communities (Santos, 2024).

Despite legal advances, challenges remain in implementing these policies. The geographic dispersion of hives, lack of producer training, and limited resources for monitoring hinder the effectiveness of these actions (Embrapa, 2025). Moreover, integration between environmental, agricultural, and research agencies is still limited, compromising the effectiveness of the PNCP and state programs. The pressure from intensive pesticide use, habitat loss, and climate change reinforces the urgency for robust and coordinated policies (Brandão, 2025; UN, 2025).

To strengthen beekeeping and meliponiculture as strategies for rural sustainability, measures that combine environmental protection with socio-economic development are necessary. These include technical training for producers, the creation of financial and fiscal incentives, promotion of research on native species resilient to climate variations, and the expansion of environmental education programs that raise awareness among farmers and consumers about the importance of bees (Pereira, 2025; Pignati et al., 2017). Implementing agroecological practices, such as crop rotation, integrated pest management, and preservation of native vegetation areas, can contribute to colony resilience and sustainable agricultural productivity.

However, their effectiveness depends on overcoming structural challenges, strengthening institutions, and engaging producers and civil society in building integrated and resilient practices (Pereira, 2025; Embrapa, 2025; UN, 2025).

3. THE HONEY SUPPLY CHAIN: INNOVATION AND SOCIO-ENVIRONMENTAL IMPACT

The honey production chain represents a convergence point between innovation, environmental conservation, and social development. This potential becomes even more relevant in the face of the alarming global decline of bee populations, caused by intensive pesticide use, climate change, and the loss of natural habitats. Responsible beekeeping emerges as a viable economic model that combines productivity with ecosystem preservation (Thomé, 2024; Noticias Ambientales, 2025). This section explores how sustainable practices, social engagement, and community empowerment are transforming the sector, highlighting cases such as organic certification.

Sustainable honey production goes beyond harvesting; it requires management that preserves biodiversity, prevents pesticide contamination, and ensures the well-being of colonies. As highlighted by InovaBee Brazil, apiaries aligned with these principles use high-quality equipment, provide beekeeper training, and are strategically located to minimize environmental impacts (Thomé, 2024). These practices not only protect bees but also strengthen the income of rural communities, with Brazil generating approximately R$ 300 million annually in this market (Thomé, 2024).

This beekeeping model strengthens communities through fair trade and organic certification, which add value to honey and ensure more equitable prices (Noticias Ambientales, 2025). However, challenges persist, such as the resistance of large-scale farmers to reducing pesticide use and the lack of effective public policies.

Beekeeping in this productive spirit combines profitability and conservation. From organic management to innovations in honey production, experiences demonstrate that valuing pollinators and beekeeping communities is vital for food security and biodiversity. To expand these models, it is necessary to:

1. Implement policies that incentivize agroecological transition;
2. Invest in technology accessible to small producers;
3. Raise consumer awareness, encouraging demand for ethical and sustainable products (Thomé, 2024; Noticias Ambientales, 2025).

Thus, every drop of honey becomes a symbol of a future where economy and ecology coexist in harmony. Over the last ten years, honey production in Brazil has grown by 80%, ranking 11th globally (SNA, 2023). In 2023 alone, Brazilian honey production reached 64.2 million kilograms, totaling approximately 908 million reais in value (IBGE, 2023), see Figure 01.

These figures highlight the economic importance of the apiculture sector for the country, showing that beekeeping not only meets domestic demand for honey and its derivatives but also significantly contributes to income generation and the strengthening of rural communities. Among producing states, Rio Grande do Sul stands out as the national leader, responsible for the majority of production, reinforcing its relevance within the Brazilian apiculture landscape.

This scenario demonstrates that apiculture is a strategic segment both for the economy and for promoting environmental sustainability, especially when combined with complementary activities such as honey tourism, which values local production and bee preservation (SNA, 2023; IBGE, 2023).

Figure 1. Honey production quantity in Brazil in 2023 and production value

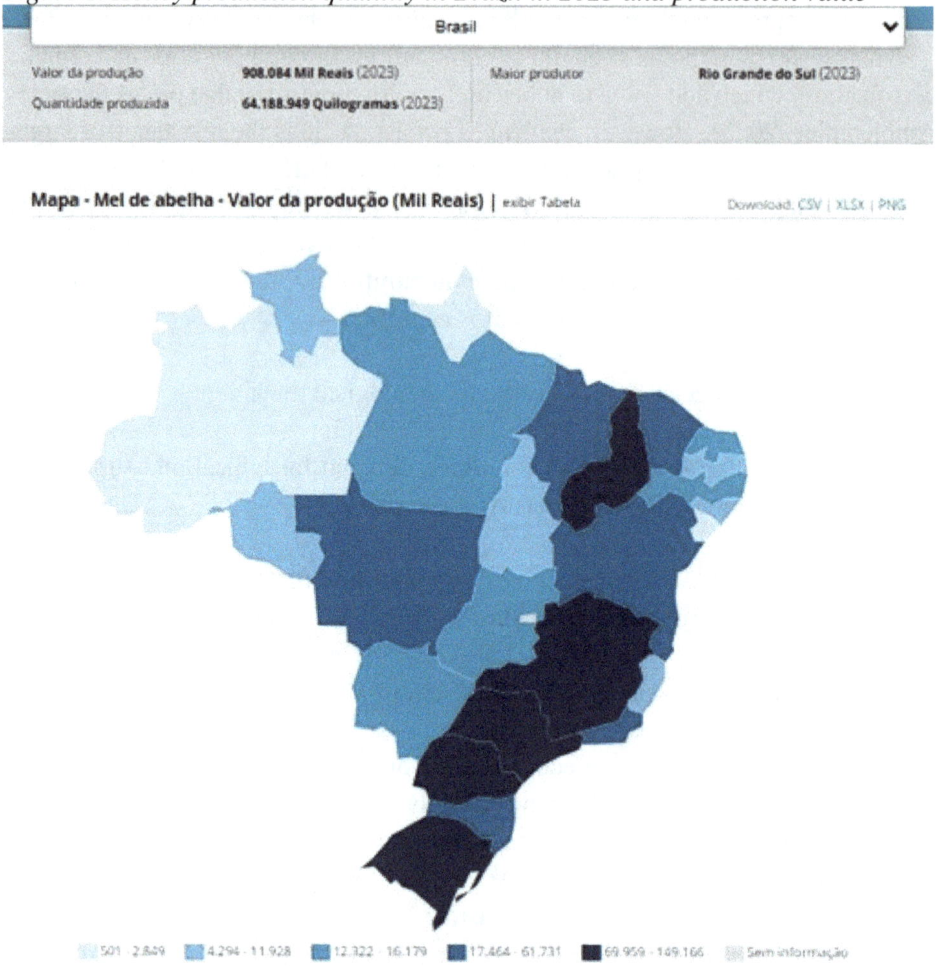

Source: IBGE, 2023

States such as Rio Grande do Sul, Paraná, São Paulo, Minas Gerais, and Piauí stand out in national production. Initiatives like Casa Apis in Piauí have promoted sustainable beekeeping practices, such as reforesting with melliferous trees to feed bees during dry periods, while maintaining organic product certifications. These projects are supported by the state government and SEBRAE, strengthening the local production chain and the income of approximately 980 beekeeping families (SNA, 2023).

Honey is valued not only for its dietary and medicinal uses but also for its application in cosmetics and natural products, which expands its economic potential. Between January and August 2023, Brazil exported 19,000 tons of honey, generating approximately USD 60 million, with the United States as the main destination, followed by Germany and Canada (SNA, 2023).

Brazilian honey, internationally recognized as one of the best in the world, suffered significant losses in the U.S. market due to increased tariffs imposed by the Trump administration, particularly affecting the Santa Catarina company Apis Nativa. In 2024, the company exported 5.9 million kilograms, 72% destined for the U.S.; in 2025, this dependence rose to 98.8%. The tariff more than doubled the price of Brazilian honey compared to Argentine competitors, threatening competitiveness, demand, and the income of around 350,000 Brazilian beekeepers. Santa Catarina accounts for almost half of national exports, with projected losses in price and export volume estimated between USD 40 and 50 million. This situation underscores the need for market diversification and government support for the sector (Figueiredo, 2025).

This vulnerability in the international market highlights the importance of diversifying income sources for Brazilian beekeepers, with honey tourism emerging as a promising strategy. By transforming apiaries and meliponaries into tourist destinations, it is possible to generate local revenue, value national production, and promote environmental education about the importance of bees, strengthening the economic and ecological sustainability of the sector.

4. HONEY TOURISM / BEE TOURISM: A STRATEGY FOR DIVERSIFICATION AND VALORIZATION OF APICULTURAL PRODUCTION

Over the past twenty years, honey tourism has emerged as an innovative strategy to enhance the value of beekeeping and meliponiculture. This activity allows producers to transform their apiaries into tourist destinations, offering educational and sensory experiences. Through guided tours, tastings, workshops, and other interactive activities, it is possible not only to promote local production and generate income for rural families but also to raise visitors' awareness about the ecological importance of bees and pollination, strengthening the economic and environmental sustainability of the apiculture sector.

Situated within the context of rural and gastronomic tourism, honey tourism highlights the value of beekeeping and its various products, such as propolis, royal jelly, mead, and cosmetics. The activity provides experiences ranging from observing bee management and honey production processes to educational activities on biodiversity conservation and the ecological role of bees, deepening the connection between visitors, local production, and environmental preservation.

In addition to promoting beekeeping and its products, honey tourism represents a concrete expression of experiential tourism, bringing visitors closer to local culture and production processes. In Brazil, this practice has already been established in several regions, including Minas Gerais, Rio Grande do Sul, Paraná, Santa Catarina, and São Paulo, through itineraries that combine guided trails, hive visits, tastings of different types of honey, and workshops on derivative products, integrating beekeepers into the tourism chain and strengthening regional identity.

Within this framework, apiecotourism, or "Bee Tourism," represents the most structured form of honey tourism, expanding over nearly two decades, particularly in the South, Southeast, and Northeast regions. According to the report *Apiecotourism: Business Opportunity* by the Sector Intelligence System (SIS) of the Brazilian Support Service for Micro and Small Enterprises (Sebrae, 2017), the activity combines environmental education, sensory experiences, hands-on participation in apiary activities, and interaction with rural culture.

Inspired by international models, such as Slovenia's *Api Routes* project, Brazilian apiecotourism includes hive visits, cooking and wax candle workshops, honey tastings, and apiary trails, constituting a form of creative tourism that connects visitors to rural realities and strengthens the sustainability of the apiculture chain (SNA, 2017).

Hotels and tourist destinations have created activities that allow visitors to interact directly with bees, such as hive observation, honey harvesting, and tasting of local apiculture products, promoting environmental awareness and valuing regional honey production (Campos, 2021). Examples include Carmel Valley Ranch in California, offering immersive educational experiences on the importance of bees, and The Brando Resort in the Tetiaroa Archipelago, French Polynesia, recognized globally for bee conservation. The first colonies were brought by boat in the 1980s with support from actor Marlon Brando, the archipelago's owner. Years later, the initiative expanded with the opening of the resort in partnership with Richard Bailey. Currently, beekeeper Stéphane Brouttier manages the apiary, which has become a flagship project in sustainable hospitality (Campos, 2021).

Properties in the Fairmont network, which install hives in gardens and rooftops to produce artisanal honey for use in their restaurants and bars, integrate sustainability and tourism innovatively. Fairmont Rio, the network's only unit in South America, partnered with small producers from Nova Friburgo to develop an exclusive artisanal honey line for the hotel, used in dishes at Marine Restô and drinks at Spirit Copa Bar. The Renaissance São Paulo also focuses on the conservation of the Jataí bee, native to Brazil, in its small urban apiary within the hotel (Campos, 2021).

Following this trend that connects sustainability, beekeeping, and tourism experiences, initiatives in rural areas of Brazil also strengthen the link between environmental preservation and hospitality. Examples include Reserva Andirá and Bee Nectar, located in Lima Duarte (MG), where honey and its derivatives are incorporated into educational tourism and nature experiences, allowing visitors to understand the role of bees in ecological balance and local production.

In addition to promoting family farming and the biodiversity of the Atlantic Forest, these spaces offer experiences aligned with community-based tourism, which will be explored in greater detail in the next section.

5. CASE STUDY OF BEE NECTAR AT RESERVA ANDIRÁ: APICULTURE, MELIPONICULTURE, AND BEE TOURISM

The municipality of Lima Duarte, located in the southeastern Zona da Mata region of Minas Gerais, Brazil, is characterized by its large territorial extent and low population density, factors that reinforce its rural and natural vocation. This setting, combined with the region's rich biodiversity, offers significant potential for the development of rural tourism and environmental conservation (IBGE, 2023; Machado et al., 2025).

Among these initiatives, Bee Nectar at the Reserva Andirá stands out. Initially created in 2014 as a personal retreat, the property has transformed into a hub for conservation, environmental education, and the promotion of beekeeping and meliponiculture. Located between the Serra Negra da Mantiqueira State Park and the Ibitipoca State Park (both in Minas Gerais), the reserve integrates beekeeping, high-quality honey production, and educational tourism experiences, highlighting the potential of honey tourism as a tool for education and environmental conservation (see Figure 02).

Figure 2. Map showing the location of Lima Duarte and Bee Nectar at Reserva Andirá (one of the rural properties of Entre Serras members)

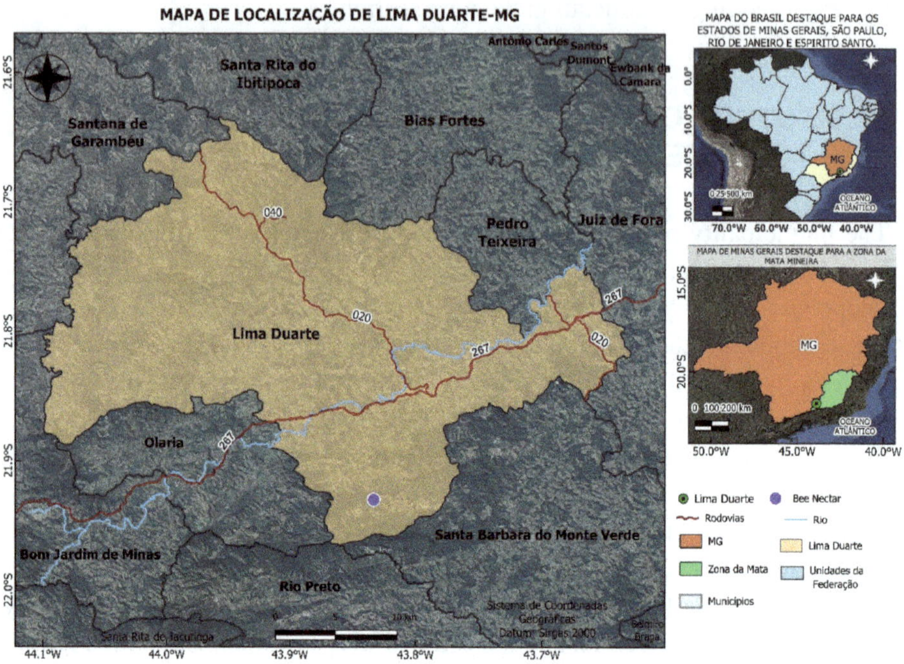

Source: Quaternary Geomorphology Laboratory – UFV (2025)

The focus of this study is Lima Duarte, which has a considerably smaller production compared to the major beekeeping hubs in the state. In 2023, Lima Duarte recorded an estimated honey production value of approximately R$ 45,000. Considering the average market price of honey, this corresponds to about 3,574 kilograms—a modest but significant quantity for production aimed at rural tourism and the promotion of local products (IBGE, 2023).

Within this context, the analysis focuses on Reserva Andirá, the property behind Bee Nectar, which represents an important portion of the municipality's honey production. The reserve stands out not only for its honey production but also for its implementation of sustainable practices, environmental education, and honey tourism, integrating conservation, local economy, and pedagogical experiences centered on native and Africanized bees.

This section was developed based on interviews with the owners of Bee Nectar and Reserva Andirá, referred to as Associate A and Associate B. In addition to the interviews, the chapter draws on direct observation by researchers, allowing the analysis of aspects of daily life on the property not explicitly mentioned by the interviewees.

Bee Nectar combines science, tradition, and hospitality with the preservation of native species and environmental awareness. The practices developed at the property enable visitors to understand the complexity of the Atlantic Forest's biodiversity, the essential role of bees in pollination and food production, and the importance of ecological conservation.

a. Beekeeping and Meliponiculture

Reserva Andirá primarily focuses on beekeeping while conducting meliponiculture in an educational and integrated manner. Beekeeping involves the management of stinging bees, specifically *Apis mellifera* (Africanized bees), for the production of honey, wax, propolis, and other products, using techniques that ensure the well-being of the insects and the pollination of agricultural and native plants. Meliponiculture, in turn, focuses on the raising of stingless bees native to the Atlantic Forest, including Jataí (*Tetragonisca angustula*), Mandaçaia (*Melipona quadrifasciata anthidioides*), Mirim (*Plebeia* sp.), Mandaguari amarela (*Scaptotrigona xanthotricha*), and Borá (*Tetragona clavipes*). Some of these species live naturally in tree trunks, where honey is not harvested, providing food for native fauna, while others are managed in hives, allowing sustainable extraction of honeys with different flavors, respecting the natural flowering cycles (Associates A and B).

The raising of native bees is complemented by educational activities that explain to visitors the importance of bees for pollination, the preservation of the Atlantic Forest, and the diversity of plant and animal species. The couple plans to expand meliponiculture in the future, with stingless bees for commercial product development, consolidating a sustainable model (Associate A).

b. Honey Tourism / Bee Tourism

Honey tourism, also known as apiecotourism, is a form of rural, gastronomic, and environmental tourism that focuses on educational and sensory experiences related to bees and honey production. At Bee Nectar and Reserva Andirá, this type of tourism goes beyond simple visitation: it integrates learning, environmental conservation, and hands-on interaction with local ecosystems.

During the visits, tourists have the opportunity to observe hives up close, always using appropriate protective clothing, such as suits and gloves, ensuring both visitor safety and the well-being of the bees in beekeeping activities. This care allows visitors to approach the colonies without interfering with their routine, promoting direct and respectful contact with nature (Associate B).

Another central experience of apiecotourism at the reserve is honey tasting, which showcases the diversity of flavors and aromas resulting from the region's different flowering plants. Visitors learn how each type of plant influences the taste of honey and how the work of bees is essential for pollination and the maintenance of local biodiversity (Associate A).

Additionally, some experiences allow tourists to observe and harvest a honeycomb, or even collect honey from stingless bees, offering practical understanding of the biological and production processes without compromising the ecological balance of the hives (see Figure 03).

Figure 3. Moments from tourists' experiences at Reserva Andirá

Source: Entre Serras, 2018

Apiecotourism at Reserva Andirá therefore combines environmental education, sensory tasting, and hands-on experiences, showing visitors the importance of bees in nature while encouraging appreciation of sustainable products and promoting rural development and Atlantic Forest conservation.

c. Sustainable Honey Production at Bee Nectar

Honey production at Bee Nectar demonstrates how sustainable beekeeping can integrate bee conservation, tourism, and income generation, creating positive environmental and socio-economic impacts. Focusing on the appreciation of biodiversity and local culture, the initiative has transformed beekeeping into an activity capable of producing high-value items for tourists and consumers who prioritize socially and environmentally responsible practices (Associate A).

Bee Nectar's portfolio is diverse and includes food and cosmetic products derived from bees, such as traditional honey, creamy honey, honeycomb, propolis, mead, and the exclusive "pingo doce"; artisanal cosmetics, including soaps, shampoos, conditioners, creams, body oils, and lip balms; as well as handcrafted candles made from natural wax. Each product reflects the project's commitment to sustainability, combining quality, authenticity, and environmental responsibility (Associate B), see Figure 04.

Figure 4. Portfolio of products crafted by Bee Nectar at Reserva Andirá

Source: Entre Serras, 2018

The practices implemented at Bee Nectar reinforce the project's socio-environmental mission. Respect for flowering periods ensures continuous and healthy food for the bees; the use of appropriate technologies, such as rational hives that simulate natural nests, optimizes management without harming the insects; and environmental education, promoted through guided tours and workshops, brings visitors and communities closer to the importance of bees and biodiversity. Additionally, partnerships with local communities strengthen the solidarity economy, value traditional knowledge, and encourage environmental conservation practices.

This case study highlights that the integration of beekeeping, stingless bee cultivation, educational tourism, and tourism that values beekeeping as a cultural, environmental, and gastronomic experience can generate significant impacts: it promotes Atlantic Forest conservation, offers transformative tourist experiences, and ensures responsible income generation. In this way, Reserva Andirá and Bee Nectar demonstrate that it is possible to reconcile high-quality artisanal production, ecological education, and environmental conservation, establishing Lima Duarte as a reference in community-based tourism and socially and environmentally responsible practices.

d. Reflections

The experience of Reserva Andirá and Bee Nectar provides an inspiring model for farmers to remain competitive in the Brazilian market, even in the face of external challenges such as international product tariffs, for example, measures implemented by the Trump administration.

By integrating beekeeping, stingless bee cultivation, honey tourism, and environmental concerns, producers are able to add value to their products, transforming honey, propolis, and natural cosmetics into differentiated items with socio-environmental and cultural appeal that attract conscious tourists and consumers. This strategy helps reduce dependence on external markets and expands local and regional marketing channels, creating income opportunities resilient to international trade fluctuations.

Furthermore, honey tourism and educational experiences enhance the visibility of production by connecting consumers directly with sustainable production processes and biodiversity conservation, ensuring that the local economy remains active and competitive even in scenarios of global market instability.

Although Bee Nectar has achieved notable results by integrating science, tradition, and hospitality around the preservation of native bees, its replicability in other contexts requires deeper analysis. One risk of such initiatives is assuming that the success achieved in one territory can automatically be reproduced in different socio-cultural, environmental, and economic realities. Replicating projects requires careful consideration of local variables, such as community engagement, the availability of specific biodiversity, tourism infrastructure, and, most importantly, the existence of institutional support that provides resources and legitimacy to the practices implemented.

Additionally, tourist demand cannot be assumed to be stable or guaranteed; market fluctuations, economic crises, and changes in visitor interests may undermine the financial viability of the model. Another central point is the environmental preservation of the region, an essential condition for sustaining stingless bee cultivation and for maintaining the sustainability narrative that underpins the Bee Nectar experience. Without healthy ecosystems, the project loses its foundation and distinctive value.

Therefore, critically reflecting on the limits and possibilities of replication does not diminish the Bee Nectar experience; on the contrary, it enhances its academic and practical relevance. Including this discussion allows for a more robust debate on how innovative models in responsible tourism can be adapted, adjusted, or even reinvented for other communities, respecting their specificities and reducing risks of failure. Ultimately, the strength of a project lies not only in its originality but also in its capacity to inspire contextualized and enduring strategies for local development.

FINAL CONSIDERATIONS

The The Bee Nectar case study at Reserva Andirá highlights the importance of bees as central elements for both food security and honey tourism. Both stinging bees (Apis mellifera) and native stingless bees (meliponines) play a crucial role in the pollination of Atlantic Forest plant species and agricultural crops, ensuring plant reproduction and food production. Thus, the preservation and proper management of hives directly contribute to maintaining biodiversity and the stability of local food systems, reinforcing the ecological significance of these insects.

In terms of sustainability, Bee Nectar demonstrates that knowledge of bee behavior and biology can be transformed into high-value products, such as specialty honeys, propolis, cosmetics, and handcrafted candles. This diversification enables rural producers to increase competitiveness, add value to their products, and develop resilient income alternatives, even in the face of external challenges such as international trade tariffs. The study shows that environmental sustainability and economic viability can go hand in hand when combined with conscious bee management and the appreciation of local knowledge.

Honey tourism, or apiecotourism, emerges as both an educational and economic tool, bringing visitors closer to the importance of bees for ecosystems and food production. The sensory and educational experience, which includes hive observation, tasting of various honeys, and participation in hive management activities, strengthens environmental awareness, encourages responsible consumption practices, and creates a direct connection between the public and sustainable production.

Therefore, the Bee Nectar case at Reserva Andirá exemplifies how bees can simultaneously act as agents of ecological preservation, food security, and socioeconomic development. The integration of beekeeping, stingless bee cultivation, and honey tourism creates a replicable model of rural tourism that values biodiversity, strengthens the local economy, and promotes transformative experiences, establishing Lima Duarte as a reference for responsible socio-environmental initiatives.

Among the chapter's strengths are the clarity in describing the case study, the presentation of relevant quantitative and qualitative data, and the emphasis on the voices of local producers. These elements provide originality, connect research to practice, and enhance the study's usefulness for researchers, public managers, and rural producers.

However, the chapter also presents areas that require attention. One of these is the limits of replicability of the model. Although Bee Nectar is inspiring, its long-term sustainability will depend on external factors such as institutional support, continuous tourist demand, and the environmental preservation of the region. Including a deeper discussion of these limitations in future works would strengthen analytical robustness and allow for a more realistic understanding of the potential for expanding the model to other territories.

Future research could explore, for example, public policies as strategies to increase producers' economic resilience in the face of global market fluctuations, or the use of emerging technologies such as remote sensing, digital beekeeping, and artificial intelligence applied to hive analysis, thereby enhancing the contemporary relevance of the topic.

ACKNOWLEDGMENT

The first author acknowledges the doctoral scholarship granted by the funding agency Capes (Coordination for the Improvement of Higher Education Personnel).

REFERENCES

Ambientales, N. (2025). *Revolução na apicultura sustentável: criam mel em pó para valorizar o produto e reduzir desperdícios.* https://noticiasambientales.com/inovacion-pt/revolucao-na-apicultura-sustentavel-criam-mel-em-po-para-valorizar-o-produto-e-reduzir-desperdicios/

Barbosa, D.. (2017). As abelhas e seu serviço ecossistêmico de polinização. *Revista Eletrônica Científica da UERGS, 3*(4), 694–703.

Beringer, J. da S., Maciel, F. L., & Tramontina, F. F. (2019). O declínio populacional das abelhas: Causas, potenciais soluções e perspectivas futuras. *Revista Brasileira de Ensino de Ciência e Tecnologia, 12*(1), pp. 17–26. Disponível em: https://revista.uergs.edu.br/index.php/revuergs/article/view/1686/411. Acesso em: 04/05/2025.

Brandão, A. (2025). *Mudança climática coloca abelhas em risco e ameaça segurança alimentar global.* Embrapa. Disponível em: https://www.embrapa.br/busca-de-noticias/-/noticia/101094052/mudanca-climatica-coloca-abelhas-em-risco-e-ameaca-seguranca-alimentar-global

Caetano, T. S. G., Franco, J. R., Oliveira, V. C., Agostinho, I. M., Almeida, I. A., & Dal Pai, E. (2024). A importância das abelhas sem ferrão na polinização das culturas agrícolas no Brasil. [Curitiba, Brasil.]. *Revista DELOS, 17*(61), 1–14.

Campos, M. (2021). *Turismo das abelhas se espalha por destinos e hotéis e defende preservação.* UOL. https://www.uol.com.br/nossa/noticias/redacao/2021/06/04/turismo-das-abelhas-se-espalha-por-destinos-e-hoteis-e-defende-preservacao.htm. Acesso em: 16 de agosto de 2025.

Carvalho, D. M. C., Amorim, L. B., Souza, D. C., & Costa, C. P. M. (2019). Apicultura em São Raimundo Nonato, Piauí. *Revista Verde de Agroecologia e Desenvolvimento Sustentável, 14*(1), 85–91.

Carvalho, R. M. A., Martins, C. F., & Mourão, J. S. (2014). Meliponiculture in Quilombola communities of Ipiranga and Gurugi, Paraíba state, Brazil: An ethnoecological approach. *Journal of Ethnobiology and Ethnomedicine, 10*(1), •••. PMID: 24410767

Chirsanova, A., Capcanari, T., Boistean, A., & Khanchel, I. (2021). Bee honey: History, characteristics, properties, benefits and adulteration in the beekeeping sector. *Journal of Social Sciences*, *4*(3), 98–114. DOI: 10.52326/jss.utm.2021.4(3).11

Cortopassi-Laurino, M.; Imperatriz-Fonseca, V. L.; Roubik, D. W.; Dollin, A.; Heard, T.; Aguilar, I.; Venturieri, G. C.; Eardley, C.; Nogueira-Neto, P. (2006). *Global meliponiculture:* challenges and opportunities. Apidologie, v. 37, n. 2, pp. 275–292, 22.

dos Santos, M. C. (2024). *O impacto dos agrotóxicos na polinização e no meio ambiente*. Mata Nativa. Disponível em: https://matanativa.com.br/impacto-dos-agrotoxicos-no-meio-ambiente/. Disponível em: 16/08/2025.

Embrapa. (2025). *Mudança climática coloca abelhas em risco e ameaça segurança alimentar global*. https://www.embrapa.br/busca-de-noticias/-/noticia/101094052/mudanca-climatica-coloca-abelhas-em-risco-e-ameaca-seguranca-alimentar-global. Acesso: em 8 de agosto de 2025.

Entre Serras – Turismo Rural. (2018). *Entre Serras No Meio Rural – Bee Nectar.* Disponível em: Https://Www.Facebook.Com/Entreserrasturismorural/?Locale=Pt_Br. Acesso: 26/09/2023.

Eroğlu, Ö., & Yuksel, S. (2020). Historical development and current status of beekeeping in Turkey and the World. *Atras Journal*, *6*, 345–354.

Estatuto Social Entre Serras Turismo No Meio Rural. (2021). *Registrado No Cartório Raul Fonseca – Lima Duarte*, Livro A-N-8, Registro 222, Pessoa Jurídica, Folhas 135 a 138. Gil, A. C. (2008). Métodos e Técnicas de Pesquisa Social. 6ed. São Paulo: Atlas.

Faita, M. R., de Moura, M. E. K., Damasco, T. de M., Poltronieri, A. S., & Nodari, R. O. (2022). *Abelhas e o ambiente: importância, nutrição e sanidade*. In J. M. B.

FAO - Food and Agriculture Organization of the United Nations. (2023). *Conselho, Centésima Septuagésima Segunda Sessão,* Roma, CL 172/5. Roma. 24 a 28 de abril de 2023. Disponível online: www.fao.org/3/nl652en/nl652en.pdf (acessado em 15 de agosto de 2023).

FAO - Food and Agriculture Organization of the United Nations. (2025). *About FAO*. Disponível em: https://www.fao.org/about/about-fao/en/. Acesso em: 10/08/2025.

Figueiredo, C. (13/08/2025). *Mel brasileiro premiado como melhor do mundo perde mercado de US$ 80 mi após tarifaço de Trump*. Gazeta do Povo. Disponível em: https://www.gazetadopovo.com.br/santa-catarina/mel-brasileiro-premiado-melhor-do-mundo-perde-mercado-apos-tarifaco-trump/. Acesso em: 16 de agosto de 2025.

Fontana, C., & Fontana, P. (2020). In Part, I., & Floris, I. (Eds.), *The first evidence: In Italian Apiculture. A Journey through History and Honey Diversity* (pp. 36–47). Accademia Nazionale Italiana di Entomologia.

Higes, M.. (2009). Honeybee colony collapse due to Nosema ceranae in professional apiaries. *Environmental Microbiology Reports, 1*(2), 110–113. PMID: 23765741

IBGE. (2023). *Produção de mel de abelha.* Disponível em: https://www.ibge.gov.br/explica/producao-agropecuaria/mel-de-abelha/br. Acesso em: 16 de agosto de 2025.

Imperatriz-Fonseca, V. L., Canhos, D. A. L., Alves, D. A., & Saraiva, A. M. (2012). *Polinizadores no Brasil: Contribuição e perspectivas para a biodiversidade, uso sustentável, conservação e serviços ambientais.* EDUSP.

IPCC. (2022). *Climate Change and Land.* https://www.ipcc.ch

Kerr, W. E.. (2010). Aspectos pouco mencionados da biodiversidade amazônica. *Parcerias Estratégicas, 6*(12), 20–41.

Kevan, P., & Imperatriz-Fonseca, V. L. (2002). *Pollinating bees: the conservation link between Agriculture and Nature.* Ministério do Desenvolvimento.

Knowledge Policy. (2021). *O Estado da Segurança Alimentar e Nutricional no Mundo 2021* (SOFI). 2021. Disponível online: https://knowledge4policy.ec.europa.eu/publication/state-food-security-nutrition-world-2021-sofi_en. Acesso: 15 de agosto de 2023.

Kösoğlu, M. (2021). *Kişisel Arı Figürlü Pul Ve Para Koleksiyonu.*

Leal Filho, W., Fedoruk, M., Eustachio, J. H. P. P., Barbir, J., Lisovska, T., Lingos, A., & Baars, C. (2023). How the war in Ukraine affects food security. *Foods, 12*(21), 3996. DOI: 10.3390/foods12213996 PMID: 37959115

Machado, A. F., de Oliveira, M. L., & de Faria, A. L. (2025). *Social Innovation Through Rural Tourism and Its Benefits for Entre Serras, Lima Duarte – MG, Brazil:* A Perspective From the Border Areas of the Territory. In B. Sousa (Ed.), Cross-Border Regions Cooperation and Implications for Organizations (pp. 339-366). IGI Global Scientific Publishing. DOI: 10.4018/979-8-3373-1912-4.ch012

Maia-Silva, C.. (2020). Stingless Bees (Melipona subnitida) Overcome Severe Drought Events in the Brazilian Tropical Dry Forest by Opting for High-Profit Food Sources. *Neotropical Entomology, 49*(4), 595–603. DOI: 10.1007/s13744-019-00756-8 PMID: 32103461

Marcelino, J., Braese, C., Christmon, K., Evans, J. D., Gilligan, T., Giray, T., Ne-arman, A., Niño, E. L., Rose, R., Sheppard, W. S., vanEngelsdorp, D., & Ellis, J. D. (2022). O movimento das abelhas ocidentais (*Apis mellifera L.*) entre estados e territórios dos EUA: História, benefícios, riscos e estratégias de mitigação. *Frontiers in Ecology and Evolution, 10*, 850600. DOI: 10.3389/fevo.2022.850600

Martel, A. C., Zeggane, S., Aurières, C., Drajnudel, P., Faucon, J. P., & Aubert, M. (2007). Acaricide residues in honey and wax after treatment of honey bee colonies with Apivar or Asuntol 50. *Apidologie, 38*, 534–544.

Melo, G. A. R. (2020). Stingless Bees (Meliponini). Encyclopedia of Social Insects, pp. 1–18.

Michener, C. D. (2007). *The bees of the word* (2nd ed.). Johns Hopkins.

Morens, D. M., & Fauci, A. S. (2020). Emerging Pandemic Diseases: How We Got to COVID-19. *Cell, 182*(5), 1077–1092. DOI: 10.1016/j.cell.2020.08.021 PMID: 32846157

National Geographic Brasil. (2022). Abelhas: por que são importantes e como podemos evitar seu desaparecimento. *National Geographic Brasil.* Disponível em: https://www.nationalgeographicbrasil.com/animais/2022/05/abelhas-por-que-sao-importantes-e-como-podemos-evitar-seu-desaparecimento. Acesso em: 05/08/2025.

Neff, J. L., & Simpson, B. B. (1993). Bees, Pollination Systems and Plant Diversity. In Lasalle, J., & Gauld, I. D. (Eds.), *Hyme-noptera and Biodiversity* (pp. 143–167). CAB International.

Nhemachena, C., Dahiya, S., Gokah, I., Echessah, P., Gichuri, M., Nhlengethwa, S., Djido, A., & Muthini, D. (2022). *Os impactos do conflito Rússia-Ucrânia nos preços dos alimentos e na segurança alimentar e nutricional na África.* Disponível online: https://agra.org/wp-content/uploads/2022/04/Impacts-of-the-Russia-Ukraine-conflict-2.pdf. Acesso: 15 de agosto de 2023.

Nobre, C. A., Sampaio, G., Borma, L. S., & Cardoso, M., & outros. (2016). Riscos de uso da terra e mudanças climáticas na Amazônia e a necessidade de um novo paradigma de desenvolvimento sustentável. *Proceedings of the National Academy of Sciences, 113*(39), 10759–10768. DOI: 10.1073/pnas.1605516113

Nogueira, D. S., Vollet Neto, A., Cassinelli, M. P., dos Santos-Silva, J. A., do Nascimento, F. S., & de Oliveira, A. L. L. (2023). *As abelhas "sem-ferrão" dos biomas brasileiros:* O Brasil possui a maior biodiversidade de abelhas "sem-ferrão" do planeta, essenciais para o funcionamento dos ecossistemas e com grande potencial econômico. *Ciência e Cultura, 75*(4), e20230053. DOI: 10.5935/2317-6660.20230053

Nogueira-Couto, R. H. (1998). *As abelhas na manutenção da biodiversidade e geração de rendas.* In: Congresso Brasileiro de Apicultura, 12, Anais [...] Salvador: p. 101.

Novais, S. M. A.. (2016). Effects of a possible pollinator crisis on food crop production in Brazil. *PLoS One, 11*(11), 1–12. PMID: 27902787

Ogilvie, J. E.. (2017). Interannual bumble bee abundance is driven by indirect climate effects on floral resource phenolo-gy. *Ecology Letters, 20*(12), 1507–1515. PMID: 29124863

ONU - United Nations. (2025). *ONU destaca papel das abelhas na segurança alimentar e na saúde de ecossistemas BR.* UN News. https://news.un.org/pt/story/2025/05/1848611

Pegoraro, A., Ferraz, M. M., Pfaw, E., Moura, M. E. K., Nunes, T. M. D., Nienow, V. V., Polak, L., & Borio, C. L. Krüg. (2017). *Aspectos práticos e técnicos da apicultura no Sul do Brasil.* Curitiba, PR: Universidade Federal do Paraná.

Pereira, F. (2025). *Resiliência das colmeias diante de mudanças climáticas: estratégias de mitigação e adaptação.* Embrapa Meio-Norte.

Pereira, S. N., Alves, L. H. S., da Costa, R. F. R., Prezoto, F., & Teixeira, E. W. (2021). Occurrence of the small hive beetle (Aethina tumida) in Melipona rufiventris colonies in Brazil. *Sociobiology, 68*(1), e6021. DOI: 10.13102/sociobiology.v68i1.6021

Pignati, W. A., Lima, F. A. N. de S., de Lara, S. S., Correa, M. L. M., Barbosa, J. R., Leão, L. H. da C., & Pignatti, M. G. (2017). Distribuição espacial do uso de agrotóxicos no Brasil: Uma ferramenta para a Vigilância em Saúde [Spatial distribution of pesticide use in Brazil: A strategy for Health Surveillance]. *Ciencia & Saude Coletiva, 22*(10), 3319–3328. DOI: 10.1590/1413-812320172210.17742017 PMID: 29069184

Pires, A. P.. (2020). Análise sensorial de méis de duas espécies de abelhas sem ferrão de Santarém, Pará. *Brazilian Journal of Development, 6*(9), 72680–72693.

Potts, S. G.. (2016). Safeguarding pollinators and their values to human well-being. *Nature, 540*(7632), 220–229. PMID: 27894123

Rao, P. V.. (2016). Biological and therapeutic effects of honey produced by honey bees and stingless bees: A comparative review. *Revista Brasileira de Farmacognosia, 26*(5), 657–664.

Ribeiro, R. E.; Silva, E. da C.; Silva, J. M.; Sousa, S. B.; Moura, T. T.; Fernandes, V. E. S. B.; Gurjão, T. A.; Matias, P. F. J.; De Assys, R. M. Da M. S.; Henrique, M. N. H. M.; Nascimento Júnior, A. A.; Januário, D. M. P.; Medeiros, A. C. de. (2023). *Contaminação do mel, cuidados e controles - revisão.* Caderno Verde de Agroecologia e Desenvolvimento Sustentável, [S. l.], v. 12, n. 1.

Ribeiro-Silva, R. C., Pereira, M., Campello, T., Aragão, É., Guimarães, J. M. de M., Ferreira, A. J. F., Barreto, M. L., & dos Santos, S. M. C. (2020). Implicações da pandemia COVID-19 para a segurança alimentar e nutricional no Brasil. *Ciencia & Saude Coletiva*, *25*(9), 3421–3430. DOI: 10.1590/1413-81232020259.22152020 PMID: 32876253

Rodger, J. G.. (2021). Widespread vulnerability of flowering plant seed production to pollinator declines. *Science Advances*, *7*(42). Advance online publication. DOI: 10.1126/sciadv.abd3524 PMID: 34644118

Rodrigues, C. A. S. (2015). *Análise morfológica do cérebro de abelhas sem ferrão Melipona Scutellarias expostas ao Tiametoxam. Trabalho de Conclusão de Curso do Curso (Instituto de Biociências) - Curso de Ciências Biológicas da Universidade Estadual Paulista Júlio de Mesquita Filho, Rio Claro*. UNESP.

Sanchez-Bayo, F., & Goka, K. (2014). Pesticide residues and bees–a risk assessment. *PLoS One*, *9*(4), •••. PMID: 24718419

Santos, J. B., Viana, M. C., Mariano, C. S. F., Menezes, R. S. T., Nery, D. G., & Brandão, S. N. (2022). *Mudanças climáticas e o declínio das abelhas.* Terræ Didática, 18(Publ. Contínua), pp. 1-12.

SNA – Sociedade Nacional de Agricultura. (2017). *Apiecoturismo: um novo negócio para produtores de mel no Brasil.* https://sna.agr.br/apiecoturismo-um-novo-negocio-para-produtores-de-mel-no-brasil/

SNA - Sociedade Nacional de Agricultura. (2023). Abemel. *Produção de mel cresceu 80% em 10 anos no Brasil.* https://sna.agr.br/abemel-producao-de-mel-cresceu-80-em-10-anos-no-brasil/. Disponível em: 16/08/2025.

Sousa Júnior, J. C., Souza, C. B., Barreira, S., & Rocha, F. R. T. (2024). Produção científica sobre apicultura numa perspectiva multidisciplinar: Uma revisão sistemática de literatura. *Revista Brasileira Multidisciplinas*, *27*(2), 133–149.

Statista Research Department. (2025). *Conflicts in the world in 2025 – statistics and facts*. Statista. Retrieved August 16, 2025, from https://www.statista.com/topics/13125/conflicts-worldwide-2025/#topFacts

Thomé, J. (2024, 6 de fevereiro). InovaBee Brazil. *Mel sustentável: para o planeta e para a comunidade*. Inovabee. https://inovabee.com/blog/mel-sustentavel

Topal, E., Adamchuk, L., Negri, I., Köso ˘glu, M., Papa, G., Dârjan, M.S., & Cornea-Cipcigan, M.; M ˘arg ˘aoan, R. (2021). Traces of Honeybees, Api-Tourism and Beekeeping: From Past to Present. *Sustainability*, *13*, 11659.

Yasmi, Y. (2025). What the Bees Are Telling Us: In Protecting Pollinators, *We Protect the Future of Food.* FAO. Disponível em: https://www.fao.org/newsroom/fao-blog/detail/fao-blog/2025/05/19/what-the-bees-are-telling-us/en. Data de Acesso: 10/05/2025.

KEY TERMS AND DEFINITIONS

Apiculture: Rearing and management of stinging bees (*Apis mellifera*) for honey, wax, propolis, and other products, focusing on pollination and hive conservation.

Apiecotourism / Honey Tourism: A form of rural and environmental tourism based on educational and sensory experiences with bees, honey, and ecosystems, integrating learning, tasting, and conservation.

Food Security: Assurance of regular access to sufficient, nutritious, and culturally appropriate food for all, promoting health and well-being.

Meliponiculture: Rearing and management of stingless bees, usually native, valuing the production of specialty honeys and local biodiversity preservation.

ENDNOTES

1 Eusocial species are those that exhibit the most complex level of social organization, characterized by the division of reproductive and labor functions, cooperative brood care, and the simultaneous coexistence of different generations within the same colony. Bees, ants, termites, and the naked mole-rat are the main examples.

Chapter 11
The Psychology of Pet-Driven Consumer Behavior

Gautam Shivaraj
https://orcid.org/0009-0000-5184-8448
Adarsh Institute of Management and Information Technology, Chamarajpet, India

Komal Bisht
https://orcid.org/0009-0009-3810-3068
Adarsh Institute of Management and Information Technology, Chamarajpet, India

M. Gurusamy
https://orcid.org/0000-0002-9425-9368
Adarsh Institute of Management and Information Technology, Chamarajpet, India

M. Harshitha
https://orcid.org/0009-0008-4368-5245
Adarsh Institute of Management and Information Technology, Chamarajpet, India

Sayantani Ghosh
https://orcid.org/0009-0004-0056-5607
Adarsh Institute of Management and Information Technology, Chamarajpet, India

K. Sankar Ganesh
https://orcid.org/0000-0003-0772-3490
Sharada University, Uzbekistan

ABSTRACT

The ongoing process of humanizing pets has turned pets into a fully-fledged member of the family turning around the consumer behavior to a major degree. With pets in the center of interests of their owners, the pet trade has exploded and covers virtually every product and service under the sun, including luxury items and health-related inventions. In this chapter, Green has examined the psychological basis of the pet driving consumer behavior that is how people make their purchase decisions under the basis of emotional attachments, attachment theory, humanization of pets. It

DOI: 10.4018/979-8-3373-4342-6.ch011

also investigates the social changes throughout the community which have helped increase the significance of pets in the contemporary homes and how they affect different industries.

1. INTRODUCTION

Over the past few decades, the interaction between peoples and pets has grown to become more than a conventional bond between a keeper and a living breathing being. Dogs and cats are the main pets which have become not only the simple companion animals, but now they have become a part of the family. As a result, a transformation has caused a boom in the pet care market, with much consumer behavior being influenced by the need of an emotional connection, as well as adjusted lifestyles coupled with the need to treat pets as children or people that should be taken care of. The pet products and pet services business is a growing industry and the pet owners are not settling with what is already there but are always looking forward to the new and innovative methods in order to pamper their furry loved ones to death. The psychology of consumer behavior based on pets deals with the emotional, cognitive as well as social components of the ownership of pets and how these elements contribute towards the consumer behavior. Ranging from pet food and grooming to high end products such as pet clothing and even pet insurance, pets are not only animals anymore, they are very much valued members of the family as well. With more growth in the pet business, companies and marketers have been giving a lot of consideration on what pet buyers are influenced to purchase based on their needs and necessity and how pets affect these purchases and how they can ultimately target the right people in this competitive market. The psychology of pet marketing is crucial to know not only by each company that aims to serve this niche market but also by policymakers, psychologists and sociologists who want to go deeper into this human-animal relationship. (Hausmann et al., 2023).The purpose of writing this chapter is to offer a thoroughly discussed study of the impact of participating in pet ownership on consumer behavior, the psychological motivation that makes consumers buy products that are related to pets, the market environment in which the pet trade is being conducted and the ethical aspects of selling products related to pet marketing. With this analysis, we will unearth the intricacies of the relationship between the consumer and pet and what the future holds of this multi-billion-dollar business.(Hummer, n.d.)

A new trend of consumerism has led to a different pattern of consumerism due to the growing culture of humanizing the pets. A psychological mechanism is explored in this paper in regard to the extent that pet ownership and attachment contribute to the forming of buying behavior. The use of consumer psychology theory, the behavioral economic theory, and social identity theories helps the study explore how emotional attachment between a human and a pet encourages the development of a spending pattern, which commercializes pet welfare, contentment, and appearance. The behavior of anthropomorphism where the consumers (the pet owners) transfers human characteristics on their pets is also examined as a consumer preference basis, such as choice of high-priced items, choice of health-based products, as well as the choice of pet-centered services. Also, the study takes into account the way marketing policies subvert the personality and feelings of pet-owner to affect their purchasing choices across the food lines, fashion, insurance, and technology. Based on survey results and behavioral information, it is believed that pet ownership not only boosts the total consumption of a household, but it also changes the mode of lifestyle choice as well as brand affiliation and online participation. These are some of the psychological factors that are important when businesses want to establish ethically sensitive and emotionally appealing marketing principles in the growing pet economy.(Yoo et al., 2024)

2. LITERATURE REVIEW

The growing human-animal connection has had a tremendous impact on the consumer market to give rise to a pet economy. The article The Psychology of Pet-Driven Consumer Behavior investigates the effect of the pet factor in the consumer behavior, decision-making process, and product buying habits. This literature review reflects the critical analysis of major findings, theoretical background and research methods given in the paper as well as literature.(Zhang et al., 2022)

Theoretical Foundations

The psychological theories that the paper is based on are:

- Attachment Theory: Assumes pets act as alternate children or companions and people buy them impulsively in an emotionally hot state of action.(Jones, 2015)
- Self-Concept Theory: Refers to the idea that pet owners usually perceive their pets as an extension of who they are and thus brand preference and social communication are affected.(Green, 2008)
- Consumer Culture Theory (CCT): Brings to the fore the cultural, and symbolic meaning of pet related consumption.(Arnould & Thompson, 2005)

Critical Evaluation:

The paper fails in this integration approach by not being deep enough in the integration of CCT with cross-cultural analysis though the use of the Attachment Theory is correct. It concentrates too much on Western situations and does not give any attention to international or non-Western consumer behavior patterns with regard to pets

Motivations Of Consumers and Behavior Patterns

Some of the consumer motivations are identified in the literature as follows:

- Emotional Satisfaction: Expenditure on pets enhances satisfaction and the emotional status of the owner.
- Anthropomorphism- Pet parents also project the human qualities to the pets, affecting their choice of birthday party, dress it up and luxury food.
- Social Status: Having a pet, particularly one of an expensive brand or "trappings" means that a person has a certain financial status that allows having such a pet.

Critical Evaluation:

Even though those reasons are reasonably justified with both qualitative and quantitative research, the paper does not test possible adverse effects, like overconsumption or petification as well as the financial burden to low-income households.

Brand and Influence in Marketing

The paper has shown that companies exploit emotional branding where customers engage themselves with the help of pets as a form of emotional appeal. Social media and pet influencers have created more awareness and spendings among pet owners.

Critical Evaluation:

It is an eloquently presented and defended section based on the current research exercises. Nevertheless, there is no deep understanding in the paper of the manner in which deceptive marketing or insufficient product regulation may take advantage of the emotional weaknesses of the consumer.(Belk et al., 1988)

Methodological Rigor

The majority of studies used are based on surveys, focus groups, and case studies, whether in urban, middle-income, and high-income environments.

Critical Evaluation:

Strengths: The relevance is increased by real life case studies and behavioral data.

Weaknesses: Weak generalizability is caused by the absence of longitudinal data, the rate of rural representation and variety of sample demographics.(Chen et al., 2012)

Ethical Considerations and Caveats

Although the literature offers recognition of emotions and psychological forces behind the consumption of pets, it does not widely take into consideration:

- Environmental effects of pet products.
- Moral issues pertaining to the Luxury pet products.
- The differences in norms that regulate pet ownership behavior depending on the culture.(Chen et al., 2012)

3. METHODOLOGICAL LIMITATIONS

3.1 Too much use of Self-Reported Data

Limitations: Most of the studies are based on self-report surveys as well as questionnaires.

Problem: These data may be subject to social desirability bias wherein respondents may claim to conduct positive behaviours (e.g. I only buy the healthiest food in the pet) excessively and negative ones less frequently.

Effect: Lowers the validity and objectivity of the results.

3.2. Cross-sectional Study Designs

Limitation: The majority of studies are cross-sectional design (the data is obtained at one time).

Problem: This denies the possibility of learning how casually a given consumer behaviour is changing over time (e.g., how spending is changing during the different periods in the life of a pet).

Impact: Hinders knowledge on behavioral natures and long-term consumer trends.

3.3 Poor Diversity in the Sample Size

Limitations: There is a tendency that the demographic aspect of respondents is typically weighted.

Urban residents Income groups- middle to high income brackets Both U.S/ European countries

Problem: There is a problem of non-representative sampling of the original data making it hard to generalize the results in different cultures, income ranges, and rural groups.

Effect: Does not pay attention to other viewpoints on pet maintenance and expenditure trends.

3.4. Unbalanced or small Sample Sizes

Limitations: In small convenience sample studies, it is common to find recruitment of the participants online or in the pet stores.

Drawback: This results in a bias of the sample and poor statistical strength.

Drug abuse: Causes a decrease in reliability and the replicability of conclusions.

3.5. Triangulation Deficiency

Weakness: Most of the researches recruit only one source of data (surveys, interviews).

Problem: The findings may be superficial and unconfirmed without the use of triangulation (combining different methods of research including observation, behavioural data and interview).

Impact: Makes the results less vigorous and thus can overlook important consumer data.

3.6. Low Utilization of Purchase and Behavioral Information

Limitations: The information regarding the actual behaviour of consumers (e.g., purchases records, transactions) is very poorly introduced in any study.

Problem: The self-reported behaviour varies frequently with real behaviour.

Effects: The study has only a limited application to marketers and product developers.

3.7. The Case of Undeveloped Theoretical Frameworks in some

Restriction: The limitation is that, although some researchers use a particular framework such as attachment theory, others are atheoretical or have little theoretical support that is based on psychological models.

Problem: It diminishes the conceptual strength and explanatory of the results.

Consequences: It inhibits the development of theory in pet related consumer behaviour.

4. GAPS IN RESEARCH

4.1. Geographic Bias and Cultural Bias

Gap: The majority of the studied literature pertains to Western or even urban consumer group (e.g. the U.S., Europe).

Why It Matters: The culture of the owned pets is very versatile. Or, say, a pet is a family in some culture, and a utilitarian or status object in the other one.

Future Direction: There need to be comparative cross-cultural studies to determine the extent of pet-driven consumer behavior that exists in the various regions, traditions, and economic situations.(Emran Shaikh, n.d.)

4.2. Socioeconomic Diversity Underrepresentation

Gap: The existing literature looks predominantly at pet owners with a medium and higher level of income.

Why It Matters: People with lower incomes or living in rural areas could behave, be limited or driven in ways that are different when it comes to spending their money on pets.

Future Direction: Put people of various socioeconomic backgrounds to know about the affordability, priorities and perceived values in pet consumption.(Gromek & Perek-Białas, 2022)

4.3. The absence of Longitudinal Studies

Gap: The majority of the research is based on cross-sectional survey and one time interview.

Why It Matters: Consumer behavior, especially the behavior that is best described as emotional, may evolve with time depending on the lifespan of the pet, the experience with pets, or life experiences.

Future Direction: The longitudinal study of consumer behavior influenced by pet ownership can be conducted in order to collect data over months or years.

4.4. Revolving Ethics and Environmental Blinds

Gap: The contribution of pet consumerism practices (e.g. excessive production of pet products, luxurious pet products, pet obesity because of indulgence, etc.) to the environment and the ethical concerns it presents are usually unmentioned in the literature.(Gromek & Perek-Białas, 2022)

Why It Matters: Conscious consumption and sustainability are on the minds of consumers in the realm of consumer psychology.

Future Direction: Include ethics and environmental sustainability into the research of pet-related consumer behavior.

5. THEORETICAL ANALYSIS ON PET CONSUMPTION PATTERNS

5.1. Attachment Theory (Attachment Theory)

The study emphasizes that, a considerable number of pet owners become quite emotionally attached to the animal and regard it like a child, best friend or life partners. This is a psychological attachment with strong determinants to the purchasing behavior, as we go towards the anthropomorphism of pets (treating pets as human beings), followed by the utilization of our spending on unnecessary products, like extravagant treats, clothing, and services in pet spas.

- Analysis: The attachment theory provides the reasons as to why the owners are eager to spend big in health care of their pets, their birthdays, and insurance covers. The resulting compensatory consumption resulting to emotional security of pets is usually an issue of those who are lonely or isolated.(Jones, 2015)

5.2. Self -Identity Expression (Self-Concept Theory)

The purchasing of pets is commonly based upon the way the owner plans their lifestyle, perception, and image. The study demonstrates that people prefer the brands and the products of pets that reflect their values: sustainability, health awareness, or luxury.

- Analysis: This correlates with self-concept theory because pet products turn into something that extenuates the identity of the owner. To give an example, a vegan owner will be more inclined to purchase pet food that is vegetarian, not only because it is an ethical thing to do but also to support personal values.(Green, 2008)

5.3. Gisele, the Cultural Wake (Symbolic Interactionism & Social Identity Theory)

In most societies pet animals act as social indicators. As shown in the literature, possession of some pets or pet accessories (United States: labrador or less glamorous pets; United Kingdom: status accessories, such as, bling-bling leads, giants traveling bags; United Kingdom: pitline breed, Parisians) may grant social status or membership in social status groups. The experiencing of social validation and community involvement, as pet content can be shared in an online environment, can be augmented.(Alves et al., 2022)

Analysis: Symbolic interactionism defines ways through which sense is built based on common social experiences. Possession of a specific breed or branded products tends to be exhortative of lifestyle would-be-trappings and enable membership of pet-owner subcultural groups (e.g., the doodle dog groups or cat cafes). (Belk et al., 2005)

5.4. Consumption Informed by Cultural Imperatives (The Consumer Culture Theory)

The research concludes that the pet-related consumption is affected by the resulting general cultural and market trends, i.e., the emergence of the culture of pet parenting or fur babies. Social media, influencers, and advertisement are a promotion of these cultural stories.

The analysis: Consumer Culture Theory (CCT) informs us that pet spending is not just anything functional but appears in culturally scripted stories about care, companionship and reponsibility. An example is that pampering of pets will be an ethical requirement and not an option.(Arnould & Thompson, 2005)

5.5. Theory of Planned Behavior- Planned Behavior and Decision-Making

As the research remarks, the willingness to spend on pets is determined by owner attitude (e.g. worry about pets welfare), subjective norms (practices of peers), and perceived behavioral control (budget prospects, access to products).

- Analysis: TPB states rational aspects of the decision-making with regard to pet consumption. Those who possess positive mindset and encourage their friends to spend on high-end products will purchase fancy items, whereas those on a budget could indulge in long-term necessities.(Ajzen, 1991)

5.6. Motivational Drivers (Maslow Hierarchy of needs)

The spending habits may indicate that buyers are motivated by a multiple of needs, which are low (food and safety) to esteem (social recognition) and even self-actualization (completing the emotional or moral aim).

- Analysis: The Maslow model can be used to establish the pyramid of spending on pets. Owners fulfilling their needs of self-psychology by taking care of pets indicate that consumption can support selfish and selfless interests, sometimes even at the same time.(Mcleod, n.d.)

6. CONSUMER TYPOLOGIES IN THE PET-RELATED CONSUMPTION

Consumers who indulge in the consumption of pet products can be grouped into or categorized into types. (Belk & Pollay, 1985)

Consumer typologies are of immeasurable value in appreciating the diverse practices, motives, and ideals of people who practice pet related consumption. There is no homogenous set of pet owners; however, they have different consumption patterns, which depends on psychological, social, cultural economic factors. The 5 key typologies of consumer types that can usually be found in the pet product and service industry are as under listed:

6.1. The Pet Parent

The Pet Parent has a strong emotional connection with the animal, and thought of the animal as family or similar to a child. These consumers are emotional and extremely active in terms of their pet health which makes them buy upmarket products like organic food, health supplements, designer clothes and insurances to their pets. This group is also known to celebrate birthdays with pets, offer grooming services to them and give them gifts on holidays. The attachment, empathy and the need to express the best care drives their consumption behavior. This typology is similar to Attachment Theory and hierarchy of needs developed by Maslow at the levels of love/belonging and esteeming.

6.2. The Utilities Owner

Utilitarian pet owners are more realistic in their attitudes towards pets by taking more instrumentalist views of pets; these people merely see useful services of pets; protection, companionship, or assistance. They are buyers whose expenses are need-oriented and they involve basic needs such as food, simple healthcare and shelter. There is an emotional attachment though not strong like pet parents. Such consumers are more concerned with the usability, the endurance and the affordability of goods. Their action tends to be dictated by the rational choice models and that theory of Planned behavior, especially the feature on Perceived behavioral control. (Melkko, n.d.)

6.3. The Ecofriend Consumer

This typology comprises of pet owners that are driven by environmental, ethical and sustainable concerns. These customers want biodegradable products, non cruel products, locally produced or organic certifications. Their decisions also show a wider belief in terms of sustainable goals and animal welfare, and they will tend to endorse the brands that stick to these principles. The behaviour of eco-conscious consumer is commonly a reflection of their own lifestyle and is guided by Consumer Culture Theory and the Self-Concept Theory whereby consumption is used as a representation of moral identity and self-ethics.(Emran Shaikh, n.d.)

6. 4. The Trend Determined Owner

Due to the emphasis on trend, the pet consumers with a trend-driven nature are highly influenced by social media, celebrity culture, and peer behaviors. They are influenced by trends, popular, trendy and aesthetics to consume. These people will be inclined to buy fashionable accessories for their pets, follow dog and cat influencers on the Internet, and will not mind something about pets being shared on social networks. To them pets are an addition to their personal brand and a social lifestyle. Symbolic Interactionism and Social Identity Theory are the only suitable approaches to explain the behavior of this group because they emphasize the significance of the social meaning and group membership.(Belk et al., 1988)

6.5. Scrimpy Sam

Economies influence the pet owners who are worried about budgets mainly. They also prioritize spending on basic yet low priced products with distinctive or discounted brands being their preferences. As they attach importance to the well-being of their pets, the availability of prices restricts their solutions, which implies strategic decision-making and value-maximization. Such consumers can do away with some luxurious purchases or turn to second-hand goods or to discounted products. Their actions are consistent with the Theory of Planned Behavior and Behavioral Economics, particularly, when connected to such issues as cost sensitivity and perceived value.(Belk et al., 2005)

Summary: Studying the consumer typologies enables the researchers and companies to better understand the psychological and the sociocultural aspect of pet consumption. Gaining a perspective on the prevailing motives and behavior trends across each segment, the marketers, the policy-makers, and the product developers will be able to frame their plans in a more focused and powerful way. In addition, the typologies provide a academic rationale on which future researches will be based on about consumer identity, lifestyle and socio-economic influences on the ever-growing pet economy.(Ajzen, 1991)

7. BACKGROUND OF HUMAN-PET INTERACTIONS

Pet Ownership in History

The relationship between people and their furry friends has existed in the human history thousands of years ago. Strongly, however, the purpose of pets in history has changed majorly. The ancient civilization made use of animals in many of the above ways including work, food and defense. Herding cattle, hunting and domestication of the homes are some of the uses that the dogs had whereas the cats were prized as a form of pest control. Such functional working relationships were of significance but they could be only functional. The cats were considered as sacred animals in ancient Egypt as they used to preserve grain from rodents. However, in these cultures the attitude towards the animals was usually based on the utility as opposed to feeling.(Lembregts & Cadario, 2024)

Only in the 18th and 19th centuries did the concept of having pets as friends have a grip. Industrial revolution caused major social reforms such as urbanization, raised income-earnings and alteration in the views on animals. Animals (which became pets) started to be regarded not only as working animals, but also as emotional pets and this trend would only continue to gain momentum in the 20th and the 21st centuries.(Farida et al., 2024)

Mental Reasoning of the Human-Animal Connection

Many psychological theories have tried to give reasons as to why man and the animal have a formidable attachment. One of the most popular theories of human-animal relationship is attachment theory, which was initially created as such in the middle of the XX century by John Bowlby. The work that Bowlby had undertaken reinforced the value of close emotional connections in the development of humans especially among children and their caretakers. According to him, this attachment is critical in the regulation of emotions, sense of security as well as social development. The theory of attachment has over the years been applied to the human animal bond where most researchers hold that pets provide a secure attachment to their owners. Owners of pets may develop emotional attachment towards the pets and use them as a source of fun and emotional support as well as companionship. Pets, in certain instances, act as substitutes to the human relationships especially to people who might be lonely and isolated. One more psychological concept in considering human-animal relationship is the concept of social support. The term social support pines the uplifting part that people get in their life through their social relationships in form of emotional, information and practical help. The emotional support offered by pets due to their being non-judgmental and unconditional source of companionship has been important to the owners who in most cases are a buffer to stress, anxiety and depression. Researchers have proved that the visitation of pets has the ability to lessen amounts of cortisol (a stress hormone) and upsurge amounts of oxytocin, which is a binding and affection hormone.(De Canio et al., 2024)

The Cultural Change in Pet keeping

The definitions and purpose of pets have also had a huge disparity in terms of cultures. The practice of anthropomorphism of pets has even been more provocative in most western cultures especially in the U.S. and Europe. In some cases, pets can be regarded as member of family with its welfare being put on par with that of other members of the family. This change in attitude is captured by the emergence of pet services such as grooming, daycare and even insurance coverage of pets as the pets are increasingly regarded as valued and emotionally attached companions. On the contrary, in most non-western societies the purpose of pets remains more utilitarian. In societies that make up a big portion of the population mainly on agriculture or in the farm lands the pets tend to be functional like guarding livestock, hunting or helping in the day-to-day activities..(López-Teijeiro et al., 2025)

8. KNOWING CONSUMER PET-DRIVEN BEHAVIOR

General Analysis of and Interpretation of the Theories of Consumer Behavior

Consumer behavior can be defined as the activity and the decision-making process of the individuals in the choice, purchase, usage and discarding of the products and services. Conventional consumer behavior explanations revolve around the fact that they concern themselves with rational models of making decisions by consumers, who are believed to make decisions based on the rational evaluation of the attributes and the costs and the advantages of using or purchasing certain products. Nevertheless, these models fail to perform well whenever it comes to purchases that are driven by emotions especially in the case of pets. The pet motivated consumer behaviour, however, is the one that contests the old models of consumer behaviour with bringing the factors of emotion and relationship in the driver of consumption. The affective bonding that the owners of pets have with their pets is major in influencing the buyers. Pet owners do not necessarily buy their products basing on the utility of a product but depending on how the utility of that product improves the welfare of the pet and increases the emotional connection between the pet and the owner. That behavior has been based on psychological component of taking care of pets and making them happy, comfortable and healthy.(De Canio et al., 2024)

On the Influences of Pet Ownership in the Emotional and Purchasing Decisions

Owning of pets is connected with strong emotional bonds. The pets are also viewed in terms of attachment theory because pets act as the safe affiliations to individuals, giving them emotional balances and constant confidants just like human relationships. Such an attachment brings about a setting where the consumers tend to perceive their pets as part of the family as opposed to the outlook that associates pets to mere animals. Therefore, the decision to buy things relating to pets is often influenced by emotional need of pampering, protecting and nursing the pets. As an example, the pet food is one of the biggest and the most stable demands in the pet industry. Nevertheless, it is not only about a supply of food; it is about the supply of the best one and the most nutritious one to pets. The pet's owner usually supports their research as they want to know which brands and in which ingredients their pets should be served. The emotional attachment towards pets also influences the food, treats, and even supplements better to purchase them at higher prices.(Hummer, n.d.)(Yoo et al., 2024)

Pet as the Members of the Family

The pets have gradually been taken as part of the family in the contemporary family. The changed culture is also replicated within the consumer behavior involving pets; where a good number of pet owners evaluate the needs and preferences of their pets as equal to that of the human members. The given perception is closely related to the phenomenon of so-called anthropomorphism when humanization of animals is proposed in a certain number of cases. Pet owners have a tendency of giving a human character to their pets; they also consider their pets as children, confidants or even partners in their day to day lives.(Dan Wu et al., 2024a) (Hummer, n.d.)

Trends in Buying Pet Product

A number of studies in the form of a case study indicate the rising role of a factor of emotional attachment in the process of buying pets. The emergence of the luxury brands of pet foods is one of such commendable examples. This trend of pet humanization has been fruitful to companies such as Blue Buffalo, hills science diet, and Wellness, which hence developed specialized and high-quality kind of food, which is demanded by pet owners that consider their pets as family members. They are usually of high-quality ingredients and health-giving properties and they are advertised to equal human-grade food. This has also happened on the pet fashion side where pet merchandise has become as common as the clothes that people wear and companies have been spawned like Petco, PetSmart, and even the smaller boutique companies that have nothing but designer products and even custom-made outfits. Most people have started using pet owners as fashion accessories they will dress up their pets using modern and trendy outfits of their own preference and the nature of the pet. Such a tendency has given rise to pet influencers who advertise pet fashion and accessories among millions of followers.(Jacobson et al., 2022)

9. PSYCHOLOGICAL MOTIVATORS OF BUYING OF PET

Attachment Theory and the Use of it in Pet Driven Consumer Decisions

The attachment theory which was created to explain touching bonds between children and their main carers has also been modified to study the strong emotional ties that take shape between human beings and their pets. The central notion of the attachment theory is that attachments to important people lead to the feeling of security and good health. To most people, pets are their source of attachment which offer emotional support, companionship as well as their personal feeling of security. A study conducted on the ownership of pets indicates that pets serve great emotional needs which in essence is met by human attachments. Pet animals provide support in emotions; free companionship and they are non-judgmental and thus they are of great value in the life of the symbiont. The attachment relationships cause certain types of behavior to be attributed to human attachment relationships that include wanting to be close to the pet, showing affection and wanting to guard the pet to prevent harm to the pet. An emotional bond that pet owners create between themselves and pets contributes to the purchase of pets to a great extent. Due to the concern of nurturing and protecting, owners of the pets will, in most cases, endeavor to purchase products that have an impact of improving the health and comfort of the pets. A good example is the purchase of a high-quality and orthopedic dog bed or a unique pet necklace bought by a pet owner where the aim of making these purchases is usually to ease the comfort of the pet and the strengthening of the bond. The more attached people are, the more money they will keep spending on the products that will help their pet in living a healthy, happy, and safe life which the attachment theory helps in explaining.

In addition, pets are in most instances a social identity of the owner. Socialization or use of pets in society is capable of sending signals alerting people of character traits of the owner. Having pets is a kind of social capital, which may emerge to affect the other people with regard to the owner. Such pet-related products as stylish pet clothes or personalized pet products are therefore frequently selected both because they are comfortable to wear or utilitarian and because they help the pet owner to improve his/her social image.(Isosuo, 2016)

The Pets Impact on the Decisions of Households

Pets are assumed to be an important part of the family and end up determining the spending on homes, timings and priorities. Studies concerning family decision making have indicated that pets are habitually used in senate on whether to purchase or go where to travel or even where to settle. Homeowners with pets can modify their living conditions in order to suit the pet and this can be done by getting pet friendly products like furniture, pet areas or getting houses with yards or parks. The control of pets on domestic affairs spreads to the budgeting and expenditure priorities. A huge percentage of the family budget is spent on pet cost which at times interferes with the other priorities of the family. Eating, medicine, grooming services and entertainment involving pets rank as some of the recurring expenses of many families. The pet owners can even change their daily activities to make sure the pet is well taken care of i.e. taking a sick pet and staying off work or modifying their eating behavior to consuming foods that are friendly towards the pet.Pets too are major influences in the purchase decisions made in houses. As an example, pet owners might opt to buy bigger houses or change their dwelling to reside in areas that are friendlier to pets where there are parks, pet hospitals and pet-friendly facilities. Such an influence on the housing choice can be an example of the accountability of pets on household behavior since household behavior is usually woven into the pet and tends to influence both action-oriented and emotion-oriented decision-making. (Isosuo, 2016)

Social Influence and Peer Pressure of Pet-based Purchase

The aspect of social influence has a great contribution in the pet-related consumer behavior. Pet owners would usually consult others when it comes to making the choice of buying in terms of their pets such as their friends, their families, their peers as well as the community over the web. This social influence may take up a number of forms. As an example, new pet owners might be inclined into buying some special goods to preserve the trends in social niches or to satisfy some external needs of other members of pet owners in the community. The social media may rise to a high level of peer pressure when it comes to pet ownership. Social media space such as Instagram, Tik Tok and Facebook have pet influencers with millions of followers promoting pet fashions, accessories and products. The idea behind this is that the pet owners are influenced by the pet related information they are exposed to on the internet and therefore they feel the need of buying related products in order to remain socially acceptable or be in line with the trends that they want to follow. This is accentuated by seeking to obtain experiences in pets on social networking sites where pets are commonly portrayed in idealistic styles. The social effect does not only involve peers, but also brand loyalty, as well as the effect of online reviews. Multitudes of pet guardians find it crucial to consult advice given at online circles of discussions, whether they feature specialized customer support, social media pages on pets or online customers appraisal on e-stores. The social influence in the consumer behavior with regard to pets often takes the form of recommending the adoption of a particular brand or product based on the recommendations given by the peers.(Hummer, n.d.)

Thinking biases in marketing of pet products

Another major motivation behind the purchase of pets is cognitive biases as systematic deviations of thinking in regard to being rational about judging. The pet industry is one of the sectors where marketers exploit the biases in the minds of consumers to influence the latter to make purchases. Halo effect, which is one of the most common cognitive biases in the pet product marketing, is carried out in such instances that the pet owners connect the brand image of a product with the general quality of the product. As an example, a notorious pet food brand could advertise itself as being high quality or premium thus making consumers assume that all their products are good albeit without direct evidence to prove that it is actually of high quality. The other cognitive bias is an anchoring effect which comes about when a consumer clings to first piece of information he or she comes across when making a decision(Bruno Sousa, 2025; Sara Pimenta, 2025). As an example, when the brand of pet food has a relatively expensive food, the consumers will perceive that the food is of high quality just by looking at the price of product without necessarily looking at the nutritional value of the food produced by the brand when compared to other lower priced alternatives. Another bias that applies in the pet-based consumer behavior is the loss aversion. With fear of loss or guilt, pet owners will have added motivation of buying products that will prevent their pets getting into discomfort or harm. As an illustration, the owners are likely to be persuaded to purchase insurance or health products to their pets despite not being clear on the advantages of the product in question as a way of preventing possible loss of the pets health.(Hummer, n.d.)

10. THE PET MARKET: THE DEVELOPMENT OF INDUSTRY AND INDUSTRY DYNAMICS

The Pet Industry that is Growing Rapidly

The animal market has grown exponentially during the last several decades and taken one of the most profitable places in the global market ever since. A combination of more pet owners and more pets being humanized has brought about a huge demand of pet-based products and services. The world market of all pet products (including pet food, toys, medical, and services) is estimated at more than 30 billion dollars a year in future years and the rates of growth remain higher than most other markets. Population, rise in disposable incomes and attitude towards pets are some of the factors growing the pet market. With the ongoing urbanization and the change in the structure of a family, pets are being viewed as inseparable house members(Paulino et al., 2025). There is also the issue of the aging population and in particular, the population in developed countries which is responsible in causing the pet industry to grow because older citizens want something to give them companionship and something to give them emotional support in the form of pets. Also, the millennials and the generation Z are more likely to spend on such categories as lifestyle products and wellness products, so they have become the main thrust of the growth of the pet market. The other element that has led to the growth of the market is the emergence of pet related services. The pet owners are not anymore buying products to use on pets but are after special services like grooming of pets, pet day care, pet training, pet sitting and, in some cases, even pet-friendly traveling facilities. The willingness to live a pet friendly living in practice and buy everything to make the pet life more satisfactory has increased the need of many more varied services towards an enhanced pet life.(Lavertu et al., 2025)

The Major Areas of the Pet Market: Toys, Food, Health Treatments, Apparel and Others

The industry is wide ranging and there are some of the key areas that have led to the growth of the industry. Every one of these industries has been innovating and changing according to the preferences of the consumers.

- **Pet Food:** The greatest part of the pet industry is represented by the pet food market where the expenditures in connection with animals are rather high. With the rise in the tendency of pet owners to identify pets as their members of the family, consumers are more prone to spend money on high quality and nutritious food. The market of pet food is as diverse as a dry kibble to a gourmet and organic meal, whereas the increasing needs and requirements are raised to the appearance of special diets (raw, grain-free, or hypoallergenic food). The increase in pet health and wellness has also influenced the need of pet food as pet owners require food that best suits the pet in terms of health requirements.
- **Pet Healthcare:** Another blistering business segment of the pet industry is the pet healthcare. With the increase of pet-since, the owners are showing increased interest in providing well-being to their pets thus leading to preventive care and wanting to provide medical care to their pets as given to human beings. The products include veterinary services, pet medications, pet insurance and products, through supplements and vitamins, which promote wellness in pets. There is a type of insurance known as pet insurance, which has developed a substantial following with pet owners since they want to avoid the financial threats of pet healthcare. In some of the developed countries (United States, the UK, and Sweden), pet insurance has become less infrequent, and the companies provide such coverage to receive regular checkups and cover emergency operations. People who own pets are more likely to afford insurance to make sure that their animals get the most professional medical treatment, which is considered the aspect of emotional involvement and the wish to get pets treated as relatives.(Han et al., 2025a)

- **Pet Toys and Accessory:** Pet toys and accessories are another booming industry in pet market. The pet toys play important role in entertaining, cognitively stimulating and physically exercising the pet, especially with those that are very active such as the dogs. The pet toys may be the ones that are as straightforward as just something to chew or the ones that have interactive activity to keep the pets busy and to prevent boredom. The manufacture of pet toys has also increased in the sophistication of high-tech toys which include automatic fetch machine, puzzle feeders, and toys which exercise the mental faculties of pets. A new market segment, which is selling pet clothing, coats, and pet shoes has also risen especially in the urban setting. People who are having pets will usually put their pets in trendy clothes during special occasions or trying to make a statement regarding the status of their pets. With the rise in the treatment of pets like a family member, pet attire has been transformed into the mode of living, and the pet fashion designers have formulated special line of clothes and the pet shop outfitters have made tailor-made clothes.
- **Pet Services:** Besides the pet-products industry, an industry comprising of pet services has grown at an alarming rate. The pet grooming, daycare, training as well as sitting services have been becoming a common feature of the pet care business industry. People who keep pets will be ready to spend on such services so that their pets remain well taken care of, happy and healthy. Pet grooming has been advanced to involve treatment of pets with a specialty like the spa services, massages and pet facials.(Yoo et al., 2024)

The Knowledge of Pet Product Innovation and Consumer Demand

There is massive demand of new pet products that is encouraging the growth of pet industry. New products and services are continually being launched by the companies to develop the changing demands of the pet owners (Bruno Sousa, 2025). The most common drivers of pet product innovation are wellness trends, technology and lifestyle trends among human beings. As an example, similar to enthusiasm about organic food, fitness tracking devices, and healthy sustainable living, the pet industry is following the same trend by allocating more interest to environmentally friendly, health-conscious, and technology driven products. Another trend which is affecting the industry is the introduction of personalized pet products. Personalization of pet collars, pet tags, pet beds and other pet clothes is gaining popularity in the pet owner segment as pet owners want to show their own personality in relation to their pets. The request to have personalized items is not a trend or unique but in a greater trend of customization of the consumer goods where personalization is treated as one of the means of self-expression and uniqueness. Innovation in the pet product is also driven by the changes in technology. The innovation of smarter pet products like automatic pet feeders, pet surveillance cameras and GPS Collars, has transformed how one takes care of the pets.(De Canio et al., 2024)

What are Pet Care and Luxury Pet Products Trends?

Luxury pet products have been seen as one of the huge segments in the pet market as the pets have become more a part of the family. Luxury pet products include high end pet beds, designer accessories, pet clothing, high end pet food and custom-made pet services. The rise in the number of people with interest to luxury products follows the growing valuations of pet owners to invest in products that improve the living quality and health status of the pets.It is also important to refer to the emergence of pet-friendly luxury. The pet owners want special travel experience and are demanding services of privately operated jets especially on behests of their pets and pet friendly resorts as well as luxury pet spas. These developments entail the rising potential of pets in determining social and leisure time activities and an upsurge of demand in high end quality specialized pet products and services.

11. EMOTIONS AND COGNITION EVERY HUMAN IS AFFECTED BY EMOTIONAL AND COGNITION RESPONSES TO PRODUCTS INVOLVING PETS

The Importance of Pets in the Emotional Response of Consumers With Respect to Advertisements

The adverts in the pet industry normally aim at evoking high emotions in consumers. The use of pets in advertisements has been very prolific in making feelings of warmth, affection and a feeling of trust. The online advertising on pets effects an emotional response, which can be explained by multiple psychological reasons, such as empathy and need to take care of other people, the need in social connection. Emotionally, pets in the advertisements make people feel cheerful and contented and even nostalgic, thus pushing shoppers to buy products depending on the emotional issue, and not on rational necessity. Pet appearance in advertising appeals to some fundamental levels in psychological reactions. A survey carried out proved that advertisements with animals have more chances of causing a positive emotional experience. The emotional pull that is generated by the pet driven advertising can be an effective tool of the brand. Purchases on the part of pet owners happen more at times when the individuals imbibe a feeling towards the pet featured in the advertisement, or when the controlled pet pet is depicted as a friendly family member in the ad. An illustration of the same could be seen in an advertisement that has been done when a pet is shown enjoying certain brand of food or play item there is an impression building that the said item will cause the same fun and happiness to the pet of the person viewing the ad.(Kasmi et al., 2023)

The Psychological Effect of Pet Product Packaging and Design

Design and packaging of pet products is very influential in the perception, as well as purchase of pet products. Packaging has been a very important element in the purchase decision because consumers tend to relate quality of products with respective packages. Packaging in the pet industry is highly instrumental in the business as consumers are attracted by designs and shapes, which in one way are used as a sales tool.

The Role of Color and Design

There is usually pet product packaging with colors and design features which are very well selected so as to evoke a particular emotion. As an example, brighter and intense colors may lead to the creation of an excited and lively atmosphere whereas more soft and pastel shades be able to express the perception of being calm and trustworthy. The right packaging of pet food can also attract consumers depending on their preference since natural colors, and earthy tones can be used to market pet food to reach consumers interested in organic or environmentally friendly foodstuff respectively. Another important feature of packaging of the pet products is the use of pictures. It is possible to establish an emotional attachment to the consumers using pictures of happy harmless pets since they would want the product to give a positive outcome to their own pets. The fact that the products will portray pets accrue delight by using the product raises the chances that the consumers will buy the products.

12. PLOTTING THE TRENDS AMONG DEMOGRAPHIC GROUPS IN PET-DRIVEN CONSUMER BEHAVIOR

To have a comprehension of the interaction of pet centered consumption among different groups of ages, it is important to understand the differences among generations. Cultural attitudes, financial level, online literacy, emotional criteria, and moral concerns play a crucial role in shaping the consumer behavior in the given sphere, and they differ within generational groups. The present section describes and evaluates the fact that there are patterns of relatedness of Generation Z, Millennials, Generation X, and Baby Boomers to pets and the matching consumption behavior.(Chen et al., 2012)

Generation z (born 1997)

The youngest adult generation Z is characterized by its digital fluency and social awareness as well as a pre occupation with identity expression. Most Gen Z breeders attribute pet ownership to emotional and mental well-being, recognizing pets as emotional support animals as opposed to the conventional family members. They consume according to the trends on Tik Tok and Instagram, where they focus on pet influencers and viral content that significantly influence the preferences of the products. They especially like customized, beautiful and ethically-produced pet products. Their main values are sustainability, the use of cruelty-free materials, and inclusivity. The Gen Z consumers with their lower purchasing power are however not afraid of paying extra to consume products that can match their own ethical standards as well as branding lifestyle. They also agree with the theory of Self Concept and Symbolic Interactionism.(Melkko, n.d.)

Millennium generation (born: 1981-1996)

The current trend on the pet market suggests that millennials are the real force of the current pet market. The present generation has more or less popularized the trend of the pet parent where pets are treated like family or even children. This emotional connection turns into additional investment in high-value goods, such as pet insurance, organic foods, grooming services, fashion accessories and technology-enhanced pet care (smart feeders, GPS tracking).

Millennials are the digital natives yet they are also focused on convenience and quality. Their consumption pattern indicates their emotional satisfaction and also the need of expressing their value through their consumption. Health-consciousness, sustainability and ethical branding are decent factors but not always paramount. Attachment Theory, Consumer Culture Theory, and Theory of Planned Behavior are the most effective ways of explaining the behavior of Millennials.(Arnould & Thompson, 2005)

Generation X (born:1965-1980)

Generation X which is regarded as being pragmatic and financially stable will tend to balance between emotional involvement and making a rational decision. They certainly do love their pet but the consumption is usually based on the thought of reliability, durability and long-term health. They spend money on quality food, veterinary care and hardwearing accessories as opposed to sense or fashion. Gen X shoppers are very faithful to their brand, and they are less vulnerable to the influence of a social media fad. They are however getting accustomed to internet purchases, particularly where this lifestyle benefits convenience. The rational choice models and Theory of Planned Behavior have greater effect on their decisions as they are cautious, goal oriented, in their style of pet ownership.(Zhang et al., 2022)

Baby Boomers (born:1946-1964)

Baby Boomers, most of who are already retired or near their retirement date, tend to perceive pets as mainly companions that offer comfort well as constancy. Their consumption on pets is usually need driven as they concentrate on necessities such as food, grooming and health among others. This generation will not be tempted to buy high-end or stylish things targeted to pets and will tend to be less active in consumption on the Internet or through social networks. Boomers like conventional retailing, and the brands they trust and follow along with personal recommendations play an important role. They act in an Attachment Theory that takes functional, as opposed to an expressive, form they are very loyal, consistent, and practical in pet keeping. Somewhere, this group is also the least occupied by a trend or ethical consumption story.(Belk et al., 2005)

The Summary and Implications: Generational mapping shows that pet-driven consumer behaviour is not uniform, but it differs based on values, technological ease or discomfort, financial earning and emotion attachment towards pets. Priorities of the Gen Z and Millennials are based on emotion, identity and digital culture with an eye on personalization and on being socially visible.

Being a balanced kind of Gen X, they are rational and emotionally invested and oriented to trust and value. Boomers like things to be simple, traditional and routine-oriented and emphasise long-term reliability rather than innovation. These data would become essential in fine-tuning promotional tactics, product development, and inclusive academic study on an age-sensitive study of pets.(Autio et al., 2014)

13. THE EXAMPLES OF PET-DRIVEN CONSUMER BEHAVIOR BETWEEN VARIOUS DEMOGRAPHICS

The role of Age, Income as well as the geographical location in the pet driven consumption Consumer behavior is affected by many forms of demography such as age, income, and geographical position but this is derived out of pet approach to product or service. All these are key determinants that contribute in the manner in which the pet owners take care of these animals especially in terms of the purchasing patterns of pet products and services they would be ready to invest in.

- **Age:** Age of people having pets can significantly affect purchasing behavior and priority of people in case of purchasing something regarding pets. Millennial and Gen Z new generations have been suggested as one of the pet obsessed groups of consumers. To these groups, pets also act like surrogate children or mates especially where young people have resorted to a delayed start of forming families, and development of small families. The tendency towards pet keeping by the Millennials has also been attributed to the fact that they seek both physical and emotional attachments thus splurging on quality products that are organic, value-added services such as wellness programs, and even luxury products that they can purchase in relation to their pets. Specifically, millennials have a high possibility of perceiving their pets as a normal family member, and as such, they tend to decide on their purchases depending on the emotional connection that they have with their pets. The age group is also technology-savvy and most of them are shopping online on pet products mostly advised and tipped by social media. The products which are interesting to the millennials, especially the ones leading to the health and wellness of pets are natural foods, grooming products, and newly developed health monitoring products.(Ajzen, 1991)
- **Income:** The level of income also has a great impact in pet led consumer behavior. The higher the income of its pet owners, the more they are willing to spend on high-rated quality products and services as it implies that they also have more disposable income which they can spend on their pets. The most popular luxury pet products are pet designer clothing, luxury pet food, and special treatments such as grooming services and are bought mostly by consumers with the higher income level who consider pets as a part of the family and should be provided with the high maintenance levels. On the other hand, pet owners who live on low income will have more priorities on necessities of their pets like food, shelter, and medical care than on luxuries. In the case of these consumers, emphasis is given to identify quality products at a low cost that will satisfy the needs of their pets without loss of any bank notes. Market approaches that attract the lower-income pet owners, such as discount pet stores, value brands and bulk purchases are often seen because these pet owners are not able to afford premium and luxury brands of pet products, nor are they financially flexible to do so. The differences in the income also affect the kind of services that will meet the pet owners. Pet owners with higher incomes are more likely to be more demanding with many services which include the pet grooming, pet day care, pet training and even the vacation

where they take the pets along with them on a vacation. Alternatively, the low-income group is likely to use cheaper services that they do themselves or use less often.(Hummer, n.d.)

- **Geographical Location:** The place also influences consumer behavior of pets greatly. Owners of pets in cities and in the rural areas tend to show varied buying experiences and desires on the basis of the accessibility of the pet products and services, purchased in addition to the lifestyle issues. People owning pets in cities have more chances of spending on luxury items and services since pets in cities are usually more expensive to keep. Cities have been pet friendly with pet friendly parks, grooming salons, pet stores and pet friendly apartments being built. Products targeting the pets in the city, including small or portable pet accessories, pet living grooming products and city traveling with pets, are more demanded in cities than in the countryside. Pet keepers in urban areas are also younger with Millennials and Gen Z comprising a huge pool of pet owners. Such pet owners are also inclined to think of their pets as their companions and fashion accessories to use high quality of both goods and services.(Isosuo, 2016)

The Millennial Pet Market and Pet Influencers

The millennials are among the most powerful demographics in the pet industry that is making a great influence in the consumer behavior trend about pets. This generation is very interested in the well-being of their pet animals and they perceive the pet animals to be part of their family. As per the survey, Millennials have more chances to do the spending on luxurious products, such as organic animal food, health care products as well as high-end pet accessories. This generation in specific is eager in products that make their pets well off, such as orthopedic beds, toy firms that can be associated with, and nutritious food products that can improve their wellbeing. Pivotal trends of the pet market of the Millennials are pet influencers. The emergence of new types of pet celebrities has been promoted by social media, which is especially true about Instagram, Tik Tok, and YouTube. These pets in most cases accompanied with their owners generate millions of followers, and when it comes to purchasing decisions, such pets endorse in their communities. Pet influencers endorse pet fashions, grooming products, brands of pet foods, etc. and make them feel that they are aspiring to live the life of these pets, the ones made popular on social media. The millennials who own pets will be more prone to online shopping, will use recommendations and reviews of social media and will refer to in flu civilization when buying a product. This age group will especially be able to be greatly involved in custom-made and tailor-made pet products, such as engraved collars, custom made beds and custom pet clothes as this reflects the personal need to provide the pet with an individualized pet experience.(Jacobson et al., 2022)

14. PET MARKETING STRATEGIES: SUCCESS, FAILURES

What Makes the Pet Marketing Campaigns Successful?

There are some very successful marketing campaigns which have best sued the attention of the consumers with the pet industry and subsequently achieved successful sales. Such campaigns tend to focus on emotional relationships, personification of pets and the growing presence of the pets in the family. Successful marketing can be used in pet industry as follows:

- **The Pedigree Adoption Drive (Pedigree):** Another really successful campaign of the pet industry is Pedigree Adoption Drive type. This campaign was aimed at creating awareness of pet adoption (one should adopt a pet instead of purchasing it at a breeder agency). Pedigree used heartwarming adverts that showed the dogs that are ready to be taken in and their new owners forming an emotional fold between the audience and the dogs that are living on the street. It was an appeal to emotions and it was obvious that a number of pet owners might be associated with the concept of taking a shelter dog to a loving home that was so close to the audience. The substantial social awareness, emotional response directed at the campaign was among the reasons of its success being associated with the popular trend in society to adhere to the pets that found themselves on the streets as a result of abandoning one by the previous owner. Besides, Pedigree collaborated with pet shelters in which part of their revenue was dedicated towards animal adoption and shelter care. The given approach was able to not only raise its sales but it also enhanced its image of a socially responsible company.(Belk & Pollay, 1985)
- **The BarkBox: The Mechanics of the Meet the Pets Campaign (BarkBox):** As an example, such a subscription service as BarkBox, providing monthly boxes that contain toys, treats, and other pet products, implemented the so-called meet the pets campaign, and it can be noted that this approach to appealing to consumers through personalization and humor worked. In the campaign, the real pets (usually, dogs) were the stars of the campaign, and each pet demonstrated their personality and particular taste to be given in some kind of treats or toys. Having actual pets as the brands of their products, BarkBox touched the emotional part of consumers, as far as their products were created based on individual needs of each pet. Humor was also em-

ployed in the campaign where pets were displayed using the product in a weird and funny manner hence making communication with social media to be facile and shareable. The targeting of Millennials in the process of selling a pet and the enhancement of the brand recognition led to the growth in sales not only among Millennium pet owners but also among the rest of the people because of the personalized and fun character of the campaign.(Chen et al., 2012)

Basic ingredients of a successful pet marketing

Out of all those examples, a number of major points can be highlighted which can help in the success of the pet marketing:

- **Emotional Appeal:** There are numerous advertisements of pet products that scored hits because of their emotional appeal to customers. The relationship between pets and their owners is so emotional and the campaigns which appeal to it tend to be successful. Emotional manipulation can be done when there is heartwarming and easy to relate to the text, like the story of adoption, pets loving their products. This can establish a tight emotional bond, which drives the consumers to buy.
- **Personalization:** Pet owners are getting interested in buying products, which are specifically shaped to the needs of their pets. Effective campaigns would even focus on customization, and that could be in customized pet food, customized pet accessories, or even in subscription services through which the likes or preferences of pet is accommodated. Personalization allows the consumers to believe that the brand knows their pet and the relationship they have with the pet, which would result in brand loyalty.
- **Social Responsibility:** Customers do not wish to disagree with the brand they are buying and hence buying the brand that supports some social cause like pet adoption or animal welfare would significantly connect with the pet owner. Consumers, especially the members of the Millennial Generation prefer to support the businesses which appear to be socially responsible. Donating at least part of the sales to charities and shelters, becoming a partner in promenades during which people can adopt animals, organizing some awareness on animal welfare, etc. can help brands to attract the increasing number of people who care about ethical matters.
- **Humor and Relationship:** To get brands to associate with a chosen consumer, humor and ability to relate with them can be used. Light-hearted manner of numerous advertisements concerning pets and performing unusual pets and funny actions help to decrease or raise the chance of sharing an ad in

social networks. Such kind of the content connects well with younger pet owners who focus on genuineness and humor in their brands.(Lavertu et al., 2025)

15. ETHICS IN PET DRIVEN MARKETING

Ethical Dilemmas Apart of Pet Product Industry

Unexpectedly, the pet product industry does not omit any ethical issues, as the commodification of pets has resulted in the concern regarding the quality of life of animals and the duty of the brands to make sure their marketing procedure complies with the ethical demands. Although the goal of pet products and services is to enhance pet life, the current dynamic development of the industry led to the emergence of the debate regarding excessive consumption, health of pets, the possibility of exploiting the animals used in pet business for profit.(Hausmann et al., 2023b)

- **Humanization of pets and its effect:** Humanization of pets is one of the major ethical concerns in the pet driven marketing. Since pets are turning into part of the family, they have become the consumers of the same kind of consumerism that human families do. It is not just pet fashion but there is even pet hotel. The emergence of what has been termed as pet pampering has raised questions as to whether this is what is best suited to the pets or otherwise. Although there is nothing wrong in pampering the pets with love and care it is the creation of a million dollar industry of luxury goods of pets that makes one to wonder whether he really needs some products. As an example, pet owners might feel obliged to buy such costly products as designer pet clothing or spa procedure or such pet furniture that might not be related to the pet care. Such tendencies are a threat to the needs of pets compared to what consumers would want, and they can give rise to unnecessary expenditure, thus establishing a market place that could be supplied by products that exploit emotions and not fulfill basic requirements of taking care of pets. Ethically, it is the responsibility of the brands not to exploit people by selling products that are not really useful to their pets but sell them because of the bonding that exists between the pet and the owner. Although the choice of purchases is left in the hands of pet owners, the marketers ought to be conscious of the possibility of playing with emotions to make profits.
- **Exhaustive exploitation of Animal Welfare in order to gain profit:** Excessive use of animals with an aim of making profits is an additional ethical concern of pet driven marketing. Certain marketing undertakings have

received criticism because of using animals in less than conducive manner. As an example, when live animals are used in advertisements or during promotion process the animation of animals may result in the fact they are treated as a subject of consumption or a thing.(Hummer, n.d.)

***Awareness of ethically and sustainable pet brands by the consumer*:** With the increased awareness of the current environmental and ethical condition of their purchases, greater interest in sustainability and humane products has been witnessed among pet owners nowadays. This encompasses pet food, pet toys and accessories, which are made of natural, organic, or eco-friendly substances and also services, which accelerate protection of animals and animal conservation. Another factor that ethically oriented pet owners would like to get is to have brands transparent on how the ingredients are sourced and how animals are ethically treated. The pet consumers have become more inclined to brands that sell cruelty-free products or those willing to collaborate with animal welfare institutions. As an example, certain brands of pet foods rely on sustainable sourcing, ingredients having been grown locally, or providing some alternative workable with plants rather than based on meat. With such concerns, the brands are able to not only increase their position in the market but they are also likely to improve animal and environmental welfare. Nevertheless, marketers should also avoid the pitfall of associating their products with environmental or ethical features when they are actually not. This would be referred to as greenwashing customers. The truth in choice of source, manufacturing, and animal welfare is what makes all the difference to the credibility in the market of pet products aimed at ethics.(Isosuo, 2016)

16. Comparison of the Major Findings

Emotional Attachment

Most of the literature affirms the fact that emotional attachment plays a central part in pet related consumption. Writing on indulgent consumption, The pet proprietors tend to commit indulgent consumption behavior as they regard pets as family members. However warns against such generalization because it is not universally true that our pets will be taken care of to the point of spending a great deal of money because of emotional attachment, other cultures exist with variations on pet-keeping practice that do not share the same behavior of being emotionally attached leading to spending.

Persona and Symbolism

The pets serve the role of symbols of identity that express the owner values, and their locations in the social structure. People tend to choose the product that is reflective of how they envision themselves: ecologically-friendly, stylish, or motherly. Yet, authorities state that such an expression of identity is more common among higher-income, urban societies and, by extension, the meaning attributed to pet ownership might be hierarchically divided by social economic status.

Influence of Marketing and Media

The increased impact of social media and pet influencers has been indicates in research, These research studies indicate that, in consumers, digital visibility, emotional narration, and influencer promotion have a significant influence on consumer tastes. however, made a further step, having argued that the consumers are not just involved in value co-creation, and that they cannot just be manipulated into it by the marketers.

Moral and Environmental Aspects

The awakening of the new type of pet consumer that prefers sustainable, cruelty-free, and ethically created pet products has occurred. However, the consideration of this ethical orientation to product behavior might conflict with convenience or aesthetic preference, and there is a gap in real-life consumer behavior because it reflects the difference in values.

Social, Economic and Cultural Factors

It emphasize income, class and culture in the formulation of pet-related consumption. Though commercial literature tends to portray a homogenized group of pet owners, scholarly evidence has indicated that low-income pet owners are subject to conditions in which they can be restricted or compelled into making trade-offs or into aspirational spending. In mainstream marketing research, these differences are mostly under-researched.

17. PREDICTIONS OF THE PET-DIRECTED CONSUMER TRENDS IN THE FUTURE

The Pet Care Technological Innovations

Technological progress is more connected with the future of pet-driven consumer patterns since it is transforming how people with pets take care of their pets. Pet care products and services are also quickly being included into the areas of technology and there is a new chance that pet owners can continue to use technology in monitoring protecting and taking care of their pets in completely new fashions.

- **Intelligent Pet products:** Smart pet products are one of the greatest technological tendencies in the pet industry. These are products which involve wearable technologies that monitor the health and activity of the pets, automated feeders which release food at a particular time and interactive toys which keeps pets entertained even when their owners are not with them. Pet care products which include the use of IoT (Internet of Things) enable pet owners to keep an eye on their pets even when they are not around them and ensure that they are fine.As would be an example, pet collars that are fitted with the GPS technology enables one to locate the position of their pets in real time hence relaxes the mind of those who are worried about their pets wanting to get lost. In the same way, pet health trackers, including Fit Bark or Whistle, can track physical activity of pets, their sleeps, and health status, which warns the owners of any strange actions and about the possible health risks. Due to increased technology savvy pet owners, it is inevitable that the demand of such smart devices will increase and new advancements in the technology are making them more usable and cost effective.(Han et al., 2025b)
- **Telemedicine and Virtual Vet Visit:** The increase of the phenomenon of telemedicine in the pet industry is another important technological trend. Consultations with veterinarians on the Internet become more and more popular and provide the pet owners with the opportunity to obtain medical consultation and not to leave the house. The COVID-19 pandemic has increased the desire of pet owners to use remote healthcare services even more, spurring this trend. Telemedicine services refers to services where pet owners shall be in a position to consult with licensed veterinarians through video call or on line. Sometimes these consultations are made out of non-emergent cases given that the case can be either a general check-up, behavior consultation or follow-up care after a medical procedure. The innovation saves time and money to the pet owners and increases the accessibility of veterinary care to people living in underserved rural areas. With the popularization of telemed-

icine, there is a chance that the owners of pets might adopt the benefits and cost-effectiveness of virtual vet shops in the future.(Han et al., 2025b)

The Pet health and Wellness Product Growth

Since pets are also perceiving to be members of the family, purchases of health and wellness products in pets have boomed. Proprietors of pets are now more concerned than before in making sure their pets live long, healthy and happy lives. This has put some products targeted to enhance the health of pets on the limelight with the popularity of such products increasing significantly owing to the fact that more people are investing in healthy supplements, natural solutions and also fitness-related products meant to keep the pet fit.

- **Pet products which are natural and organic:** The trend in the natural and organic pet product segment can also be found in the consumer trend as more pet owners have grown aware of the ingredients of the food and products, they consumer. The popularity of organic pet food as a type made using human-grade ingredients and without artificial preservatives and other additives is at a high level. Companies such as The Honest Kitchen and Blue Buffalo are only taking advantage of the emerging need of healthy and sustainable pet food. The same goes with natural health supplements to pets, which take the form of joint health supplementation, probiotics, and supplements infused with CBD. The pet owners resort to the products in order to reduce various health problems, including digestive issues, anxiety, pain management, etc. The increase in the popularity of these wellness products is indicative of the general want of the consumer to be healthy as well as environmentally conscious, and it should intently increase as pet owners entrench on preventative pet care services.(SAMPLE et al., 2025)
- **Mental and Physical Health Products Pet:** Due to the increment in knowledge of pet owners of the significance of mental and physical activities of their pets, the demand of physical fitness and mental stimulation of pets products has increased many folds. These products are interactive toys and puzzle feeders to activity trackers that supervise the degree of exercise by pets. Pet owners are taking up the top priority to make sure their pets have active and stimulating lives where the kind of products made to entertain the pets physically and mentally are becoming popular. To illustrate, Pet Safe has various puzzle toys that make dogs engage in critical thinking and to earn their treats, and Furbo also produces pet cameras with the help of which pet owners can observe and communicate with their pets when they are not at home. Due to an increasing tendency of putting pets, most of whom are dogs, in the same

position as members of a family, pet owners will tend to spend more on products that will ensure that their pets remain entertained, healthy and happy.

Personalizing and Customizing of Pet

It is believed that customized pet products will stay popular as pet owners strive to ensure their differentiation of the connection between them and their pets. The benefit of customization is that pet owners will have the possibility to make unique products that show the personality, their pet and its needs and style. Personalizing of pets is motivated by the wants of people to grow much attached to their pets and it presents a virtue by the brands to respond to the move of establishing a uniqueness in pet products.

- **personalized pet accessories and clothes:** Pet clothes that used to be considered as a gimmick is booming in the market, especially for dogs. There is an increasing trend in customized clothes of pets i.e. personalized pet collars, coats and even pet-owner matching outfits. Such brands as Petco and BarkBox introduce personalized pet accessories, such as engraved pet tags, monogrammed beds and custom-made pet clothing. There is also the tendency of consumers using customized pet goods such as designer collars, harnesses, and pet carriers that allow the consumers to satisfy the unique needs and style of the pet. Customized products such as pet portraits or personalized pet beds have also become an essential trend in the recent years through which a pet owner expresses his or her very own relationship with its pet.
- **Individualized Pet Food and Sub crisis:** Another growth trend is pet food customization. The subscription model (i.e., The Farmer s Dog, Ollie) provides individual food sequences depending on a pet s breed, age, size, and the diet. The services of the organization will be relevant to the pet owners who wish to know that their pets can get the most ideal nutrition as per the needs of the pet. Through the provision of personalized, fresh and natural food choices such companies are taking into consideration the pet humanization trend as well as the growth in the demand of customized pet care solutions. (Dodd et al., 2025)

Green Products and Eco-Friendly Products

As the prospect of environmental issues is gaining greater relevance in the world discourse, a trend of sustainability and environmentally-friendly pets-related business is starting to emerge. The consumer market wants more products that are being made ethically and with the minimal effect on the environment. These are biodegradable pet products, eco-friendly packaging of the pet products, and organic-based and plant-derived pet food ingredients. Products made by brands that are environmentally friendly and fully transparent should enjoy more demand among environmentally conscious buyers. The trend is in line with the current trends in the general society towards being sustainable and responsible consumers. Pet brands which are bringing in eco-friendly initiatives, i.e. the recycles of the materials being used in toys, bedding materials or the packaging itself, have a high chance of connecting with an increasing number of environmentally conscious consumers of pets.

Future Trends in Consumer Behavior in Combination With Pets

Technological innovation, personalization, and growing popularity of the pet health/wellness have defined the future of the consumer behavior that is driven by pets. As the pet ownership progresses further, it is possible to expect that only brands concerned about the emotional and physical welfare of pets and appreciating sustainable and ethical business both will be in a better position to succeed. These trends whereby pets are increasingly being humanized coupled with evolvement of technology will further increase the consumer needs of quality and tailor-made pet products and services. Following the increasing scale of education among consumers, regarding the well-being of animals, not only in matters of the product production but also on the environment, the pet business industry will have to change in order to satisfy these new demands. In sum, the adapted up-to-date strategy of the pet industry that consists of innovation, sustainability and knowledge on the emotional connection between pets and their owners is going to determine the future of the sector. Knowing that this market is still flourishing, brands that have adopted these changes will not only make consumers think of engaging in it, but also act in a more responsible, caring and ethical manner towards the pet care business process.(Dan Wu et al., 2024b)

18. CONCLUSION

Throughout this chapter, we have been able to learn more about the rich dynamic nature of pets and pet consumer behavior, and how pets affect the purchasing choice of the owner, and general trends that affect the pet industry as a whole. The emergence of pet humanization has transformed the relationship between the pet owners and the pet products and services offerings fundamentally whereby majority of the pet owners represent the pets as part of the family. This emotional attachment between the pet and the owner is the major trigger that drives purchase behavior of pet owner and makes a difference between purchasing the daily pet feed like pet food and grooming products and the luxury like the pet designer fashions and pet high-tech accessories.

REFERENCES

Ajzen, I. (1991). The theory of planned behavior. *Organizational Behavior and Human Decision Processes, 50*(2), 179–211. DOI: 10.1016/0749-5978(91)90020-T

Alves, H. M., Sousa, B., Carvalho, A., Santos, V., Dias, Á. L., & Valeri, M. (2022). Encouraging brand attachment on consumer behaviour: Pet-friendly tourism segment. *Journal of Tourism. Heritage and Services Marketing*, *8*(2), 16–24. DOI: 10.5281/zenodo.7357978

Arnould, E. J., & Thompson, C. J. (2005). Consumer Culture Theory (CCT): Twenty years of research. *The Journal of Consumer Research, 31*(4), 868–882. DOI: 10.1086/426626

Autio, J., Kuismin, A., Autio, M., Syrjälä, H., & Kylkilahti, E. (2014). *Consumer value journey with pet in multiple service touchpoints.*

Belk, R. W., Ger, G., & Askegaard, S. (2005). The Fire of Desire: A Multisited Inquiry into Consumer Passion. SSRN *Electronic Journal.* https://doi.org/DOI: 10.2139/ssrn.354640

Belk, R. W., & Pollay, R. W. (1985). Images of Ourselves: The Good Life in Twentieth Century Advertising. *The Journal of Consumer Research, 11*(4), 887. DOI: 10.1086/209024

Belk, R. W., Sherry, J. F.Jr, & Wallendorf, M. (1988). A Naturalistic Inquiry into Buyer and Seller Behavior at a Swap Meet. *The Journal of Consumer Research, 14*(4), 449. DOI: 10.1086/209128

Chen, A., Hung, K. P., & Peng, N. (2012). A cluster analysis examination of pet owners consumption values and behavior - Segmenting owners strategically. *Journal of Targeting. Measurement and Analysis for Marketing*, *20*(2), 117–132. DOI: 10.1057/jt.2012.10

De Canio, F., Viglia, G., & Lombart, C. (2024). Package-free products: How to improve pro-environmental buying behaviors among consumers. *Technological Forecasting and Social Change*, *198.* Advance online publication. DOI: 10.1016/j.techfore.2023.122995

Dodd, M., Fowler, A., & Lottridge, D. (2025). Purr-ogrammed love: A narrative review of virtual pets. *Entertainment Computing*, *54.* Advance online publication. DOI: 10.1016/j.entcom.2025.100958

Emran Shaikh, M. (n.d.). *A STUDY ON CONSUMER PERCEPTION AND PREFERENCES TOWARDS PET CARE INDUSTRY IN INDIA CAPSTONE PROJECT REPORT MASTER OF MANAGEMENT STUDIES SIES COLLEGE OF MANAGEMENT STUDIES NERUL, NAVI MUMBAI-400706.*

Farida, Y., Siswanto, N., & Vanany, I. (2024). Reverse logistics toward a circular economy: Consumer behavioral intention toward polyethylene terephthalate (PET) recycling in Indonesia. *Case Studies in Chemical and Environmental Engineering, 10.* Advance online publication. DOI: 10.1016/j.cscee.2024.100807

Green, M. S. (2008). Self-Expression. In *Self-Expression.* Oxford University Press., DOI: 10.1093/acprof:oso/9780199283781.001.0001

Gromek, N., & Perek-Białas, J. (2022). Why is pet goods consumption imperceptible for economists? A scoping review. In *SN Business and Economics* (Vol. 2, Issue 11). Springer Nature. https://doi.org/DOI: 10.1007/s43546-022-00349-5

Han, J., Zuo, J., Zillante, G., Chang, R., & Du, L. (2025a). A systematic review of PET circularity technologies and management strategies: Challenges and future directions. In *Resources, Conservation and Recycling* (Vol. 219). Elsevier B.V. https://doi.org/DOI: 10.1016/j.resconrec.2025.108280

Han, J., Zuo, J., Zillante, G., Chang, R., & Du, L. (2025b). A systematic review of PET circularity technologies and management strategies: Challenges and future directions. In *Resources, Conservation and Recycling* (Vol. 219). Elsevier B.V. https://doi.org/DOI: 10.1016/j.resconrec.2025.108280

Hausmann, A., Cortés-Capano, G., & Di Minin, E. (2023a). Exploring the effects of market scarcity on consumers' demand for rarity in the wildlife trade. In *Global Ecology and Conservation* (Vol. 48). Elsevier B.V., DOI: 10.1016/j.gecco.2023.e02744

Hausmann, A., Cortés-Capano, G., & Di Minin, E. (2023b). Exploring the effects of market scarcity on consumers' demand for rarity in the wildlife trade. In *Global Ecology and Conservation* (Vol. 48). Elsevier B.V., DOI: 10.1016/j.gecco.2023.e02744

Hummer, R. L. (n.d.). *Pets in Today's Society.*

Isosuo, H. (2016). *Social media influencer marketing.*

Jacobson, J., Hodson, J., & Mittelman, R. (2022). Pup-ularity contest: The advertising practices of popular animal influencers on instagram. *Technological Forecasting and Social Change, 174.* Advance online publication. DOI: 10.1016/j.techfore.2021.121226

Jones, S. M. (2015). Attachment Theory. In *The International Encyclopedia of Interpersonal Communication* (pp. 1–5). Wiley., DOI: 10.1002/9781118540190.wbeic161

Lavertu, L., Kulow, K., Cowan, K., & Marder, B. (2025). Petfluencers, the Fur-Mula for Sincere Endorsements: Examining How and When Pets Exhibit Greater Persuasion as Influencers. *Journal of Advertising Research*, , 1–16. DOI: 10.1080/00218499.2025.2463707

Lembregts, C., & Cadario, R. (2024). Consumer-driven climate mitigation: Exploring barriers and solutions in studying higher mitigation potential behaviors. *International Journal of Research in Marketing*, *41*(3), 513–528. DOI: 10.1016/j.ijresmar.2024.04.001

López-Teijeiro, A., Barreiro-Piñeiro, N., Eibes, G., & Martínez-Costas, J. (2025). Nearly complete depolymerization of untreated post-consumer plastic with an immobilized and reusable PET hydrolase. *Journal of Hazardous Materials*, *495*. Advance online publication. DOI: 10.1016/j.jhazmat.2025.138789 PMID: 40466280

Mcleod, S. (n.d.). *Maslow's Hierarchy of Needs*. https://doi.org/DOI: 10.5281/zenodo.15240897

Melkko, A. (n.d.). *CONSUMER BEHAVIOR AMONG DOG OWNERS How trends spread from the US to small businesses in Finland.*

Paulino, E., Gocuyo, N., Rington, D., Isip, L., Mazo, P. N., Romero, R., Tan, R., & Boquila, L.-R. (2025). Mapping the Fur Landscape: A Dual Cluster Analysis of Relationship-Driven and Purchase-Based Segmentation of the Pet Care Market. *Journal of Business and Management Studies*, *7*(3), 107–119. DOI: 10.32996/jbms.2025.7.3.10

SAMPLE. K. L., SEVILLA, J., & HAWS, K. L. (2025). Clear views, clear gains: Exterior transparency's role in increasing consumer entry for retail environments. *Journal of Retailing*. Advance online publication. DOI: 10.1016/j.jretai.2025.01.005

Sara Pimenta, A. C. M. F. B. S. (2025). *Neurosensory and Neuromarketing Impacts on Consumer Behavior*. IGI Global.

Sousa, B. (2025). *Neurosensory and Neuromarketing Impacts on Consumer Behavior*. IGI Global.

Wu, D., Liu, Y., & Yang, T. (2024a). Pet ownership: A sign of superior socioeconomic position? Evidences from six cities in China. *Preventive Veterinary Medicine*, *225*. Advance online publication. DOI: 10.1016/j.prevetmed.2024.106140 PMID: 38350165

Wu, D., Liu, Y., & Yang, T. (2024b). Pet ownership: A sign of superior socioeconomic position? Evidences from six cities in China. *Preventive Veterinary Medicine*, *225*. Advance online publication. DOI: 10.1016/j.prevetmed.2024.106140 PMID: 38350165

Yoo, S., Pu, K., & Truong, K. N. (2024, May 11). Behind the Pup-ularity Curtain: Understanding the Motivations, Challenges, and Work Performed in Creating and Managing Pet Influencer Accounts. *Conference on Human Factors in Computing Systems - Proceedings*. https://doi.org/DOI: 10.1145/3613904.3642367

Zhang, W., Cao, H., & Lin, L. (2022). *Analysis of the Future Development Trend of the Pet Industry*.

KEY TERMS AND DEFINITIONS

Attachment Theory: A psychological system which relates how people attach to each other emotionally and is usually applied so as to relate human beings and animals.

Behavioral Economics: The science of the processes that define how an individual makes a decision based on the psychological, emotional, and social backgrounds or conditions they face with regards to owning and caring about pets.

Consumer Culture Theory (CCT): This is a theoretical approach that helps to look at the cultural, social and emotional meaning of consumption behaviour such as consumption of pets.

Emotional Support Animals: These are pets that are used to give emotional support to individuals mostly with a mental condition and the pets have an impact on consumer behavior concerning pet ownership.

Ethical Consumption: It is a form of consumption where the consumers refer to sustainability, animals, and ethics when making decisions to buy products, notwithstanding pet-related products.

Generation Z (Gen Z): A group of people, who have a certain trend in consumption of pets, and this trend is usually predetermined by online media and social media.

Pet Parent: The name given to pet parents who consider their pets as members of their family and highly emotionally attached to their pet.

Pet Related Consumption: Pet related-consumption is a behavior of buying pet products and pet services based on emotional, social and psychological motivations.

Self-Concept Theory: It is the theory that implies that individuals purchase, even to pet-related products, to define and reinforce their self-concept and identity.

Symbolic Interactionism: A sociological theory which implies that individuals are perceived to make meaning based on their interaction with others, as well as how pets and products associated with pets are regarded in social provisions.

Chapter 12
Digital Marketing Trends in the Pet Industry

Arvinder Kour Mehta
https://orcid.org/0000-0002-7428-0346
Yeshwantrao Chavan College of Engineering, India

Shiney Chib
https://orcid.org/0000-0001-7648-9963
Datta Meghe Institute of Management Studies, India

Sujay Mugaloremutt Jayadeva
https://orcid.org/0000-0003-2252-9071
JSS Academy of Higher Education and Research, India

Amruta Mahalle
https://orcid.org/0009-0001-4246-4060
Datta Meghe Institution of Management Studies, India

Tanmay Waghmare
Datta Meghe Institute of Management Studies, India

P. Selvakumar
https://orcid.org/0000-0002-3650-4548
Department of Science and Humanities, Nehru Institute of Technology, Coimbatore, India

T. C. Manjunath
https://orcid.org/0000-0003-2545-9160
Rajarajeswari College of Engineering, India

ABSTRACT

As pet owners increasingly rely on the internet to seek information, shop for products, and engage with services, the digital shift in this sector has presented a wealth of opportunities for businesses to enhance their reach, improve customer experiences, TikTok, where pet brands and service providers now engage directly with millions of potential customers. These platforms not only allow companies to showcase their products and services but also enable them to create emotionally resonant connections with pet owners through storytelling, user-generated content, and interactive

DOI: 10.4018/979-8-3373-4342-6.ch012

campaigns. Influencer marketing has emerged as a key strategy within the pet industry, where influencers and pet personalities create authentic connections with their followers, endorsing products that resonate with their audiences. This form of marketing is particularly, and reach wider markets. As pet owners increasingly rely on the internet to seek information, shop for products, and engage with services, the digital shift in this sector has presented a wealth of opportunities for businesses.

INTRODUCTION

As pet owners increasingly rely on the internet to seek information, shop for products, and engage with services, the digital shift in this sector has presented a wealth of opportunities for businesses to enhance their reach, improve customer experiences, TikTok, where pet brands and service providers now engage directly with millions of potential customers. These platforms not only allow companies to showcase their products and services but also enable them to create emotionally resonant connections with pet owners through storytelling, user-generated content, and interactive campaigns. Influencer marketing has emerged as a key strategy within the pet industry, where influencers and pet personalities create authentic connections with their followers, endorsing products that resonate with their audiences. This form of marketing is particularly, and reach wider markets. As pet owners increasingly rely on the internet to seek information, shop for products, and engage with services, the digital shift in this sector has presented a wealth of opportunities for businesses to enhance their reach, improve customer experiences, and streamline their operations. (Aghaei et al., 2025)These With more consumers turning to online shopping for pet supplies, food, toys, and healthcare products, businesses have capitalized on digital marketing strategies such as search engine optimization (SEO), pay-per-click advertising (PPC), and targeted email campaigns to increase their visibility and drive sales. The convenience of online shopping, coupled with subscription services for recurring products like pet food, has further driven growth in the pet industry, making it more accessible for pet owners to access everything their pets need from the comfort of their homes.Data analytics has become an essential tool in digital marketing within the pet industry, enabling businesses to gain insights into customer behavior, preferences, and trends. Through the collection and analysis of data, companies can personalize their marketing strategies, offering tailored product recommendations, promotions, and services to specific customer segments. This data-driven approach has not only improved customer satisfaction but also enhanced customer retention, as businesses can continuously refine their strategies based on real-time insights.Mobile(Anderson, 2025) applications have also played a pivotal role in the digital shift in the pet industry. From pet health tracking apps to online vet consultations, businesses have embraced mobile solutions that allow pet owners to manage their pets' health and well-being more efficiently. With increased access to information and product options, pet owners now expect greater transparency, authenticity, and convenience from the brands they choose to support. (Athavale et al., 2025) The emphasis on sustainability, ethical sourcing, and eco-friendly practices in the pet industry has well-positioned for long-term success. The rapid expansion of digital platforms and technologies has not only opened up new avenues for reaching customers but also provided valuable tools for building stronger relationships with pet owners, creating more meaningful experiences, and fostering loyalty. In this rapidly evolving landscape, the key to thriving in the pet industry will lie in understanding and leveraging the power of digital marketing to meet the evolving needs of pet owners while remaining agile enough to adapt to the constant changes in technology and consumer behavior.

THE RISE OF PET HUMANIZATION: DIGITAL MARKETING IMPLICATIONS

Understanding pet owners' online behavior is crucial for businesses within the pet industry, as the digital landscape has dramatically reshaped how consumers interact with products, services, and brands. As more pet owners turn to the internet to meet their pet-related needs, businesses must recognize the nuances of these behaviors to develop effective digital marketing strategies. The habits of pet owners online reflect a blend of convenience, information-seeking, emotional connection, and social influence, which play a pivotal role in shaping purchasing decisions and brand loyalty. In this context, understanding these behaviors provides businesses with a competitive advantage in delivering more personalized and targeted experiences that resonate with their audiences.At the heart of pet owners' online behavior is a profound reliance on the internet for information. Pet owners today are highly informed consumers, often turning to search engines, review sites, and online forums to research products, services, and health-related issues before making any purchases. This trend reflects a shift from traditional methods of acquiring information, such as word-of-mouth or in-store consultations, to a more self-guided approach where users seek trusted, expert opinions and reviews from online sources. According to surveys, a significant portion of pet owners regularly consult online resources to learn about pet care, health tips, and product effectiveness. (Blue Dogs Media, 2025) This behavior underscores the importance of businesses creating educational and valuable content, whether it's in the form of blog posts, how-to guides, customer testimonials, or videos. Brands that can offer useful, credible, and easy-to-digest content are more likely to build trust with. Pet owners have become accustomed to the convenience of browsing, comparing prices, and making purchases with minimal effort, and they expect the same level of ease when engaging with pet brands. As a result, businesses in the pet industry must ensure that their websites and online stores are optimized for a smooth, seamless experience across various devices, especially mobile phones, where the majority of online shopping now takes place. Another significant aspect of pet owners' online behavior is their increasing reliance on social media platforms for inspiration, product discovery, and brand engagement.

Social media channels like Instagram, Facebook, Pinterest(Chakraborty, 2025), and TikTok have become key platforms for pet owners to connect with brands, discover new products, and share their experiences. Pet owners frequently follow pet influencers, participate in online communities, and engage in conversations around their pets, which allows businesses to tap into these spaces through organic content, paid advertisements, and influencer collaborations. emotions of pet owners, offering both entertainment and educational value, as well as promoting community-driven initiatives like pet adoption or charity events.Pet owners' online behaviors are also influenced by their desire for social proof, which means they place significant value on online reviews and testimonials. Pet product reviews are some of the most important factors in making purchase decisions. Pet owners trust the opinions of fellow consumers, especially those with similar pets or needs, and are more likely to purchase a product with positive feedback. This behavior aligns with the broader trend of consumer decision-making in the digital age, where peer recommendations and authentic user experiences hold more weight than traditional advertising. As such, businesses in the pet industry must actively manage their online reputation, encouraging customers to leave reviews, sharing user-generated content, and engaging in transparent dialogue with their audiences. (Chandel & Vats, 2025) Positive reviews and community engagement not only build trust but also drive higher conversion rates. Emotional connections also play a significant role in pet owners' online behavior. The bond between pets and their owners is often deeply emotional, and pet-related products and services are frequently marketed not just as functional, but as part of the emotional well-being of both the pet and the owner. Pet owners often share their pets' stories, milestones, and challenges on social media and in online forums, seeking advice, support, or just the joy of sharing their experiences with others. In turn, brands that can tap into these emotions by positioning their products as solutions that contribute to the happiness and well-being of pets are more likely to resonate with pet owners. Emotional advertising and storytelling are becoming increasingly popular in the pet industry, with brands using heartwarming narratives, showcasing real-life pet stories, and aligning themselves with causes that matter to pet owners, such as animal welfare and sustainability. The increasing importance of personalization in digital experiences is another defining characteristic of pet owners' unique needs, fostering a sense of trust and loyalty Additional, pet owners are increasingly adopting online subscription services, which have grown in popularity as a convenient way to ensure they never run out of essential pet products like food, litter, or medications.

Subscription services also cater to the convenience factor, allowing pet owners to have regular deliveries of products they use consistently, without the need to reorder or make frequent trips to the store. Businesses in the pet industry are capitalizing on this behavior by offering subscription options for a wide range of pet-related products, from grooming supplies to health and wellness items. Finally, privacy concerns and ethical considerations are also shaping pet owners' online behavior. (Dobuss Agency, 2025) As with other consumer sectors, pet owners are becoming more conscious of how their personal data is used and shared. Many pet owners are increasingly concerned about the transparency and ethical practices of the brands they support, particularly when it comes to data security, environmental impact, and the treatment of animals. Businesses in the pet industry must be transparent about their practices, offering clear privacy policies, and demonstrating a commitment to sustainable and ethical practices. Pet owners are increasingly drawn to brands that align with their personal values and ethics, including those that promote animal welfare, environmental sustainability, and cruelty-free practices.In conclusion, understanding the online behavior of pet owners is essential for businesses in the pet industry. Pet owners today are informed, emotionally connected, and value convenience and personalization. They rely heavily on online platforms for research, shopping, and community engagement, and they trust the experiences and recommendations of other pet owners. To succeed in this rapidly evolving market, pet businesses must leverage digital marketing strategies that cater to these habits and preferences, ensuring that their online presence is engaging, educational, convenient, and emotionally resonant

SOCIAL MEDIA MARKETING FOR PET BUSINESSES: BEST PRACTICES

This phenomenon, driven by evolving societal attitudes toward pets, has led to a profound shift in how businesses market their products and services to pet owners. As pets are increasingly seen as integral members of the family, the expectations placed on pet products and services have expanded, and the digital marketing strategies designed to target pet owners have had to adapt to these new realities. (Global Gurus, 2025)Traditional marketing in the pet industry often emphasized functionality and utility—products designed to meet the basic needs of pets, such as food, grooming products, and toys. However, with the rise of pet humanization, pet owners now view their pets as more than just animals; they are companions deserving of care, attention, and comfort similar to the way human family members are treated. As a result, pet brands have shifted their focus to positioning their products as not just functional but also as enhancing the quality of life for pets, supporting their emotional and physical well-being. This emotional connection between pet owners and their pets has led to the creation of luxury pet products, from gourmet pet foods to stylish clothing, bedding, and accessories, which are marketed as ways to pamper pets and ensure their happiness. For digital marketers, this means that the emotional tone of advertising and promotional materials has become more important than ever. Brands now often emphasize the bond between pets and owners, with marketing messages that highlight the love, care, and joy shared between humans and their pets.As pets are increasingly treated like family, content marketing strategies have evolved to reflect these emotional connections. Pet brands now create content that resonates with pet owners on a deeply personal level, tapping into the growing desire for connection, comfort, and shared experiences. For example, storytelling has become a key element of many pet brands' marketing campaigns, with ads that feature real-life stories about pets and their owners. These stories may highlight a pet's journey from adoption to becoming an integral part of a family or showcase the emotional challenges that pet owners face, such as dealing with a pet's illness or loss. (HuffPost España, 2025) Through storytelling, brands can evoke empathy, strengthen their emotional bond with customers, and create a sense of community human-like lives, often dressed in clothing, participating in activities, or even featured in humorous or heartwarming posts that reflect the personalities of their owners. Pet accounts with millions of followers—often referred to as "pet influencers"—have become powerful marketing tools in the digital space. (IGI Global Scientific Publishing, 2025) These pet influencers often feature products, services, or experiences in a way that feels organic and authentic, which resonates deeply with their audience of pet owners. The success of these pet influencer accounts has led many pet brands to collaborate with popular pets or pet-focused influencers as part of their digital marketing strategies. Influencer marketing in the pet industry, which focuses on using pet influencers or human influencers who resonate with pet owners, has proven to be a highly effective way of reaching a large and engaged audience, particularly on social media platforms.The rise of pet humanization has also driven the growth of niche markets within the pet industry, which digital marketers are keen to tap into.

As pets are viewed as family members, specialized services and products that cater to specific needs have gained popularity. For example, there has been a surge in demand for pet wellness products, including natural and organic pet foods, pet supplements, and even pet therapy services. Furthermore, there is an increasing interest in pet fashion, with many pet owners investing in designer pet clothing, accessories, and grooming products. Pet owners also seek out services that mirror human care, such as pet spas, pet massages, and even pet-friendly hotels and vacation spots. Digital marketing campaigns in these niche markets need to be highly targeted and personalized, emphasizing the luxury, quality, and human-like care that these products and services offer. Brands have to cater to the growing demand for premium, specialized, and often customized products and services that align with the pet humanization trend. (Just Food for Dogs, 2025) Data analytics plays an important role in understanding the shift toward pet humanization and tailoring digital marketing strategies accordingly. Through the collection of data from online shopping behaviors, social media interactions, and consumer feedback, businesses can gain valuable insights into the preferences, values, and needs of pet owners who treat their pets as family members. The ability to personalize content and offerings has become a significant aspect of digital marketing in the pet industry, allowing businesses to connect with their audience in a more meaningful and individualized way.he rise of pet humanization has also influenced how brands communicate with pet owners on a customer service level. (Koppaka, 2025) Pet owners who treat their pets like family members expect a higher level of customer care and service from the brands they choose to support. Businesses in the pet industry must be responsive, empathetic, and accommodating when interacting with pet owners, whether through social media, email, or live chat. Offering personalized recommendations, addressing concerns with compassion, and providing high-quality support for pet-related issues are crucial to maintaining customer loyalty. Pet owners often seek out brands This has led to the adoption of more empathetic and inclusive branding strategies that celebrate the bond between humans and animals. The tone of messaging has shifted from a more clinical or utilitarian approach to one that is warm, caring, and emotionally engaging. As a result, brands in the pet industry often focus on themes such as compassion, love, and community in their messaging, emphasizing that pets deserve the best, just like any human family member. Additionally, many pet brands now align with social causes related to animal welfare, sustainability, and environmental consciousness, which are values that resonate strongly with pet owners who view their pets as part of a larger ethical and social responsibility.Finally, the rise of pet humanization has reshaped the e-commerce experience in the pet industry. With pet owners willing to spend more on their pets' well-being and lifestyle, there has been an increasing demand for more premium, high-end pet products. Online pet retailers must cater to this demand by offering curated selections of premium items, luxury brands, and exclusive collections, all of which need to be showcased in a way that appeals to the emotions and desires of pet owners. (Laetro, 2025) This might include offering personalized shopping experiences, creating exclusive online communities for pet owners, or offering limited-edition products. In addition, subscription models, where pet owners can receive regular deliveries of premium products, have become increasingly popular, allowing businesses to cater to the convenience and ongoing needs of pet

INFLUENCER MARKETING IN THE PET INDUSTRY: TRENDS AND TIPS

This allows businesses to tailor their messaging and content to specific groups, creating more relevant and compelling posts that resonate with followers.For example, pet owners who are passionate about sustainability might respond well to posts that emphasize eco-friendly pet products or sustainable practices within the pet care industry. On the other hand, pet owners of specific breeds may appreciate content that addresses their pet's unique needs, such as tips on breed-specific nutrition or training advice. Understanding these nuances helps brands avoid generic posts and instead develop targeted campaigns that speak directly to their followers' interests and values.often the most engaging types of content on platforms like Instagram and TikTok, which are designed to showcase rich media. Posts that feature pets—whether they are adorable, funny, or heartwarming—tend to generate more engagement than standard product advertisements. (Mehta et al., 2025) Pet businesses should leverage the cuteness factor, as well as the emotional bond between owners and their pets, to create content that appeals to pet owners' love for their animals.Moreover, pet-related content that is shareable tends to perform better, as users enjoy sharing cute, relatable, or informative posts with their friends and family. Creating content that elicits emotional responses, such as funny pet videos, heartwarming stories, or tips that improve the lives of pets, can enhance a brand's visibility through organic reach. User-generated content, where followers share photos or videos of their pets using a brand's products, can also be highly effective in amplifying reach and fostering community involvement.in the pet community—offer businesses an authentic way to promote their products or services. (NielsenIQ, 2024a)Pet influencers often have highly engaged audiences that trust their recommendations, and their endorsements can create a significant impact on sales and brand awareness. When working with influencers, Micro-influencers are often seen as more relatable and approachable, which can drive deeper connections with their audience. (NielsenIQ, 2024b) Moreover, their content tends to feel more personal and authentic, which can be an advantage for brands looking to engage with consumers on a more human level.. This interaction shows that the business cares about its customers and values their input, which can help strengthen brand loyalty. A great way to encourage engagement is by creating interactive content that invites followers to participate. For example, businesses can encourage followers to share photos of their pets using a particular product, host contests or challenges (such as a "cutest pet" contest), or ask for feedback on new product ideas. When customers feel heard and involved, they are more likely to share their positive experiences with others and remain loyal to the brand. Additionally, establishing a sense of community is crucial in the pet industry, where owners often seek support, advice, or companionship. should As with any marketing strategy, measuring the effectiveness of social media campaigns is crucial for understanding what works and what doesn't. Social media platforms offer a wealth of data and analytics tools that allow businesses to track key metrics such as engagement rates, follower growth, website traffic, and conversion rates. By analysing these metrics, businesses can assess which types of content resonate most with their audience, determine the best times to post, and refine their strategies to improve results. Regularly reviewing analytics ensures that businesses can adjust their social media marketing efforts in real-time, optimizing campaigns for maximum impact.For example, if pet businesses notice that videos showcasing funny or heartwarming pet moments receive significantly more engagement than product-focused posts, they can adjust their content strategy accordingly. Similarly, if

CONTENT MARKETING FOR PET BUSINESSES: ENGAGING AND RELEVANT CONTENT

In many cases, these pets have become celebrities in their own right, attracting millions of followers on platforms like Instagram, TikTok, and YouTube. Pets like Jiff the Pomeranian, Nala the Cat, and Doug the Pug have amassed legions of fans, many of whom eagerly await their daily posts, videos, and adventures. These pets are often featured in a variety of content types, ranging from cute and humorous videos to informative content related to pet care, health, and lifestyle.Pet influencers play an important role in influencer marketing because their popularity and relatability drive engagement. Their audience often views them as genuine, authentic, and fun-loving, and as a result, the endorsement of products by these pets is seen as more personal and credible than traditional advertising. The emotional connection that pet owners have with these influencers makes them more likely to trust recommendations for pet products or services, particularly when these influencers align with their own values or interests.In addition to individual pets, pet-related content created by human influencers has also gained traction in the pet industry. (Omnichannel Retail, 2025) These influencers are typically pet owners who have garnered large followings due to their expertise, lifestyle content, or personality, and their influence extends to a wide range of pet care and pet-related products. They may be veterinarians, pet groomers, or animal lovers who share insights, advice, and personal experiences about their pets. The partnership between pet brands and these human influencers can 10,000 and 100,000 followers, while nano-influencers have fewer than 10,000. Despite their smaller audiences, these influencers often have higher engagement rates, with their followers tending to trust their recommendations more due to the perceived authenticity of their content. As a result, working with micro and nano-influencers can help pet brands reach niche segments of the pet-owning community and drive more meaningful interactions., or ethical pet care. Brands that work with influencers in these categories are able to target consumers who are passionate about these topics, which can lead to more successful campaigns. (PawPrint Digital, 2025) For example, a pet brand offering eco-friendly pet products might partner with an influencer who is dedicated to sustainability and ethical pet care, reaching an audience that is already aligned with the brand's values. They are drawn to influencers who show their pets in relatable, unscripted moments and who provide honest feedback about products and services.For brands, this trend means that influencer partnerships need to be based on transparency. Influencers who only promote products they truly believe in, or that they have personally used and benefited from, tend to build stronger, long-term relationships with their followers causes through influencer partnerships. Influencers in the pet space are often vocal advocates for adoption, rescue, and responsible pet ownership, and brands that partner with influencers who promote these causes are able to tap into this growing segment of socially conscious consumers. This trend is beneficial for both pet brands and the influencers themselves, as it allows them to build goodwill and trust within the pet-owning community. (Pet Business Guide, 2025) For example, a pet brand might collaborate with an influencer to raise awareness about the benefits of adopting pets from shelters, and in turn, the influencer's audience might be more likely to support the brand because of its commitment to animal welfare. These collaborations also often lead to viral campaigns that highlight charitable initiatives or support for rescue organizations.

THE ROLE OF AI IN PET INDUSTRY DIGITAL MARKETING

Content marketing in the pet industry is a crucial strategy for businesses seeking to connect with their target audience, build brand awareness, and foster customer loyalty. As the pet industry continues to grow and evolve, pet businesses must adopt effective content marketing strategies to stay competitive bond. In the digital age, content marketing has become an essential part of any pet business's strategy, as it helps companies establish trust, educate consumers, and build long-term relationships with their audience.it helps establish the brand as an authority in the pet space by providing valuable information that pet owners can trust. Whether it's advice on pet nutrition, tips on training, or information about the latest trends in pet care, creating content that addresses the pain points and interests of pet owners allows businesses to position themselves as experts. This trust-building aspect is particularly important in the pet industry, where consumers are highly invested in the well-being of their pets and are constantly seeking reliable sources of information. Furthermore, content marketing enables businesses to connect with pet owners on a deeper emotional level. Pet owners often view their animals as members of the family, and content that speaks to this emotional bond can help strengthen relationships with customers. (Pet Care Marketing Pros, 2025) Engaging content, such as heartwarming stories, inspiring pet care advice, or funny and relatable pet moments, not only encourages social sharing but also helps create a sense of community around the brand. When pet businesses create content that resonates emotionally with consumers, it fosters brand loyalty and increases the likelihood that customers will return for future purchases. Another key advantage of content marketing is its ability to improve search engine rankings through search engine optimization (SEO). is a key benefit of content marketing, as it allows businesses to attract new customers while building an enduring online presence. That addresses a variety of customer needs, while maintaining consistency and relevancy. (Pradeep et al., 2025) Below are several types of content that have proven effective in capturing the attention of pet owners:and health. Educational blog posts not only help inform and educate pet owners, but they also provide businesses with the opportunity to showcase their expertise and build trust with their audience. For example, a pet food company might publish blog posts that explain the benefits of a particular type of diet for pets, or a pet grooming business could write articles on how to properly care for a pet's coat. (Zoetis, 2025) To be effective, blog posts should be optimized for search engines, incorporating relevant keywords that pet owners are likely to search for. By providing in-depth, valuable content that answers common questions or solves common problems how-to guides provide actionable and valuable information that pet owners can use immediately. For example, a pet business that sells pet accessories could create a tutorial on how to properly fit a dog harness, while a pet health company could produce a guide on how to recognize common signs of illness in pets. These guides not only educate pet owners but also position the business as a trusted resource for practical pet care information., and they love sharing stories, pictures, and videos of their pets. By encouraging customers to share their experiences with a brand's products or services, pet businesses can generate authentic content that resonates with other pet owners. User-generated content can take many forms, including photos of pets using a product, videos of pets enjoying a particular activity, or personal stories shared by customers. Pet businesses can feature UGC on their website

PERSONALIZATION IN PET MARKETING: TAILORING MESSAGES AND OFFERS

AI applications are helping brands rise to this challenge by providing tools that allow for more efficient, scalable, and targeted marketing strategies. This analysis explores the various ways in which AI is being utilized in digital marketing within the pet industry, including customer segmentation, personalized content delivery, chatbots, predictive analytics, and even the development of AI-powered pet products and services. It also considers the implications of these technologies for consumer behavior and the future of digital marketing in the pet space. And target potential customers. Traditional segmentation strategies often rely on broad demographic factors like age, income, and location. However, AI goes beyond this by using more nuanced data points to segment customers based on their behaviors, preferences, and interactions with brands. This approach allows for highly personalized marketing strategies, which are especially important in the pet industry, where customer needs and interests can vary widely depending on pet types, breed preferences, pet care philosophies, and lifestyle factors.Machine learning algorithms can analyze vast amounts of data, including browsing habits, purchase histories, social media interactions, and even the time a consumer spends on certain pages of a website., such as past purchases, browsing history, and even feedback from customer reviews, AI can suggest products that are tailored to each customer's preferences. If a pet owner has purchased specific dog food in the past, AI can recommend similar products, complementary items such as treats or supplements, or offer discounts on the next purchase to increase customer retention. Similarly, in email marketing, AI can segment audiences based on their interactions with the brand and send targeted offers or content, such as articles on dog training tips or promotions for specific pet-related products. These personalized experiences increase engagement and drive sales by offering consumers what they are most likely to be interested in at a particular moment. Additionally, (Wearable Pet Health Monitors, 2025) AI can help pet businesses optimize pricing strategies by dynamically adjusting prices based on factors such as demand, customer behavior, and competitor pricing. This means businesses can offer personalized discounts or promotions to individual customers, further enhancing the customer experience and encouraging repeat purchases. With customers in a conversational manner, answering their questions, providing recommendations, and even processing orders. Chatbots are particularly useful in the pet industry, where customers often have a range of specific questions about pet products, services, or care. For example, a pet retailer might use a chatbot to answer questions about the ingredients in its pet food products or provide information on how to properly groom a specific breed of dog.Chatbots can be available 24/7, providing immediate assistance to customers regardless of time zones or office hours. This is particularly important in the pet industry, where pet owners may need quick answers to urgent questions, especially in cases related to pet health or safety. (User-Generated Content, 2025) AI-powered virtual assistants can also help customers navigate websites more efficiently, guiding Facebook or Instagram.The use of AI chatbots not only improves customer satisfaction but also allows businesses to handle a high volume of inquiries with fewer resources, reducing the need for human customer service representatives and lowering operational costs.

Pet Industry Marketing on Instagram: Visual Storytelling

Whether it's demonstrating a product in action, telling an inspiring story, or providing helpful tips, video content resonates strongly with pet owners who are passionate about their pets' health, happiness, and well-being. (Top Pet Industry Trends, 2025) This makes video marketing an indispensable tool for pet businesses looking to enhance their visibility, increase engagement, and drive sales. Facebook, and TikTok has made video content even more prevalent and accessible. These platforms have not only become spaces where consumers seek entertainment and information but also places where they discover new brands, products, and services. For pet businesses, creating engaging video content allows brands to tap into the immense traffic these platforms generate while leveraging the viral nature of videos to expand their reach. Lives of their pets. Whether it's a demonstration of a pet grooming product, a pet food brand showing how their ingredients are sourced and prepared, or a tutorial on proper pet care, video allows businesses to provide detailed, informative content that is often more effective than written descriptions alone. Video is also an excellent way to highlight the emotional connection pet owners have with their pets, which is central to many purchasing decisions in the pet industry. more. Video marketing allows pet businesses to tailor their content to specific niches, creating highly targeted videos that speak directly to the unique needs and interests of different customer segments. Additionally, video is an inclusive medium that appeals to different age groups and demographic profiles, making it a versatile tool for reaching a broad audience. It's also inherently shareable—audiences are more likely to share a video that resonates with them, whether it's a funny clip of a pet doing something adorable or an informative video on pet care.the most of video marketing, pet businesses must create diverse and compelling video content that aligns with their brand message, appeals to their target audience, and showcases the unique value of their products and services. Below are several types of video content that have proven to be effective in engaging pet owners:a product in action, allowing businesses to highlight its features, benefits, and ease of use. For example, a pet food company might create a video demonstrating how their food is prepared and explaining the nutritional benefits for pets. Similarly, a brand that sells pet grooming products could produce a video showing how easy it is to use their brushes or shampoos on different breeds of dogs or cats.Tutorials are also a popular type of video content that offers actionable advice content.

Figure 1. Pet Stores Can Leverage Digital Marketing to Grow Their Online Presence

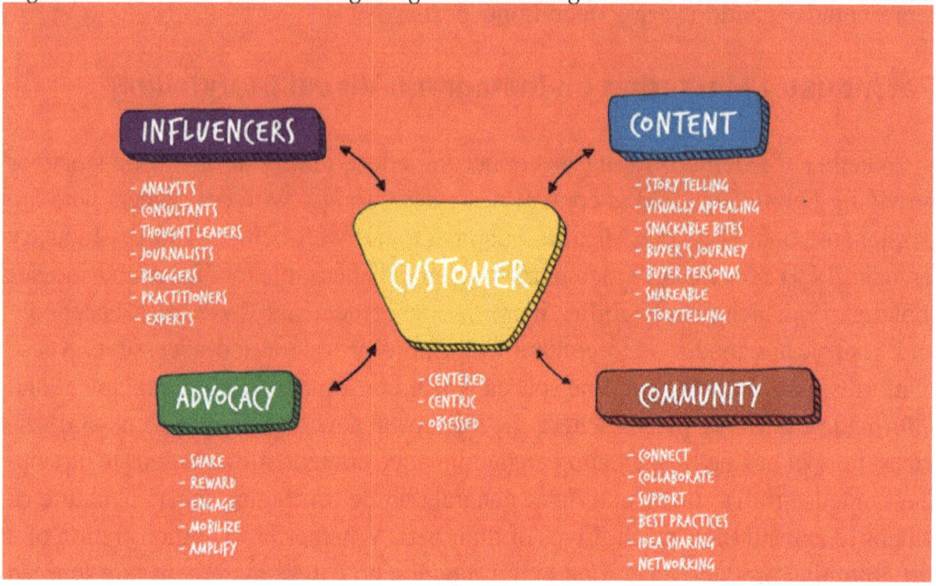

Pet businesses can encourage their customers to share videos of their pets using the brand's products, and these videos can then be repurposed in social media posts, advertisements, or even on the brand's website.Customer testimonials in video format are also incredibly powerful. (Subramanian et al., 2025)Pet owners are more likely to be influenced by the positive experiences of others, especially when they can see the impact that a product or service has had on a pet's well-being. For instance, a pet health brand could feature a video. For example, a pet food company might create a video that highlights its commitment to sustainability, featuring stories of how it works with local farmers to source ingredients and help animals in need. These types of videos allow consumers to align with the brand's values, deepening their connection and increasing brand loyalty.and can quickly go viral, helping brands reach a wider audience. For example, a pet toy company might create a playful video showcasing pets interacting with their toys in an amusing way. These types of videos appeal to the emotional side of pet ownership, tapping into the affection people have for their pets and creating positive associations with the brand.Emotional storytelling also works well in the pet industry. Videos that highlight the bond between pet owners and their pets, showcase heartwarming rescue stories, or demonstrate the transformative effects of a particular product on a pet's life can resonate deeply with audiences. These emotional appeals can create a lasting impression and inspire viewers to take action, whether that's purchasing a product, sharing the video, or simply expressing support for the brand.

Facebook Advertising for Pet Businesses: Targeting and Optimization

The key to successful Instagram marketing in the pet industry lies in visual storytelling. Visual storytelling is an art form that uses images, videos, and captions to convey a brand's message, values, and products in an engaging and emotionally resonant way. (Quality Pet Products, 2025) For pet businesses, this means showcasing the bond between pets and their owners, telling inspiring stories about animals, and using eye-catching visuals to promote products or services. Instagram's features—such as posts, stories, reels, and live streams—offer various ways for pet businesses to create dynamic content that appeals to their target audience. Through visual storytelling, pet brands can not only build awareness and trust but also foster deeper connections with their customers. This analysis delves into how pet businesses can effectively leverage Instagram's platform to craft visual narratives that engage, inspire, and ultimately drive sales.a significant amount of time, effort, and money into ensuring their pets' well-being, which makes them highly receptive to content that showcases the happiness, health, and joy of their pets. Instagram, being a predominantly image- and video-based platform, taps directly into this emotional connection by allowing pet businesses to share visual content that stirs positive emotions. Whether it's showcasing a cute puppy playing with a new toy or a cat enjoying a healthy meal, visual content has the power to capture attention and spark feelings of warmth and affection, which translate into stronger engagement and brand loyalty. visual understanding of the service's impact. Similarly, a pet food brand can post vibrant, colorful images of their products, accompanied by information on the nutritional benefits, to visually emphasize the quality and health advantages of their offerings. (Shende et al., 2025)The use of filters, interactive stickers, polls, and hashtags can further engage the audience while reinforcing the brand's identity. beyond just sharing individual posts. (Ranjitha et al., 2025)The use of Instagram Stories, which allows for more spontaneous and behind-the-scenes content, adds an extra layer of connection. Brands can showcase pet-friendly events, product launches, or customer testimonials in real-time, giving followers an insider look into the business's world. The ephemeral nature of Instagram Stories, which disappear after 24 hours, creates a sense of urgency and exclusivity, making followers more likely to engage with the content before it disappears. creativity in a quick, fun format. For pet businesses, Reels present an opportunity to capture attention with visually captivating, entertaining, and educational content that is easily shareable and highly engaging.The playful and fun nature of Instagram Reels aligns perfectly with the pet industry. Pet brands can create humorous or heartwarming videos featuring pets interacting with their products, demonstrating product features, or showing the bond between pets and their owners. Reels can also be used for trending challenges or collaborations with influencers, which can significantly boost the brand's visibility and reach on the platform. Pet businesses that create high-quality, entertaining Reels have the potential to go viral, reaching a wide audience and attracting new followers.For example, a pet toy company might create a Reel showing a pet trying out different toys, with each toy demonstrating its unique features in an amusing way. Alternatively, a pet grooming business could create a Reel that shows a dog getting a bath and trim, emphasizing the transformation with before-and-after shots. The fun and engaging nature of Reels, coupled with the platform's algorithm, makes this content format highly effective in driving engagement and increasing brand awareness. for engaging with followers on Instagram. UGC is content that comes directly from customers or followers, rather than the brand itself, and it plays a crucial role in building trust and authenticity. For pet businesses, UGC could include photos or videos of pets using the brand's products, such as a dog playing with a new toy or a cat enjoying a meal from a pet food brand.

MEASURING DIGITAL MARKETING SUCCESS IN THE PET INDUSTRY

Whether through newsletters, special promotions, or personalized offers, email marketing enables pet businesses to maintain consistent engagement with their customers, enhance brand loyalty, and create an environment for repeat business. With the vast number of pet owners seeking new products, services, and advice for their beloved animals, leveraging email marketing can prove to be a game-changer for businesses in the competitive pet industry.decisions, email marketing offers a unique opportunity to foster that connection. Emails can serve as a direct line to potential customers, allowing pet businesses to deliver tailored messages that resonate with specific segments of their audience. Whether it's a pet store promoting new pet toys, a grooming service offering seasonal discounts, or a pet food brand sending a reminder about an upcoming product launch, email marketing provides a way to communicate essential information while reinforcing a brand's value and building trust.One of the core benefits of email marketing is its ability to deliver content directly to a subscriber's inbox, offering businesses an opportunity to be in front of their customers when they are most engaged. With an open rate higher than many social media platforms, email allows for more control over messaging and timing, allowing businesses to design campaigns that align with customers' interests, preferences, and buying behaviors.Moreover, email marketing in the pet industry enables businesses to communicate with a highly targeted audience. of topics, including pet care tips, product recommendations, industry news, and special events. For example, a pet grooming business might send a monthly newsletter offering grooming tips, new services, and advice on maintaining a pet's coat during different seasons. A pet food brand could use a newsletter to share articles on the benefits of specific ingredients, nutrition tips, and customer success stories.Newsletters help businesses stay in constant contact with their customers, keeping the brand top-of-mind. Regularly delivered, well-designed newsletters also show that the business is engaged with its audience and committed to providing value, which in turn builds brand loyalty. Importantly, newsletters allow businesses to deliver content that adds value beyond the typical sales pitch, helping to establish trust and credibility. When customers feel that they are receiving helpful information, they are more likely to develop a lasting relationship with the brand.where new products, seasonal offers, and discounts are a constant part of the business cycle. Whether launching a new product line or offering a limited-time discount, promotional emails allow pet businesses to directly communicate these offers to their audience.

These emails should be designed to grab the attention of the reader with compelling visuals, concise messaging, and clear calls-to-action (CTAs).pet toys or accessories, or a pet grooming service may offer a discount on seasonal grooming packages. Additionally, promotional emails can be used to announce flash sales, bundle deals, or special events like pet adoption drives or charity events. By leveraging urgency and exclusivity, promotional emails can create a sense of excitement and encourage subscribers to take immediate action. behavior, purchase history, and preferences, pet businesses can create tailored offers that resonate with each individual. For example, a dog food company might send a special offer for dog treats to dog owners, while a pet accessory store might send promotions related to cat toys for their cat-owning customers. Personalizing the content not only increases the chances of engagement but also enhances the customer experience, showing them that the business understands their specific needs.step in building a strong relationship with new customers. It's an opportunity to thank them for joining the community and to offer a warm introduction to the brand's values, products, and services.a free guide on pet care could also be included as an incentive to encourage the recipient to make a first purchase or engage with the business. A personalized touch, such as using the recipient's first name or recommending specific products based on their interests, can make the welcome email feel more tailored and engaging.their lost sales and turning potential customers into loyal ones.can offer special promotions, new product updates, or personalized content to entice recipients to return to the business's website or make a purchase.For example, a pet business could send an email offering a limited-time discount on popular products to subscribers who haven't interacted with the brand in a while. Another approach might be to send a survey asking for feedback on why the customer hasn't made a purchase recently and offering a special incentive to encourage them to re-engage. Re-engagement emails serve as a reminder to customers of the value the brand provides, which can reignite their interest and re-establish a connection To ensure email marketing campaigns are effective, pet businesses should follow best practices that maximize engagement, improve deliverability, and drive conversions. Below are some essential tips for successful email marketing: personalization, and engaging content, businesses can create highly effective email campaigns that not only build connections with pet owners but also enhance their bottom line. With the right strategy, email marketing can be a powerful and rewarding channel for pet businesses of all sizes.

Return on Investment (ROI) Analysis for Pet Industry Digital Marketing

In the increasingly competitive and data-rich landscape of digital marketing, optimizing consumer behavior is influenced by emotional connections with pets, evolving trends, and an ever-expanding digital ecosystem. Businesses must continually refine their digital marketing strategies to ensure they are not only reaching the right audience but also engaging them effectively, patterns in customer behavior, and adjust strategies in real-time to achieve better results. The key to successful optimization lies in harnessing the vast amounts of data available, analyzing it effectively, and using it to inform decision-making at every stage of the customer journey.from social media networks to search engines, provide businesses with a wealth of information about their audiences, campaign performance, and customer interactions. This data is often collected in real-time, allowing businesses to analyze results quickly and adapt their campaigns as needed. The goal of data-driven optimization is not just to adjust tactics but to understand the underlying factors that contribute to success and failure.For pet businesses, this can mean tracking data points across multiple channels, such as website traffic, social media engagement, email open rates, conversion rates, and customer behavior on the website. By combining data from various sources, businesses can gain a comprehensive understanding of their customers and marketing efforts, allowing for more precise targeting and improved outcomes. The effectiveness of digital marketing campaigns depends largely on how well businesses can interpret and act on the data they collectin the pet industry. Each of these strategies helps businesses identify areas for improvement, boost engagement, and ensure that marketing two different product images in a Facebook ad campaign. Testing different headlines, images, CTAs, or product descriptions allows pet businesses to optimize not only creative elements but also the overall user experience. Beyond A/B testing, multivariate testing allows businesses to test multiple variables at once. For instance, instead of just testing two versions of an email subject line, multivariate testing allows for testing different combinations of subject lines, body copy, images, and CTAs. This approach can reveal more nuanced insights into how different elements of a campaign work together and provide more granular data for optimization.For pet businesses, segmentation is crucial for delivering personalized content and offers that resonate with each specific by name; it involves delivering the right message to the right person at the right time based on their specific needs and behaviorConversion rate optimization (CRO) is the process of improving the percentage of website visitors who complete a desired action, whether that action is making a purchase, signing up for a newsletter, or scheduling a service appointment. In the pet industry, where competition is fierce, even small increases in conversion rates can lead to significant improvements in revenue and customer acquisition.To optimize conversions, businesses need to analyze user behavior on their website and identify potential obstacles that might prevent users from completing a desired action. Heatmaps, session recordings, and click-tracking tools can help businesses understand how visitors are interacting with their website. For example, if a pet store's checkout process has a high abandonment rate, it could be due to a complex or lengthy form, lack of trust signals, or unanticipated shipping fees.

CONCLUSION

The adoption of these technologies and the ability to understand and anticipate the preferences and behaviors of pet owners will be critical for success. The future will also bring greater focus on creating stronger connections between brands and consumers through social responsibility, authenticity, and purpose-driven marketing.continued rise of artificial intelligence (AI) and automation technologies. AI has the potential to revolutionize how pet businesses communicate with customers, personalize content, and optimize marketing campaigns. Machine learning algorithms can analyze vast amounts of customer data, providing actionable insights into customer preferences, behaviors, and purchase patterns. This enables pet businesses to create highly personalized marketing messages, product recommendations, and promotions that resonate with individual customers.In particular, AI-driven tools are already being used to enhance customer experiences on websites and e-commerce platforms. Chatbots and virtual assistants, powered by natural language processing, allow businesses to engage with customers in real time, answering their questions, offering personalized recommendations, and assisting with product purchases. AI can also enhance social media marketing by identifying trends, automating content creation, and analyzing the effectiveness of campaigns. For example, a pet food company could use AI to analyze customer reviews and feedback to identify common issues or preferences, allowing them to refine their product offerings and marketing messages accordingly.Automation will also play a crucial role in streamlining and scaling digital marketing to worry about reordering. Pet businesses can leverage digital marketing strategies to promote these subscription models, using targeted ads, email campaigns, and social media engagement to reach potential subscribers. Subscription-based models also enable businesses to generate predictable revenue streams while increasing customer loyalty.products, and build brand awareness. However, as platforms become more saturated and competition increases, marketers will need to adapt and explore new ways to stand out. The future of social media marketing in the pet industry will focus on deeper engagement, authentic storytelling, and community-building, rather than just pushing products.Influencer marketing is another trend that will continue to evolve in the pet industry. While influencer partnerships with popular pet influencers and animal celebrities have been widely successful, the future of influencer marketing will be more focused on micro-influencers and niche communities. Pet businesses will increasingly collaborate with smaller influencers who have highly engaged, loyal followings within specific niches, such as eco-conscious pet owners, dog trainers, or owners of specific dog breeds. These micro-influencers often provide a higher level of trust and authenticity, which resonates more with their audience.websites, enabling customers to try out products virtually. For example, a pet store could develop an app that lets dog owners visualize how different dog collars would look on their pets. This type of interactive experience enhances the customer journey, reduces the uncertainty associated with online shopping, and boosts confidence in purchasing decisions.Furthermore, virtual reality (VR) could be leveraged to provide immersive experiences for pet owners. For example, a pet care brand could use VR to simulate the experience of visiting a pet spa or training facility, giving customers a feel for the service before booking an appointment. Similarly, pet insurance providers could offer VR-based simulations to educate pet owners about the importance of various types of coverage, making the decision-making process more engaging and informativeIn the future, the use of data-driven Personalized marketing has already proven effective in the pet industry, but as data collection and analytics tools become more sophisticated, businesses will be able to create even more precise and relevant experiences for their customers. Customers will increasingly expect businesses to understand their preferences and offer personalized solutions that enhance their pet ownership experience.embracing emerging trends and prioritizing personalization, transparency, and customer engagement, pet businesses can capitalize on these opportunities, drive customer loyalty, and create memorable experiences that resonate with today's tech.

REFERENCES

Aghaei, R., Kiaei, A. A., Boush, M., Vahidi, J., Zavvar, M., Barzegar, Z., & Rofoosheh, M. (2025). Harnessing the Potential of Large Language Models in Modern Marketing Management: Applications, Future Directions, and Strategic Recommendations. arXiv. https://arxiv.org/abs/2501.10685

Anderson, J. (2025). The Rise of Biotics—Pre, Post, and Pro: Enhancing Pet Health. Forbes. https://www.forbes.com/councils/forbescommunicationscouncil/2023/05/02/6-trends-driving-the-pet-industry-takeaways-from-global-pet-expo/

Athavale, V. A., Selvakumar, P., Poorani, S., Anand, T., & Rathore, D. S. (2025). Designing chatbots for educational leadership. In Musundire, A. (Ed.), *Chatbots in educational leadership and management* (pp. 181–204). IGI Global Scientific Publishing., DOI: 10.4018/979-8-3693-8734-4.ch008

Blue Dogs Media. (2025). Digital Marketing Trends to Watch in 2025. Blue Dogs Media. https://bluedogsmedia.com/digital-marketing-trends-to-watch-in-2025/

Chakraborty, S. (Ed.). (2025). *Ethical AI Solutions for Addressing Social Media Influence and Hate Speech*. IGI Global Scientific Publishing.

Chandel, P. S., & Vats, C. (2025). Empowering Social Media Users With Ethical AI. In Chakraborty, S. (Ed.), *Ethical AI Solutions for Addressing Social Media Influence and Hate Speech* (pp. 91–118). IGI Global Scientific Publishing., DOI: 10.4018/979-8-3693-9904-0.ch005

Content, U.-G. Leveraging Customer Engagement. (2025). Podium. https://www.podium.com/article/pet-care-marketing-trends/

Dobuss Agency. (2025). Las tendencias emergentes en el marketing digital para 2025. Huffington Post España. https://www.huffingtonpost.es/tecnologia/las-tendencias-emergentes-marketing-digital-2025-agencia-dobuss.html

Global Gurus. (2025). 8 Pet Industry Trends in the Future. Global Gurus. https://globalgurus.org/8-pet-industry-trends-in-the-future/

HuffPost España. (2025). Las tendencias emergentes en el marketing digital para 2025. Huffington Post España. https://www.huffingtonpost.es/tecnologia/las-tendencias-emergentes-marketing-digital-2025-agencia-dobuss.html

IGI Global Scientific Publishing. (2025). *Ethical AI Solutions for Addressing Social Media Influence and Hate Speech*. IGI Global Scientific Publishing.

Just Food for Dogs. (2025). Personalized Nutrition: Tailored Meal Plans for Pets. Just Food for Dogs. https://www.forbes.com/councils/forbescommunicationscouncil/2023/05/02/6-trends-driving-the-pet-industry-takeaways-from-global-pet-expo/

Koppaka, A. K. (2025). Empowering Social Media Users With Ethical AI. In Chakraborty, S. (Ed.), *Ethical AI Solutions for Addressing Social Media Influence and Hate Speech* (pp. 91–118). IGI Global Scientific Publishing., DOI: 10.4018/979-8-3693-9904-0.ch005

Laetro. (2025). Digital Marketing Trends 2025. Laetro. https://www.laetro.com/blog/digital-marketing-trends-2025

Mehta, A. K., Yashoda, L., Selvakumar, P., Mishra, B. R., Das, A., & C. T. C., M. (2025). Teaching methods: Techniques for disadvantaged learners. In S. Hai-Jew (Ed.), Mitigating learner disadvantages in teaching and learning (pp. 181–206). IGI Global Scientific Publishing. https://doi.org/DOI: 10.4018/979-8-3693-8623-1.ch007

Nielsen, I. Q. (2024). The Full View of The Pet Industry: A Comprehensive Analysis of Consumer and Product Trends. NielsenIQ. [https://nielseniq.com/global/en/insights/analysis/2024/the-full-view-of-the-pet-industry-a-comprehensive-analysis-of-consumer-and-product-trends/](https://nielseniq.com/global/en/insights/analysis/2024/the-full-view-of-the-pet

Nielsen, I. Q. (2024). Pet Care Growing Faster Than Other Departments. Pet Food Processing. https://www.petfoodprocessing.net/articles/18052-nielseniq-pet-care-growing-faster-than-other-departments

Nielsen, I. Q. (2024). Unveils Trending Consumer Searches. Pet Food Processing. https://www.petfoodprocessing.net/articles/15722-nielseniq-unveils-trending-consumer-searches

PawPrint Digital. (2025). 2025 Trends and Innovations Shaping the Future of Pet Care. PawPrint Digital. https://pawprint.digital/p/2025-trends-innovations

Pet Business Guide. (2025). Top 5 Marketing Trends Pet Businesses Can't Ignore in 2025. Pet Business Guide. https://petbusinessguide.com/top-5-marketing-trends-pet-businesses-cant-ignore-in-2025/

Pet Care Marketing Pros. (2025). 5 Explosive Digital Marketing Strategies for Pet Care Businesses in 2025. Pet Care Marketing Pros. https://petcaremarketingpros.com/5-explosive-digital-marketing-strategies-for-pet-care-businesses-in-2025/

Pradeep, E., Mukherjee, S. K., Selvakumar, P., Koppaka, A. K., Chandel, P. S., & Vats, C. (2025). Empowering social media users with ethical AI. In Chakraborty, S. (Ed.), *Ethical AI solutions for addressing social media influence and hate speech* (pp. 91–118). IGI Global Scientific Publishing., DOI: 10.4018/979-8-3693-9904-0.ch005

Quality Pet Products. (2025). Sustainable Practices in Pet Product Manufacturing. Quality Pet Products. https://www.qualitypetproducts.com/

Ranjitha, P. K., Selvakumar, P., Anute, N., Manjunath, T., Sureshkrishna, G., & Pougajendy, S. (2025). Transportation challenges in islands tourism. In Hassan, V. (Ed.), *Navigating mass tourism to island destinations: Preservation and cultural heritage challenges* (pp. 287–312). IGI Global Scientific Publishing., DOI: 10.4018/979-8-3693-9107-5.ch011

Retail, O. Meeting Customers Where They Shop. (2025). MultiDev. https://multidev.com/blog/pet-industry-trends/

Shende, A. D., Tekade, S. A., Deshmukh, A. A., Tembhurkar, S. P., & Selvakumar, P. (2025). Water quality monitoring and control with AI. In Ruiz-Vanoye, J., & Díaz-Parra, O. (Eds.), *Smart water technology for sustainable management in modern cities* (pp. 51–80). IGI Global Scientific Publishing., DOI: 10.4018/979-8-3693-8074-1.ch003

Subramanian, M., Portia, R., Mishra, B. R., & Selvakumar, P. P. V., R., & T. C., M. (2025). Assessment and evaluation in personalized STEAM education. In N. Son (Ed.), Integrating personalized learning methods into STEAM education (pp. 103–122). IGI Global Scientific Publishing. https://doi.org/DOI: 10.4018/979-8-3693-7718-5.ch005

Top Pet Industry Trends. Omnichannel, Sustainability & Technology. (2025). MultiDev. https://multidev.com/blog/pet-industry-trends/

wearable Pet Health Monitors: Advancements in Pet Care. (2025). Grand View Research. https://www.grandviewresearch.com/

Zoetis. (2025). Advancements in Veterinary Pharmaceuticals. Zoetis. https://www.zoetis.com

Compilation of References

Aaker, D. A. (1996). Measuring Brand Equity across Products and Markets. *California Management Review*, *38*, 102–120. DOI: 10.2307/41165845

Aaker, D. A. (2012). *Building strong brands*. Simon and schuster.

Abdukayumov, A., Maturazov, I. S., & Yaronova, N. V. (2023). Improvement of the Aircraft Aviation Equipment Diagnostic System after Flight. In S. S. & S. P. Saint Petersburg Electrotechnical University LETI Prof. Popov Str. 5 (Eds.), *Proceedings of the Seminar on Information Systems Theory and Practice, ISTP 2023* (pp. 9 – 13). Institute of Electrical and Electronics Engineers Inc. https://doi.org/DOI: 10.1109/ISTP60767.2023.10427496

Abdulluh, M. N. A., & Saud, Z. Y. (2025). Branding and its Relationship with Ethical Marketing: An Empirical Study on Iraqi Delivery Companies. *International Journal of Research and Innovation in Social Science*, *IX*(IV), 5354–5363. DOI: 10.47772/IJRISS.2025.90400384

Abeer, H., & Malkawi. (2025). The use of conceptual metaphors in advertising: A cognitive approach to persuasive language. *Journal of Humanities and Political Science*, *5*(2). Advance online publication. DOI: 10.63332/joph.v5i2.469

Abidin, C. (2016). "Aren't These Just Young, Rich Women Doing Vain Things Online?": Influencer Selfies as Subversive Frivolity. *Social Media + Society*, *2*(2), 2056305116641342. DOI: 10.1177/2056305116641342

Abidin, C. (2021). Mapping Internet Celebrity on TikTok: Exploring Attention Economies and Visibility Labours. *Cultura e Scuola*, *12*(1), 77–103. DOI: 10.5334/csci.140

Adamkiewicz, J., Kochańska, E., Adamkiewicz, I., & Łukasik, R. M. (2022). Greenwashing and sustainable fashion industry. *Current Opinion in Green and Sustainable Chemistry*, *38*. Advance online publication. DOI: 10.1016/J.COGSC.2022.100710

Afzal, B., Xiao, W., Nazir, A., Junaid, D., & Silva, L. J. O. (2024). Analyzing the Impact of Social Media Influencers on Consumer Shopping Behavior: Empirical Evidence from Pakistan. *Sustainability*, *16*(14), 6079. DOI: 10.3390/su16146079

Agarwal, P., Tikkha, V., & Rajwanshi, R. (2025). A Study to Explore the Effect of Brand Label Vs. Information Label in the Food and Beverage Industry Towards Greenwashing Practices. *International Journal of Agriculture and Environmental Research*, *11*(1), 1–15. DOI: 10.51193/IJAER.2025.11101

Aggarwal, P., & McGill, A. L. (2007). Is That Car Smiling at Me? Schema Congruity as a Basis for Evaluating Anthropomorphized Products. *The Journal of Consumer Research*, *34*(4), 468–479. DOI: 10.1086/518544

Aggerholm, H. K., & Thomsen, C. (2024). Strategic communication in contexts of high sustainability pressure: Balancing purposefulness, transparency and participation in pursuit of organizational legitimacy. *Journal of Communication Management (London)*, *28*(1), 58–73. DOI: 10.1108/JCOM-12-2022-0131

Aghaei, R., Kiaei, A. A., Boush, M., Vahidi, J., Zavvar, M., Barzegar, Z., & Rofoosheh, M. (2025). Harnessing the Potential of Large Language Models in Modern Marketing Management: Applications, Future Directions, and Strategic Recommendations. arXiv. https://arxiv.org/abs/2501.10685

Ahlström, H., Williams, A., Wassénius, E., & Downing, A. S. (2025). Deepening the Conversation on Systemic Sustainability Risks: A Social-Ecological Systems Approach. *Journal of Business Ethics*, *199*(3), 495–506. DOI: 10.1007/S10551-024-05860-3/FIGURES/1

Ajoykumar, K. N., Singh, G., & Shackira, A. M. (2022). Corporate Social Accountability in Waste Production and Management. *Utilization of Waste Biomass in Energy, Environment and Catalysis*, 305–334. https://doi.org/DOI: 10.1201/9781003196358-15

Ajzen, I. (1991). The theory of planned behavior. *Organizational Behavior and Human Decision Processes*, *50*(2), 179–211. DOI: 10.1016/0749-5978(91)90020-T

Aksak, E. O., Ferguson, M. A., & Duman, S. A. (2016). Corporate social responsibility and CSR fit as predictors of corporate reputation: A global perspective. *Public Relations Review*, *42*(1), 79–81. DOI: 10.1016/j.pubrev.2015.11.004

Alassani, R., & Göretz, J. (2019). "Product placements by micro and macro influencers on Instagram" in *International conference on human-computer interaction* (Cham: Springer), 251–267

Albert, J.-F., Gómez-Fernández, N., & Boto-García, D. (2025). Up in the air: How do carbon policy shocks affect air travel? *Transport Policy, 168*, 54–68. DOI: 10.1016/j.tranpol.2025.04.003

Allal-Chérif, O., Puertas, R., & Carracedo, P. (2023). Intelligent influencer marketing: How AI-powered virtual influencers outperform human influencers. *Technological Forecasting and Social Change, 200*, 123113. DOI: 10.1016/j.techfore.2023.123113

Allenbacher, J., & Berg, N. (2023). How assessment and cooperation practices influence suppliers' adoption of sustainable supply chain practices: An inter-organizational learning perspective. *Journal of Cleaner Production, 403*, 136852. DOI: 10.1016/J.JCLEPRO.2023.136852

Almestarihi, R. (2024). Eco friendly branding and digital marketing strategies in Jordanian assessment. *Journal of Infrastructure. Policy and Development, 8*(7). Advance online publication. DOI: 10.24294/JIPD.V8I7.4843

Altinay, L., & Paraskevas, A. (2008). *Planning Research in Hospitality and Tourism* (1st ed.). Elsevier, Ltd.

Alves, H. M., Sousa, B., Carvalho, A., Santos, V., Dias, Á. L., & Valeri, M. (2022). Encouraging brand attachment on consumer behaviour: Pet-friendly tourism segment. *Journal of Tourism. Heritage and Services Marketing, 8*(2), 16–24. DOI: 10.5281/ZENODO.7357978

Alves, M. C. A. (2019). *Relação de Trabalho Responsável: Responsabilidade social empresarial e a afirmação dos direitos fundamentais no trabalho*. Editora JH Mizuno.

Aman, H. M. (2024). Cultural identities in Marketing and Branding: Appreciation vs. Appropriation. *Proceedings of the 8th International Visual Methods Conference*, 170–177. https://doi.org/DOI: 10.21467/PROCEEDINGS.168.19

Amazon Prime Video. (2021, 25 de novembro). Prime Video celebrates an unlikely friendship in its first ever Christmas advert for Europe [Press release]. https://press.aboutamazon.com/uk/2021/11/prime-video-celebrates-an-unlikely-friendship-in-its-first-ever-christmas-advert-for-europe

Ambientales, N. (2025). *Revolução na apicultura sustentável: criam mel em pó para valorizar o produto e reduzir desperdícios*. https://noticiasambientales.com/inovacion-pt/revolucao-na-apicultura-sustentavel-criam-mel-em-po-para-valorizar-o-produto-e-reduzir-desperdicios/

Amer, F., Khalifa, H. E. S., Elahmady, M., ElBadawy, N. E., Zahran, W. A., Abdelnasser, M., Rodríguez-Morales, A. J., Wegdan, A. A., & Tash, R. M. E. (2023). Mpox: Risks and approaches to prevention. *Journal of Infection and Public Health, 16*(6), 901–910. DOI: 10.1016/j.jiph.2023.04.001 PMID: 37062165

Amoako, G. K., Bawuah, J., Asafo-Adjei, E., & Ayimbire, C. (2023). Internal audit functions and sustainability audits: Insights from manufacturing firms. *Cogent Business & Management, 10*(1). Advance online publication. DOI: 10.1080/23311975.2023.2192313

Ampuero-Canellas, O., González-Del-Río, J., & Tarazona-Belenguer, N. (2023). Communicating Sustainability through Packaging Graphic Design: Associated Sociodemographic Factors. *Design Principles & Practices, 17*(1), 1–21. DOI: 10.18848/1833-1874/CGP/V17I01/1-21

Anantharaman, M. (2022). Is it sustainable consumption or performative environmentalism? *Consumption and Society, 1*(1), 120–143. DOI: 10.1332/LTTT8626

Anderson, J. (2025). The Rise of Biotics—Pre, Post, and Pro: Enhancing Pet Health. Forbes. https://www.forbes.com/councils/forbescommunicationscouncil/2023/05/02/6-trends-driving-the-pet-industry-takeaways-from-global-pet-expo/

Andika, A. D. P., Lestari, E. I. P., & Wiliam, A. (2024). Analyzing the Role of Influencers in Digital Marketing Strategy: A Case Study in the Online Fashion Industry. *Ilomata International Journal of Social Science, 5*(2), 444. DOI: 10.61194/ijss.v5i2.1166

Anisimova, T., & Vrontis, D. (2024). The food you can trust: The moderating role of age in the relationship between consumer values and organic food trust. *Journal of Business Research, 182*. Advance online publication. DOI: 10.1016/J.JBUSRES.2024.114803

Antoniou, A. (2024). When likes go rogue: Advertising standards and the malpractice of unruly social media influencers. *Journal of Medicine and Law, 16*(1), 74. DOI: 10.1080/17577632.2024.2361517

Ao, L., Bansal, R., Pruthi, N., & Khaskheli, M. B. (2023). Impact of Social Media Influencers on Customer Engagement and Purchase Intention: A Meta-Analysis. *Sustainability, 15*(3), 2744. DOI: 10.3390/su15032744

Arantes, L., & Sousa, B. (2021). Digital Marketing and Tourism. *Case Study Applied to Barcelos.*, (June), 23–26.

Arayess, S., & De Boer, A. (2022). How to Navigate the Tricky Landscape of Sustainability Claims in the Food Sector. *European Journal of Risk Regulation*, *13*(4), 643–664. DOI: 10.1017/ERR.2022.6

Arman, S. M., & Mark-Herbert, C. (2024). Ethical Consumption: A Review and Research Agenda. *International Journal of Consumer Studies*, *48*(5). Advance online publication. DOI: 10.1111/IJCS.13079

Arnould, E. J., & Thompson, C. J. (2005). Consumer Culture Theory (CCT): Twenty years of research. *The Journal of Consumer Research*, *31*(4), 868–882. DOI: 10.1086/426626

Ashtiani, J. (2012). Social Media Marketing for an Artist: Using Engagement to Build a Loyal Fan Base.https://www.theseus.fi/bitstream/handle/10024/55945/Thesis?sequence=1

Athavale, V. A., Selvakumar, P., Poorani, S., Anand, T., & Rathore, D. S. (2025). Designing chatbots for educational leadership. In Musundire, A. (Ed.), *Chatbots in educational leadership and management* (pp. 181–204). IGI Global Scientific Publishing., DOI: 10.4018/979-8-3693-8734-4.ch008

Audrezet, A., de Kerviler, G., & Guidry Moulard, J. (2020). Authenticity under threat: When social media influencers need to go beyond self-presentation. *Journal of Business Research*, *117*, 557–569. DOI: 10.1016/j.jbusres.2018.07.008

Autio, J., Kuismin, A., Autio, M., Syrjälä, H., & Kylkilahti, E. (2014). *Consumer value journey with pet in multiple service touchpoints.*

Aw, E. C., & Agnihotri, R. (2023). Influencer marketing research: Review and future research agenda. *Journal of Marketing Theory and Practice*, *32*(4), 435. DOI: 10.1080/10696679.2023.2235883

Ayob, N. A., Kamaruddin, N. A., & Zaidi, M. Z. H. M. (2023). Social Influencer Factors that Affect Young Adult Buying Behaviour. *International Journal of Academic Research in Business & Social Sciences*, *13*(1). Advance online publication. DOI: 10.6007/ijarbss/v13-i1/14610

Azazz, A. M. S., Elshaer, I. A., Al Thani, A., Algezawy, M., Mahrous, A. A., Mansour, M. A., Abdel Moneim, A., & Fayyad, S. (2024). The Influence of Green Demarketing on Brand Credibility, Green Authenticity, and Greenwashing in the Food Industry. *Sustainability*, *16*(21), 1–17. DOI: 10.3390/SU16219215

Azzari, V., & Pelissari, A. S. (2020). Does brand awareness influence purchase intention? The mediation role of brand equity dimensions. *Brazilian Business Review*, *17*(6), 669–685. DOI: 10.15728/bbr.2020.17.6.4

Babadoğan, B. (2024). Exploring the Role of AI in Automating Content Marketing: Unlocking Opportunities and Navigating Challenges. *Next Frontier.*, *8*(1), 67. DOI: 10.62802/gkj6f352

Bailey, R., Hillman, C., Arent, S., & Petitpas, A. (2013). Physical activity: An underestimated investment in human capital? *Journal of Physical Activity & Health*, *10*(3), 289–308. PMID: 23620387

Bailey, R., Wise, K., & Bolls, P. (2009). How avatar customizability affects children's arousal and subjective presence during junk food-sponsored online video games. *Cyberpsychology & Behavior*, *12*, 277–283. DOI: 10.1089/cpb.2008.0292 PMID: 19445632

Bakir, N., El Nemar, S., Gehchan, F. B., Samrouth, K., & Vrontis, D. (2025). Optimizing airline services: Leveraging data-driven strategies for enhanced customer satisfaction and engagement. *Journal of Asia Business Studies*, *19*(2), 487–510. DOI: 10.1108/JABS-09-2024-0559

Bandura, A. (2002). Social cognitive theory in cultural context. *Applied Psychology*, *51*, 269–290. DOI: 10.1111/1464-0597.0009

Bao, T., Chang, T.-L. S., Kim, A. J., & Moon, S. H. (2019). The characteristics and business impact of children's electronic word of mouth in marketing communications. *International Journal of Advertising*, *38*, 731–759. DOI: 10.1080/02650487.2018.1559558

Barbosa, D.. (2017). As abelhas e seu serviço ecossistêmico de polinização. *Revista Eletrônica Científica da UERGS*, *3*(4), 694–703.

Bardin, L. (1977). *Análise de Conteúdo*. Presses Universitaires de France.

Barreda, A. A., Bilgihan, A., Nusair, K., & Okumus, F. (2015). Generating brand awareness in online social networks. *Computers in Human Behavior*, *50*, 600–609. DOI: 10.1016/j.chb.2015.03.023

Batra, R., & Ahtola, O. T. (1991). Measuring the hedonic and utilitarian sources of consumer attitudes. *Marketing Letters*, *2*, 159–170. DOI: 10.1007/BF00436035

Batra, R., Ahuvia, A., & Bagozzi, R. P. (2012). Brand Love. *Journal of Marketing*, *76*(2), 1–16. DOI: 10.1509/jm.09.0339

Bauer, A., & Woodward, L. (2007). People and Their Pets: A Relational Perspective on Interpersonal Complementarity and Attachment in Companion Animal Owners. *Society & Animals*, *15*(2), 169–189. https://doi.org/https://doi.org/10.1163/156853007X187117

BBC. (2019). *Grumpy Cat internet legend dies*. BBC NEWS. https://www.bbc.com/news/world-us-canada-48308638

Beetz, A., Uvnäs-Moberg, K., Julius, H., & Kotrschal, K. (2012). Psychosocial and psychophysiological effects of human-animal interactions: The possible role of oxytocin. *Frontiers in Psychology, 3*, 234. PMID: 22866043

Belk, R. W., Ger, G., & Askegaard, S. (2005). The Fire of Desire: A Multisited Inquiry into Consumer Passion. SSRN *Electronic Journal*. https://doi.org/DOI: 10.2139/ssrn.354640

Belk, R. W. (1988). Possessions and the Extended Self. *The Journal of Consumer Research, 15*(2), 139–168. DOI: 10.1086/209154

Belk, R. W., & Pollay, R. W. (1985). Images of Ourselves: The Good Life in Twentieth Century Advertising. *The Journal of Consumer Research, 11*(4), 887. DOI: 10.1086/209024

Belk, R. W., Sherry, J. F.Jr, & Wallendorf, M. (1988). A Naturalistic Inquiry into Buyer and Seller Behavior at a Swap Meet. *The Journal of Consumer Research, 14*(4), 449. DOI: 10.1086/209128

Ben Lahouel, B., & Taleb, L. (2025). Beyond the linear link: Threshold effects of CSR on financial performance. *International Review of Economics & Finance, 100*, 104086. Advance online publication. DOI: 10.1016/j.iref.2025.104086

Bennetts, S. K., Crawford, S. B., Howell, T. J., Burgemeister, F., Chamberlain, C., Burke, K., & Nicholson, J. M. (2022). Parent and child mental health during COVID-19 in Australia: The role of pet attachment. *PLoS ONE, 17*(7 July). https://doi.org/DOI: 10.1371/journal.pone.0271687

Beringer, J. da S., Maciel, F. L., & Tramontina, F. F. (2019). O declínio populacional das abelhas: Causas, potenciais soluções e perspectivas futuras. *Revista Brasileira de Ensino de Ciência e Tecnologia, 12*(1), pp. 17–26. Disponível em: https://revista.uergs.edu.br/index.php/revuergs/article/view/1686/411. Acesso em: 04/05/2025.

Berry, L. L. (1983). Relationship Marketing. In Berry, L. L., Shostack, G. L., & Upala, G. D. (Eds.), *Emerging Perspectives on Services Marketing* (pp. 25–80). American Marketing Association.

Beverland, M. (2006). The 'real thing': Branding authenticity in the luxury wine trade. *Journal of Business Research, 59*(2), 251–258. https://doi.org/https://doi.org/10.1016/j.jbusres.2005.04.007

Bishop, K. J., & Carlson, K. M. (2022). The role of third-party audits in ensuring producer compliance with the Roundtable on Sustainable Palm Oil (RSPO) certification system. *Environmental Research Letters*, *17*(9). Advance online publication. DOI: 10.1088/1748-9326/AC8B96

Bishop, S. (2020). Algorithmic Experts: Selling Algorithmic Lore on YouTube. *Social Media + Society*, *6*(1), 2056305119897323. DOI: 10.1177/2056305119897323

Blue Dogs Media. (2025). Digital Marketing Trends to Watch in 2025. Blue Dogs Media. https://bluedogsmedia.com/digital-marketing-trends-to-watch-in-2025/

Bodie, M. T. (2022). Labor Relations at the Woke Corporation. SSRN *Electronic Journal*, 1–30. https://doi.org/DOI: 10.2139/SSRN.4298588

Bonamigo, A., Makhija, H., Theocharis, D., & Tsekouropoulos, G. (2025). Sustainable Consumption and Branding for Gen Z: How Brand Dimensions Influence Consumer Behavior and Adoption of Newly Launched Technological Products. *Sustainability*, *17*(9), 1–40. DOI: 10.3390/SU17094124

Borkfelt, S., Kondrup, S., Röcklinsberg, H., Bjørkdahl, K., & Gjerris, M. (2015). Closer to Nature? A Critical Discussion of the Marketing of "Ethical" Animal Products. *Journal of Agricultural & Environmental Ethics*, *28*, 1053–1073. DOI: 10.1007/S10806-015-9577-4

Borsa, Z., & Walls, J. L. (2022). Sustainability Branding: Challenges with Building and Maintaining Stakeholder Trust. Https://Doi.Org/10.5465/AMBPP.2022.16111abstract, *2022*(1). https://doi.org/DOI: 10.5465/AMBPP.2022.16111ABSTRACT

Bowler, H. (2022, June 14). World's best ads ever: 'Monty the Penguin' becomes John Lewis's most iconic. The Drum. https://www.thedrum.com/news/2022/06/14/world-s-best-ads-ever-43-monty-the-penguin-becomes-john-lewis-s-most-iconic

Brambilla, M., Badrizadeh, H., Mohammadi, N. M., & Sabet, A. J. (2022). Analyzing Brand Awareness Strategies on Social Media in the Luxury Market: The Case of Italian Fashion on Instagram. *Digital*, *3*(1), 1. DOI: 10.3390/digital3010001

Brandão, A. (2025). *Mudança climática coloca abelhas em risco e ameaça segurança alimentar global*. Embrapa. Disponível em: https://www.embrapa.br/busca-de-noticias/-/noticia/101094052/mudanca-climatica-coloca-abelhas-em-risco-e-ameaca-seguranca-alimentar-global

Brandão, F., & Costa, C. (2014). Inovação em Turismo: Uma Abordagem Sistémica e Territorial. In Z. Costa, Carlos; Brandão, Filipa; Costa, Rui; e Breda (Ed.), *Produtos e Competitividade do Turismo na Lusofonia* (pp. 69–91). Escolar Editora.

Braun, V., & Clarke, V. (2006). Using thematic analysis in psychology. *Qualitative Research in Psychology, 3*(2), 77–101. DOI: 10.1191/1478088706qp063oa

Brown, Stephen, Kozinets, R. V, & SherryJr., John F. (2003). Teaching Old Brands New Tricks: Retro Branding and the Revival of Brand Meaning. *Journal of Marketing, 67*(3), 19–33. DOI: 10.1509/jmkg.67.3.19.18657

Buenavista, D. P., Dinopol, N. M. A., Mollee, E., & McDonald, M. (2021). From poison to food: On the molecular identity and indigenous peoples' utilisation of poisonous "Lab-o" (Wild Yam, Dioscoreaceae) in Bukidnon, Philippines. *Cogent Food & Agriculture, 7*(1). Advance online publication. DOI: 10.1080/23311932.2020.1870306

Bühler, A., & Nufer, G. (2015). Relationship marketing in sports: Building and establishing longstanding relations in the business of sports. In *Routledge handbook of sports marketing* (pp. 207–221). Routledge.

Burton, L., & Collins, F. L. (2014). Mediated animal geographies: Symbolism, manipulation and the imaginary in advertising. *Social & Cultural Geography, 16*(3), 276–298. DOI: 10.1080/14649365.2014.979863

Caetano, T. S. G., Franco, J. R., Oliveira, V. C., Agostinho, I. M., Almeida, I. A., & Dal Pai, E. (2024). A importância das abelhas sem ferrão na polinização das culturas agrícolas no Brasil. [Curitiba, Brasil.]. *Revista DELOS, 17*(61), 1–14.

Cai, T. (2025). Analysis of digital marketing strategies in the pet food industry: A comparative study of different brands. Advances in Economics [AEMPS]. *Management and Political Sciences, 151*. Advance online publication. DOI: 10.54254/2754-1169/2024.19411

Campbell, C., & Farrell, J. R. (2020). More than meets the eye: The functional components underlying influencer marketing. *Business Horizons, 63*(4), 469–479. DOI: 10.1016/j.bushor.2020.03.003

Campbell, C., & Grimm, P. E. (2018). The Challenges Native Advertising Poses: Exploring Potential Federal Trade Commission Responses and Identifying Research Needs. *Journal of Public Policy & Marketing, 38*(1), 110–123. DOI: 10.1177/0743915618818576

Campos, M. (2021). *Turismo das abelhas se espalha por destinos e hotéis e defende preservação*. UOL. https://www.uol.com.br/nossa/noticias/redacao/2021/06/04/turismo-das-abelhas-se-espalha-por-destinos-e-hoteis-e-defende-preservacao.htm. Acesso em: 16 de agosto de 2025.

Carvalho, D. M. C., Amorim, L. B., Souza, D. C., & Costa, C. P. M. (2019). Apicultura em São Raimundo Nonato, Piauí. *Revista Verde de Agroecologia e Desenvolvimento Sustentável, 14*(1), 85–91.

Carvalho, R. M. A., Martins, C. F., & Mourão, J. S. (2014). Meliponiculture in Quilombola communities of Ipiranga and Gurugi, Paraíba state, Brazil: An ethnoecological approach. *Journal of Ethnobiology and Ethnomedicine, 10*(1), •••. PMID: 24410767

Casaló, L. V., Flavián, C., & Ibáñez-Sánchez, S. (2020). Influencers on Instagram: Antecedents and consequences of opinion leadership. *Journal of Business Research, 117*, 510–519. https://doi.org/https://doi.org/10.1016/j.jbusres.2018.07.005

Chae, J. (2018). Explaining Females' Envy Toward Social Media Influencers. *Media Psychology, 21*(2), 246–262. DOI: 10.1080/15213269.2017.1328312

Chakraborty, S. (Ed.). (2025). *Ethical AI Solutions for Addressing Social Media Influence and Hate Speech.* IGI Global Scientific Publishing.

Chamberlin, K. G., & Plant, E. A. (2023). Systemic sexism recognition and antisexism encourage gender equality activism: An adaptation of bystander intervention theory. *Journal of Applied Social Psychology, 53*(10), 911–924. DOI: 10.1111/JASP.12976

Chambers, N., Kashefpakdel, E. T., Rehill, J., & Percy, C. (2018). *Drawing the future: Exploring the career aspirations of primary school children from around the world.* Education and Employers., Available at https://www.educationandemployers.org/wp-content/uploads/2018/01/Drawing-the-Future-FINAL-REPORT.pdf

Chase, B. (2020). *Strategy First: How Businesses Win Big.* Greenleaf Book Group. https://books.google.co.in/books?hl=en&lr=&id=Pcv1DwAAQBAJ&oi=fnd&pg=PT12&dq=Some+have+popped+up+in+Super+Bowl+ads,+teamed+up+with+giants+like+Amazon+or+Mercedes-Benz,+or+launched+their+own+pet+accessory+lines&ots=h71RdIDTAC&sig=Bko2YT3XW1fDlbWtDG8RlxHso_4&redir_esc=y#v=onepage&q&f=false

Chen, A., Hung, K. P., & Peng, N. (2012). A cluster analysis examination of pet owners consumption values and behavior - Segmenting owners strategically. *Journal of Targeting. Measurement and Analysis for Marketing, 20*(2), 117–132. DOI: 10.1057/jt.2012.10

Chen, K. K., & Zhang, J. J. (2011). Examining consumer attributes associated with collegiate athletic facility naming rights sponsorship: Development of a theoretical framework. *Sport Management Review, 14*(2), 103–116.

Chen, Y., Qin, Z., Yan, Y., & Yi, H. (2024). The Power of Influencers: How Does Influencer Marketing Shape Consumers' Purchase Intentions? *Sustainability*, *16*(13), 5471. DOI: 10.3390/su16135471

Cheung, M. Y., Luo, C., Sia, C. L., & Chen, H. (2009). Credibility of electronic word-of-mouth: Informational and normative determinants of on-line consumer recommendations. *International Journal of Electronic Commerce*, *13*, 9–38. DOI: 10.2753/JEC1086-4415130402

Chevalier, M., & Mazzalovo, G. (2008). *Luxury brand management*. Franco Angeli.

Chirsanova, A., Capcanari, T., Boistean, A., & Khanchel, I. (2021). Bee honey: History, characteristics, properties, benefits and adulteration in the beekeeping sector. *Journal of Social Sciences*, *4*(3), 98–114. DOI: 10.52326/jss.utm.2021.4(3).11

Choraria, C. A. R., Jain, M., & Goel, C. A. P. (2020). Global Fashion Brands: Does Sustainability Make Business Sense? [IJRTE]. *International Journal of Recent Technology and Engineering*, *9*(1), 895–903. DOI: 10.35940/IJRTE.A1476.059120

Chowdhury, R. H. (2024). Sustainability Marketing and Ethical Branding in the Digital Space. *Journal of Trends in Applied Science and Advanced Technologies*, *1*(1), 18–27. DOI: 10.61784/ASAT3002

Chu, S. C., Kim, H., & Kim, Y. (2023). When brands get real: The role of authenticity and electronic word-of-mouth in shaping consumer response to brands taking a stand. *International Journal of Advertising*, *42*(6), 1037–1064. DOI: 10.1080/02650487.2022.2138057

Clément, G. R., Boyle, R. D., George, K. A., Nelson, G. A., Reschke, M. F., Williams, T. J., & Paloski, W. H. (2020). Challenges to the central nervous system during human spaceflight missions to Mars. *Journal of Neurophysiology*, *123*(5), 2037–2063. DOI: 10.1152/JN.00476.2019 PMID: 32292116

Coelho, J., Figueira, L., & Costa, C. (2014). O Turismo Militar e a Ativação Turística do Património: Conceitos, Perspetivas e Tendências. *Revista Turismo & Desenvolvimento (Aveiro)*, *I*, 113–120.

Colliander, J., & Dahlén, M. (2011). Following the Fashionable Friend: The Power of Social Media. *Journal of Advertising Research*, *51*(1), 313–320. DOI: 10.2501/jar-51-1-313-320

Collis, J., & Hussey, J. (2005). *Pesquisa em Administração* (2ª). São Paulo: Artmed Editora.

Comission, E. (2024). *Influencer Legal Hub*. https://commission.europa.eu/live-work-travel-eu/consumer-rights-and-complaints/influencer-legal-hub_en

Content, U.-G. Leveraging Customer Engagement. (2025). Podium. https://www.podium.com/article/pet-care-marketing-trends/

Cornish, A., Raubenheimer, D., & McGreevy, P. (2016). What We Know about the Public's Level of Concern for Farm Animal Welfare in Food Production in Developed Countries. *Animals (Basel)*, *6*. Advance online publication. DOI: 10.3390/ani6110074

Cortopassi-Laurino, M.; Imperatriz-Fonseca, V. L.; Roubik, D. W.; Dollin, A.; Heard, T.; Aguilar, I.; Venturieri, G. C.; Eardley, C.; Nogueira-Neto, P. (2006). *Global meliponiculture:* challenges and opportunities. Apidologie, v. 37, n. 2, pp. 275–292, 22.

Costa, C. (2005). Turismo e cultura: Avaliação das teorias e práticas culturais do sector do turismo (1990-2000). *Analise Social*, *XL*(175), 279–295.

Cotter, K. (2018). Playing the visibility game: How digital influencers and algorithms negotiate influence on Instagram. *New Media & Society*, *21*(4), 895–913. DOI: 10.1177/1461444818815684

Cottingham, M. D. (2012). Interaction ritual theory and sports fans: Emotion, symbols, and solidarity. *Sociology of Sport Journal*, *29*(2), 168–185.

Cravidão, F. (2014). Velho(s) Território(s): Novo(s) Turismo(s). In R. B. Costa, Carlos; Brandão, Filipa; Costa (Ed.), *Turismo nos Países Lusófonos: Conhecimento, Estratégia e Territórios* (pp. 59–69). Escolar Editora.

Creator, I. Q. Connect. (2025). *The State of Creator Marketing Report: Trends and Trajectory 2024-2025*. https://www.creatoriq.com/white-papers/state-of-creator-marketing-trends-2025?creative=721461056566&keyword=influencer marketing&matchtype=p&network=g&device=c&_bt=721461056566&_bk=influencer marketing&_bm=p&_bn=g&_bg=171923138873&utm_term=influencer mark

Creswell, J. W. (2013). Qualitative inquiry and research design: choosing among five approaches (3rd Edition). *SAGE Publications.* ENAME Charter, 1 (2008).

Crozet, G., Lacoste, M.-L., Rivière, J., Robardet, E., Cliquet, F., & Dufour, B. (2021). Management practices of dog and cat owners in France (pet traveling, animal contact rates and medical monitoring): Impacts on the introduction and the spread of directly transmitted infectious pet diseases. *Transboundary and Emerging Diseases*. Advance online publication. DOI: 10.1111/tbed.14088 PMID: 33787076 da Silva Pereira, I., & Sousa, B. B. (2020). Corporate social responsibility in the field of sports marketing: A study applied to SC Braga. In *Statistical Modelling and Sports Business Analytics* (pp. 108–118). Routledge.

da Silva, E. C., & Las Casas, A. L. (2020). Key elements of sports marketing activities for sports events. *International Journal of Business Administration, 11*(1), 11–21.

Dabbous, A., & Barakat, K. (2020). Bridging the online offline gap: Assessing the impact of brands' social network content quality on brand awareness and purchase intention. *Journal of Retailing and Consumer Services, 53*, 101966. DOI: 10.1016/j.jretconser.2019.101966

Dadhich, J. P., Smith, J. P., Iellamo, A., & Suleiman, A. (2021). Climate Change and Infant Nutrition: Estimates of Greenhouse Gas Emissions From Milk Formula Sold in Selected Asia Pacific Countries. *Journal of Human Lactation, 37*(2), 314–322. DOI: 10.1177/0890334421994769 PMID: 33586512

Dagalp, I., & Hartmann, B. J. (2022). From "aesthetic" to aestheticization: A multi-layered cultural approach. *Consumption Markets & Culture, 25*(1), 1–20. DOI: 10.1080/10253866.2021.1935900

Das, A., & Albinsson, P. A. (2023). Consumption Culture and Critical Sustainability Discourses: Voices from the Global South. *Sustainability, 15*(9), 1–19. DOI: 10.3390/SU15097719

Dashper, K. (2016). *Human-animal relationships in equestrian sport and leisure*. Routledge.

Davenport, T. H., & Beck, J. C. (2021). *The attention economy: Understanding the new currency of business*. Harvard Business Press. https://www.hbs.edu/faculty/Pages/item.aspx?num=

Davies, I., Oates, C. J., Tynan, C., Carrigan, M., Casey, K., Heath, T., Henninger, C. E., Lichrou, M., McDonagh, P., McDonald, S., McKechnie, S., McLeay, F., O'Malley, L., & Wells, V. (2020). Seeking sustainable futures in marketing and consumer research. *European Journal of Marketing, 54*(11), 2911–2939. DOI: 10.1108/EJM-02-2019-0144

de Brito Silva, M. J., de Oliveira Ramos Delfino, L., Alves Cerqueira, K., & de Oliveira Campos, P. (2022). Avatar marketing: A study on the engagement and authenticity of virtual influencers on Instagram. *Social Network Analysis and Mining, 12*(1), 130. DOI: 10.1007/s13278-022-00966-w

De Canio, F., Viglia, G., & Lombart, C. (2024). Package-free products: How to improve pro-environmental buying behaviors among consumers. *Technological Forecasting and Social Change*, *198*. Advance online publication. DOI: 10.1016/j.techfore.2023.122995

de Droog, S. M., Buijzen, M., & Valkenburg, P. M. (2012). Use a rabbit or a rhino to sell a carrot? The effect of character–product congruence on children's liking of healthy foods. *Journal of Health Communication*, *17*, 1068–1080. DOI: 10.1080/10810730.2011.65083 PMID: 22650613

de Droog, S. M., Valkenburg, P. M., & Buijzen, M. (2011). Using brand characters to promote young children's liking of and purchase requests for fruit. *Journal of Health Communication*, *16*, 79–89. DOI: 10.1080/10810730.2010.529487 PMID: 21058143

De Veirman, M., & Hudders, L. (2020). Disclosing sponsored Instagram posts: The role of material connection with the brand and message-sidedness when disclosing covert advertising. *International Journal of Advertising*, *39*(1), 94–130. DOI: 10.1080/02650487.2019.1575108

del Río, C., González-Álvarez, K., & López-Arceiz, F. J. (2024). Examining greenwashing and SDG-washing: An analysis of corporate engagement with the SDGs. *Sustainability Accounting. Management and Policy Journal*, *15*(2), 412–456. DOI: 10.1108/SAMPJ-02-2023-0080

Dessart, L. (2017). Social media engagement: A model of antecedents and relational outcomes. *Journal of Marketing Management*, *33*(5–6), 375–399. DOI: 10.1080/0267257X.2017.1302975

Dessart, L., & Standaert, W. (2023). Strategic storytelling in the age of sustainability. *Business Horizons*, *66*(3), 371–385. DOI: 10.1016/J.BUSHOR.2023.01.005

Di Cioccio, M., Pozharliev, R., & De Angelis, M. (2024). Pawsitively powerful: Why and when pet influencers boost social media effectiveness. *Psychology and Marketing*. Advance online publication. DOI: 10.1002/mar.22000

Diaz-Bustamante-Ventisca, M., Carcelén-García, S., Díaz-Soloaga, P., & Kolotouchkina, O. (2025). Greenwashing perception in Spanish fast-fashion brands' communication: Modelling sustainable behaviours and attitudes. *International Journal of Fashion Design, Technology and Education*, *18*(2), 179–189. DOI: 10.1080/17543266.2024.2343934

Dibble, J. L., Hartmann, T., & Rosaen, S. F. (2016). Parasocial Interaction and Parasocial Relationship: Conceptual Clarification and a Critical Assessment of Measures. *Human Communication Research*, *42*(1), 21–44. DOI: 10.1111/hcre.12063

Dickson, G., & Zhang, J. J. (2021). Sports and urban development: An introduction. *International Journal of Sports Marketing & Sponsorship*, *22*(1), 1–9.

Dicu, A. M., Rad, D., Barbu, F., Cuc, L. D., Feher, A., Roman, D., Mazuru, L., Sanda, G., & Pîrvulescu, L. (2025). From Attachment to Action: Consumer Identification and the Sustainable Buying of Rural Brand Products Like "Pită de Pecica.". *Sustainability*, *17*(9), 1–19. DOI: 10.3390/SU17094133

Djafarova, E., & Rushworth, C. (2017). Exploring the credibility of online celebrities' Instagram profiles in influencing the purchase decisions of young female users. *Computers in Human Behavior*, *68*, 1–7. https://doi.org/https://doi.org/10.1016/j.chb.2016.11.009

Dobuss Agency. (2025). Las tendencias emergentes en el marketing digital para 2025. Huffington Post España. https://www.huffingtonpost.es/tecnologia/las-tendencias-emergentes-marketing-digital-2025-agencia-dobuss.html

Dodd, M., Fowler, A., & Lottridge, D. (2025). Purr-ogrammed love: A narrative review of virtual pets. *Entertainment Computing*, *54*. Advance online publication. DOI: 10.1016/j.entcom.2025.100958

Dondapati, A., & Dehury, R. K. (2024). Virtual vs. Human influencers: The battle for consumer hearts and minds. *Computers in Human Behavior Artificial Humans*, *2*(1), 100059. DOI: 10.1016/j.chbah.2024.100059

Donmez, K., Kaplan, Z., Cetek, F. A., Rogošic, T., Juricic, B., & Francetic, I. (2022). Service Quality and Efficiency-Oriented Training Design in Air Traffic Management. In P. M., D. I., & C. A.L. (Eds.), *Transportation Research Procedia* (Vol. 64, Issue C, pp. 345 – 355). Elsevier B.V. https://doi.org/DOI: 10.1016/j.trpro.2022.09.038

dos Santos, M. C. (2024). *O impacto dos agrotóxicos na polinização e no meio ambiente*. Mata Nativa. Disponível em: https://matanativa.com.br/impacto-dos-agrotoxicos-no-meio-ambiente/. Disponível em: 16/08/2025.

dos Santos, R. M., & Murça, M. C. R. (2025). Airport capacity prediction and optimal allocation for strategic air traffic flow management at Sao Paulo/Guarulhos International Airport. *Case Studies on Transport Policy*, *20*. Advance online publication. DOI: 10.1016/j.cstp.2025.101414

Doshi, R., Ramesh, A., & Rao, S. (2022). Modeling Influencer Marketing Campaigns in Social Networks. *IEEE Transactions on Computational Social Systems*, *10*(1), 322. DOI: 10.1109/tcss.2022.3140779

Drossos, D., Coursaris, C. K., & Kagiouli, E. (2023). Social media marketing content strategy: A comprehensive framework and empirically supported guidelines for brand posts on Facebook pages. *Journal of Consumer Behaviour*, *23*(3), 1175. DOI: 10.1002/cb.2269

Drury, M., Fuller, J., & Hoeks, J. (2023). Embedding animals within a definition of sustainability. *Sustainability Science*, *18*(4), 1925–1938. DOI: 10.1007/S11625-023-01310-7/FIGURES/1

Duan, Y., Aloysius, J. A., & Mollenkopf, D. A. (2022). Communicating supply chain sustainability: Transparency and framing effects. *International Journal of Physical Distribution & Logistics Management*, *52*(1), 68–87. DOI: 10.1108/IJPDLM-04-2020-0107

Dzreke, S. S., & Dzreke, S. E. (2025). Influence of Social Media on Consumer Behavior: Investigating How Social Media Platforms Shape Consumer Purchasing Decisions and Loyalty. *Open Journal of Business and Management*, *13*(2), 1154. DOI: 10.4236/ojbm.2025.132061

Edwards, S. (2007). Role of organic agriculture in preventing and reversing land degradation. *Environmental Science and Engineering*, 523–536. https://www.scopus.com/inward/record.uri?eid=2-s2.0-85108904023&partnerID=40&md5=127c3fb4c7afdf38c7ae715f361592d7

Effendy, V., & Xiao, Z. (2025). How Does Cultural Sustainability Promote Fashion Consumers' Purchase Intention? *Sustainability*, *17*(5), 1–7. DOI: 10.3390/SU17052034

Eidelson, R. J., & Eidelson, J. I. (2003). Dangerous ideas: Five beliefs that propel groups toward conflict. *The American Psychologist*, *58*(3), 182. DOI: 10.1037/0003-066X.58.3.182 PMID: 12772423

El-adaway, I. H., & Jennings, M. (2022). Professional and Organizational Leadership Role in Ethics Management: Avoiding Reliance on Ethical Codification and Nurturing Ethical Culture. *Science and Engineering Ethics*, *28*(4), 1–30. DOI: 10.1007/S11948-022-00385-2/METRICS PMID: 35939145

Embrapa. (2025). *Mudança climática coloca abelhas em risco e ameaça segurança alimentar global*. https://www.embrapa.br/busca-de-noticias/-/noticia/101094052/mudanca-climatica-coloca-abelhas-em-risco-e-ameaca-seguranca-alimentar-global. Acesso: em 8 de agosto de 2025.

Emran Shaikh, M. (n.d.). *A STUDY ON CONSUMER PERCEPTION AND PREFERENCES TOWARDS PET CARE INDUSTRY IN INDIA CAPSTONE PROJECT REPORT MASTER OF MANAGEMENT STUDIES SIES COLLEGE OF MANAGEMENT STUDIES NERUL, NAVI MUMBAI-400706*.

Entre Serras – Turismo Rural. (2018). *Entre Serras No Meio Rural – Bee Nectar*. Disponível em: Https://Www.Facebook.Com/Entreserrasturismorural/?Locale=Pt_Br. Acesso: 26/09/2023.

Epley, N., Waytz, A., & Cacioppo, J. T. (2007). On seeing human: A three-factor theory of anthropomorphism. *Psychological Review*, *114*(4), 864–886. DOI: 10.1037/0033-295X.114.4.864

Eroğlu, Ö., & Yuksel, S. (2020). Historical development and current status of beekeeping in Turkey and the World. *Atras Journal*, *6*, 345–354.

Escalas, J. E., & Bettman, J. R. (2005). Self-construal, reference groups, and brand meaning. *The Journal of Consumer Research*, *32*(3), 378–389. DOI: 10.1086/497549

Estatuto Social Entre Serras Turismo No Meio Rural. (2021). *Registrado No Cartório Raul Fonseca – Lima Duarte*, Livro A-N-8, Registro 222, Pessoa Jurídica, Folhas 135 a 138. Gil, A. C. (2008). Métodos e Técnicas de Pesquisa Social. 6ed. São Paulo: Atlas.

Evans, N. J., Hoy, M. G., & Childers, C. C. (2018). Parenting "YouTube natives": The impact of pre-roll advertising and text disclosures on parental responses to sponsored child influencer videos. *Journal of Advertising*, *47*, 326–346. DOI: 10.1080/00913367.2018.1544952

Fair, L. (2019a). FTC-FDA warning letters: Influential to influencers and marketers. Available at: https://www.ftc.gov/news-events/blogs/business-blog/2019/06/ftc-fda-warning-letters-influential-influencers-marketers (Accessed November 21, 2019).

Fair, L. (2019b). Great American Fake-Off? FTC cases challenge bogus influencer metrics and fake reviews. Available at: https://www.ftc.gov/news-events/blogs/business-blog/2019/10/great-american-fake-ftc-cases-challenge-bogus-influencer (Accessed November 21, 2019).

Faisal, A., & Ekawanto, I. (2022). *The role of Social Media Marketing in increasing Brand Awareness, Brand Image and Purchase Intention.* Indonesian Management and Accounting Research., DOI: 10.25105/imar.v20i2.12554

Faita, M. R., de Moura, M. E. K., Damasco, T. de M., Poltronieri, A. S., & Nodari, R. O. (2022). *Abelhas e o ambiente: importância, nutrição e sanidade.* In J. M. B.

Fang, Z. (2023). Ananlysing the Effectiveness of Anime-like Virtual Influencer. *Advances in Economics. Management and Political Sciences, 33*(1), 232–239. DOI: 10.54254/2754-1169/33/20231660

FAO - Food and Agriculture Organization of the United Nations. (2023). *Conselho, Centésima Septuagésima Segunda Sessão,* Roma, CL 172/5. Roma. 24 a 28 de abril de 2023. Disponível online: www.fao.org/3/nl652en/nl652en.pdf (acessado em 15 de agosto de 2023).

FAO - Food and Agriculture Organization of the United Nations. (2025). *About FAO.* Disponível em: https://www.fao.org/about/about-fao/en/. Acesso em: 10/08/2025.

Farida, Y., Siswanto, N., & Vanany, I. (2024). Reverse logistics toward a circular economy: Consumer behavioral intention toward polyethylene terephthalate (PET) recycling in Indonesia. *Case Studies in Chemical and Environmental Engineering, 10.* Advance online publication. DOI: 10.1016/j.cscee.2024.100807

Fazenda, N. (2014). Turismo em Portugal: Reflexões para uma Política Nacional de Turismo. In Costa, C. (Ed.), *Turismo nos Países Lusófonos: Conhecimento, Estratégia e Territórios* (pp. 293–312). Escolar Editora.

Federal Trade Comission. (2025). *Disclosures 101 for Social Media Influencers.* https://www.ftc.gov/business-guidance/resources/disclosures-101-social-media -influencers

Fennell, D. A. (2022). Animal-informed consent: Sled dog tours as asymmetric agential events. *Tourism Management, 93.* Advance online publication. DOI: 10.1016/J. TOURMAN.2022.104584

Ferrand, A., & McCarthy, S. (2008). *Marketing the sports organisation: Building networks and relationships.* Routledge.

Figueira, L. (2010). *Manual para Elaboração de roteiros de Turismo Cultural.* Instituto Politécnico de Tomar.

Figueira, L. M. (2013). Roteirização do Turismo: Uma Abordagem Preliminar à "apresentação-interpretação" do território. *Revista Turismo & Desenvolvimento (Aveiro), 1*(20), 121–133.

Figueiredo, C. (13/08/2025). *Mel brasileiro premiado como melhor do mundo perde mercado de US$ 80 mi após tarifaço de Trump*. Gazeta do Povo. Disponível em: https://www.gazetadopovo.com.br/santa-catarina/mel-brasileiro-premiado-melhor-do-mundo-perde-mercado-apos-tarifaco-trump/. Acesso em: 16 de agosto de 2025.

Foltz, R. (2014). *Animals in Islamic tradition and Muslim cultures*. Simon and Schuster.

Fontana, C., & Fontana, P. (2020). In Part, I., & Floris, I. (Eds.), *The first evidence: In Italian Apiculture. A Journey through History and Honey Diversity* (pp. 36–47). Accademia Nazionale Italiana di Entomologia.

Fournier, S. (1998). Consumers and Their Brands: Developing Relationship Theory in Consumer Research. *The Journal of Consumer Research*, *24*(4), 343–353. DOI: 10.1086/209515

Fournier, S., & Alvarez, C. (2012). Brands as relationship partners: Warmth, competence, and in-between. *Journal of Consumer Psychology*, *22*(2), 177–185. DOI: 10.1016/j.jcps.2011.10.003

Francioni, B., De Cicco, R., Curina, I., & Cioppi, M. (2025). *The strength of stance: The impact of brand activism on resistance to negative information, purchasing, and premium paying intents across different types of failures*. University of Urbino Carlo Bo., DOI: 10.1016/j.jretconser.2024.104102

Franklin, A. (1999). *Animals and Modern Cultures: A Sociology of Human–Animal Relations in Modernity*. SAGE Publications Ltd., DOI: 10.4135/9781446217764

Frig, M. M., & Jaakkola, M. (2024). Between conspicuous and conscious consumption: The sustainability paradox in the intermediary promotional work of an online lifestyle site. *Journal of Consumer Culture*, *24*(1), 3–23. DOI: 10.1177/14695405231170684/ASSET/0F8CA3F7-8E6F-4422-9A41-0AE9DA59A5C4/ASSETS/IMAGES/LARGE/10.1177_14695405231170684-FIG1.JPG

Fuchs, C. (2014). *Social Media: A Critical Introduction*. SAGE Publications Ltd., DOI: 10.4135/9781446270066

Gaiato, G., Ardigó, C. M., & Limberger, P. F. (2023). Animal Welfare Certification Seal and the Effect on Brand Equity: Consumer Perspective of Chicken Commodity. *Journal of Food Products Marketing*, *29*(6), 197–218. DOI: 10.1080/10454446.2023.2227583

Gálvez-Sánchez, F. J., Molina-Prados, A., Molina-Moreno, V., & Moral-Cuadra, S. (2024). Exploring the three-dimensional effect of corporate social responsibility on brand equity, corporate reputation, and willingness to pay: A study of the fashion industry. *Journal of Retailing and Consumer Services*. Advance online publication. DOI: 10.1016/j.jretconser.2024.103836

García-Madariaga, J., Moya, I., Recuero, N., & Blasco, M.-F. (2020). Revealing Unconscious Consumer Reactions to Advertisements That Include Visual Metaphors. A Neurophysiological Experiment. *Frontiers in Psychology*, *11*, 760. DOI: 10.3389/fpsyg.2020.00760

Gashi, A. (2025). Sports Marketing Strategies, Navigating the Intersection of Globalization and Internationalization. *Interdisciplinary Journal of Research and Development*, *12*(1), 190–190.

Giannitrapani, A. (2018). Cat Cafes and Dog Restaurants. In Marrone, G., & Mangano, D. (Eds.), *SEMIOTICS OF ANIMALS IN CULTURE: ZOOSEMIOTICS 2.0* (Vol. 17, pp. 91–102)., DOI: 10.1007/978-3-319-72992-3_7

Gil, C. (2021). *The end of marketing: Humanizing your brand in the age of social media*. Kogan Page Publishers. https://scholar.google.com/scholar?hl=en&as_sdt=0%2C5&q=Platforms+like+Instagram%2C+TikTok%2C+YouTube%2C+and+Facebook+have+changed+the+game%2C+moving+away+from+old-school+ads+to+something+more+personal%2C+genuine%2C+and+engaging&btnG=

Giles, D. (2018). Twenty-First Century Celebrity: Fame In Digital Culture. In *Twenty-First Century Celebrity: Fame In Digital Culture* (pp. 207–235). Emerald Publishing Limited. https://doi.org/DOI: 10.1108/978-1-78743-708-120181018

Gleim, M., Sreen, N., & Pant, L. (2022). Is Doing Right All that Matters in Sustainability Marketing? The Role of Fit in Sustainable Marketing Strategies. SSRN *Electronic Journal*. https://doi.org/DOI: 10.2139/SSRN.4093796

Global Gurus. (2025). 8 Pet Industry Trends in the Future. Global Gurus. https://globalgurus.org/8-pet-industry-trends-in-the-future/

Golob, U., Podnar, K., & Zabkar, V. (2023). Sustainability communication. *International Journal of Advertising*, *42*(1), 42–51. DOI: 10.1080/02650487.2022.2144035

Gomes, S., Lopes, J. M., & Nogueira, S. (2023). Willingness to pay more for green products: A critical challenge for Gen Z. *Journal of Cleaner Production*, *390*. Advance online publication. DOI: 10.1016/J.JCLEPRO.2023.136092

Gonçalves, A. R., Dorsch, L. L. P., & Figueiredo, M. (2022). Digital Tourism: An Alternative View on Cultural Intangible Heritage and Sustainability in Tavira, Portugal. *Sustainability (Switzerland), 14*(5). Advance online publication. DOI: 10.3390/su14052912

Gonçalves, F. (2018). *A Interpretação do Património como fator de desenvolvimento do Turismo Cultural e Criativo. O caso do Galo de Barcelos.* Tese de Doutoramento, Universidade de Aveiro.

Gonçalves, F., & Costa, C. (2016). Galo de Barcelos: Património e destino turístico. *Revista Turismo & Desenvolvimento (Aveiro).*

Gonçalves, F., & Costa, C. (2019a). Modelo de Desenvolvimento e Implementação do Turismo Criativo. O caso do Galo de Barcelos. *Revista Turismo & Desenvolvimento (Aveiro), 32*(52), 25–36.

Gonçalves, F., & Costa, C. (2019b). O Contributo da Interpretação do Património Para o Desenvolvimento do Turismo Criativo. O Caso do Galo de Barcelos. *Revista Portuguesa de Estudos Regionais, 52*, 25–36.

Gonçalves, F., & Costa, C. (2020). Contribution of Caminos de Santiago to the sustainable development of Tourism, in Barcelos. *Journal of Tourism & Development, 34*, 65–79.

Gonçalves, F., & Costa, C. (2022). Barcelos, Cidade Criativa da UNESCO: Contributo para o desenvolvimento sustentável do Artesanato através do Turismo Criativo Creative City sustainable development Creative Tourism. *Revista Turismo & Desenvolvimento (Aveiro)*, •••, 107–128.

Gowda.V, S., & H., A. (2024). The role of brand storytelling in creating emotional connections. *ShodhKosh: Journal of Visual and Performing Arts, 5*(1), 1843–1848. https://doi.org/DOI: 10.29121/SHODHKOSH.V5.I1.2024.4576

Gracias, A., Olukemi, A., & Bell, C. (2024). Influencer Marketing ROI: Measurement Techniques and Optimization Strategies. SSRN Electronic Journal. DOI: 10.2139/ssrn.4907402

Green, M. S. (2008). Self-Expression. In *Self-Expression*. Oxford University Press., DOI: 10.1093/acprof:oso/9780199283781.001.0001

Greger, M. (2007). The long haul risks associated with livestock transport. *Biosecurity and Bioterrorism, 5*(4), 301–312. DOI: 10.1089/bsp.2007.0028 PMID: 18081490

Gromek, N., & Perek-Białas, J. (2022). Why is pet goods consumption imperceptible for economists? A scoping review. In *SN Business and Economics* (Vol. 2, Issue 11). Springer Nature. https://doi.org/DOI: 10.1007/s43546-022-00349-5

Grönroos, C. (2004). The relationship marketing process: Communication, interaction, dialogue, value. *Journal of Business and Industrial Marketing*, *19*(2), 99–113. DOI: 10.1108/08858620410523981

Gross, J., Cui, Z., & von Wangenheim, F. (2023). How to Make Influencer Advertising Engaging on Instagram: Emotional Storytelling in Sponsored Posts. *Journal of Interactive Advertising*, *23*(4), 388–408. DOI: 10.1080/15252019.2023.2211579

Gu, C., & Duan, Q.-T. (2024). Exploring the dynamics of consumer engagement in social media influencer marketing: From the self-determination theory perspective. *Humanities & Social Sciences Communications*, *11*(1). Advance online publication. DOI: 10.1057/s41599-024-03127-w

Guerra-Tamez, C. R., Flores, K. K., Serna-Mendiburu, G. M., Robles, D. C., & Cortés, J. I. (2024). Decoding Gen Z: AI's influence on brand trust and purchasing behavior. *Frontiers in Artificial Intelligence*, *7*. Advance online publication. DOI: 10.3389/frai.2024.1323512 PMID: 38500672

Guinness World Records. (2023). *Most followers on Instagram for a cat*. Guiness World Records. https://www.guinnessworldrecords.com/world-records/465511-most-followers-for-a-cat-on-instagram

Guo, C., Chen, F., & Wang, Y. (2025). The Psychological Impact of Competitive Sports Participation on Adolescent Athletes: An Analysis of Coping Mechanisms and Performance Outcomes. *Journal of Rational-Emotive & Cognitive-Behavior Therapy*, *43*(2), 24.

Guttmann, A. (2019). Spending on advertising to children worldwide from 2012 to 2021, by format (in billion U.S. dollars). Available at: https://www.statista.com/statistics/750865/kids-advertising-spending-worldwide/ (Accessed November 21, 2019).

Haghani, M. (2022). Crowd dynamics research in the era of Covid-19 pandemic: Challenges and opportunities. *Safety Science*, *153*. Advance online publication. DOI: 10.1016/j.ssci.2022.105818 PMID: 35582429

Han, J., Zuo, J., Zillante, G., Chang, R., & Du, L. (2025a). A systematic review of PET circularity technologies and management strategies: Challenges and future directions. In *Resources, Conservation and Recycling* (Vol. 219). Elsevier B.V. https://doi.org/DOI: 10.1016/j.resconrec.2025.108280

Haraway, D. (2008). *When species meet University of Minne*. sota Press, Minneapolis MN.

Hardey, M. (2024). What Is Influencer Marketing? DOI: 10.4135/9781071959664

Hartama, E. (2021). Possibilities of influencer marketing through pet Instagram accounts: a fast lane to a pet owner's pocket? https://urn.fi/URN:NBN:fi-fe2021072241653

Hassan, S. M. (2024). Greenwashing in ESG: Identifying and Addressing False Claims of Sustainability. *Journal of Business and Strategic Management*, *9*(8), 90–105. DOI: 10.47941/JBSM.2390

Hasson, G. (2017). *Emotional intelligence pocketbook: Little exercises for an intuitive life*. John Wiley & Sons. url: https://books.google.co.in/books?hl=en&lr=&id=o-jFDQAAQBAJ&oi=fnd&pg=PA1&dq=Pets+spark+universal+emotions+joy,+laughter,+maybe+a+little+%E2%80%9Caww%E2%80%9D+that+brands+love+to+link+to+their+image&ots=NfyEew17BW&sig=S_Ue-ILEvxXlGx9CwDU3BAYlv5E&redir_esc=y#v=onepage&q&f=false

Hasudungan, A., & Saragih, H. S. (2023). Brand awareness and relationship intention: The moderating role of perceived corporate social responsibility dimensions. *Asia Pacific Journal of Marketing and Logistics*. Advance online publication. DOI: 10.1108/APJML-03-2022-0184

Hausmann, A., Cortés-Capano, G., & Di Minin, E. (2023a). Exploring the effects of market scarcity on consumers' demand for rarity in the wildlife trade. In *Global Ecology and Conservation* (Vol. 48). Elsevier B.V., DOI: 10.1016/j.gecco.2023.e02744

Hebden, L., King, L., & Kelly, B. (2011). Art of persuasion: An analysis of techniques used to market foods to children. *Journal of Paediatrics and Child Health*, *47*, 776–782. DOI: 10.1111/j.1440-1754.2011.02025.x PMID: 21707822

Heidenstrøm, N. (2024). Green marketing in the fashion industry: A critical analysis of sustainability narratives. *Consumption Markets & Culture*, *27*(5), 488–504. DOI: 10.1080/10253866.2024.2440557

Hicham, N., Nassera, H., & Karim, S. (2023). Strategic Framework for Leveraging Artificial Intelligence in Future Marketing Decision-Making. *Journal of Intelligent Management Decision*, *2*(3), 139. DOI: 10.56578/jimd020304

Higes, M.. (2009). Honeybee colony collapse due to Nosema ceranae in professional apiaries. *Environmental Microbiology Reports*, *1*(2), 110–113. PMID: 23765741

Hochstein, R. E., Veresiu, E., & Harmeling, C. M. (2025). Moralizing Everyday Consumption: The Case of Self-Care. *The Journal of Consumer Research*, *52*(1), 219–242. DOI: 10.1093/JCR/UCAE056

Hoffner, C. (2008). *"Parasocial and online social relationships" in The handbook of children, media and development* (Calvert, S. L., & Wilson, B. J., Eds.). Blackwell-Wiley.

Hoffner, C., & Buchanan, M. (2005). Young adults' wishful identification with television characters: The role of perceived similarity and character attributes. *Media Psychology*, *7*, 325–351. DOI: 10.1207/S1532785XMEP0704_2

Hofverberg, H., Franzén, J., & Maivorsdotter, N. (2023). Education for sustainable clothing consumerism?: A critical examination of educational material for design and craft education. *FormAkademisk*, *16*(5), 1–21. DOI: 10.7577/FORMAKADEMISK.5234

Holbrook, M. B. (2008). Pets and people: Companions in commerce? *Journal of Business Research*, *61*(5), 546–552. DOI: 10.1016/j.jbusres.2007.07.010

Holbrook, M. B., & Hirschman, E. C. (1982). The experiential aspects of consumption: Consumer fantasies, feelings, and fun. *The Journal of Consumer Research*, *9*(2), 132–140. DOI: 10.1086/208906

Holbrook, M. B., & Schindler, R. M. (2003). Nostalgic bonding: Exploring the role of nostalgia in the consumption experience. *Journal of Consumer Behaviour*, *3*(2), 107–127. DOI: 10.1002/cb.127

Hölker, S., Meyer-Höfer, M., & Spiller, A. (2019). Inclusion of Animal Ethics into the Consumer Value-Attitude System Using the Example of Game Meat Consumption. *Food Ethics*, •••, 1–23. DOI: 10.1007/S41055-019-00036-6

Hollebeek, L. D., Glynn, M. S., & Brodie, R. J. (2014). Consumer Brand Engagement in Social Media: Conceptualization, Scale Development and Validation. *Journal of Interactive Marketing*, *28*(2), 149–165. DOI: 10.1016/j.intmar.2013.12.002

Holt, D. B. (2004). *How brands become icons: The principles of cultural branding*. harvard business press.

Horton, D., & Richard Wohl, R. (1956). Mass Communication and Para-Social Interaction. *Psychiatry*, *19*(3), 215–229. DOI: 10.1080/00332747.1956.11023049 PMID: 13359569

Hoyer, W. D., & Brown, S. P. (1990). Effects of brand awareness on choice for a common, repeat-purchase product. *The Journal of Consumer Research*, *17*(2), 141–148. DOI: 10.1086/208544

Hu, X. (2024). Presenting Global Brands with Celebrity Endorsement through Impression Management and Storytelling Techniques: A Case Study of 12 Brand Archetypes in Personal Care Product Category (Doctoral dissertation, Bangkok University). http://dspace.bu.ac.th/jspui/handle/123456789/5767

Huang, W. H., & Hsieh, S. Y. (2023). The impact of animal metaphors on consumer response to courtesy advertising. *Journal of Retailing and Consumer Services*, *75*. Advance online publication. DOI: 10.1016/J.JRETCONSER.2023.103485

Huang, W.-H. (2024). I am not an animal: How animal metaphors backfire in product advertising. *Psychology and Marketing*, *41*(12), 3009–3023. DOI: 10.1002/mar.22100

HuffPost España. (2025). Las tendencias emergentes en el marketing digital para 2025. Huffington Post España. https://www.huffingtonpost.es/tecnologia/las-tendencias-emergentes-marketing-digital-2025-agencia-dobuss.html

Hummer, R. L. (n.d.). *Pets in Today's Society.*

IBGE. (2023). *Produção de mel de abelha.* Disponível em: https://www.ibge.gov.br/explica/producao-agropecuaria/mel-de-abelha/br. Acesso em: 16 de agosto de 2025.

ICOMOS International Cultural Tourism Charter. (1999). https://www.icomos.org/charters/tourism_e.pdf

Ilieva, G., Yankova, T., Ruseva, M., Dzhabarova, Y., Klisarova-Belcheva, S., & Bratkov, M. (2024). Social Media Influencers: Customer Attitudes and Impact on Purchase Behaviour. *Information (Basel)*, *15*(6), 359. DOI: 10.3390/info15060359

Imperatriz-Fonseca, V. L., Canhos, D. A. L., Alves, D. A., & Saraiva, A. M. (2012). *Polinizadores no Brasil: Contribuição e perspectivas para a biodiversidade, uso sustentável, conservação e serviços ambientais*. EDUSP.

Inês, A., Diniz, A., & Moreira, A. C. (2023). A review of greenwashing and supply chain management: Challenges ahead. *Cleaner Environmental Systems*, *11*. Advance online publication. DOI: 10.1016/J.CESYS.2023.100136

Influencer Marketing Hub. (2024). *The State of Influencer Marketing 2022: Benchmark Report*. Influencer Marketing Hub. https://influencermarketinghub.com/influencer-marketing-benchmark-report-2022/

Ingale, A. (2024). The Role of Influencer Marketing in Brand Building. SSRN Electronic Journal. DOI: 10.2139/ssrn.4972626

IPCC. (2022). *Climate Change and Land.* https://www.ipcc.ch

Iqbal, A., Aslam, S., Jalali, W. U. B., Saboor, A., & Haider, W. (2023). Unveiling the Power of Influencer Marketing: A Systematic review of Influencer Marketing Antecedents, Outcomes, Theoretical Framework and the Future Research Directions [Review of Unveiling the Power of Influencer Marketing: A Systematic review of Influencer Marketing Antecedents, Outcomes, Theoretical Framework and the Future Research Directions]. *Research Journal for Societal Issues, 5*(2), 362. DOI: 10.56976/rjsi.v5i2.119

Iqbal, N., Arif, M., Abbas, Q., Mahmood, Q., Naseem Anwar, M., Mansoor, M., & Khan, D. (2025). Green Influencers. *The Power of Social Media in Shaping Eco-Conscious Communities., 3*(02), 402–412. DOI: 10.55966/assaj.2025.3.2.001

Ismael, Z. N. (2022). Marketing strategy: The influence of corporate social responsibility on brand awareness. *International Journal of Engineering Business Management, 6*(5), 43–48. DOI: 10.22161/ijebm.6.5.6

Ismail, K. (2018). Social media influencers: mega, macro, micro or nano. Available at: https://www.cmswire.com/digital-marketing/social-media-influencers-mega-macro-micro-or-nano/ (Accessed November 21, 2019).

Ismail, S. A., & Mohamed, M. (2024). Analyzing the effects of influencer marketing on consumer behavior: Insights from social influence theory in TikTok Campaigns. *World Journal of Advanced Research and Reviews, 24*(3), 2116. DOI: 10.30574/wjarr.2024.24.3.3926

Isosuo, H. (2016). *Social media influencer marketing.*

Jacobson, J., Hodson, J., & Mittelman, R. (2022). Pup-ularity contest: The advertising practices of popular animal influencers on Instagram. *Technological Forecasting and Social Change, 174*, 121226. DOI: 10.1016/j.techfore.2021.121226

Jacobson, M. (2019). *Marketing madness: A survival guide for a consumer society.* Routledge., DOI: 10.4324/9780429038938

Jacobs, T. P., Humphrey, B. T., & McConnell, A. R. (2023). Nature's Best Friend: Viewing Pets as Having Greater Emotional Experience Increases Ecological Concern. *Anthrozoos, 36*(4), 625–639. DOI: 10.1080/08927936.2023.2200647

Jain, V., Roy, S., Daswani, A., & Sudha, M. (2011). What really works for teenagers: Human or fictional celebrity? *Young Consumers, 12*, 171–183. DOI: 10.1108/17473611111141623

Janssens, M. (2021). Animal Business: An Ethical Exploration of Corporate Responsibility Towards Animals. *Food Ethics, 7*. Advance online publication. DOI: 10.1007/s41055-021-00094-9

Javed, U. (2022). Linking Perceived Greenwashing with Brand Credibility: An Empirical Evidence from Pakistan. *International Journal of Business and Economic Affairs*, *7*(3), 1–10. DOI: 10.24088/IJBEA-2022-73001

Javed, U., Rashid, M. A., Hussain, G., & Shafique, S. (2024). Consumers' perception of green brand attributes and its outcomes: A sustainable perspective. *Journal of Environmental Planning and Management*, *67*(8), 1655–1677. DOI: 10.1080/09640568.2023.2178882

Jeffery, T., Hirche, M., Faulkner, M., Page, B., Trinh, G., Bruwer, J., & Lockshin, L. (2024). Branding consistency across product portfolios in the wine industry. *International Journal of Wine Business Research*, *36*(4), 473–488. DOI: 10.1108/IJWBR-11-2023-0067

Jestratijevic, I., Uanhoro, J. O., & Rana, M. R. I. (2024). Transparency of sustainability disclosures among luxury and mass-market fashion brands: Longitudinal approach. *Journal of Cleaner Production, 436*. https://doi.org/ https://doi.org/DOI: 10.1016/J.JCLEPRO.2023.140481

Jiang, Y. (2023). The Research on the Current Situation and Trends of Social Media Marketing. In Advances in Social Science, Education and Humanities Research/ Advances in social science, education and humanities research (p. 348). DOI: 10.2991/978-2-38476-062-6_44

Jiang, Y., Yang, X., & Jia, L. (2022). The Pet Exposure Effect: Exploring the Differential Impact of Dogs Versus Cats on Consumer Mindsets. *Journal of Marketing*.

Jin, S. V., Muqaddam, A., & Ryu, E. (2019). Instafamous and social media influencer marketing. *Marketing Intelligence & Planning*, *37*(5), 567–579. DOI: 10.1108/MIP-09-2018-0375

Jochen, W., & Christopher, L. (2022). *Services marketing: People, technology, strategy*. World Scientific Publishing.

Jones, S. M. (2015). Attachment Theory. In *The International Encyclopedia of Interpersonal Communication* (pp. 1–5). Wiley., DOI: 10.1002/9781118540190.wbeic161

Joshi, Y., Lim, W. M., Jagani, K., & Kumar, S. (2023). Social media influencer marketing: Foundations, trends, and ways forward. *Electronic Commerce Research*. Advance online publication. DOI: 10.1007/s10660-023-09719-z

Judijanto, L., Suroso, A., & Choerudin, A. (2024). The Evolution of Sustainable Business Practices: A Bibliometric Study on Corporate Social Responsibility and Green Marketing. *Sciences Du Nord Economics and Business*, *1*(02), 83–91. DOI: 10.58812/SNEB.V1I2.33

Jung, C. G. (2014). *The Archetypes and the Collective Unconscious.* Routledge., DOI: 10.4324/9781315725642

Jurgena, I., & Mikainis, Z. (2011). Consumer Citizenship Education for Sustainable Development in Higher Education in Latvia. *The China Business Review*, *10*(12). Advance online publication. DOI: 10.17265/1537-1506/2011.12.011

Just Food for Dogs. (2025). Personalized Nutrition: Tailored Meal Plans for Pets. Just Food for Dogs. https://www.forbes.com/councils/forbescommunicationscouncil/2023/05/02/6-trends-driving-the-pet-industry-takeaways-from-global-pet-expo/

Kádeková, Z., & Holienčinová, M. (2018). Influencer marketing as a modern phenomenon creating a new frontier of virtual opportunities. *Communication Today, 9*(2). url: https://www.ceeol.com/search/article-detail?id=715881

Kamins, M. A. (2010). An investigation into the "match-up" hypothesis in celebrity advertising: When beauty may be only skin deep. *Journal of Advertising*, *19*, 4–13. DOI: 10.1080/00913367.1990.10673175

Kansara, T. (2024). *Awwvertising strategy: exploring how cuteness impacts influencer marketing* (Doctoral dissertation, Concordia University). https://spectrum.library.concordia.ca/id/eprint/994095/1/Kansara_MSc_F2024.pdf

Kapferer, J.-N. (2012). *The new strategic brand management: Advanced insights and strategic thinking*. Kogan page publishers.

Kassier, L. (2024). Identifying transitions in corporate sustainability reporting: a content analysis of JSE/FTSE multinational sustainability reports from 2016 to 2021. *International Journal of Corporate Social Responsibility 2024 9:1, 9*(1), 1–23. https://doi.org/DOI: 10.1186/S40991-024-00099-7

Kaushik, M., Choudhary, S., & Choudhary, M. (2024). Impact of emotional marketing on consumer decision making: A review (Article No. IJFMR240213659). [IJFMR]. *International Journal for Multidisciplinary Research*, *6*(2). https://www.ijfmr.com

Keen, S. (2011). Fast tracks to narrative empathy: Anthropomorphism and dehumanization in graphic narratives. *SubStance*, *40*(1), 135–155.

Keller, B., & Gierl, H. (2020). *Effectiveness of Animal Images in Advertising*. Marketing ZFP.

Kelman, H. C. (2006). *"Interests, relationships, identities: three central issues for individuals and groups in negotiating their social environment" in Annual review of psychology* (Fiske, S. T., Kazdin, A. E., & Schacter, D. L., Eds.). Vol. 57). Annual Reviews.

Kerr, W. E.. (2010). Aspectos pouco mencionados da biodiversidade amazônica. *Parcerias Estratégicas*, *6*(12), 20–41.

Kevan, P., & Imperatriz-Fonseca, V. L. (2002). *Pollinating bees: the conservation link between Agriculture and Nature*. Ministério do Desenvolvimento.

Khamis, S., Ang, L., & Welling, R. (2017). Self-branding, 'micro-celebrity' and the rise of Social Media Influencers. *Celebrity Studies*, *8*(2), 191–208. DOI: 10.1080/19392397.2016.1218292

Kharabsheh, R. (2024). Strategic Green Marketing: Exploring Consumer Perceptions and Preferences for Sustainable Products. *International Journal of Green Management and Business Studies*, *4*(1). Advance online publication. DOI: 10.56830/IJGMBS06202405

Ki, C.-W. (Chloe), Cuevas, L. M., Chong, S. M., & Lim, H. (2020). Influencer marketing: Social media influencers as human brands attaching to followers and yielding positive marketing results by fulfilling needs. *Journal of Retailing and Consumer Services, 55*, 102133. https://doi.org/https://doi.org/10.1016/j.jretconser.2020.102133

Kim, C. G., & Yang, O. S. (2024). Global Companies' Dynamic Response to Business Environment Uncertainty through Digital Transformation: Sustainable Digital Quality–Customer Value–Market Performance Relationships. *Sustainability*, *16*(15), 1–32. DOI: 10.3390/SU16156541

Kim, D.-G., & Wang, Z. (2023). The ethics of virtuality: Navigating the complexities of human-like virtual influencers in the social media marketing realm. *Frontiers in Communication*, *8*. Advance online publication. DOI: 10.3389/fcomm.2023.1205610

Kim, J.-Y., Ko, S.-H., & Choi, Y. (2024). Unveiling the power of social influencers in brand trust and brand identification. *South African Journal of Business Management*, *55*(1), 4087.

Kim, M., & Kim, J. (2020). How does a celebrity make fans happy? Interaction between celebrities and fans in the social media context. *Computers in Human Behavior*, *111*, 106419. DOI: 10.1016/j.chb.2020.106419

Kinnunen, J., Saunila, M., Ukko, J., & Rantanen, H. (2022). Strategic sustainability in the construction industry: Impacts on sustainability performance and brand. *Journal of Cleaner Production, 368*, 133063. DOI: 10.1016/J.JCLEPRO.2022.133063

Kirk, C. P. (2019). Dogs have masters, cats have staff: Consumers' psychological ownership and their economic valuation of pets. *Journal of Business Research, 99*, 414–429. DOI: 10.1016/j.jbusres.2019.02.057

KIRKSEY. S. E., & HELMREICH, S. (2010). THE EMERGENCE OF MULTISPECIES ETHNOGRAPHY. *Cultural Anthropology, 25*(4), 545–576. https://doi.org/https://doi.org/10.1111/j.1548-1360.2010.01069.x

Knowledge Policy. (2021). *O Estado da Segurança Alimentar e Nutricional no Mundo 2021* (SOFI). 2021. Disponível online: https://knowledge4policy.ec.europa.eu/publication/state-food-security-nutrition-world-2021-sofi_en. Acesso: 15 de agosto de 2023.

Knudson, D., Cable, T., & Beck, L. (2003). Interpretation of Cultural and Natural Resources. In *2ª Ed., Pennsylvania, Venture Publishing, Inc.*

Koch, N. (2025). The symbolic power of sustainability: Gulf megaprojects and the case of Expo City Dubai. *Cambridge Journal of Regions, Economy and Society, 18*(2), 279–292. DOI: 10.1093/CJRES/RSAE046

Kösoğlu, M. (2021). *Kişisel Arı Figürlü Pul Ve Para Koleksiyonu.*

Ko, T., Lee, J., Park, D., & Ryu, D. (2023). Supply chain transparency as a signal of ethical production. *Managerial and Decision Economics, 44*(3), 1565–1573. DOI: 10.1002/MDE.3765

Kothari, H., Choudhary, A., Jain, A., Singh, S., Prasad, K. D. V., & Vani, U. K. (2025). Impact of social media advertising on consumer behavior: Role of credibility, perceived authenticity, and sustainability. *Frontiers in Communication, 10*. Advance online publication. DOI: 10.3389/FCOMM.2025.1595796/BIBTEX

Kronenberg, J., & Bocian, M. (2022). Animal and plant images in corporate marketing communications are ecosystem services that should be paid for. *Ecosystem Services, 55*, 101464. DOI: 10.1016/j.ecoser.2022.101464

Kronrod, A., & Danziger, S. (2013). "Wii Will Rock You!" The Use and Effect of Figurative Language in Consumer Reviews of Hedonic and Utilitarian Consumption. *The Journal of Consumer Research, 40*(4), 726–739. DOI: 10.1086/671998

Kumar, K. (2019). A study of Veterinary Scholars' Perception of MOOCs. *Information and Learning Science, 120*(11–12), 743–757. DOI: 10.1108/ILS-04-2019-0031

Kumar, P., Oberoi, S., & Jaitly, R. C. (2023). Impact of Social Media Influencers on Consumer Engagement and Its Consequences in the Emerging Environment of Metaverse. In *Advances in marketing, customer relationship management, and e-services book series* (p. 225). IGI Global., DOI: 10.4018/978-1-6684-8898-0.ch014

Kundi, V., & Ernszt, I. (2024). The Phenomenon of Greenwashing: An Analysis of the Hungarian Regulation. *Journal of Sustainability Research, 6*(4). Advance online publication. DOI: 10.20900/JSR.20240066

Kwak, D. H., Kim, Y. K., & Hirt, E. R. (2011). Exploring the role of emotions on sport consumers' behavioral and cognitive responses to marketing stimuli. *European Sport Management Quarterly, 11*(3), 225–250.

Kwon, S., & Ha, S. (2023). Examining identity- and bond-based hashtag community identification: The moderating role of self-brand connections. *Journal of Research in Interactive Marketing, 17*(1), 78–93. DOI: 10.1108/JRIM-07-2021-0183

Labrecque, L. I. (2014). Fostering Consumer–Brand Relationships in Social Media Environments: The Role of Parasocial Interaction. *Journal of Interactive Marketing, 28*(2), 134–148. DOI: 10.1016/j.intmar.2013.12.003

Laetro. (2025). Digital Marketing Trends 2025. Laetro. https://www.laetro.com/blog/digital-marketing-trends-2025

Lafferty, B. A. (2001). Emotional Branding: The New Paradigm for Connecting Brands to People20011Marc Gobé. Emotional Branding: The New Paradigm for Connecting Brands to People. New York, NY: Allworth Press 2001. iii + 319 pp., ISBN: ISBN: 1-58115-078-4 US $24.95. *Journal of Product and Brand Management, 10*(7), 466–469. DOI: 10.1108/jpbm.2001.10.7.466.1

Łaszkiewicz, A. (2023). THE USE OF INFLUENCER MARKETING IN MARKETING COMMUNICATION OF PLACES. *Scientific Papers of Silesian University of Technology Organization and Management Series, 2023*(173), 445. DOI: 10.29119/1641-3466.2023.173.29

Laurent-Simpson, A. (2021). "This Is My Son Rosenberg". In Just Like Family.

Lavertu, L., Kulow, K., Cowan, K., & Marder, B. (2025). Petfluencers, the fur-mula for sincere endorsements: Examining how and when pets exhibit greater persuasion as influencers. *Journal of Advertising Research*, •••, 1–16.

Lavertu, L., Kulow, K., Cowan, K., & Marder, B. (2025). Petfluencers, the fur-mula for sincere endorsements: Examining how and when pets exhibit greater persuasion as influencers. *Journal of Consumer Behaviour*. Advance online publication. DOI: 10.1080/00218499.2025.2463707

LBBOnline. (2021). How Erste Group's Christmas ads became a festive favourite. https://lbbonline.com/news/how-erste-groups-christmas-ads-became-a-festive-favourite

Leal Filho, W., Fedoruk, M., Eustachio, J. H. P. P., Barbir, J., Lisovska, T., Lingos, A., & Baars, C. (2023). How the war in Ukraine affects food security. *Foods*, *12*(21), 3996. DOI: 10.3390/foods12213996 PMID: 37959115

Lee, H. H. (2023). *How Do Ad-Blockers Affect Various Stakeholders? Perspectives from Consumers, Marketers, and Legal Professionals*. Indiana University. https://www.proquest.com/openview/f2b2946ccf14ad8e4ad9f8766f20246b/1?pq-origsite=gscholar&cbl=18750&diss=y

Lee, S. Y., Kim, Y., & Kim, Y. (2021). Engaging consumers with corporate social responsibility campaigns: The roles of interactivity, psychological empowerment, and identification. *Journal of Business Research*, *134*, 507–517. DOI: 10.1016/j.jbusres.2021.05.062

Leite, E. T. (2025). The power of strategies in sports marketing sponsorship, licensing, and advertising in action. *Brazilian Journal of Development*, *11*(5), e79628–e79628.

Lelo de Larrea, G., & Smith, S. J. (2025). Bear E. Drooley: Achieving Business Growth With the Help of Pets-In-Residence and Resort Mascots. *Journal of Hospitality & Tourism Cases*, *13*(1), 3–11. DOI: 10.1177/21649987231221484

Lembregts, C., & Cadario, R. (2024). Consumer-driven climate mitigation: Exploring barriers and solutions in studying higher mitigation potential behaviors. *International Journal of Research in Marketing*, *41*(3), 513–528. DOI: 10.1016/j.ijresmar.2024.04.001

Levy, S. J. (2014). How new, how dominant? In *The Service-Dominant Logic of Marketing* (pp. 57–64). Routledge.

Liang, L., & Cheong, C. Y. M. (2025). Brand identity construction through the heritage of Chinese destination logos. *Semiotica*, *2025*(263), 241–277.

Liang, Y., Xu, Y., Lai, D., Hua, G., Huang, D., Wang, H., Li, H., & Han, L. (2022). Emerging market for pork with animal welfare attribute in China: An ethical perspective. *Meat Science*, *195*, 108994. DOI: 10.1016/j.meatsci.2022.108994

Liao, H., Lyon, C. J., Ying, B., & Hu, T. (2024). Climate change, its impact on emerging infectious diseases and new technologies to combat the challenge. *Emerging Microbes & Infections*, *13*(1). Advance online publication. DOI: 10.1080/22221751.2024.2356143 PMID: 38767202

Lindimore, J. (2020). People, Property, Or Pet-Influencers? *J. Animal & Env't L.*, *12*, 44. https://heinonline.org/HOL/LandingPage?handle=hein.journals/jael12&div=7&id=&page=

Li, R. K. (2025). The Impact of Social Media Influencers on Gen Z's Online Purchase Decisions. *Advances in Economics Management and Political Sciences*, *150*(1), 178. DOI: 10.54254/2754-1169/2024.19299

Liu, L., & Zhao, H. (2024). Research on consumers' purchase intention of cultural and creative products—Metaphor design based on traditional cultural symbols. *PLoS One*. Advance online publication. DOI: 10.1371/journal.pone.0301678

Liu, P. (2024). Optimizing E-commerce Operational Efficiency and Customer Experience Through Data Analytics and Technological Innovation. *Advances in Economics Management and Political Sciences*, *100*(1), 14. DOI: 10.54254/2754-1169/100/20241121

Liu, Y., Chang, X., Yang, S., Li, Z., & Wu, Y. (2024). "Pets make you spend more!" Impact of pet ownership on consumer purchase decisions. *Journal of Business Research*, *174*, 114838. DOI: 10.1016/j.jbusres.2024.114838

Lloyd, S., & Woodside, A. G. (2013). Animals, archetypes, and advertising (A3): The theory and the practice of customer brand symbolism. *Journal of Marketing Management*, *29*(1-2), 5–25.

Looi, J., & Kahlor, L. A. (2024). Artificial Intelligence in Influencer Marketing: A Mixed-Method Comparison of Human and Virtual Influencers on Instagram. *Journal of Interactive Advertising*, *24*(2), 107. DOI: 10.1080/15252019.2024.2313721

Lopez, D. V. (2024). Well-being and Sustainable Development: An Exploratory Approach from a Marketing Perspective. *European Journal of Sustainable Development*, *13*(1), 205–205. DOI: 10.14207/EJSD.2024.V13N1P205

López-Teijeiro, A., Barreiro-Piñeiro, N., Eibes, G., & Martínez-Costas, J. (2025). Nearly complete depolymerization of untreated post-consumer plastic with an immobilized and reusable PET hydrolase. *Journal of Hazardous Materials*, *495*. Advance online publication. DOI: 10.1016/j.jhazmat.2025.138789 PMID: 40466280

Lotun, S. (2022). *Social media for social good: Understanding, creating, and harnessing the strength of parasocial relationships* (Doctoral dissertation, University of Essex). https://repository.essex.ac.uk/33077/

Lou, C., & Yuan, S. (2019). Influencer Marketing: How Message Value and Credibility Affect Consumer Trust of Branded Content on Social Media. *Journal of Interactive Advertising*, *19*(1), 58–73. DOI: 10.1080/15252019.2018.1533501

Loureiro, S. M. C., & Lopes, J. (2019). How corporate social responsibility initiatives in social media affect awareness and customer engagement. *Journal of Promotion Management, 25*(3), 378–403. DOI: 10.1080/10496491.2019.1557815

Luckerson, V. (2014, february 3). This was the most successful commercial of the Super Bowl. TIME. https://time.com/3870/budweiser-puppy-love-super-bowl-commercial

Luna-Amador, J., Caraballo-Payares, A., & Escobar-Espinoza, A. (2025). *Brand activism: Research trends and cluster analysis.* Departamento de Economía y Administración, Universidad de Cartagena., DOI: 10.1016/j.iedeen.2025.100279

Machado, A. F., de Oliveira, M. L., & de Faria, A. L. (2025). *Social Innovation Through Rural Tourism and Its Benefits for Entre Serras, Lima Duarte – MG, Brazil:* A Perspective From the Border Areas of the Territory. In B. Sousa (Ed.), Cross-Border Regions Cooperation and Implications for Organizations (pp. 339-366). IGI Global Scientific Publishing. DOI: 10.4018/979-8-3373-1912-4.ch012

Maddox, J. (2022). *The Internet is for cats: How animal images shape our digital lives.* Rutgers University Press., https://books.google.co.in/books?hl=en&lr=&id=zsaHEAAAQBAJ&oi=fnd&pg=PP1&dq=When+it+comes+to+petfluencers,+these+connections+hit+harder+because+animals+come+off+as+sweet,+harmless,+and+funny&ots=EGdl6LFK5p&sig=W2z7bpuaATZEihKzhpRuRftuBH4&redir_esc=y#v=onepage&q&f=false

Maghsoudi, M., Shokouhyar, S., Sanaee, N., & Shokoohyar, S. (2025). Enhancing sustainability reporting practices in the notebook manufacturing industry: A multi-faceted analysis integrating traditional reports and social media data. *Annals of Operations Research, 345*(1), 317–349. DOI: 10.1007/S10479-024-06343-4/METRICS

Maia-Silva, C.. (2020). Stingless Bees (Melipona subnitida) Overcome Severe Drought Events in the Brazilian Tropical Dry Forest by Opting for High-Profit Food Sources. *Neotropical Entomology, 49*(4), 595–603. DOI: 10.1007/s13744-019-00756-8 PMID: 32103461

Malamud, R. (2012). *Animal movies guide.* Greenwood.

Malancus, R. N., Arsenoaia, V. N., & Ghita, M. (2024). Comparative analysis of stress responses in dogs and cats during the covid-19 pandemic: A focus on cortisol, total leukocytes, eosinophils, and behavioral changes; [Análise comparativa das respostas ao estresse em cães e gatos durante a pandemia de covid-. *Arquivo Brasileiro de Medicina Veterinária e Zootecnia, 76*(3). Advance online publication. DOI: 10.1590/1678-4162-13153

Mansoor, M., Paul, J., Khan, T. I., Abukhait, R., & Hussain, D. (2025). Customer evangelists: Elevating hospitality through digital competence, brand image, and corporate social responsibility. *Journal of Business Research, 165*, 113181. DOI: 10.1016/j.ijhm.2025.104085

Marcelino, J., Braese, C., Christmon, K., Evans, J. D., Gilligan, T., Giray, T., Nearman, A., Niño, E. L., Rose, R., Sheppard, W. S., vanEngelsdorp, D., & Ellis, J. D. (2022). O movimento das abelhas ocidentais (*Apis mellifera L.*) entre estados e territórios dos EUA: História, benefícios, riscos e estratégias de mitigação. *Frontiers in Ecology and Evolution, 10*, 850600. DOI: 10.3389/fevo.2022.850600

Mardani, P. B., Ayuningtyas, F., & Putri, J. N. (2019). Creative Strategies to Drive Brand Awareness (Case of "Forever Against Animal Testing Campaign" The Body Shop Indonesia). International Journal of Multicultural and Multireligious Understanding.

Margaron, A. (2024). *The Eye, the Heart, and the Network: the Humanistic Blogging of Tumblr's Webweaving Community* (Doctoral dissertation, Concordia University). Margaron_MA_F2024.pdf

Mark, M., & Pearson, C. S. (2022). *The hero and the outlaw: Building extraordinary brands through the power of archetypes*. McGraw Hill-Ascent Audio.

Martel, A. C., Zeggane, S., Aurières, C., Drajnudel, P., Faucon, J. P., & Aubert, M. (2007). Acaricide residues in honey and wax after treatment of honey bee colonies with Apivar or Asuntol 50. *Apidologie, 38*, 534–544.

Martin, D., Palakshappa, N., & Woodside, A. (2019). Consumer metaphoria: Uncovering the automaticity of animal, product/brand, and country meanings. *Australasian Marketing Journal, 27*(2). Advance online publication. DOI: 10.1016/j.ausmj.2018.08.001

Martini, E., Shidqi, M. N., Hurriyati, R., & Widjajanta, B. (2022). *The Impact of Brand Experience on Consumer Engagement*. Advances in Economics, Business and Management Research/Advances in Economics, Business and Management Research., DOI: 10.2991/aebmr.k.220701.062

Martins, A. M., & Cró, S. (2022). Airline stock markets reaction to the COVID-19 outbreak and vaccines: An event study. *Journal of Air Transport Management, 105*. Advance online publication. DOI: 10.1016/j.jairtraman.2022.102281 PMID: 36034526

Marvin, S., Sorenson, K., & Stevens, J. R. (2022). Bringing human-animal interaction to sport: Potential impacts on athletic performance. *European Journal of Sport Science*, *22*(7), 955–963. PMID: 33840355

Marwick, A. E. (2015). Instafame: Luxury Selfies in the Attention Economy. *Public Culture*, *27*(1), 137–160. DOI: 10.1215/08992363-2798379

Masilamani, N., & Ganapathy, D. (2020). Knowledge and awareness about MERS-CoV among the dental students in Chennai. *International Journal of Research in Pharmaceutical Sciences, 11*(Special Issue 1), 847–851. https://doi.org/DOI: 10.26452/ijrps.v11iSPL1.3091

Maulidian, M., Zahra, S. F., Nadela, A. T., & Fitriani, A. (2023). Content categories on Instagram: From promotional to interactivity for business development. *Journal of Enterprise and Development*, *5*(1), 15. DOI: 10.20414/jed.v5i1.6774

Mayo, D. T., Helms, M., & Mayo, C. (2009). Pets in Print Advertising-Are We Seeing More of Rover and Fluffy? A Content Analysis of Four Popular Magazines. *Academy of Marketing Studies Journal*.

Mbiti, J. S. (1990). *African religions & philosophy*. Heinemann.

McCracken, G. (1986). Culture and Consumption: A Theoretical Account of the Structure and Movement of the Cultural Meaning of Consumer Goods. *The Journal of Consumer Research*, *13*(1), 71–84. DOI: 10.1086/209048

McEwen, W. J. (2005). *Married to the brand: Why consumers bond with some brands for life*. Simon and Schuster. https://books.google.co.in/books?hl=en&lr=&id=ydpDCwAAQBAJ&oi=fnd&pg=PA1&dq=That+makes+them+perfect+for+industries+like+pet+care,+lifestyle,+wellness,+or+even+travel,+where+their+authentic+appeal+turns+fans+into+loyal+customers.&ots=TKYWITQ3iY&sig=KQNUrs96UdRVyM9hzW79yEKUFUs&redir_esc=y#v=onepage&q&f=false

McGrane, C., Hjorth, L., & Murray, P. (2024). "We Make Them Our Kin": Australian Older Adult's Playful Kinship Practices Through Sharing Animal Images on Social Media. *Social Media + Society*, *10*(4). Advance online publication. DOI: 10.1177/20563051241306540/ASSET/B3196695-E21C-4311-93DC-D567875D3A0D/ASSETS/IMAGES/LARGE/10.1177_20563051241306540-FIG5.JPG

Mcleod, S. (n.d.). *Maslow's Hierarchy of Needs*. https://doi.org/DOI: 10.5281/zenodo.15240897

Mehta, A. K., Yashoda, L., Selvakumar, P., Mishra, B. R., Das, A., & C. T. C., M. (2025). Teaching methods: Techniques for disadvantaged learners. In S. Hai-Jew (Ed.), Mitigating learner disadvantages in teaching and learning (pp. 181–206). IGI Global Scientific Publishing. https://doi.org/DOI: 10.4018/979-8-3693-8623-1.ch007

Melkko, A. (n.d.). *CONSUMER BEHAVIOR AMONG DOG OWNERS How trends spread from the US to small businesses in Finland.*

Melo, G. A. R. (2020). Stingless Bees (Meliponini). Encyclopedia of Social Insects, pp. 1–18.

Melo, D. (2001). *Salazarismo e Cultura Popular (1933 - 1958).* Instituto de Ciências Sociais da Universidade de Lisboa.

Menon, J., Shanmugam, N., Patel, K., Hakeem, A., Reddy, M. S., & Rela, M. (2020). Awareness and concerns about novel coronavirus disease 2019 (COVID-19) among parents of pediatric liver transplant recipients. *Pediatric Transplantation, 24*(8). Advance online publication. DOI: 10.1111/petr.13805 PMID: 32663351

Merskin, D. (2021). Circle of responsibility: Animals as stakeholders. In Bowen, D., Hayward, A. M., & James, K. (Eds.), *Public relations for social responsibility.* Emerald Publishing., DOI: 10.1108/9781800431676

Mesiranta, N., Mattila, M., Koskinen, O., & Närvänen, E. (2024). Circular Consumption Practices as Matters of Care. *Journal of Business Ethics, 200*(1), 13–30. DOI: 10.1007/S10551-024-05888-5/TABLES/1

Michener, C. D. (2007). *The bees of the word* (2nd ed.). Johns Hopkins.

Mick, D. G. (1986). Consumer research and semiotics: Exploring the morphology of signs, symbols, and significance. *The Journal of Consumer Research, 13*(2), 196–213.

Micle, B. G. (2020). The Influencer Role of Charismatic Renewal in the Spirituality of Post-Covid Society. *Dialogo, 7*(2), 247-259. https://www.ceeol.com/search/article-detail?id=964351

Migkos, S. P., Giannakopoulos, N. T., & Σακάς, Δ. Π. (2025). Impact of Influencer Marketing on Consumer Behavior and Online Shopping Preferences. DOI: 10.20944/preprints202504.0787.v1

Mimoso, J. M. (2010). Origem e Evolução do Galo de Barcelos. *Olaria: Estudos Arqueológicos, Históricos e Etnológicos*, 143–159.

Möhrer, M. (2022). *Shared Value Statement: New Perspectives on Measuring Business Value Creation.* 111–131. https://doi.org/DOI: 10.1007/978-3-030-86526-9_7

Morens, D. M., & Fauci, A. S. (2020). Emerging Pandemic Diseases: How We Got to COVID-19. *Cell, 182*(5), 1077–1092. DOI: 10.1016/j.cell.2020.08.021 PMID: 32846157

Mota-Rojas, D., Mariti, C., Zdeinert, A., Riggio, G., Mora-Medina, P., Reyes, A. del M., Gazzano, A., Domínguez-Oliva, A., Lezama-García, K., José-Pérez, N., & Hernández-Ávalos, I. (2021). Anthropomorphism and its adverse effects on the distress and welfare of companion animals. *Animals (Basel), 11*(11), 3263. DOI: 10.3390/ani11113263

Muniz, F., Guzmán, F., Paswan, A. K., & Crawford, H. J. (2019). The immediate effect of corporate social responsibility on consumer-based brand equity. *Journal of Product and Brand Management*. Advance online publication. DOI: 10.1108/JPBM-09-2018-2036

Murár, P., & Kubovics, M. (2023). Using AI to Create Content Designed for Marketing Communications. European Conference on Innovation and Entrepreneurship, 18(1), 660. DOI: 10.34190/ecie.18.1.1638

Myers, S., Sen, S., Syrdal, H., & Woodroof, P. (2022). The impact of persuasion knowledge cues on social media engagement: A look at pet influencer marketing. *Journal of Interactive Advertising*, *22*(1), 43–60. DOI: 10.1080/10696679.2022.2093224

Naderer, B., Matthes, J., & Zeller, P. (2018). Placing snacks in children's movies: Cognitive, evaluative, and conative effects of product placements with character product interaction. *International Journal of Advertising*, *37*, 852–870. DOI: 10.1080/02650487.2017.1348034

Nairn, A., & Fine, C. (2008). Who's messing with my mind? *International Journal of Advertising*, *27*, 447–470. DOI: 10.2501/S0265048708080062

Nassani, A. A., Yousaf, Z., Grigorescu, A., & Popa, A. (2023). Green and Environmental Marketing Strategies and Ethical Consumption: Evidence from the Tourism Sector. *Sustainability*, *15*(16), 1–13. DOI: 10.3390/SU151612199

National Geographic Brasil. (2022). Abelhas: por que são importantes e como podemos evitar seu desaparecimento. *National Geographic Brasil*. Disponível em: https://www.nationalgeographicbrasil.com/animais/2022/05/abelhas-por-que-sao-importantes-e-como-podemos-evitar-seu-desaparecimento. Acesso em: 05/08/2025.

Neff, J. L., & Simpson, B. B. (1993). Bees, Pollination Systems and Plant Diversity. In Lasalle, J., & Gauld, I. D. (Eds.), *Hyme-noptera and Biodiversity* (pp. 143–167). CAB International.

Nejati, M., & Shafaei, A. (2023). Why do employees respond differently to corporate social responsibility? A study of substantive and symbolic corporate social responsibility. *Corporate Social Responsibility and Environmental Management, 30*(4), 2066–2080. DOI: 10.1002/CSR.2474

Nhemachena, C., Dahiya, S., Gokah, I., Echessah, P., Gichuri, M., Nhlengethwa, S., Djido, A., & Muthini, D. (2022). *Os impactos do conflito Rússia-Ucrânia nos preços dos alimentos e na segurança alimentar e nutricional na África*. Disponível online: https://agra.org/wp-content/uploads/2022/04/Impacts-of-the-Russia-Ukraine-conflict-2.pdf. Acesso: 15 de agosto de 2023.

Nielsen, I. Q. (2024). Pet Care Growing Faster Than Other Departments. Pet Food Processing. https://www.petfoodprocessing.net/articles/18052-nielseniq-pet-care-growing-faster-than-other-departments

Nielsen, I. Q. (2024). The Full View of The Pet Industry: A Comprehensive Analysis of Consumer and Product Trends. NielsenIQ. [https://nielseniq.com/global/en/insights/analysis/2024/the-full-view-of-the-pet-industry-a-comprehensive-analysis-of-consumer-and-product-trends/](https://nielseniq.com/global/en/insights/analysis/2024/the-full-view-of-the-pet

Nielsen, I. Q. (2024). Unveils Trending Consumer Searches. Pet Food Processing. https://www.petfoodprocessing.net/articles/15722-nielseniq-unveils-trending-consumer-searches

Nirupama, M. I., Galdolage, B. S., Al-Daoud, K., Vasudevan, A., Mohammad, S., Vasumathi, A., & Qin, P. (2025). The effect of conspicuous consumption on social identity formation in the branded clothing sector: The mediating effect of product symbolism. *Uncertain Supply Chain Management, 13*, 395–408. DOI: 10.5267/j.uscm.2024.9.013

Nittono, H., Fukushima, M., Yano, A., & Moriya, H. (2012). The Power of Kawaii: Viewing Cute Images Promotes a Careful Behavior and Narrows Attentional Focus. *PLoS One, 7*(9), e46362. DOI: 10.1371/journal.pone.0046362 PMID: 23050022

Noble, C. H., Bing, M. N., & Bogoviyeva, E. (2013). The effects of brand metaphors as design innovation: A test of congruency hypotheses. *Journal of Product Innovation Management, 31*(1), 32–45. DOI: 10.1111/jpim.12067

Nobre, C. A., Sampaio, G., Borma, L. S., & Cardoso, M., & outros. (2016). Riscos de uso da terra e mudanças climáticas na Amazônia e a necessidade de um novo paradigma de desenvolvimento sustentável. *Proceedings of the National Academy of Sciences, 113*(39), 10759–10768. DOI: 10.1073/pnas.1605516113

Nogueira-Couto, R. H. (1998). *As abelhas na manutenção da biodiversidade e geração de rendas.* In: Congresso Brasileiro de Apicultura, 12, Anais [...] Salvador: p. 101.

Nogueira, D. S., Vollet Neto, A., Cassinelli, M. P., dos Santos-Silva, J. A., do Nascimento, F. S., & de Oliveira, A. L. L. (2023). *As abelhas "sem-ferrão" dos biomas brasileiros:* O Brasil possui a maior biodiversidade de abelhas "sem-ferrão" do planeta, essenciais para o funcionamento dos ecossistemas e com grande potencial econômico. *Ciência e Cultura, 75*(4), e20230053. DOI: 10.5935/2317-6660.20230053

Novais, S. M. A.. (2016). Effects of a possible pollinator crisis on food crop production in Brazil. *PLoS One, 11*(11), 1–12. PMID: 27902787

Odoom, R., Odoom, P. T., Amu, P. Y., & Adams, M. (2025). Sustainable digital marketing practices and consumer brand engagement – a brand reputation mediation investigation. *Journal of Strategic Marketing, 33*(2), 254–270. DOI: 10.1080/0965254X.2025.2453690

Ogilvie, J. E.. (2017). Interannual bumble bee abundance is driven by indirect climate effects on floral resource phenolo-gy. *Ecology Letters, 20*(12), 1507–1515. PMID: 29124863

Ogle, A. D., Graham, D. J., Lucas-Thompson, R. G., & Roberto, C. A. (2017). Influence of cartoon media characters on children's attention to and preference for food and beverage products. *Journal of the Academy of Nutrition and Dietetics, 117*, 265–270. DOI: 10.1016/j.jand.2016.08.01 PMID: 27793520

Oleárová, M., & Bačík, R. (2023). A Relationship Between Social Media Marketing and Brand Awareness Increase. 15TH GLOBAL CONFERENCE ON BUSINESS AND SOCIAL SCIENCES ON 14 - 15 SEPTEMBER 2023. *NOVOTEL BANGKOK PLATINUM PRATUNAM, THAILAND., 184.* Advance online publication. DOI: 10.35609/gcbssproceeding.2023.1

Oliver, R. L. (1999). Whence consumer loyalty? *Journal of Marketing, 63*(Special Issue), 33–44. DOI: 10.2307/1252099

Omasta, M., & Chappell, D. (Eds.). (2015). *Play, performance, and identity: How institutions structure ludic spaces.* Routledge.

ONU - United Nations. (2025). *ONU destaca papel das abelhas na segurança alimentar e na saúde de ecossistemas BR.* UN News. https://news.un.org/pt/story/2025/05/1848611

Onyas, W. I., & Ryan, A. (2015). Exploring the brand's world-as-assemblage: The brand as a market shaping device. *Journal of Marketing Management, 31*, 141–166. DOI: 10.1080/0267257X.2014.977333

Oppong-Tawiah, D., & Webster, J. (2023). Corporate Sustainability Communication as 'Fake News': Firms' Greenwashing on Twitter. *Sustainability*, *15*(8), 1–26. DOI: 10.3390/SU15086683/S1

Osmanova, I., Ozerden, S., Dalal, B., & Ibrahim, B. (2023). Examining the Relationship between Brand Symbolism and Brand Evangelism through Consumer Brand Identification: Evidence from Starbucks Coffee Brand. *Sustainability*, *15*(2), 1–15. DOI: 10.3390/SU15021684

Oxman, E. (2010). Sensing the image: Roland Barthes and the affect of the visual. *SubStance*, *39*(2), 71–90. DOI: 10.1353/sub.0.0083

Palladino, A., Lee, M., & Zhou, X. (2022). An analysis of Olympic mascot design toward attitude and purchase intention. *International Journal of Sport Communication*, *15*(3), 190–196. DOI: 10.1123/ijsc.2022-0052

Palmer, C. (2003). *Ethics and animals*. Oxford University Press.

Palusuk, N., Koles, B., & Hasan, R. (2019). 'All you need is brand love': A critical review and comprehensive conceptual framework for brand love. *Journal of Marketing Management*, *35*(1–2), 97–129.

Park, H. W., Lim, C. V., Zhu, Y. P., & Omar, M. (2024). Decoding the Relationship of Artificial Intelligence, Advertising, and Generative Models. DOI: 10.20944/preprints202401.0373.v1

Paulino, E., Gocuyo, N., Rington, D., Isip, L., Mazo, P. N., Romero, R., Tan, R., & Boquila, L.-R. (2025). Mapping the Fur Landscape: A Dual Cluster Analysis of Relationship-Driven and Purchase-Based Segmentation of the Pet Care Market. *Journal of Business and Management Studies*, *7*(3), 107–119. DOI: 10.32996/jbms.2025.7.3.10

Pawle, J., & Cooper, P. (2006). Measuring Emotion—Lovemarks, The Future Beyond Brands. *Journal of Advertising Research*, *46*(1), 38–48. DOI: 10.2501/S0021849906060053

PawPrint Digital. (2025). 2025 Trends and Innovations Shaping the Future of Pet Care. PawPrint Digital. https://pawprint.digital/p/2025-trends-innovations

Payne, A., & Frow, P. (2013). *Strategic customer management: Integrating relationship marketing and CRM*. Cambridge University Press., DOI: 10.1017/CBO9781139057417

Pegoraro, A., Ferraz, M. M., Pfaw, E., Moura, M. E. K., Nunes, T. M. D., Nienow, V. V., Polak, L., & Borio, C. L. Krüg. (2017). *Aspectos práticos e técnicos da apicultura no Sul do Brasil.* Curitiba, PR: Universidade Federal do Paraná.

Peng, C. (2023). Influencer Marketing: Statistics and Skepticism. *Open Journal of Business and Management, 11*(2), 744. DOI: 10.4236/ojbm.2023.112040

Pereira, F. (2025). *Resiliência das colmeias diante de mudanças climáticas: estratégias de mitigação e adaptação*. Embrapa Meio-Norte.

Pereira, S. N., Alves, L. H. S., da Costa, R. F. R., Prezoto, F., & Teixeira, E. W. (2021). Occurrence of the small hive beetle (Aethina tumida) in Melipona rufiventris colonies in Brazil. *Sociobiology*, *68*(1), e6021. DOI: 10.13102/sociobiology.v68i1.6021

Pet Business Guide. (2025). Top 5 Marketing Trends Pet Businesses Can't Ignore in 2025. Pet Business Guide. https://petbusinessguide.com/top-5-marketing-trends-pet-businesses-cant-ignore-in-2025/

Pet Care Marketing Pros. (2025). 5 Explosive Digital Marketing Strategies for Pet Care Businesses in 2025. Pet Care Marketing Pros. https://petcaremarketingpros.com/5-explosive-digital-marketing-strategies-for-pet-care-businesses-in-2025/

Petty, R. E., & Cacioppo, J. T. (2012). *Communication and persuasion: Central and peripheral routes to attitude change*. Springer Science & Business Media.

Pew Research Center. (2018). Many turn to YouTube for children's content, news, how-to lessons. Available at: https://www.pewinternet.org/2018/11/07/many-turn-to-youtube-for-childrens-content-news-how-to-lessons/ (Accessed November 21, 2019).

Pignati, W. A., Lima, F. A. N. de S., de Lara, S. S., Correa, M. L. M., Barbosa, J. R., Leão, L. H. da C., & Pignatti, M. G. (2017). Distribuição espacial do uso de agrotóxicos no Brasil: Uma ferramenta para a Vigilância em Saúde [Spatial distribution of pesticide use in Brazil: A strategy for Health Surveillance]. *Ciencia & Saude Coletiva*, *22*(10), 3319–3328. DOI: 10.1590/1413-812320172210.17742017 PMID: 29069184

Pilley, J. W., & Hinzmann, H. (2014). *Chaser: Unlocking the genius of the dog who knows 1000 words*. Simon and Schuster. https://books.google.co.in/books?hl=en&lr=&id=Cve7DwAAQBAJ&oi=fnd&pg=PT10&dq=%E2%80%A2%09Pilley,+J.+W.,+%26+Hinzmann,+H.+(2014).+Chaser:+Unlocking+the+genius+of+the+dog+who+knows+1000+words.+Simon+and+Schuster.&ots=ve7kZg5lKl&sig=HMAdj40B31hRcF0C7ZG26trylYE&redir_esc=y#v=onepage&q&f=false

Pires de Lima, F. (1965). *A Lenda do Senhor do Galo de Barcelos e o Milagre do Enforcado*. Gabinete de Etnografia da FNAT.

Pires, A. P.. (2020). Análise sensorial de méis de duas espécies de abelhas sem ferrão de Santarém, Pará. *Brazilian Journal of Development*, *6*(9), 72680–72693.

Podhovnik, E. (2023). *Purrieties of Language*. Cambridge University Press., https://books.google.co.in/books?hl=en&lr=&id=womzEAAAQBAJ&oi=fnd&pg=PR12&dq=Petfluencers+shine+at+spinning+short,+-captivating+tales+through+photos,+videos,+or+gifs&ots=ineT4xT-5vO&sig=98PxxlO8o6-qCp-ZT7ioxa9C8ys&redir_esc=y#v=onepage&q&f=false

Popp, B., Germelmann, C. C., & Jung, B. (2016). We love to hate them! Social media-based anti-brand communities in professional football. *International Journal of Sports Marketing & Sponsorship*, *17*(4), 349–367.

Potts, S. G.. (2016). Safeguarding pollinators and their values to human well-being. *Nature*, *540*(7632), 220–229. PMID: 27894123

Pradeep, E., Mukherjee, S. K., Selvakumar, P., Koppaka, A. K., Chandel, P. S., & Vats, C. (2025). Empowering social media users with ethical AI. In Chakraborty, S. (Ed.), *Ethical AI solutions for addressing social media influence and hate speech* (pp. 91–118). IGI Global Scientific Publishing., DOI: 10.4018/979-8-3693-9904-0.ch005

Prihatiningrum, R. R. Y., Supraptiningsih, J. D., Lutfi, L., Imron, A., & Fithoni, A. (2024). Sustainable Marketing Strategies: Aligning Brand Values with Consumer Demand for Environmental Responsibility. *Global International Journal of Innovative Research*, *2*(9), 2271–2283. DOI: 10.59613/GLOBAL.V2I9.304

Provensi, T., Marcon, M. L., Schmidt, J. L., Rodrigues, C. de O., & Sehnem, S. (2024). Sustainability and Innovation in the Pet Industry: An Analysis from the Perspective of Ecological Modernization Theory. *Revista de Administração de Empresas, 64*(3), e2023-0247. https://doi.org/DOI: 10.1590/S0034-759020240301

Putra Pratama, A., & Koentoro Djati, D. (2021). Balanced messaging for experienced laptop consumers. *Jurnal Sosioteknologi*, *20*(3), 299–311. DOI: 10.5614/SOSTEK.ITBJ.2021.20.3.2

Quality Pet Products. (2025). Sustainable Practices in Pet Product Manufacturing. Quality Pet Products. https://www.qualitypetproducts.com/

Rafique, N., Hassan, I., & Adil, M. (2025). *Flight PK8303 crash: a disastrous failure of human factors*. CASE Journal., DOI: 10.1108/TCJ-08-2024-0234

Rani, A., Roy, A., Boaler, M., & Itam, U. J. (2022). Determinants of Influencer Credibility and Platform Credibility to Understand the Effectiveness of Indian Fashion Influencers. *International Journal of Online Marketing*, *12*(1), 1. DOI: 10.4018/ijom.299399

Ranjitha, P. K., Selvakumar, P., Anute, N., Manjunath, T., Sureshkrishna, G., & Pougajendy, S. (2025). Transportation challenges in islands tourism. In Hassan, V. (Ed.), *Navigating mass tourism to island destinations: Preservation and cultural heritage challenges* (pp. 287–312). IGI Global Scientific Publishing., DOI: 10.4018/979-8-3693-9107-5.ch01

Rao, P. V.. (2016). Biological and therapeutic effects of honey produced by honey bees and stingless bees: A comparative review. *Revista Brasileira de Farmacognosia*, *26*(5), 657–664.

Raso, G., & Cherubini, D. (2024). The sport tourism and regional economic development: A systematic review. *Scientific Journal of Sport and Performance*, *3*(1), 108–121.

Rausch, T. M., & Kopplin, C. S. (2021). Bridge the gap: Consumers' purchase intention and behavior regarding sustainable clothing. *Journal of Cleaner Production*, *278*. Advance online publication. DOI: 10.1016/J.JCLEPRO.2020.123882

Recabarren, J. I., Castillo, E., García, A., & Cantallopts, J. (2024). Product differentiation in mineral commodities based on sustainability indicators: The case of copper mining. *Journal of Cleaner Production*, *476*, 143786. DOI: 10.1016/J.JCLEPRO.2024.143786

Reddy, B. V. V., & A. S., S. (2023). Delineation on Celebrity Endorsement and Brand Mascot Towards Attitudes, Beliefs, Purchase Intention and Behaviour of the Consumers. SSRN *Electronic Journal*. https://doi.org/DOI: 10.2139/SSRN.4330745

Reddy, B. V. V., & Sathish, A. S. (2023). Creating Connections Through Characters: A Study of Brand Mascots and Their Influence on Consumer Purchase Intentions. *Advances in Decision Sciences*, *27*(4), 1–17.

Reis, T. dos S. M., Drumond, M. V. G., Gomes, P. R., Tonacio, C. M. S. de P., & Junior, P. C. T. (2025). Environmental Compliance, ESG Practices, and Stakeholder Capitalism: Challenges For Sustainable Corporate Management. *Revista de Gestão - RGSA*, *19*(3). https://doi.org/DOI: 10.24857/rgsa.v19n3-071

Resende, R. (2016). Técnica de Investigação Qualitativa: ETCI. *Journal of Sport Pedagogy & Research*, *1*, 50–57.

Retail, O. Meeting Customers Where They Shop. (2025). MultiDev. https://multidev.com/blog/pet-industry-trends/

Rexhepi, G., Kurtishi, S., & Bexheti, G. (2013). Corporate social responsibility (CSR) and innovation: The drivers of business growth? *Procedia: Social and Behavioral Sciences, 75*, 532–541. DOI: 10.1016/j.sbspro.2013.04.058

Ribeiro, R. E.; Silva, E. da C.; Silva, J. M.; Sousa, S. B.; Moura, T. T.; Fernandes, V. E. S. B.; Gurjão, T. A.; Matias, P. F. J.; De Assys, R. M. Da M. S.; Henrique, M. N. H. M.; Nascimento Júnior, A. A.; Januário, D. M. P.; Medeiros, A. C. de. (2023). *Contaminação do mel, cuidados e controles - revisão.* Caderno Verde de Agroecologia e Desenvolvimento Sustentável, [S. l.], v. 12, n. 1.

Ribeiro-Silva, R. C., Pereira, M., Campello, T., Aragão, É., Guimarães, J. M. de M., Ferreira, A. J. F., Barreto, M. L., & dos Santos, S. M. C. (2020). Implicações da pandemia COVID-19 para a segurança alimentar e nutricional no Brasil. *Ciencia & Saude Coletiva, 25*(9), 3421–3430. DOI: 10.1590/1413-81232020259.22152020 PMID: 32876253

Richards, G. (2011). Creativity and tourism. The state of the art. *Annals of Tourism Research, 38*(4), 1225–1253. DOI: 10.1016/j.annals.2011.07.008

Robehmed, N., & Berg, M. (2018). Highest-Paid YouTube Stars 2018: Markiplier, Jake Paul, PewDiePie and More. Available at: https://www.forbes.com/sites/natalierobehmed/2018/12/03/highest-paid-youtube-stars-2018-markiplier-jake-paul-pewdiepie-and-more/#563480c2909a (Accessed November 21, 2019).

Rocha Peixoto. (1966). *As olarias de Prado.* Museu Regional de Cerâmica.

Rodger, J. G.. (2021). Widespread vulnerability of flowering plant seed production to pollinator declines. *Science Advances, 7*(42). Advance online publication. DOI: 10.1126/sciadv.abd3524 PMID: 34644118

Rodrigues, C. A. S. (2015). *Análise morfológica do cérebro de abelhas sem ferrão Melipona Scutellarias expostas ao Tiametoxam. Trabalho de Conclusão de Curso do Curso (Instituto de Biociências) - Curso de Ciências Biológicas da Universidade Estadual Paulista Júlio de Mesquita Filho, Rio Claro.* UNESP.

Romaniuk, J., Wight, S., & Faulkner, M. (2017). Brand awareness: Revisiting an old metric for a new world. *Journal of Product and Brand Management, 26*(5), 469–476. DOI: 10.1108/JPBM-06-2016-1242

Rosado-Pinto, F., & Loureiro, S. M. C. (2024). Authenticity: Shedding light on the branding context. *EuroMed Journal of Business, 19*(3), 544–570. DOI: 10.1108/EMJB-08-2021-0115

Rose, P. (2016). A lifetime in airline revenue management. *Journal of Revenue and Pricing Management, 15*(3–4), 197–202. DOI: 10.1057/rpm.2016.21

Sah, R., Hada, V., Mohanty, A., Alshahrani, N. Z., Chakraborty, S., Bhattacharya, M., Chakraborty, C., & Dhama, K. (2022). Recent first report of human-to-dog transmission of Monkeypox virus emphasizes an urgent need of enhancing surveillance and strengthen further explorative research to reveal its real magnitude of reverse zoonosis from other animals including pets as like. *International Journal of Surgery, 106*. Advance online publication. DOI: 10.1016/j.ijsu.2022.106949 PMID: 36174830

Salhab, H. A. (2024). Social media marketing—Rise of social media influencer marketing and Instagram. *Journal of Infrastructure Policy and Development, 8*(8), 3783. DOI: 10.24294/jipd.v8i8.3783

Salinas, G., & Abril, C. (2025). Integrating sustainability into brand valuation models: an integrative literature review. *European Journal of Management and Business Economics*. https://doi.org/DOI: 10.1108/EJMBE-03-2024-0104/1249822/INTEGRATING-SUSTAINABILITY-INTO-BRAND-VALUATION

Saluja, G., & Chan, E. Y. (2025). Going against the tide: How self-construal moderates receptivity towards popular brand activism. *Journal of Business Research, 171*, 114129. DOI: 10.1016/j.jbusres.2025.115228

SAMPLE. K. L., SEVILLA, J., & HAWS, K. L. (2025). Clear views, clear gains: Exterior transparency's role in increasing consumer entry for retail environments. *Journal of Retailing*. Advance online publication. DOI: 10.1016/j.jretai.2025.01.005

Sanchez-Bayo, F., & Goka, K. (2014). Pesticide residues and bees–a risk assessment. *PLoS One, 9*(4), •••. PMID: 24718419

SanMiguel, P., & Sádaba, T. (2024). Who is Accountable for the Negative Effects of Influencer Marketing? Voices of the Influencer Ecosystem. Revista ICONO14, 22(1). DOI: 10.7195/ri14.v22i1.2103

Sansome, K., Conduit, J., & Wilkie, D. (2025). Consumers demand transparency… but do they actually engage? Exploring motives and interactions with brand transparency information. *Journal of Business Research, 194*, 115386. DOI: 10.1016/j.jbusres.2025.115386

Santos, J. B., Viana, M. C., Mariano, C. S. F., Menezes, R. S. T., Nery, D. G., & Brandão, S. N. (2022). *Mudanças climáticas e o declínio das abelhas*. Terræ Didática, 18(Publ. Contínua), pp. 1-12.

Santos, C., Coelho, A., & Marques, A. (2024). The greenwashing effects on corporate reputation and brand hate, through environmental performance and green perceived risk. *Asia-Pacific Journal of Business Administration*, *16*(3), 655–676. DOI: 10.1108/APJBA-05-2022-0216

Saputra, O., Azhar, A., & Saputa, O. (2025). ANALYSIS OF THE ROLE OF SOCIAL MEDIA IN BRAND MANAGEMENT AND MARKETING. Pedagogic Research-Applied Literacy Journal. https://doi.org/.DOI: 10.70574/tdbrer63

Saputra, A. I., & Asfiah, N. (2025). Bibliometric Analysis of Green Marketing Strategies: Innovative Approaches to Improve Sustainability. *Jurnal Ekuisci*, *2*(3), 158–170. DOI: 10.62885/EKUISCI.V2I3.589

Sara Pimenta, A. C. M. F. B. S. (2025). *Neurosensory and Neuromarketing Impacts on Consumer Behavior*. IGI Global.

Savona, N., Thompson, C., Smith, D., & Cummins, S. (2017). Proportional responsibility versus individual responsibility for healthy eating: A complex systems analysis. *Lancet*, *390*. Advance online publication. DOI: 10.1016/s0140-6736(17)33015-5

Schroll, R., Schnurr, B., & Grewal, D. (2018). Humanizing Products with Handwritten Typefaces. *The Journal of Consumer Research*. Advance online publication. DOI: 10.1093/jcr/ucy014

Schultz, B., & Sheffer, M. L. (2018). The mascot that wouldn't die: A case study of fan identification and mascot loyalty. *Sport in Society*, *21*(3), 482–496.

Setyawati, R. L., & Anindita, R. (2022). Developing Customer Engagement Through Instagram Social Media on Local Coffee Shop. *Majalah Ilmiah Bijak*, *19*(2), 168. DOI: 10.31334/bijak.v19i2.2539

Sha, L. (2024). Design of a Brand Emotional Connection System Based on Visual Communication. *Proceedings - 2024 International Conference on Computers, Information Processing and Advanced Education, CIPAE 2024*, 430–435. https://doi.org/DOI: 10.1109/CIPAE64326.2024.00084

Shamayleh, G. (2019). *Engagement and Monetization on Instagram Pet Influencer Communities* (Doctoral dissertation, Concordia University). Shamayleh_MSc_F2019.pdf

Shamayleh, G., & Arsel, Z. (2025). Digital Affective Encounters: The Relational Role of Content Circulation on Social Media. *The Journal of Consumer Research*. Advance online publication. DOI: 10.1093/JCR/UCAF023

Shank, M. D., & Lyberger, M. R. (2014). *Sports marketing: A strategic perspective*. Routledge.

Sharma, A., Kumar, K., & Dwesar, R. (2025). "Keenly aware of environmental issues, yet wavering in conviction": Understanding the factors influencing the consumers' willingness to pay for green energy. *Sustainable Futures : An Applied Journal of Technology, Environment and Society*, *9*. Advance online publication. DOI: 10.1016/J.SFTR.2024.100427

Shende, A. D., Tekade, S. A., Deshmukh, A. A., Tembhurkar, S. P., & Selvakumar, P. (2025). Water quality monitoring and control with AI. In Ruiz-Vanoye, J., & Díaz-Parra, O. (Eds.), *Smart water technology for sustainable management in modern cities* (pp. 51–80). IGI Global Scientific Publishing., DOI: 10.4018/979-8-3693-8074-1.ch003

Sherfudeen, N. (2025). Sustainable Supply Chain Management: Assessing Environmental Impact Using Data Analytics. *Journal of Information Systems Engineering & Management*, *10*(12s), 313–323. DOI: 10.52783/JISEM.V10I12S.1813

SIMION, R. (2024). Eco-Frauds: The Ethics and Impact of Corporate Greenwashing. *Studia Universitatis Babe -Bolyai Philosophia*, *69*, 7–26. DOI: 10.24193/SUBBPHIL.2024.2.01

Simões-Coelho, M., Figueira, A. R., & Russo, E. (2023). Motivations for a sustainable ethos: Evidence from the globally present Brazilian multinational Natura &Co. *Environment Systems & Decisions*, *43*(3), 321–336. DOI: 10.1007/S10669-022-09890-Y/METRICS PMID: 36628130

Singer, A. E. (2024). Marketing objects as talking machines: The performative capacity of product packages. *Marketing Theory*, *24*(3), 481–497. DOI: 10.1177/14705931231207319

SINGH, P. K. (2024). The Role of Artificial Intelligence in Personalized Marketing Strategies of AMAZON. INTERANTIONAL JOURNAL OF SCIENTIFIC RESEARCH IN ENGINEERING AND MANAGEMENT, 8(4), 1. DOI: 10.55041/ijsrem32818

Singh, C., Park, H., & Joyner Martinez, C. M. (2022). Love letters to Patagonia: Fostering sustainable consumption via consumer–brand relationships. *International Journal of Sustainable Fashion & Textiles*, *1*(1), 41–62. DOI: 10.1386/SFT/0003_1

Singh, S., & Singh, A. K. (2025). Regulations and Prevention – "Green Washing and Green Marketing. *IJFMR - International. Journal of Multidisciplinary Research*, *7*(3). Advance online publication. DOI: 10.36948/IJFMR.2025.V07I03.41968

Sipos, D. (2024). The Role of Social Media in Promoting Sustainable Brands: Influencing Consumer Perceptions and Behavior Towards Sustainable Products. *Technium Sustainability*, *8*, 1–11. DOI: 10.47577/SUSTAINABILITY.V8I.11741

Skinner, J., Zakus, D. H., & Cowell, J. (2008). Development through sport: Building social capital in disadvantaged communities. *Sport Management Review*, *11*(3), 253–275.

Smith, A. C., Stavros, C., & Westberg, K. (2017). *Brand Fans. Lessons from the Worlds Greatest Sporting Brands*. RMIT University.

SNA – Sociedade Nacional de Agricultura. (2017). *Apiecoturismo: um novo negócio para produtores de mel no Brasil*. https://sna.agr.br/apiecoturismo-um-novo-negocio-para-produtores-de-mel-no-brasil/

SNA - Sociedade Nacional de Agricultura. (2023). Abemel. *Produção de mel cresceu 80% em 10 anos no Brasil*. https://sna.agr.br/abemel-producao-de-mel-cresceu-80-em-10-anos-no-brasil/. Disponível em: 16/08/2025.

Sousa Júnior, J. C., Souza, C. B., Barreira, S., & Rocha, F. R. T. (2024). Produção científica sobre apicultura numa perspectiva multidisciplinar: Uma revisão sistemática de literatura. *Revista Brasileira Multidisciplinas*, *27*(2), 133–149.

Spears, N. E., Mowen, J. C., & Chakraborty, G. (1996). Symbolic role of animals in print advertising: Content analysis and conceptual development. *Journal of Business Research*, *37*(1), 87–95. DOI: 10.1016/0148-2963(96)00060-4

Spee, L. B., Hazel, S. J., Dal Grande, E., Boardman, W. S., & Chaber, A. L. (2019). Endangered exotic pets on social media in the Middle East: Presence and impact. *Animals (Basel)*, *9*(8), 480. PMID: 31344918

Statista Research Department. (2025). *Conflicts in the world in 2025 – statistics and facts*. Statista. Retrieved August 16, 2025, from https://www.statista.com/topics/13125/conflicts-worldwide-2025/#topFacts

Stavleu, D. C., Mulder, R. L., Kruimer, D. M., Kremer, L. C. M., Tissing, W. J. E., & Loeffen, E. A. H. (2024). Less restrictions in daily life: A clinical practice guideline for children with cancer. *Supportive Care in Cancer*, *32*(7). Advance online publication. DOI: 10.1007/s00520-024-08537-9 PMID: 38850341

Štofejová, L., Kráľ, Š., Fedorko, R., Bačík, R., & Tomášová, M. (2023). Sustainability and Consumer Behavior in Electronic Commerce. *Sustainability*, *15*(22), 1–16. DOI: 10.3390/SU152215902

Stutey, D. M., Solis, A. E., Notestine, L., & Wehrman, J. (2022). The Impact of Therapy Dogs on Graduate-Level, Military-Affiliated Students. *Society & Animals*, *32*(3), 309–327. DOI: 10.1163/15685306-BJA10106

Subramanian, M., Portia, R., Mishra, B. R., & Selvakumar, P. P. V., R., & T. C., M. (2025). Assessment and evaluation in personalized STEAM education. In N. Son (Ed.), Integrating personalized learning methods into STEAM education (pp. 103–122). IGI Global Scientific Publishing. https://doi.org/DOI: 10.4018/979-8-3693-7718-5.ch005

Sugumaran, K. M. D., & Pandiyarajan, V. Y. B. S., Selvakumar, P., & M. S. (2024). Analysis of electromyography signals for control of mechanical prosthesis using machine learning techniques. In 2024 2nd International Conference on Intelligent Data Communication Technologies and Internet of Things (IDCIoT) (pp. 1059–1067). IEEE. https://doi.org/DOI: 10.1109/IDCIoT59759.2024.10467707

Suijkerbuijk, A. W. M., Mangen, M.-J. J., Haverkate, M. R., Luppino, F. S., Bantjes, S. E., Visser, L. G., Swaan, C. M., Ruijs, W. L. M., & Over, E. A. B. (2020). Rabies vaccination strategies in the Netherlands in 2018: A cost evaluation. *Eurosurveillance*, *25*(38). Advance online publication. DOI: 10.2807/1560-7917.ES.2020.25.38.1900716 PMID: 32975187

Sun, B., Xu, Z., Wei, M., & Wang, X. (2025). A study on the strategic behavior of players participating in air-rail intermodal transportation based on evolutionary games. *Journal of Air Transport Management*, *126*. Advance online publication. DOI: 10.1016/j.jairtraman.2025.102793

Sun, D., Yang, D., Wang, J., & Tan, F. (2024). How animal metaphors increase tourists' waste classification intention. *Environmental Research Communications*, *6*(10), 105012. DOI: 10.1088/2515-7620/ad82b0

Sundar, S. S., Kang, J., & Oprean, D. (2017). Being There in the Midst of the Story: How Immersive Journalism Affects Our Perceptions and Cognitions. *Cyberpsychology, Behavior, and Social Networking*, *20*(11), 672–682. DOI: 10.1089/cyber.2017.0271 PMID: 29125787

Suo, D., Dai, J., & Gong, S. (2025). Doing good with flow: Unlocking brand passion through virtual CSR co-creation participation and immersive experiences. *Corporate Social Responsibility and Environmental Management*, *32*(1), 1309–1324. DOI: 10.1002/CSR.3023

Suoheimo, M., Walter, S., Backer, H., Kotaniemi, S., & Pyykkö, H. (2025). Service Designing Transitions to More Sustainable Supply Chains: A Systematic Literature Review through the Lens of Systemic Design Approach. *Journal of Sustainability Research*, *7*(2). Advance online publication. DOI: 10.20900/JSR20250020

Suparto, Y. (2024). *The Role of Social Media in Increasing Brand Awareness: A Literature Review*. Maneggio., DOI: 10.62872/bry58b32

Syahribulan, S., Elliyana, E., & Rosmiati, R. (2025). The Role of Social Media Influencers in Shaping Sustainable Purchasing Behavior: Genuine Consumer Interest or Impulsive Trends? *Journal of Production. Operations Management and Economics*, *5*(1), 63–77. DOI: 10.55529/JPOME.51.63.77

Ta, A. H., Aarikka-Stenroos, L., & Litovuo, L. (2022). Customer Experience in Circular Economy: Experiential Dimensions among Consumers of Reused and Recycled Clothes. *Sustainability*, *14*(1), 1–18. DOI: 10.3390/SU14010509

Tchelidze, L. (2023). Influence of Brand Activities through Social Media on Consumer Awareness. Journal of International Business Research and Marketing. https://doi.org/.DOI: 10.18775/jibrm.1849-8558.2015.81.3001

The Marketing Explainer. (2024, july 2). Budweiser's marketing strategy explained. https://www.marketingexplainers.com/budweisers-marketing-strategy-explained/

The Mill. (2021). Amazon Prime – Unlikely Friendship [Portfólio de produção]. https://www.themill.com/the-mill/work/amazon-prime-unlikely-friendship/

Theaker, A. (2020). The public relations handbook. In *The Public Relations Handbook*. Taylor and Francis., DOI: 10.4324/9780429298578

Thomé, J. (2024, 6 de fevereiro). InovaBee Brazil. *Mel sustentável: para o planeta e para a comunidade*. Inovabee. https://inovabee.com/blog/mel-sustentavel

Thomson, M., MacInnis, D. J., & Whan Park, C. (2005). The Ties That Bind: Measuring the Strength of Consumers' Emotional Attachments to Brands. *Journal of Consumer Psychology*, *15*(1), 77–91. DOI: 10.1207/s15327663jcp1501_10

Thu, N. N. Q., Kadirov, D., Fam, K. S., & Tho, N. D. (2023). Firms' Sustainability Marketing Commitment: The Roles of Chief Marketing Officers' Future Focus and Prosocial Motivation. *Journal of Macromarketing*, *43*(3), 306–321. DOI: 10.1177/02761467231174027

Tilden, F. (2007). Interpreting our Heritage (4th Ed.). The University of North Carolina Press. (Original publicado em 1957).

Tolstoy, D., Melén Hånell, S., & Ghauri, P. N. (2025). Unpacking the Role of Ethical Leadership in the Era of Sustainable Development Goals and Values-Based Marketing. *Journal of International Marketing, 33*(2), 19–38. DOI: 10.1177/1069031X241296468/ASSET/5755ECDA-2A24-4226-84CA-04F927A9F496/ASSETS/IMAGES/LARGE/10.1177_1069031X241296468-FIG2.JPG

Top Pet Industry Trends. Omnichannel, Sustainability & Technology. (2025). MultiDev. https://multidev.com/blog/pet-industry-trends/

Topal, E., Adamchuk, L., Negri, I., Köso ˘glu, M., Papa, G., Dârjan, M.S., & Cornea-Cipcigan, M.; M ˘arg ˘aoan, R. (2021). Traces of Honeybees, Api-Tourism and Beekeeping: From Past to Present. *Sustainability, 13*, 11659.

Tseng, T. A., Fang, H. Y., Shen, C. C., & Chang, Y. C. (2024). Peer bonds and nature's embrace: Exploring the influence of pet caregiving on social well-being and nature connection among Taiwanese children. *Frontiers in Public Health, 12*. Advance online publication. DOI: 10.3389/FPUBH.2024.1431939/BIBTEX PMID: 39498111

Tu, J. C., Cui, Y., Liu, L., & Yang, C. (2024). Perceived Greenwashing and Its Impact on the Green Image of Brands. *Sustainability, 16*(20), 1–17. DOI: 10.3390/SU16209009

Turner, G. (2014). *Understanding Celebrity*. SAGE Publications Ltd., DOI: 10.4135/9781473957855

Tyagi, V. K., Kumar, S., Gulyani, M., & Gahlawat, R. (2023). E-SERV-EX: A Multi-item Scale for Measuring Customer Expectations from the Online Retail Services. *NMIMS Management Review, 31*(2), 131–144. DOI: 10.1177/09711023231197795

Tymowsk, G. (2013). The virtue of compassion: Animals in sport, hunting as sport, and entertainment. In *Sport, animals, and society* (pp. 140–154). Routledge.

Ubb Negotia, S., Lxix; E, & Harmati, A. (2024). Pets In Advertising or How to Influence Consumers? *Studia Universitatis Babe -Bolyai Negotia, 69*(1), 55–68. DOI: 10.24193/SUBBNEGOTIA.2024.1.03

Umbelino, J. (2014). Os Valores do Território no Lazer e no Turismo. In Z. Costa, C. Brandão, F., Costa, R., & Breda (Ed.), *Produtos e Competividade do Turismo na Lusofonia* (pp. 203–216). Lisboa: Escolar Editora.

Ünalmış, E., Dirsehan, T., & Erdoğmuş, İ. E. (2024). Consequences of influencer-created content on influencers' authenticity in the beauty and personal care industry. *Journal of Marketing Communications, 1*. Advance online publication. DOI: 10.1080/13527266.2024.2371833

Underwood, P. J. (2000). Pet Travel Scheme. *The Veterinary Record, 146*(9), 263. https://www.scopus.com/inward/record.uri?eid=2-s2.0-0034716454&partnerID=40&md5=aabe276cb445522ab465e806e2977857 PMID: 10737301

Vala, J. (1986). A Análise de Conteúdo. In Santos Silva, A., & Madureira Pinto, J. (Eds.), *Metodologia das Ciências Sociais* (pp. 101–128). Edições Afrontamento.

van der Harst, J. P., & Angelopoulos, S. (2024). Less is more: Engagement with the content of social media influencers. *Journal of Business Research, 181*, 114746. DOI: 10.1016/j.jbusres.2024.114746

Varenna, S., Li, H., Ribeiro, M., & Santos, B. F. (2025). Stochastic discrete event simulation of airline network and maintenance operations. *Journal of Air Transport Management, 125*. Advance online publication. DOI: 10.1016/j.jairtraman.2025.102789

Velicia Martin, F., Toledo, L. D., & Palos-Sanchez, P. (2020). How deep is your love? Brand love analysis applied to football teams. *International Journal of Sports Marketing & Sponsorship, 21*(4), 669–693.

Vieira, C. B., & Sousa, B. (2020). The brand attachment and consumer behaviour in sports marketing contexts: The case of football fans in Portugal. *International Journal of Sport Management and Marketing, 20*(1-2), 29–46.

Vienová, R., & Mišík, M. (2025). *Far-right greenwashing: the twisting of sustainability*. Sustainability Accounting, Management and Policy Journal., DOI: 10.1108/SAMPJ-10-2024-1184/1256108/FAR-RIGHT-GREENWASHING-THE-TWISTING-OF

Vigneau, L., & Adams, C. A. (2023). The failure of transparency as self-regulation. *Sustainability Accounting. Management and Policy Journal, 14*(4), 852–876. DOI: 10.1108/SAMPJ-01-2022-0051

Visnes, T., Benítez-Buelga, C., Cázares-Körner, A., Sanjiv, K., Hanna, B. M. F., Mortusewicz, O., Rajagopal, V., Albers, J. J., Hagey, D. W., Bekkhus, T., Eshtad, S., Baquero, J. M., Masuyer, G., Wallner, O., Müller, S., Pham, T., Göktürk, C., Rasti, A., Suman, S., & Helleday, T. (2021). Targeting OGG1 arrests cancer cell proliferation by inducing replication stress. *Nucleic Acids Research, 48*(21), 12234–12251. DOI: 10.1093/nar/gkaa1048 PMID: 33211885

Vladimirova, K. (2022). Behind 11 million likes: Sustainable fashion on Instagram – A critical analysis of actors and discourses on fashion, sustainability and social change. *International Journal of Sustainable Fashion & Textiles, 1*(1), 107–148. DOI: 10.1386/SFT/0006_1

Waltenrath, A. (2024). Consumers' ambiguous perceptions of advertising disclosures in influencer marketing: Disentangling the effects on current and future social media engagement. *Electronic Markets, 34*(1). Advance online publication. DOI: 10.1007/s12525-023-00679-8

Walter, N., Föhl, U., Sander, F., & Nies, A. (2024). Act as you preach! Authentic brand purpose versus "woke washing's" impact on brand credibility: The moderating role of cause involvement and consumer skepticism. *Journal of Business Research, 184*. Advance online publication. DOI: 10.1016/J.JBUSRES.2024.114868

Wandelt, S., Wang, S., Chen, X., Zheng, C., Chang, S., & Sun, X. (2025). Network structures in air transportation: A comprehensive review of applications and challenges. *Journal of Air Transport Management, 126*. Advance online publication. DOI: 10.1016/j.jairtraman.2025.102794

Wang, X. (2024). Visual Communication and Branding: The Role of Graphic Design in Building Brand Image and Recognition. *Highlights in Art and Design, 8*(2), 19–22. DOI: 10.54097/QWY32G44

wearable Pet Health Monitors: Advancements in Pet Care. (2025). Grand View Research. https://www.grandviewresearch.com/

Weaver, H. (2013). Becoming in Kind": Race, Class, Gender, and Nation in Cultures of Dog Rescue and Dogfighting. *American Quarterly, 65*(3), 689–709. DOI: 10.1353/aq.2013.0034

Weber, D. (2016). *Brand seduction: How neuroscience can help marketers build memorable brands*. Red url: Wheel/Weiser.https://books.google.co.in/books?hl=en&lr=&id=sd9EDwAAQBAJ&oi=fnd&pg=PT10&dq=Their+posts+are+wholesome,+fun,+and+tug+at+your+heartstrings,+making+them+perfect+for+brands+wanting+to+create+warm,+fuzzy+feelings&ots=Gn_gnnzzz0&sig=zDuYQwKqyv8YFwWLdC1E6MkA4eA&redir_esc=y#v=onepage&q&f=false

Weder, F. (2023). The Evolution of the Sustainability Story: Strategic Sustainability Communication as Niche Construction. *International Journal of Strategic Communication, 17*(3), 228–244. DOI: 10.1080/1553118X.2023.2229304

Wei, W., Zhang, L., Ying, T., & Zheng, Y. (2025). Pet influencer marketing appeal in hotel booking: Exploring the power of message appeal and boundary conditions. *International Journal of Hospitality Management, 126*, 104094. DOI: 10.1016/j.ijhm.2025.104094

White, E. J. (2020). *A unified theory of cats on the internet*. Stanford University Press., https://books.google.co.in/books?hl=en&lr=&id=fuD5DwAAQBAJ&oi=fnd&pg=PA1934&dq=Doug+the+Pug,+rocking+goofy+outfits+with+his+squishy+face,+Tuna+the+Chiweenie,+whose+quirky+looks+became+an+internet+sensation,+or+Nala+Cat,+a+fluffy+feline+with+a+talent+for+melting+hearts&ots=ax0W5X3MSl&sig=fKYVPNP3Ykwx6d2OssomIFYfB7g&redir_esc=y#v=onepage&q&f=false

Williams, J. (2024). Greenwashing: Appearance, illusion and the future of 'green' capitalism. *Geography Compass*, *18*(1), e12736. DOI: 10.1111/GEC3.12736

Winit, W., Kantabutra, S., & Kantabutra, S. (2023). Toward a Sustainability Brand Model: An Integrative Review. *Sustainability*, *15*(6), 1–25. DOI: 10.3390/SU15065212

Winter, C. (2020). A review of research into animal ethics in tourism: Launching the Annals of Tourism Research curated collection on animal ethics in tourism. *Annals of Tourism Research*, *84*, 102989. DOI: 10.1016/j.annals.2020.102989

Wojdynski, B. W., & Evans, N. J. (2016). Going native: Effects of disclosure position and language on the recognition and evaluation of online native advertising. *Journal of Advertising*, *45*, 157–168. DOI: 10.1080/00913367.2015.1115380

Wolf, S. M., Pruett, T. L., McVan, C. C., Brister, E., Callier, S. L., Capron, A. M., Childress, J. F., Goodwin, M. B., Hyun, I., Isasi, R., Maynard, A. D., Oye, K. A., Thompson, P. B., & Tiersch, T. R. (2024). Anticipating Biopreservation Technologies that Pause Biological Time: Building Governance & Coordination Across Applications. *The Journal of Law, Medicine & Ethics*, *52*(3), 534–552. DOI: 10.1017/jme.2024.129 PMID: 39676361

Wong, J. C. (2019). 'It's not play if you're making money': how Instagram and YouTube disrupted child labor laws. Available at: https://www.theguardian.com/media/2019/apr/24/its-not-play-if-youre-making-money-how-instagram-and-youtube-disrupted-child-labor-laws (Accessed November 21, 2019)

Wong, W. (2017). Brand Mascots and Other Marketing Animals, Stephen Brown & Sharon Ponsonby-McCabe (Eds.). Journal of Design History, 30(2), 241–242. https://doi.org/DOI: 10.1093/jdh/epx015

Woodside, A., & Lloyd, S. (2013). Animals, archetypes, and advertising (A3): The theory and the practice of customer brand symbolism. Journal of Marketing Management.

Wu, D., Liu, Y., & Yang, T. (2024a). Pet ownership: A sign of superior socioeconomic position? Evidences from six cities in China. *Preventive Veterinary Medicine*, *225*. Advance online publication. DOI: 10.1016/j.prevetmed.2024.106140 PMID: 38350165

Xie-Carson, L., Benckendorff, P., & Hughes, K. (2023). Not so different after all? A netnographic exploration of user engagement with non-human influencers on social media. *Journal of Business Research*, *167*, 114149. DOI: 10.1016/j.jbusres.2023.114149

Xie, Z., Liu, Y., Liu, Y., & Xu, L. (2024). Unveiling greenwashing dynamics: Exploring the nexus between transparent corporate practices, employee perspectives, and ethical leadership impact. *Environment, Development and Sustainability*, *2024*, 1–25. DOI: 10.1007/S10668-024-04665-8

Xu, S. (2024). Research on marketing strategies in the pet food industry: A case study based on existing brands. SHS Web of Conferences, 207, 1002. DOI: 10.1051/shsconf/202420701002

Xu, J., Tong, Z., Rehman, M., & Hussain, T. (2025). Informational or emotional? The influencing mechanism of digital corporate social responsibility related interactive content on product purchase intention. *Journal of Business Research*. Advance online publication. DOI: 10.1016/j.actpsy.2025.104988

Yang, J., Zhang, J., & Zhang, Y. (2024). Engagement That Sells: Influencer Video Advertising on TikTok. *Marketing Science*. Advance online publication. DOI: 10.1287/mksc.2021.0107

Yasmi, Y. (2025). What the Bees Are Telling Us: In Protecting Pollinators, *We Protect the Future of Food.* FAO. Disponível em: https://www.fao.org/newsroom/fao-blog/detail/fao-blog/2025/05/19/what-the-bees-are-telling-us/en. Data de Acesso: 10/05/2025.

Yeboah, A. Y. O., Jibril, A. B., & Novak, P. (2022). A strategic framework for developing sustainable value propositions. *Problems and Perspectives in Management*, *20*(4), 407–421. DOI: 10.21511/PPM.20(4).2022.31

Ye, C. (2025). Mapping out digital luxury marketing: A systematic review and future research agenda. *Marketing Intelligence & Planning*, **•••**, 1–24.

Ye, Y., & Lau, K. H. (2022). Competitive Green Supply Chain Transformation with Dynamic Capabilities—An Exploratory Case Study of Chinese Electronics Industry. *Sustainability*, *14*(14), 1–23. DOI: 10.3390/SU14148640

Ying, T., Tang, J., Wen, J., Ye, S., Zhou, Y., & Li, F. (Sam). (2021). Traveling with pets: Constraints, negotiation, and learned helplessness. *Tourism Management, 82*. Advance online publication. DOI: 10.1016/j.tourman.2020.104183

Yoo, S., Pu, K., & Truong, K. N. (2024, May 11). Behind the Pup-ularity Curtain: Understanding the Motivations, Challenges, and Work Performed in Creating and Managing Pet Influencer Accounts. *Conference on Human Factors in Computing Systems - Proceedings*. https://doi.org/DOI: 10.1145/3613904.3642367

Yoo, S., Pu, K., & Truong, K. N. (2024, May). Behind the Pup-ularity Curtain: Understanding the Motivations, Challenges, and Work Performed in Creating and Managing Pet Influencer Accounts. In *Proceedings of the 2024 CHI Conference on Human Factors in Computing Systems* (pp. 1-17).

Yoo, W.-S. (2024). The Impact of Artificial Intelligence on Marketing Strategies. *International Journal of Science and Research Archive, 13*(1), 3211. DOI: 10.30574/ijsra.2024.13.1.2042

Yue, S., Liao, W., Ji, Q., & Wang, C. (2025). The effect of financial performance on aviation carbon emissions. *Journal of Air Transport Management, 126*. Advance online publication. DOI: 10.1016/j.jairtraman.2025.102800

Yu, J., & Meng, T. (2025). Image Generative AI in Tourism: Trends, Impacts, and Future Research Directions. *Journal of Hospitality & Tourism Research (Washington, D.C.)*. Advance online publication. DOI: 10.1177/10963480251324676

Zaman, S. U., Asif, H., & Alam, S. H. (2025). Beyond Influence: The Behavioral Blueprint of Ethical and Sustainable Consumer Decision-Making. *Journal of Social and Organizational Matters, 4*(2), 254–279. DOI: 10.56976/JSOM.V4I2.219

Zhang, W., Cao, H., & Lin, L. (2022). *Analysis of the Future Development Trend of the Pet Industry*.

Zhang, L., Wei, W., Rathjens, B., & Zheng, Y. (2023). Pet influencers on social media: The joint effect of message appeal and narrator. *International Journal of Hospitality Management, 110*, 103453. DOI: 10.1016/j.ijhm.2023.103453

Zhang, L., Yang, H., & Bian, L. (2025). Complex network analysis of China's domestic air cargo network based on actual flight data. *Transport Policy, 168*, 133–156. DOI: 10.1016/j.tranpol.2025.04.015

Zhang, X. (2023). Influencer Marketing: Assessing Effectiveness and Exploring Potential Drawbacks in Advertising Strategies. *Highlights in Business Economics and Management, 23*, 171. DOI: 10.54097/t83twa35

Zhang, Y. (2015). The impact of brand image on consumer behavior: A literature review. *Open Journal of Business and Management, 3*(1), 58–62.

Zheng, Y. (2024). The Impact of Brand Loyalty on Consumer Purchase Decisions and Analysis of Sustainable Consumption Strategies. *Frontiers in Business, Economics and Management, 15*(2), 219–222. DOI: 10.54097/PS4YA869

Ziakis, C., & Vlachopoulou, M. (2023). Artificial Intelligence in Digital Marketing: Insights from a Comprehensive Review [Review of Artificial Intelligence in Digital Marketing: Insights from a Comprehensive Review]. Information, 14(12), 664. Multidisciplinary Digital Publishing Institute. DOI: 10.3390/info14120664

Zniva, R., Weitzl, W., & Lindmoser, C. (2023). Be constantly different! How to manage influencer authenticity. *Electronic Commerce Research, 23*(3), 1485. DOI: 10.1007/s10660-022-09653-6

Zoetis. (2025). Advancements in Veterinary Pharmaceuticals. Zoetis. https://www.zoetis.com

Zürn, M., Buder, F., & Unfried, M. (2023). Brand Purpose and Brand Success. *NIM Marketing Intelligence Review, 15*(1), 54–59. DOI: 10.2478/NIMMIR-2023-0008

About the Contributors

Luzia Arantes (lamorim@ua.pt) as a PhD in Applied Psychology from the University of Minho, Portugal, in addition, she is doing a PhD in Marketing and Strategy at the same institution. She is currently a researcher at Ekonomikas un Kulturas Augstskola (Serbia) and a lecturer at Polytechnic University of Cávado and Ave and at University of Aveiro, Portugal. She has published book chapters in IGI Global on marketing, tourism, consumer behaviour, sustainability and artificial intelligence. He has published in the Journal of International Journal of Marketing, Corporate Social Responsibility and Environmental Management, Journal of Cultural Heritage Management and Sustainable Development, Journal of International Consumer Marketing, Sustainability and the European Journal of Applied Business Management. She has received several awards, including the Best Paper Award in Sustainable Marketing & Digital Perspectives and the Best Paper Award in Consumer Behaviour.

Bruno Sousa (bsousa@ipca.pt) is Adjunct Professor of Marketing at Polytechnic Institute of Cavado and Ave (IPCA), Portugal and PhD in Marketing and Strategy in Universidade do Minho, Portugal. Head of Master Program - Tourism Management (IPCA) and Tourism Marketing Master. CiTUR research member. Bruno Sousa has published several chapters at IGI Global over the past 5 years, on topics of marketing, tourism and management. He has published in the Journal of Enterprising Communities, Tourism Management Perspectives, Current Issues in Tourism, Journal of Organizational Change Management, World Review of Entrepreneurship, Management and Sust. Development, among others.

***

Nilesh Anute is an Associate Professor at Sri Balaji University, Pune, where he brings a wealth of academic expertise and industry insight to the field of management education. With a strong commitment to teaching and research, Dr. Anute has played a significant role in shaping future business leaders through his dynamic approach to pedagogy. His academic contributions and dedication to excellence have made him a respected figure in the university's academic community.

Komal Bisht Designation is a dedicated Assistant Professor specializing in Human Resource Management, has over five years of teaching experience at institutions such as Shri Guru Ram Rai University and Dev Bhoomi Group of Institutions in Dehradun. Currently pursuing a Ph.D. in Human Resource Management, Komal holds an MBA from Graphic Era Hill University. Throughout her career, she has developed and implemented comprehensive lesson plans and mentored students. Additionally, Komal has significant experience in recruitment and selection, having led a team at Placement Dehradun. She has also attended various national workshops, FDPs, and conferences and has been recognized for her exceptional student mentorship and leadership skills.

Shiney Chib is a respected academic in the Department of Management at Datta Meghe Institute of Management Studies, situated in Nagpur, Maharashtra. With a strong foundation in management education and a commitment to academic excellence, Dr. Chib plays a vital role in shaping future business leaders through her teaching and mentorship. Her dedication to research, innovation, and student-centric learning reflects her deep involvement in the field of management studies.

Prashant Chordiya is an Associate Professor at Dr. D.Y. Patil Institute of Master of Computer Application and Management, located in Akurdi, Pune. With a strong academic background and extensive teaching experience, he plays a vital role in guiding students in the fields of computer applications and management. Dr. Chordiya is known for his research-oriented approach and commitment to academic excellence, contributing significantly to the development of future professionals through innovative teaching and mentorship.

Carlos Costa is a Full Professor at the University of Aveiro. He is also the Scientific and Technical Director of IDTOUR and the Editor of the journal Tourism & Development. He holds a PhD in Tourism from the University of Surrey (United Kingdom).

Renata Costa has a PhD and Master's in Veterinary Hygiene and Technological Processing of Animal-Origin Products from Fluminense Federal University (UFF). Bachelor's in Veterinary Medicine from Fluminense Federal University (UFF). Sector Coordinator of Zoosanitary Surveillance and Disease Control and Manager of the Herbivore Rabies Control Program at the State Secretariat of Agriculture, Livestock, and Supply.

Janderson Damaceno dos Reis is a Ph.D. in Applied Economics from the University of São Paulo (USP). Master's degree in Applied Economics from the Federal University of Viçosa (UFV); Bachelor's degree in Animal Science from the Federal University of Viçosa (UFV). Associate Professor at the Department of Rural Economics (UFV).

André Faria is a PhD in Agronomy (Soils and Plant Nutrition) from the Federal University of Viçosa (2010). Currently an Associate Professor at the Federal University of Viçosa. Coordinator of the Quaternary Geomorphology Laboratory (DGE/UFV). Coordinator of the Research Group on Continental and Coastal Landscapes.

Sayantani Ghosh, an assistant professor at Adarsh Institute of Management and Technology, Bengaluru, and has prior experience working t at NIT Silchar. She specializes in marketing management, Human Resource Management, business regulation, service marketing, and research methodology, etc. She has guided numerous MBA students and actively participated in curriculum development, mentoring and student-centric initiatives. She is pursuing Ph.D. in Marketing from NIT Silchar and also an MBA in Marketing from NIT Silchar, an Institute of National Importance Along with a B.Tech in Agricultural Engineering from Assam University. She has also cleared UGC NET (2024) in Management. Beyond academia, she has industry experience of 3 years. Her research contribution includes publications in 4 Scopus-indexed journals on topics related to green marketing, acoustic textiles, and the circular economy, and many more. She has authored 1 book and many book chapters.

Francisco Gonçalves holds a Ph.D. in Tourism from the University of Aveiro and teaches several courses on Tourism at the School of Hospitality and Tourism of the Polytechnic Institute of Cávado e Ave in Barcelos, Portugal.

M. Gurusamy, with a comprehensive academic background including an MBA, M.Phil, Ph.D., and a D.Litt. in Marketing, brings an impressive 20 years of teaching experience alongside a brief stint in the industry of 9 months. Currently serving as a Professor and Chairperson for Marketing and Entrepreneurship at the Adarsh Institute of Management and Information Technology in Bangalore, Karnataka, India, he has distinguished himself in the academic and research fields. Dr. Gurusamy has significantly contributed to the intellectual property domain with nine patents in India and 5 in Australia, underscoring his innovative approach to research and development. His scholarly output is remarkable, with 12 articles published in Web of Science journals, 32 in Scopus-indexed journals, and many articles in other national and international journals, totalling 40 books published. As an academic leader, he has evaluated Ph.D. theses and served as an external examiner, showcasing his expertise in guiding research scholars. Dr. Gurusamy's role as a resource person and chairperson in 90 instances, along with his editorial and reviewer memberships in 14 and 16 journals respectively, reflects his esteemed position in the academic community. Additionally, his contributions extend to academic advisory boards and visiting professorships, demonstrating a commitment to enhancing educational standards. His achievements have been recognized with 30 awards, affirming his influence and excellence in marketing and research. Dr. Gurusamy's professional journey is a testament to his dedication to academia, research, and the practical applications of marketing principles in the evolving business landscape.

Lakshmi H is currently working as an Associate Professor in the Department of Management Studies and Research Centre at NITTE Meenakshi Institute of Technology, Bangalore. She holds PhD from Visvesvaraya Technological University, MBA (Marketing), Post-Graduation in Airline and Airport Management (Gold medalist) from Anna University, and Bachelor of Engineering in Electrical and Electronics from Avinashilingam Deemed University. She has 15+ years of Corporate & Academics Experience. She has published various Research papers on Web of science, Scopus and authored book chapters. Her area of Research area Interest lies in Retail 4.0, Consumer Behavior, Social media marketing, M commerce. She has successfully completed research projects under KSCST, Government of Karnataka

Sujay M.J. holds a Ph.D., MBA, UGC-NET (Management), and a B.E. in Computer Science. He is currently serving as an Associate Professor in the Department of Health System Management Studies, Faculty of Management Studies, at JSS Academy of Higher Education & Research, Mysuru. With over six years of corporate experience and more than 14 years of teaching experience, Dr. Sujay has a strong academic and professional background in the field of Management, spanning both undergraduate and postgraduate education.

K. Sankar Ganesh – Registrar & Dean, Faculty of Management, Sharda University Uzbekistan Dr. K. Sankar Ganesh is a distinguished academician and administrator with over two decades of experience in management education, research, and academic leadership. Holding a Ph.D. in Marketing Management and multiple postgraduate degrees in business and personnel management, he brings a wealth of knowledge in marketing, human resource management, and strategic planning. Throughout his illustrious career, Dr. Sankar Ganesh has served in pivotal academic and administrative roles including Dean (Academic and Management), Head of the Department, Admission Head, and Public Relations Officer. His dynamic leadership is marked by his commitment to academic excellence, innovation, and societal impact. With an impressive portfolio of 74 journal publications (including 11 in Scopus), 6 books, 3 patents, and numerous keynote addresses, Dr. Sankar Ganesh is a prolific contributor to academia. He has mentored Ph.D. scholars, spearheaded international conferences, signed MOUs, and led consultancy projects. His dedication to fostering academic collaborations and nurturing young minds stands as a testament to his visionary approach.

Arvinder Kour Mehta is a distinguished faculty member in the Department of Management & Humanities at Yeshwantrao Chavan College of Engineering, located in Nagpur, Maharashtra. With a strong academic background and a passion for interdisciplinary education, Dr. Mehta brings valuable insights into the integration of management principles within the technical education landscape. Her contributions to teaching, research, and student development reflect her commitment to academic excellence and holistic learning.

Harshitha M is a dedicated academician with a strong passion for teaching and research. She holds an M.Com from Sita Devi Ratanchand Nahar Adarsh College and a B.Com with a commendable CGPA, providing her with a solid academic foundation. Her professional experience includes roles as a Front Office Executive and Account Executive at IMSMTC, where she gained practical insights into administration and finance. She has also explored dynamic fields such as financial modeling and digital marketing, reflecting her adaptability to evolving industry trends. Harshitha has authored two books titled Digital Marketing and Financial Planning, and has published over 22 research articles in reputed national and international journals. Her active participation in various seminars, workshops, Faculty Development Programs (FDPs), Management Development Programs (MDPs), and academic conferences showcases her ongoing commitment to professional growth and academic excellence.

Annaelise Machado PhD Candidate in the Rural Extension Program at the Federal University of Viçosa (UFV) – CAPES Scholarship Holder (Coordination for the Improvement of Higher Education Personnel, Brazil). Master's in Tourism Management from the Polytechnic Institute of Cávado and Ave – Portugal (IPCA). Bachelor's in Tourism from FACTUR – Fundação Educacional São José. Bachelor's in Business Administration from Estácio de Sá University. E-mail: annaelise.machado@ufv.br;

Amruta Mahalle is currently serving as an Assistant Professor at Datta Meghe Institute of Management Studies, Nagpur. With a strong academic foundation and a passion for teaching, she specializes in the areas of Marketing and Human Resource Management.Her academic journey is marked by a commitment to developing industry-relevant knowledge and fostering practical learning among management students. She actively engages in research and scholarly activities, contributing to academic publications and participating in conferences and seminars. Amruta is known for her dynamic teaching approach, blending theoretical insights with real-world applications to enhance student engagement and understanding. Her interests include consumer behavior, digital marketing strategies, financial planning, and investment analysis. She is dedicated to continuous learning and professional development and aims to bridge the gap between academic theory and industry practices. Amruta Mahalle's contributions are instrumental in nurturing future business leaders and promoting academic excellence in the field of management education.

T.C. Manjunath did his BE from RV College of Engg. in 1989, ME in Robotics & Automation from LD College of Engg. in 1992 with First Rank and PhD in Systems & Control Engg. from IIT Bombay in the year 2007. He is currently working as the Dean Research R D and as Professor in the Dept. of Computer Science & Engineering with specialization in IoT, Cyber Security & Blockchain Technology in Rajarajeswari College of Engineering, Bengaluru, Karnataka. He has completed B.E. Degree from R.V. College of Engg., M.E. Govt.'s LD College of Engg., Gujarat Univ., Ahmedabad in First Rank and Ph.D. in Systems and Control Engineering from the Indian Institute of Technology Bombay IIT Bombay He has got a teaching academic, research and administrative experience of more than 35+ years 10 years as Principal, 8 years as HoD rest as faculty and has published more than 1200+ research papers in various national & international journals and conferences, with 175+ patents, 25 book-chapters, 25 awards and also published 25 text books in various field of science, engineering and technology, completed projects worth Rs. 9 Crores till date apart from guiding 10 PhD scholars. He is a member of 30 Professional Society Chapters and is a fellow of IE, IETE, AMIEE and a chartered engineer. He got the best research scholar award in 2006 in IIT Bombay amongst all the research scholars of the institute. He has got 10 awards in academics and research activities.

Geetha Manoharan is currently working in Telangana as an assistant professor at SR University. She is the university-level PhD program coordinator and has also been given the additional responsibility of In Charge Director of Publications and Patents under the Research Division at SR University.

Marcelo Oliveira is a PhD in Social Sciences from CPDA at the Federal Rural University of Rio de Janeiro. Master's in Rural Extension from the Federal University of Viçosa. Specialization in Brazilian History Post-1930 from the Fluminense Federal University. Bachelor's in Business Administration from the Federal University of Lavras. E-mail: marcelo.romarco@ufv.br;

P. Selvakumar is currently an Associate Professor in the Department of Science and Humanities at Nehru Institute of Technology, Coimbatore, Tamil Nadu, India. Prior to joining Nehru Institute of Technology, he held positions as an Assistant Professor in the Department of Science and Humanities various engineering colleges in Coimbatore, Tamil Nadu, India, spanning from 2011 to 2023. Dr.P. Selvakumar's academic and research interests lie primarily in the field of phytochemistry. He has made significant contributions to his field, with an impressive record that includes 30 journal publications, 12 patents, and 20 conference papers. Additionally, he has organized 5 seminars and conferences, further demonstrating his commitment to academic and scientific exchange. Throughout his career, Dr. P.Selvakumar has been recognized for his dedication and excellence in teaching, having been honored with several awards, including the Best Teacher Awards. He holds a prominent position in the academic community, contributing actively to research.

Sérgio Pereira has a Master's in Animal Biology from the Federal Rural University of Rio de Janeiro (UFRRJ). Bachelor's in Biological Sciences (Teaching Degree) from Centro Universitário Geraldo Di Biase, Barra do Piraí-RJ Campus. Bachelor's in Biological Sciences from Universidade Severino Sombra, Vassouras-RJ Campus. Staff member at the State Secretariat of Agriculture, Livestock, and Supply – SEAPA-RJ. Basic education teacher at SEEDUC-RJ (Biology and Chemistry). E-mail: spereirabio@gmail.com;

Gautam Shivaraj, with a comprehensive academic background including a Bachelor's in Mechanical Engineering, Master of Engineering Management (Australia), MBA and also pursuing Ph.D, brings an impressive 06 years of teaching experience alongside a brief stint in the industry of 3 years. Currently serving as an Assistant Professor at the Adarsh Institute of Management and Information Technology in Bangalore, Karnataka, India, he has distinguished himself in the academic and research fields. Prof.Gautam Shivaraj professional journey is a testament to his dedication to academia, research, in the evolving world.

Tanmay Waghmare is a student in the MBA program at Datta Meghe Institute of Management Studies, located in Nagpur, Maharashtra. He is currently pursuing his postgraduate studies with a focus on developing strong managerial and leadership skills. Tanmay is dedicated to building a solid foundation in business management and aims to contribute meaningfully to the corporate sector. His academic journey reflects a commitment to learning, professional growth, and excellence in the field of management.

Anjel Raj Y is an Assistant Professor at GNA Business School, GNA University. She holds a Ph.D. in Social Media Marketing, reflecting her expertise in the evolving intersection of digital platforms and consumer behaviour. With over one year and six months of industry experience and one year and five months in academia, Dr. Anjel brings a balanced perspective that bridges practical insights with academic rigour. Her academic contributions are noteworthy. She has published over three research papers indexed in Scopus, showcasing her active engagement in scholarly research. In addition, she has authored two book chapters and served as the editor of one academic book, further demonstrating her commitment to knowledge creation and dissemination in the field of marketing and digital communication. Dr. Anjel has also got best paper award from Vels Institute of Science and Technology. Dr. Anjel's work reflects a strong foundation in digital marketing trends, consumer engagement, and the strategic use of social media platforms, making her a valuable contributor to both academic and industry discussions on modern marketing practices.

Index

A

B

C

D

E

G